W Juliet

Volume 8

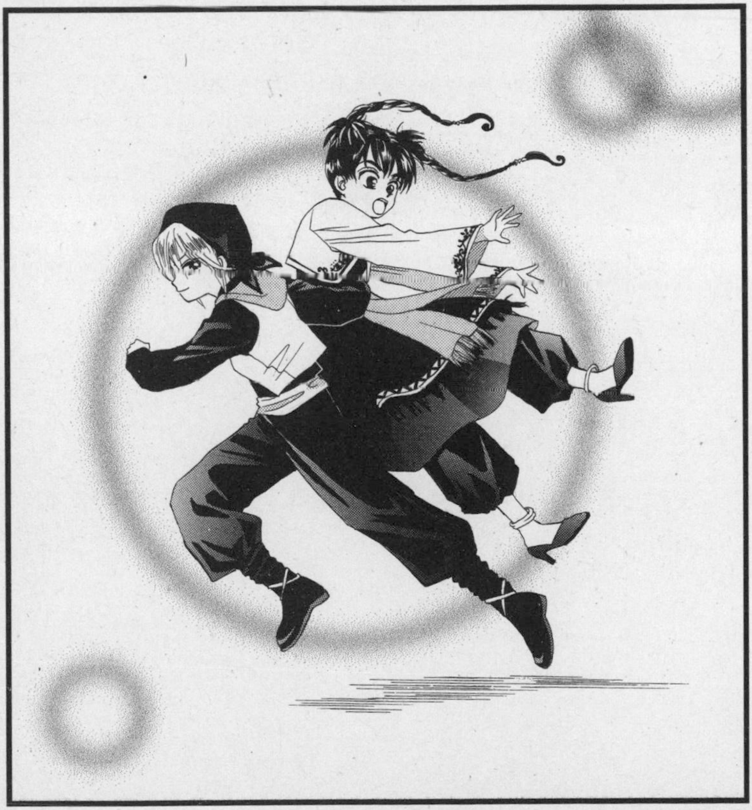

Story & Art by Emura

W Juliet
Volume 8

Story and Art by Emura

Translation & English Adaptation/Naomi Kokubo & Jeff Carlson
Touch-up Art & Lettering/Mark McMurray
Graphic Design/Hidemi Sahara
Editor/Carrie Shepherd

Managing Editor/Annette Roman
Director of Production/Noboru Watanabe
Vice President of Publishing/Alvin Lu
Sr. Director of Acquisitions/Rika Inouye
Vice President of Sales & Marketing/Liza Coppola
Publisher/Hyoe Narita

W Juliet by Emura © Emura 2000. All rights reserved.
First published in Japan in 2001 by HAKUSENSHA, Inc., Tokyo. English language translation
rights in America and Canada arranged with HAKUSENSHA, Inc., Tokyo.
The W JULIET logo is a trademark of VIZ Media, LLC.
The stories, characters and incidents mentioned in this publication are entirely fictional.

Printed In Canada

Published by VIZ Media, LLC
P.O. Box 77010
San Francisco, CA 94107

10 9 8 7 6 5 4 3 2 1
First printing, December 2005

www.viz.com
store.viz.com

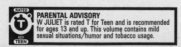

PARENTAL ADVISORY
W JULIET is rated T for Teen and is recommended
for ages 13 and up. This volume contains mild
sexual situations/humor and tobacco usage.

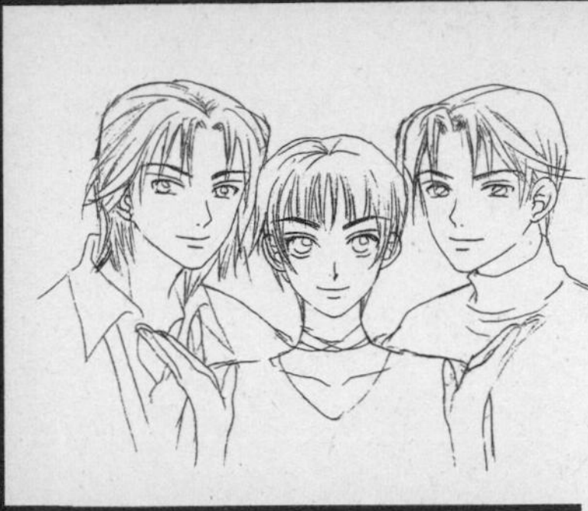

↑ 2001 Telephone Card, draft

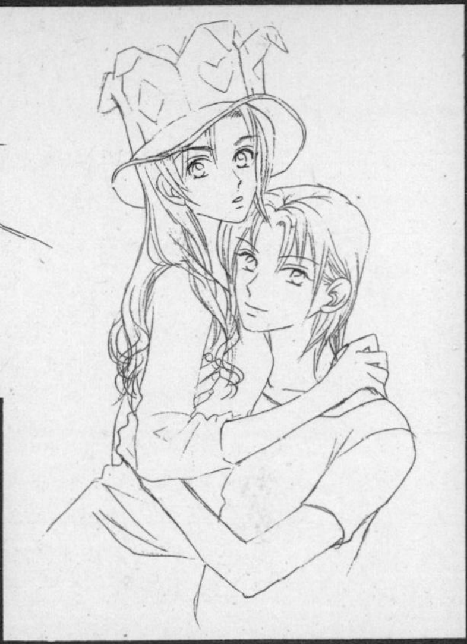

Hana to Yume No. 3 cover art,
↓ draft (B4 size)

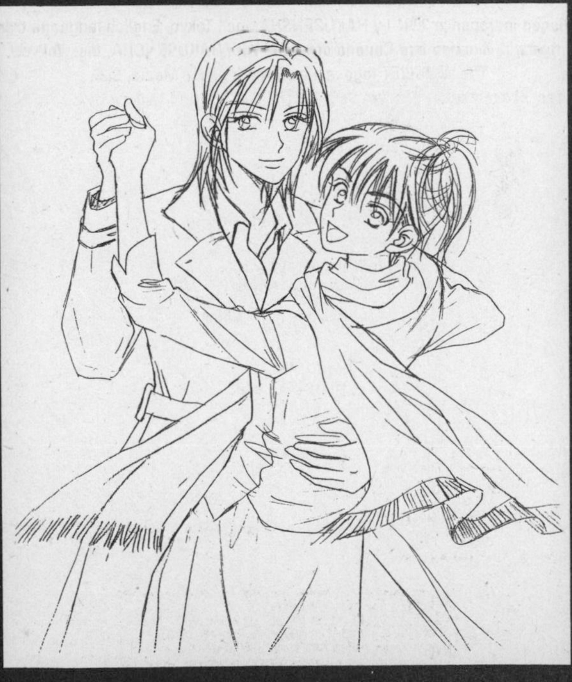

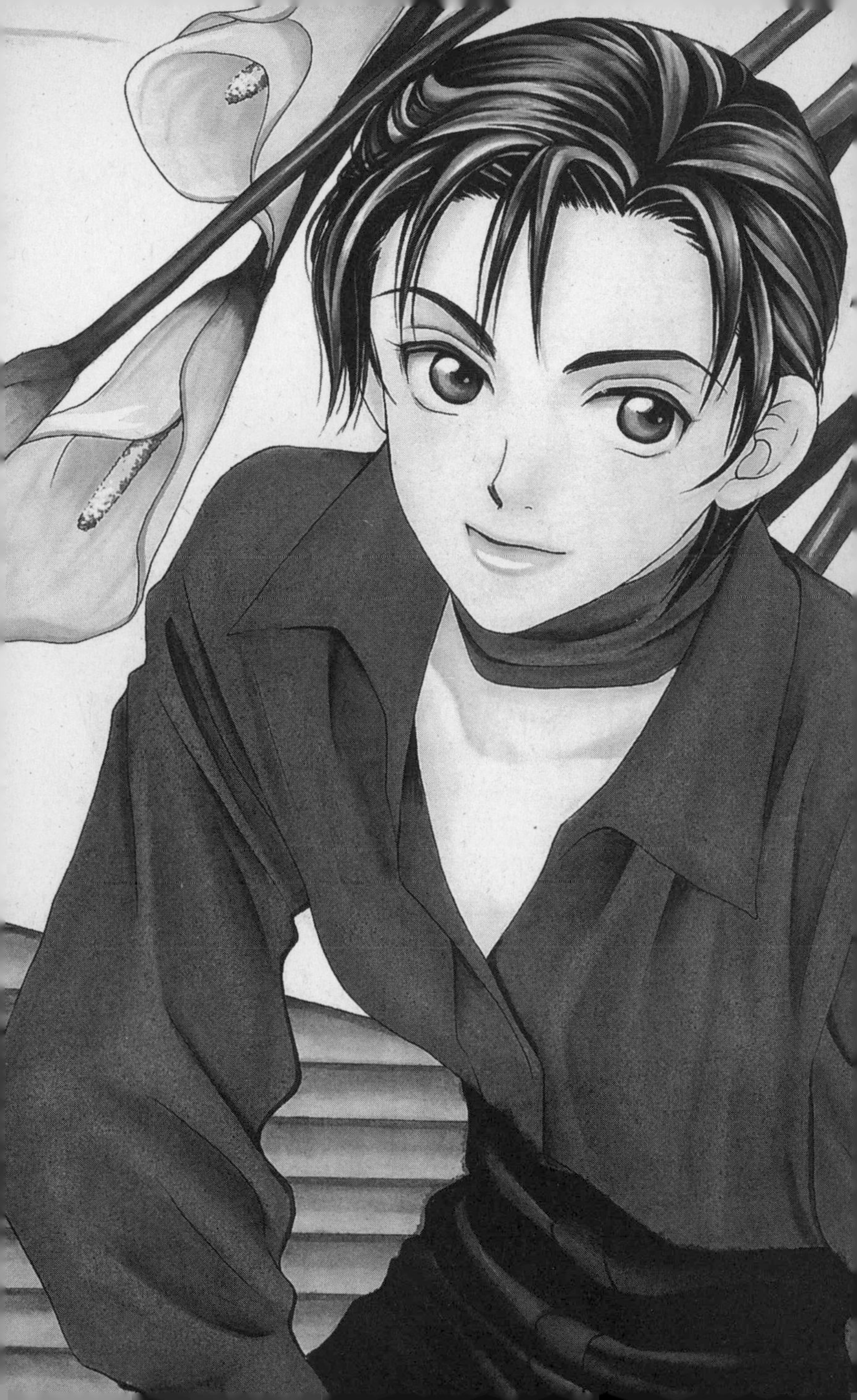

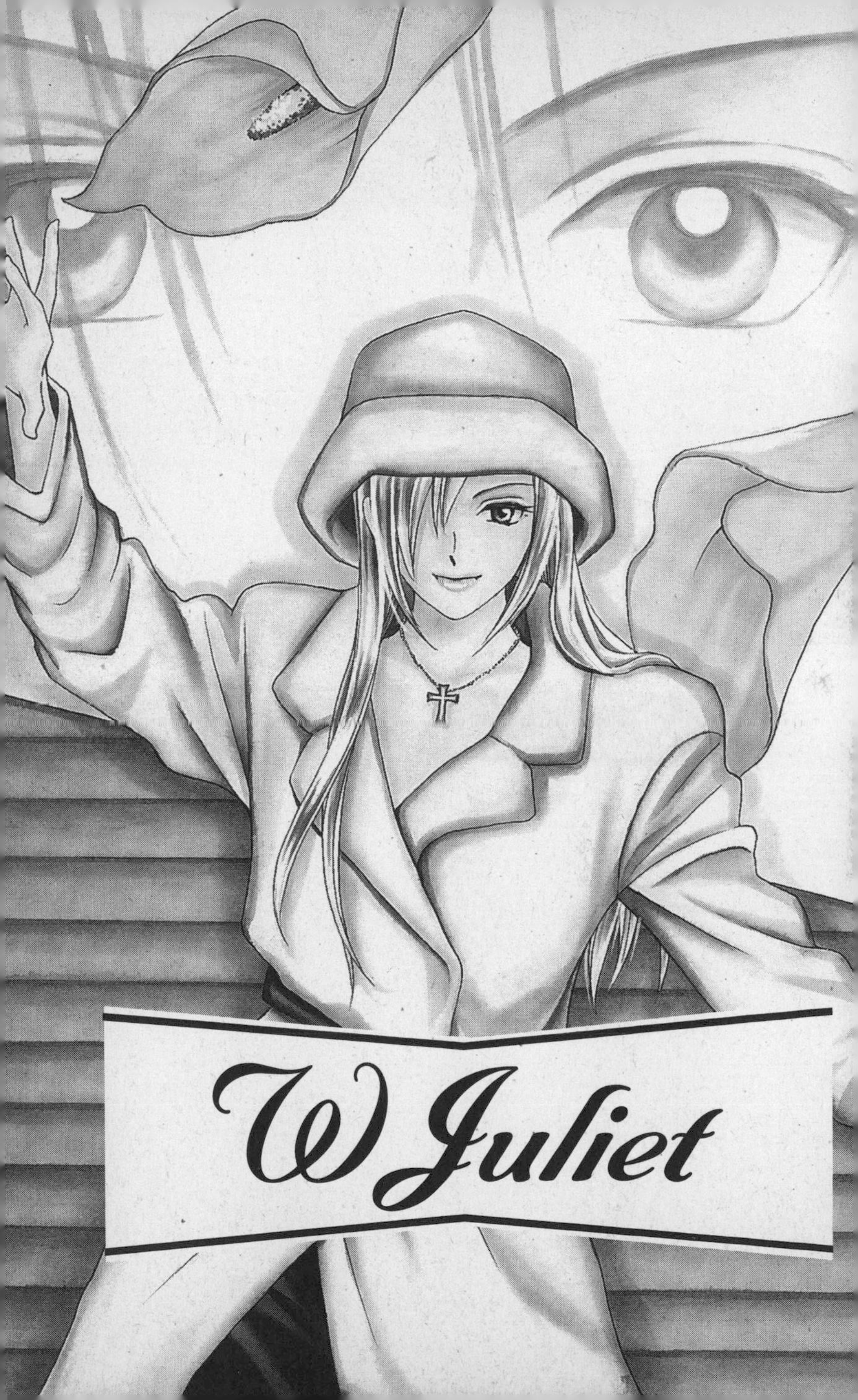
W Juliet

↑ Rejected draft

↓ 2001 Hana to Yume No. I opening art (Draft B5 size) Final draft.

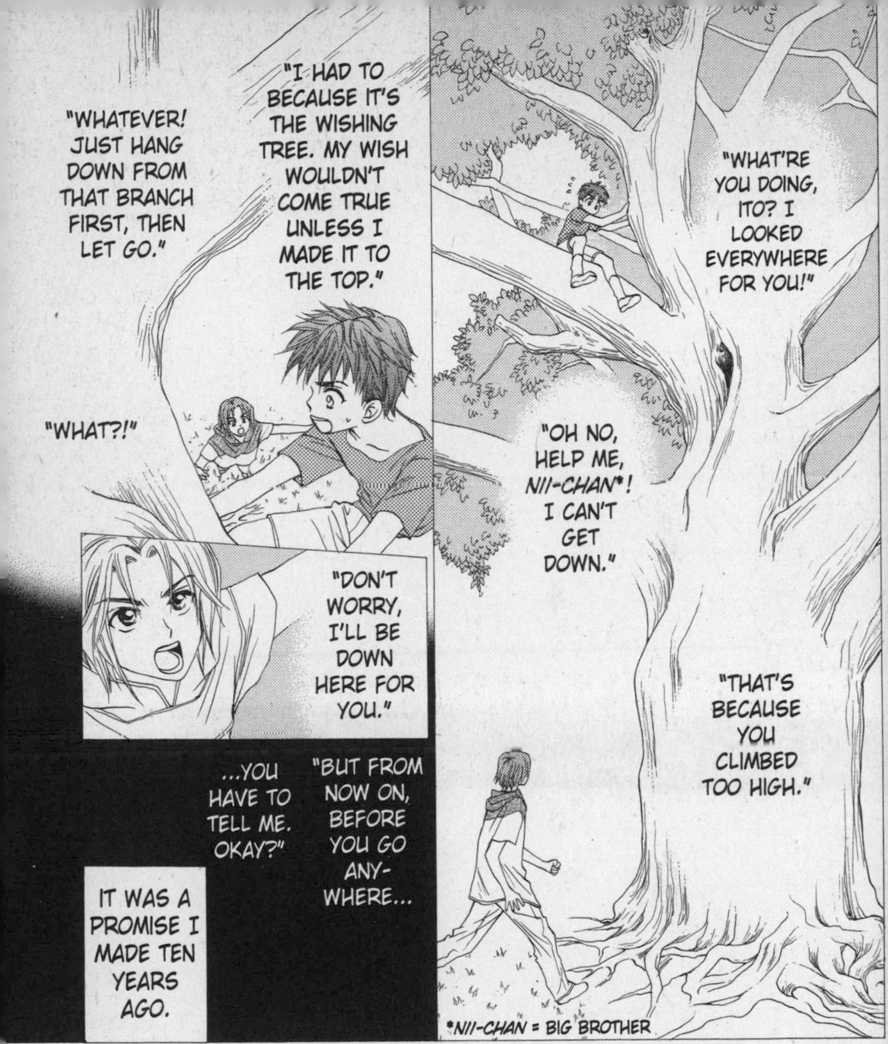
"WHAT'RE YOU DOING, ITO? I LOOKED EVERYWHERE FOR YOU!"
"OH NO, HELP ME, NII-CHAN*! I CAN'T GET DOWN."
"THAT'S BECAUSE YOU CLIMBED TOO HIGH."
*NII-CHAN = BIG BROTHER
"I HAD TO BECAUSE IT'S THE WISHING TREE. MY WISH WOULDN'T COME TRUE UNLESS I MADE IT TO THE TOP."
"WHATEVER! JUST HANG DOWN FROM THAT BRANCH FIRST, THEN LET GO."
"WHAT?!"
"DON'T WORRY, I'LL BE DOWN HERE FOR YOU."
"BUT FROM NOW ON, BEFORE YOU GO ANYWHERE...
...YOU HAVE TO TELL ME. OKAY?"
IT WAS A PROMISE I MADE TEN YEARS AGO.

-Behind the Scenes Story- ①

What a story. It reminds me of my old days... Ah ha ha! When I was in high school, I used to break curfew, and my father would reprimand me as soon as I set foot in the house. The thing is, the curfew was 7 P.M. (oh dear!), and I might call and tell my parents that I'd be late, but by the time I got home, it was like 11 P.M. Yes, my parents were in a complete rage. Ahh, it was scary!! When I was in middle school, just like Ito, there were times when they forced me back home. One day, when I got home late because of a game, after 9:30, they said, "If you didn't return by 10 P.M., we were going to call the police." It's no laughing matter. And they may still be a bit overprotective. But I have no more curfew, that's for sure.

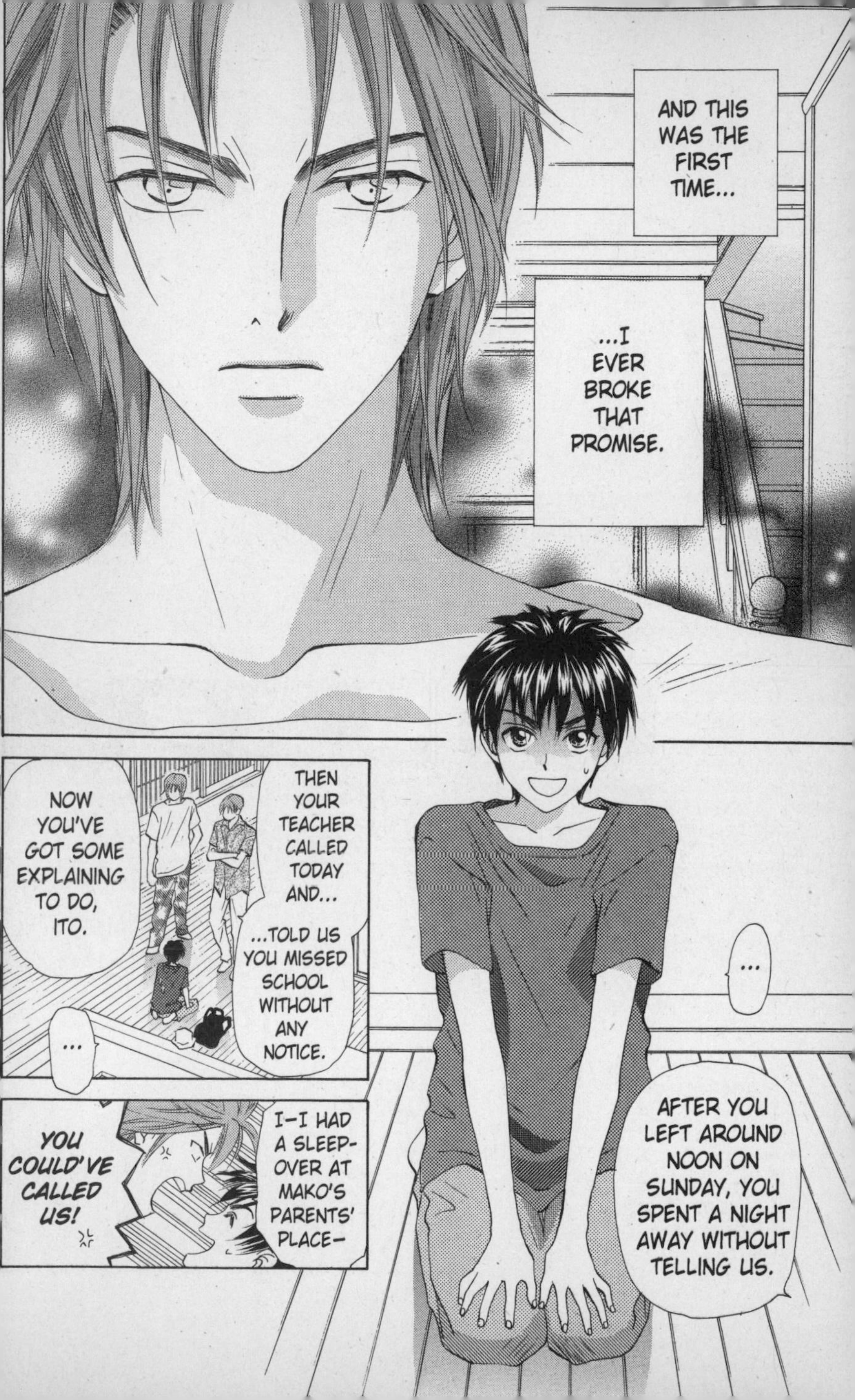
AND THIS WAS THE FIRST TIME...
...I EVER BROKE THAT PROMISE.
...
AFTER YOU LEFT AROUND NOON ON SUNDAY, YOU SPENT A NIGHT AWAY WITHOUT TELLING US.
THEN YOUR TEACHER CALLED TODAY AND...
...TOLD US YOU MISSED SCHOOL WITHOUT ANY NOTICE.
NOW YOU'VE GOT SOME EXPLAINING TO DO, ITO.
...
I-I HAD A SLEEP-OVER AT MAKO'S PARENTS' PLACE-
YOU COULD'VE CALLED US!

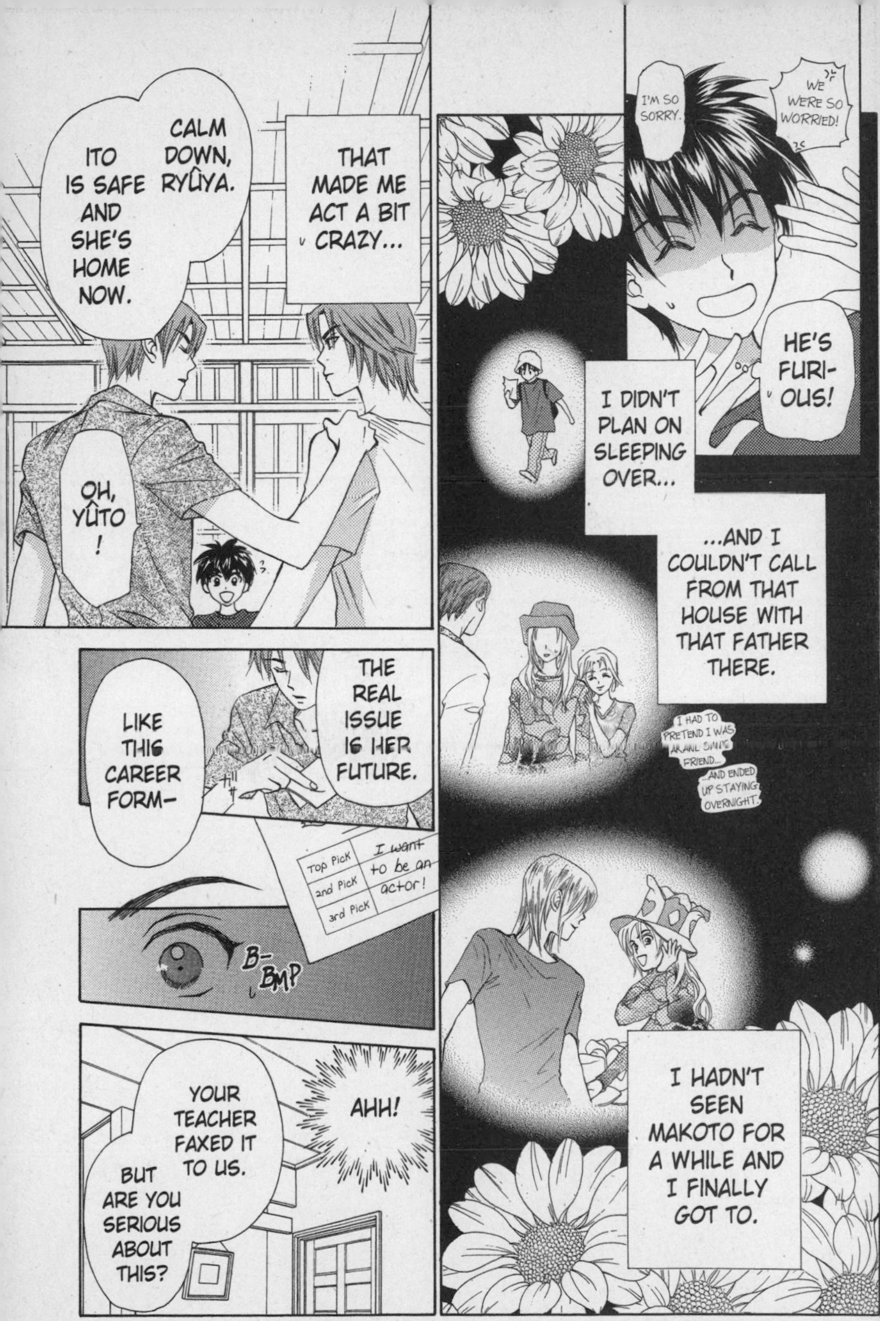
I'M SO SORRY.
WE WERE SO WORRIED!
HE'S FURIOUS!
I DIDN'T PLAN ON SLEEPING OVER...
...AND I COULDN'T CALL FROM THAT HOUSE WITH THAT FATHER THERE.
I HAD TO PRETEND I WAS AKANE FRIEND...
...AND ENDED UP STAYING OVERNIGHT.
I HADN'T SEEN MAKOTO FOR A WHILE AND I FINALLY GOT TO.
THAT MADE ME ACT A BIT CRAZY...
CALM DOWN, RYÛYA.
ITO IS SAFE AND SHE'S HOME NOW.
OH, YÛTO!
THE REAL ISSUE IS HER FUTURE.
LIKE THIS CAREER FORM—
Top Pick
2nd Pick
3rd Pick
I want to be an actor!
B-BMP
AHH!
YOUR TEACHER FAXED IT TO US.
BUT ARE YOU SERIOUS ABOUT THIS?

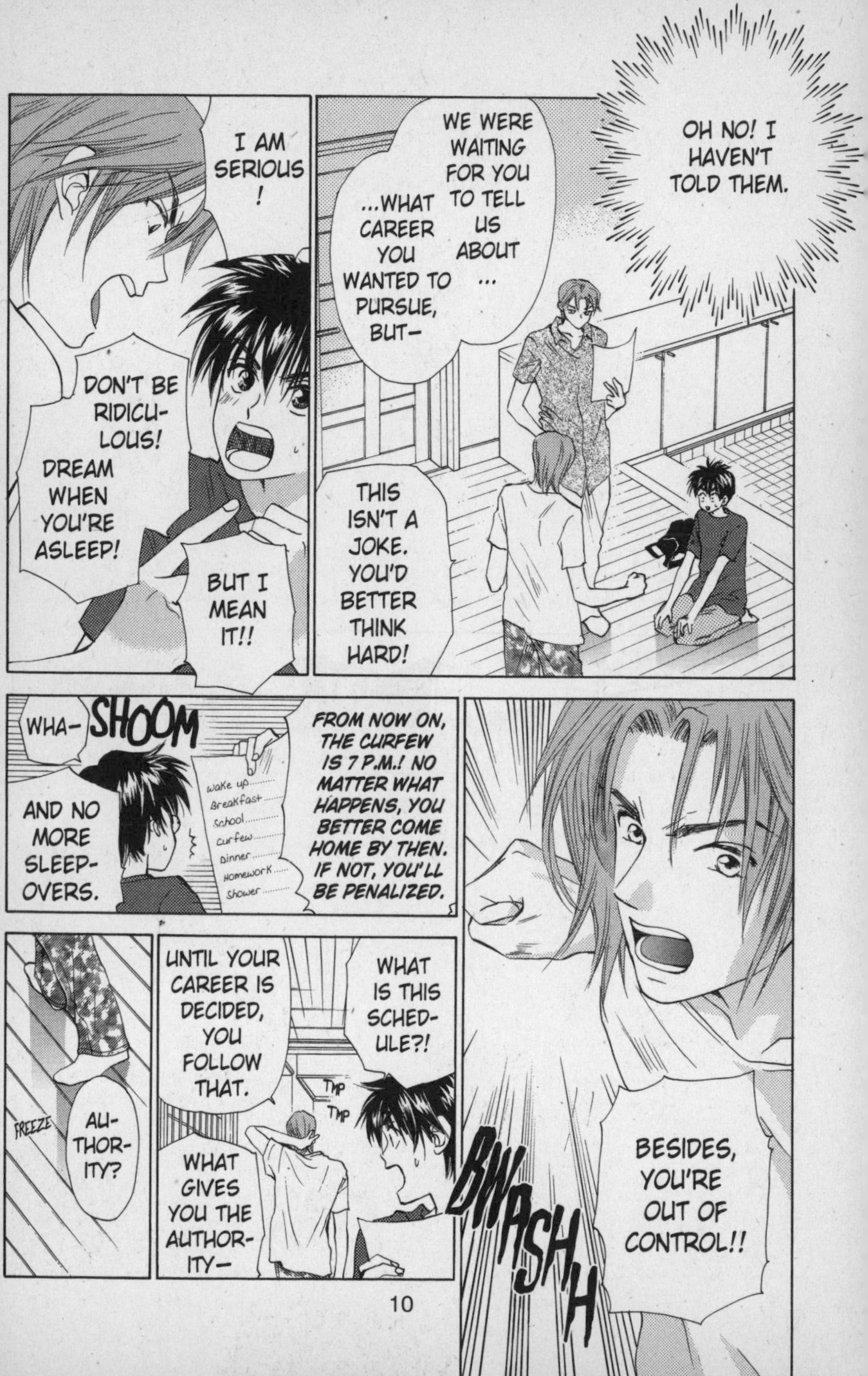
OH NO! I HAVEN'T TOLD THEM.
WE WERE WAITING FOR YOU TO TELL US ABOUT ...
...WHAT CAREER YOU WANTED TO PURSUE, BUT—
THIS ISN'T A JOKE. YOU'D BETTER THINK HARD!
I AM SERIOUS!
DON'T BE RIDICULOUS! DREAM WHEN YOU'RE ASLEEP!
BUT I MEAN IT!!
BESIDES, YOU'RE OUT OF CONTROL!!
BWASHH
FROM NOW ON, THE CURFEW IS 7 P.M.! NO MATTER WHAT HAPPENS, YOU BETTER COME HOME BY THEN. IF NOT, YOU'LL BE PENALIZED.
Wake up
Breakfast
School
Curfew
Dinner
Homework
Shower
SHOOM
WHA—
AND NO MORE SLEEP-OVERS.
WHAT IS THIS SCHED-ULE?!
UNTIL YOUR CAREER IS DECIDED, YOU FOLLOW THAT.
TMP TMP
WHAT GIVES YOU THE AUTHOR-ITY—
FREEZE
AU-THOR-ITY?

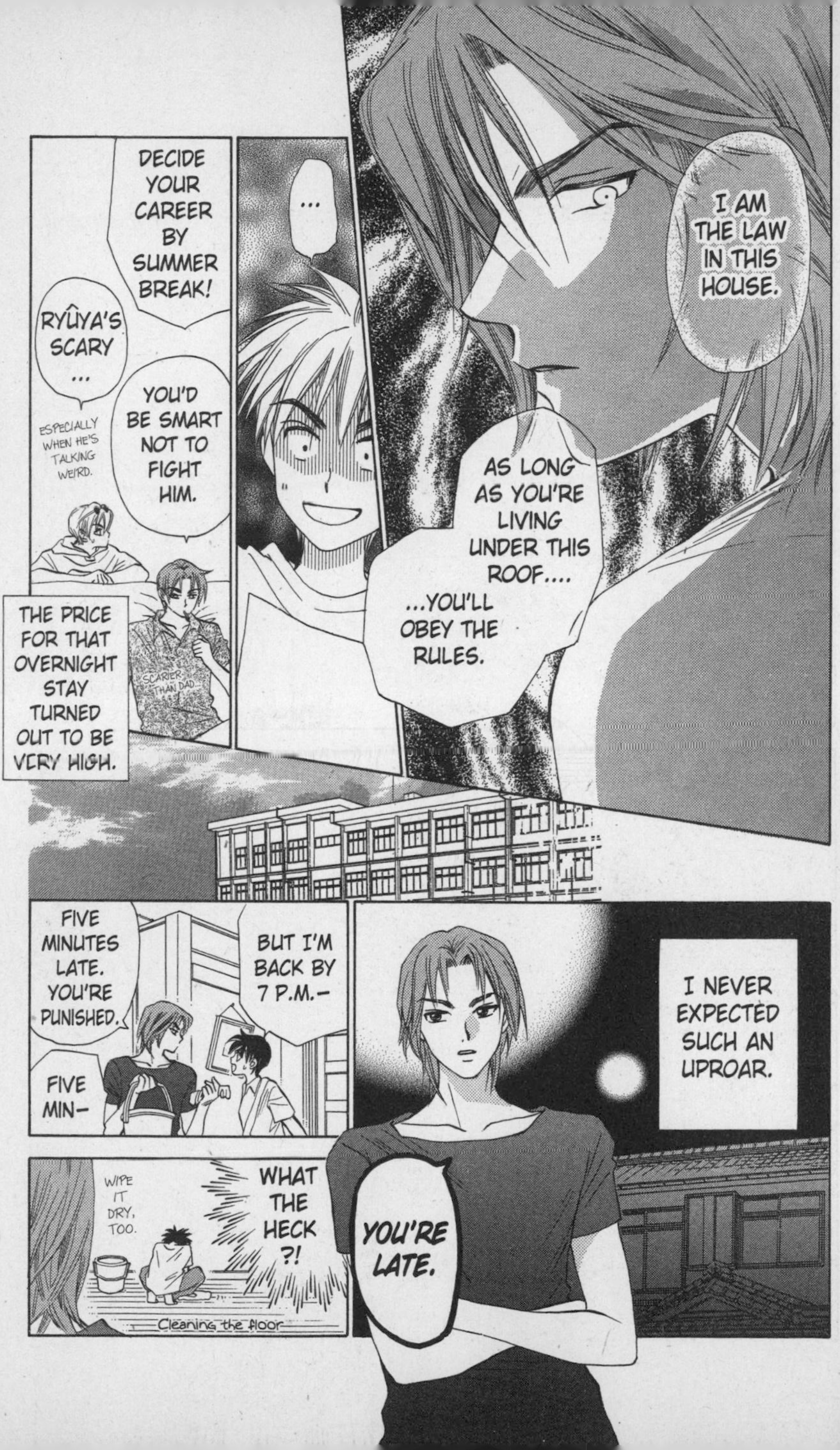
I AM THE LAW IN THIS HOUSE.
AS LONG AS YOU'RE LIVING UNDER THIS ROOF....
...YOU'LL OBEY THE RULES.
...
DECIDE YOUR CAREER BY SUMMER BREAK!
YOU'D BE SMART NOT TO FIGHT HIM.
RYÛYA'S SCARY ...
ESPECIALLY WHEN HE'S TALKING WEIRD.
SCARIER THAN DAD...
THE PRICE FOR THAT OVERNIGHT STAY TURNED OUT TO BE VERY HIGH.
I NEVER EXPECTED SUCH AN UPROAR.
YOU'RE LATE.
BUT I'M BACK BY 7 P.M.–
FIVE MINUTES LATE. YOU'RE PUNISHED.
FIVE MIN–
WHAT THE HECK ?!
WIPE IT DRY, TOO.
Cleaning the floor

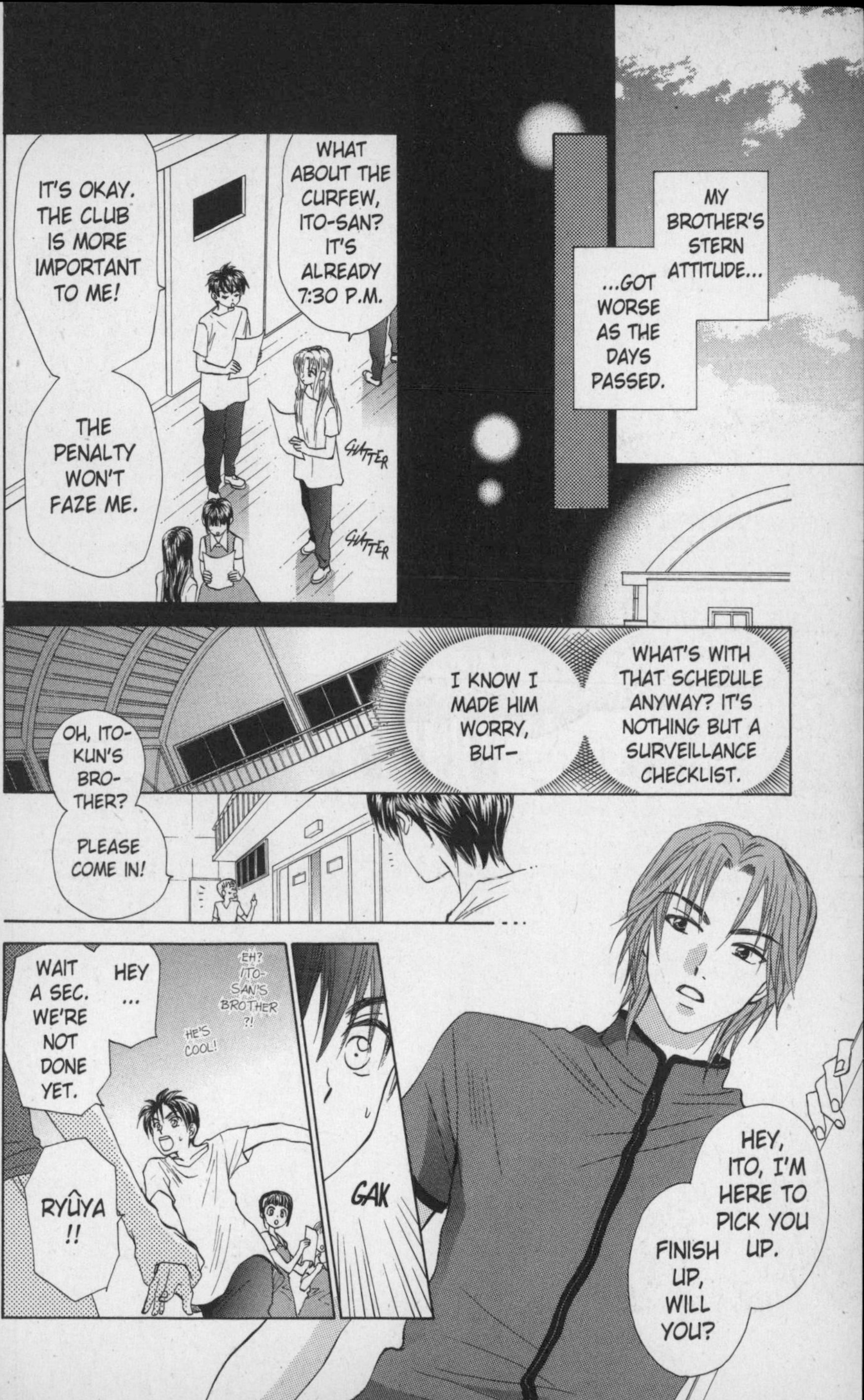
MY BROTHER'S STERN ATTITUDE...
...GOT WORSE AS THE DAYS PASSED.
WHAT ABOUT THE CURFEW, ITO-SAN? IT'S ALREADY 7:30 P.M.
IT'S OKAY. THE CLUB IS MORE IMPORTANT TO ME!
THE PENALTY WON'T FAZE ME.
CHATTER
CHATTER
WHAT'S WITH THAT SCHEDULE ANYWAY? IT'S NOTHING BUT A SURVEILLANCE CHECKLIST.
I KNOW I MADE HIM WORRY, BUT-
OH, ITO-KUN'S BROTHER?
PLEASE COME IN!
HEY, ITO, I'M HERE TO PICK YOU UP.
FINISH UP, WILL YOU?
GAK
EH? ITO-SAN'S BROTHER?!
HE'S COOL!
HEY...
WAIT A SEC. WE'RE NOT DONE YET.
RYÛYA!!

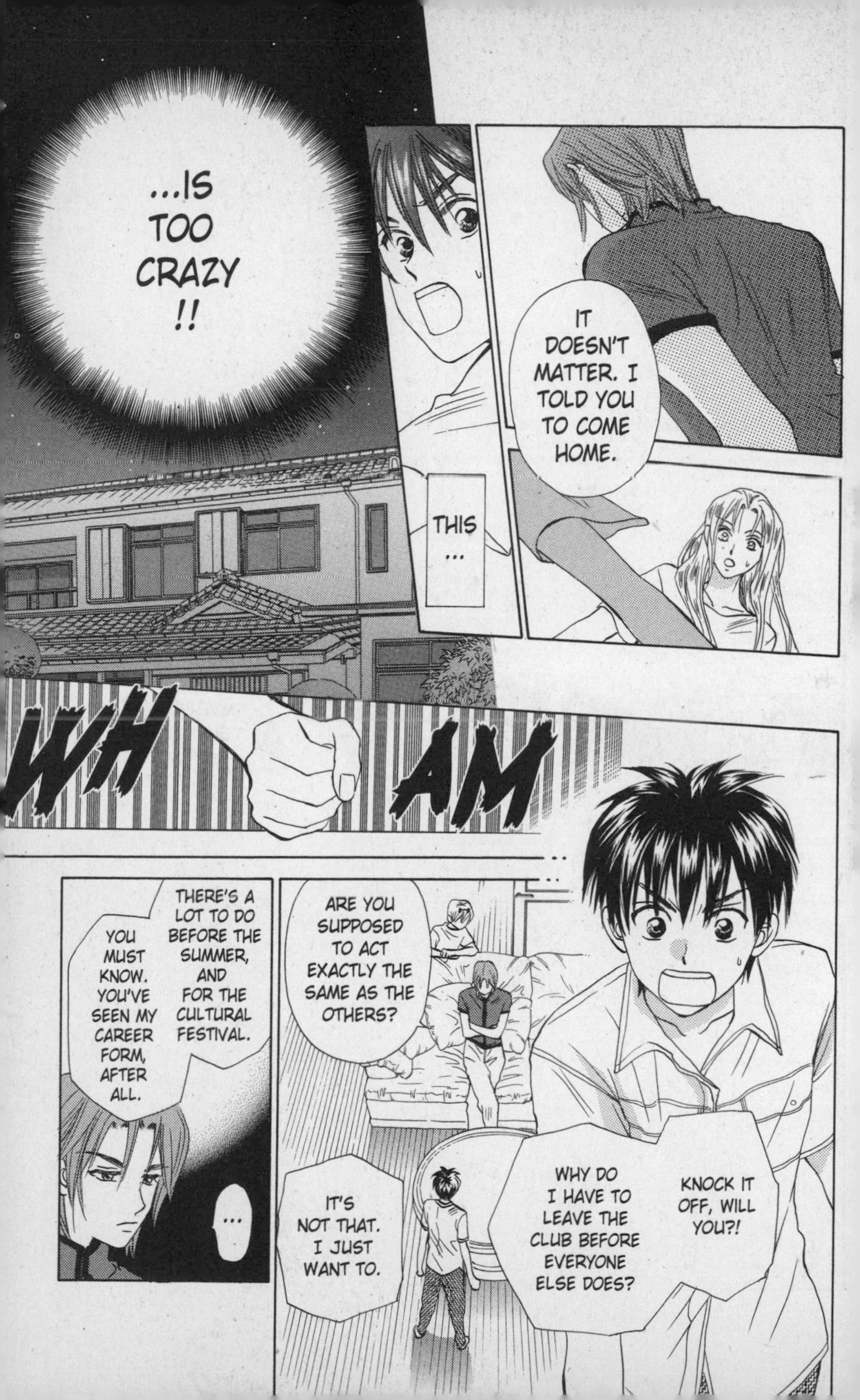
IT DOESN'T MATTER. I TOLD YOU TO COME HOME.
THIS ...
...IS TOO CRAZY !!
WHAM
KNOCK IT OFF, WILL YOU?!
WHY DO I HAVE TO LEAVE THE CLUB BEFORE EVERYONE ELSE DOES?
IT'S NOT THAT. I JUST WANT TO.
ARE YOU SUPPOSED TO ACT EXACTLY THE SAME AS THE OTHERS?
THERE'S A LOT TO DO BEFORE THE SUMMER, AND FOR THE CULTURAL FESTIVAL.
YOU MUST KNOW. YOU'VE SEEN MY CAREER FORM, AFTER ALL.
...

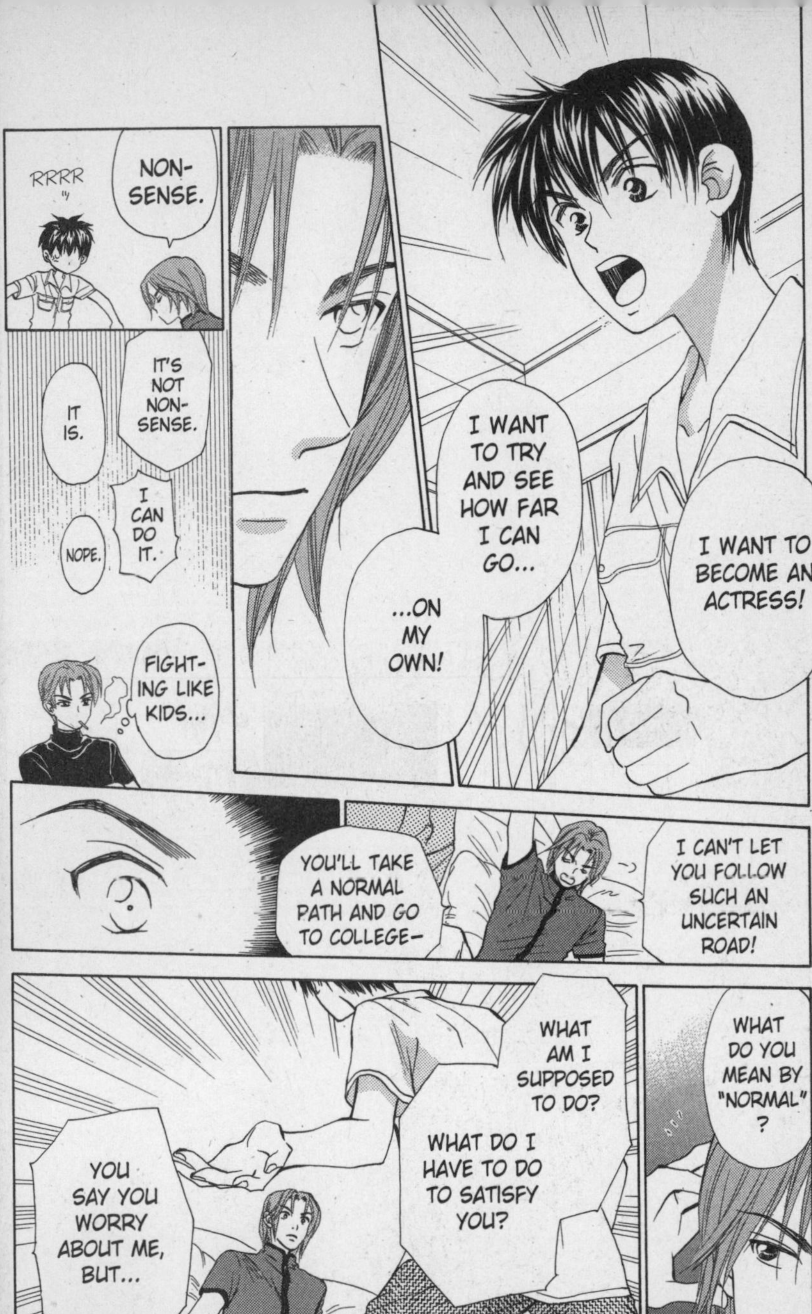
I WANT TO BECOME AN ACTRESS!
I WANT TO TRY AND SEE HOW FAR I CAN GO...
...ON MY OWN!
RRRR
NON-SENSE.
IT'S NOT NON-SENSE.
IT IS.
I CAN DO IT.
NOPE.
FIGHT-ING LIKE KIDS...
I CAN'T LET YOU FOLLOW SUCH AN UNCERTAIN ROAD!
YOU'LL TAKE A NORMAL PATH AND GO TO COLLEGE–
WHAT DO YOU MEAN BY "NORMAL"?
WHAT AM I SUPPOSED TO DO?
WHAT DO I HAVE TO DO TO SATISFY YOU?
YOU SAY YOU WORRY ABOUT ME, BUT...

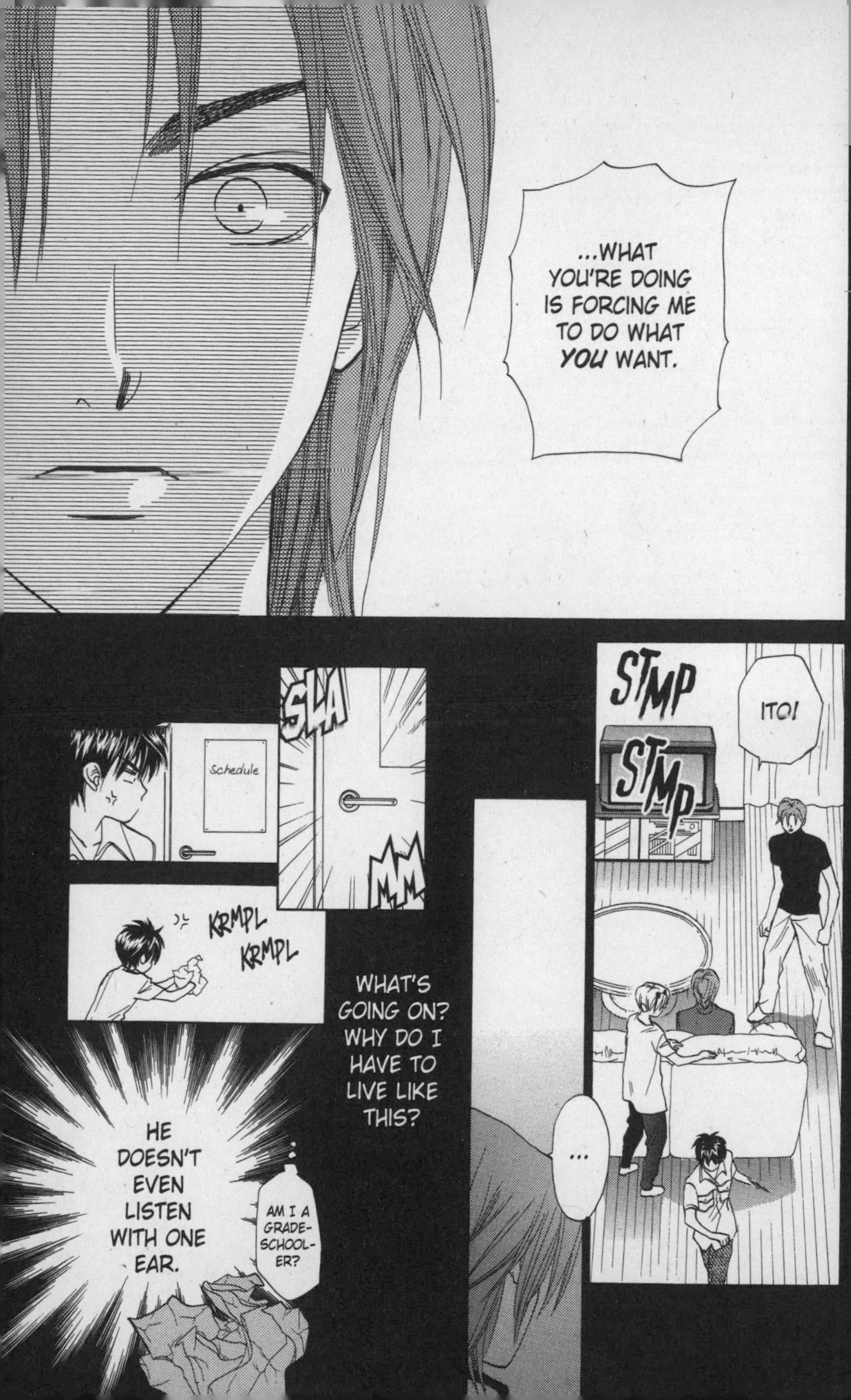
...WHAT YOU'RE DOING IS FORCING ME TO DO WHAT *YOU* WANT.
STMP
STMP
ITO!
...
SLA
MM
Schedule
KRMPL
KRMPL
WHAT'S GOING ON? WHY DO I HAVE TO LIVE LIKE THIS?
HE DOESN'T EVEN LISTEN WITH ONE EAR.
AM I A GRADE-SCHOOL-ER?

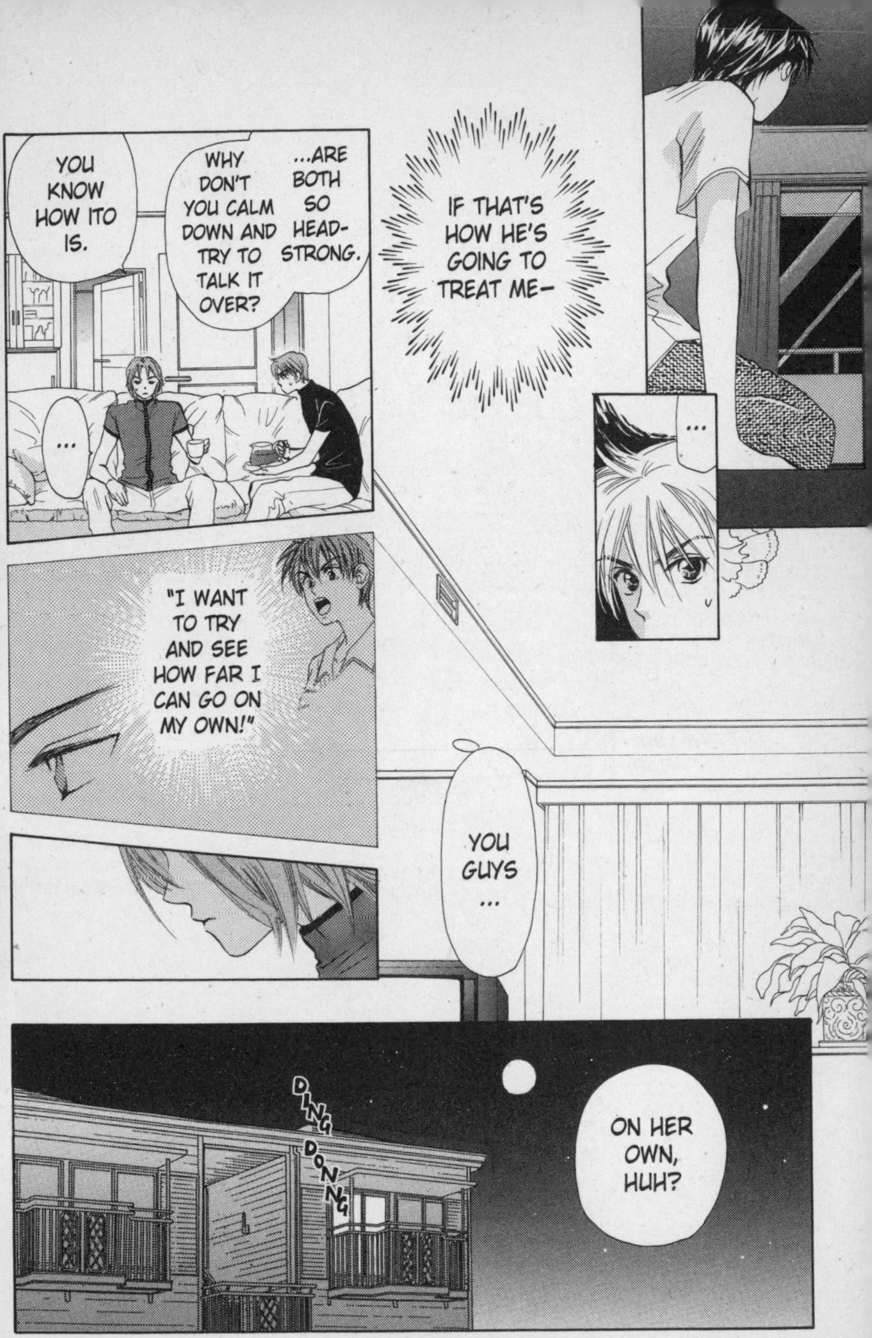
IF THAT'S HOW HE'S GOING TO TREAT ME—
...
...ARE BOTH SO HEAD-STRONG.
WHY DON'T YOU CALM DOWN AND TRY TO TALK IT OVER?
YOU KNOW HOW ITO IS.
...
YOU GUYS ...
"I WANT TO TRY AND SEE HOW FAR I CAN GO ON MY OWN!"
ON HER OWN, HUH?
DING DONG

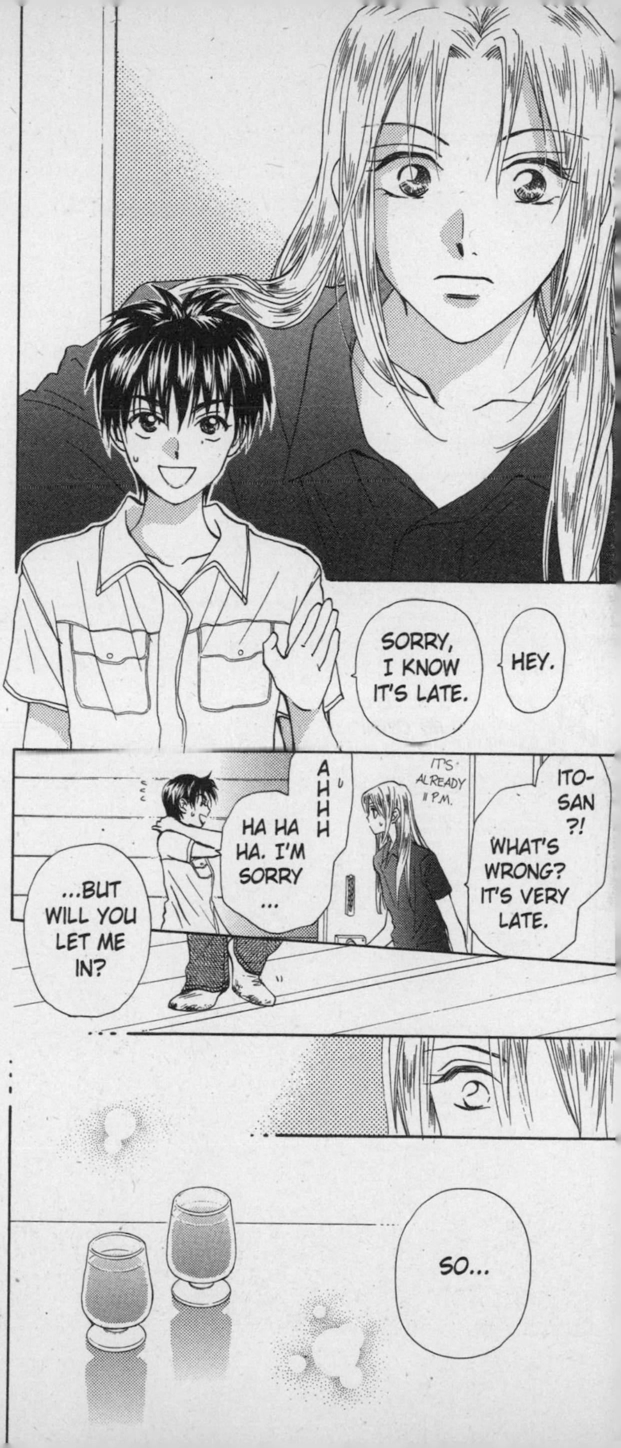
HEY.
SORRY, I KNOW IT'S LATE.
ITO-SAN?! WHAT'S WRONG? IT'S VERY LATE.
IT'S ALREADY 11 P.M.
AHHH
HA HA HA. I'M SORRY...
...BUT WILL YOU LET ME IN?
SO...

GREETINGS

Hello.
This is Emura.
We finally reached volume 8!

I say this every time, don't I?

This volume made me happy because it let me tell stories about the subcharacters. I have a feeling I might hear from you saying, "Why are there hardly any love moments between the two?!" (And sure enough, I did hear it.) Please excuse me. I think it's okay to have stories like this too. Treats taste better when you get them occasionally. By the way, I'm the type who saves them until later. But I know, it's tempting to eat dessert before the meal. I mean, I'm starving at the moment. I should go get some breakfast. My story is beginning to meander. Oh well, please enjoy volume 8. ♥

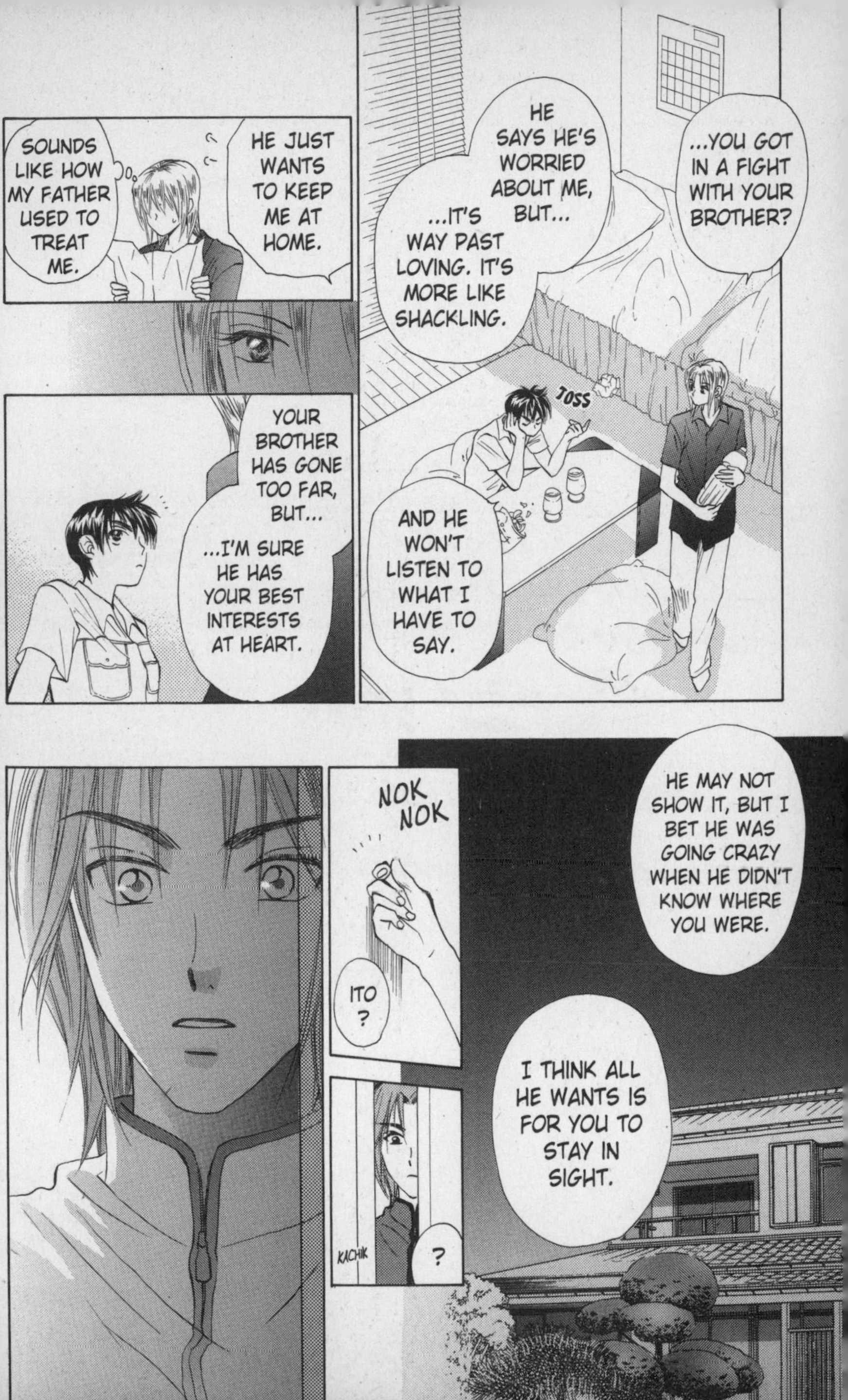
...YOU GOT IN A FIGHT WITH YOUR BROTHER?
HE SAYS HE'S WORRIED ABOUT ME, BUT...
...IT'S WAY PAST LOVING. IT'S MORE LIKE SHACKLING.
TOSS
AND HE WON'T LISTEN TO WHAT I HAVE TO SAY.
HE JUST WANTS TO KEEP ME AT HOME.
SOUNDS LIKE HOW MY FATHER USED TO TREAT ME.
YOUR BROTHER HAS GONE TOO FAR, BUT...
...I'M SURE HE HAS YOUR BEST INTERESTS AT HEART.
HE MAY NOT SHOW IT, BUT I BET HE WAS GOING CRAZY WHEN HE DIDN'T KNOW WHERE YOU WERE.
I THINK ALL HE WANTS IS FOR YOU TO STAY IN SIGHT.
NOK NOK
ITO ?
KACHIK
?

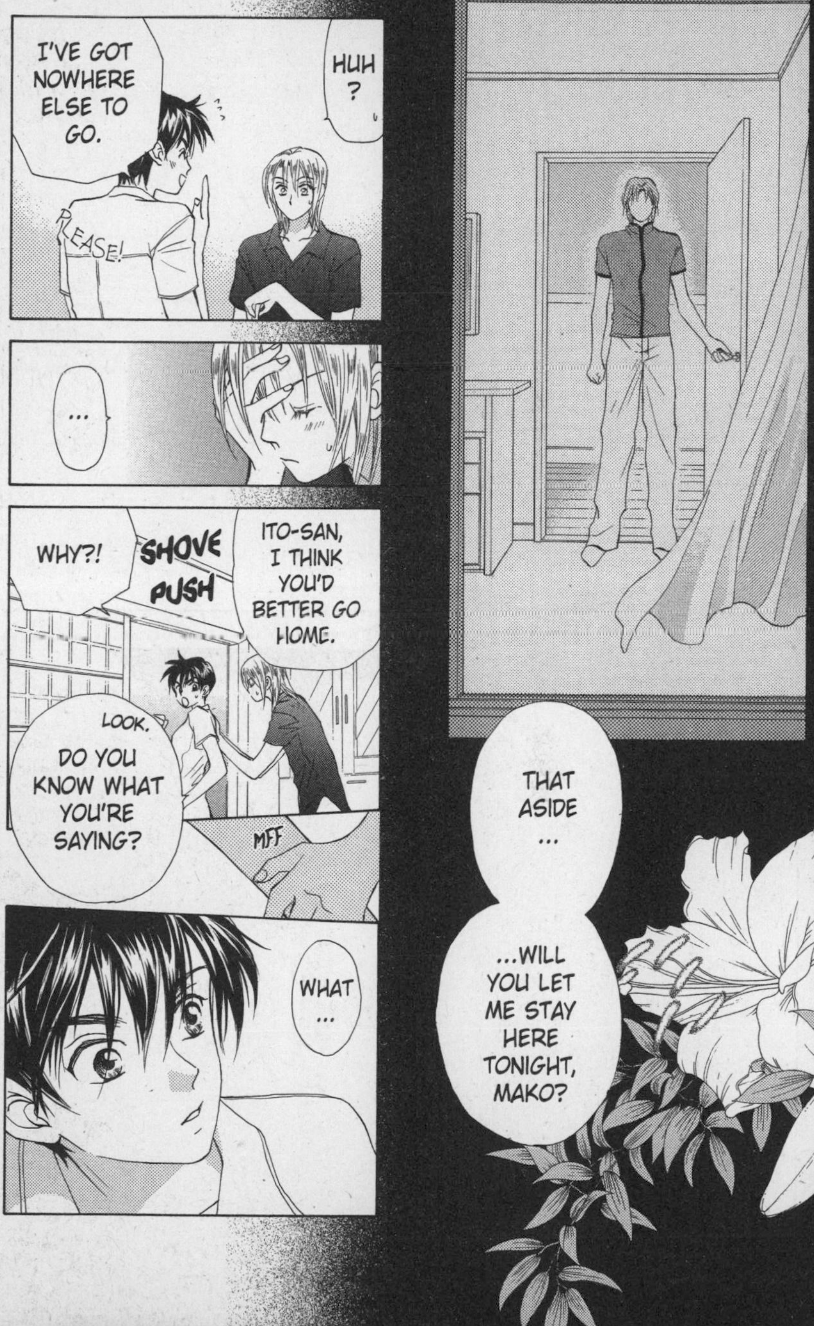
THAT ASIDE ...
...WILL YOU LET ME STAY HERE TONIGHT, MAKO?
HUH ?
I'VE GOT NOWHERE ELSE TO GO.
PLEASE!
...
ITO-SAN, I THINK YOU'D BETTER GO HOME.
SHOVE
PUSH
WHY?!
LOOK.
DO YOU KNOW WHAT YOU'RE SAYING?
MFF
WHAT ...

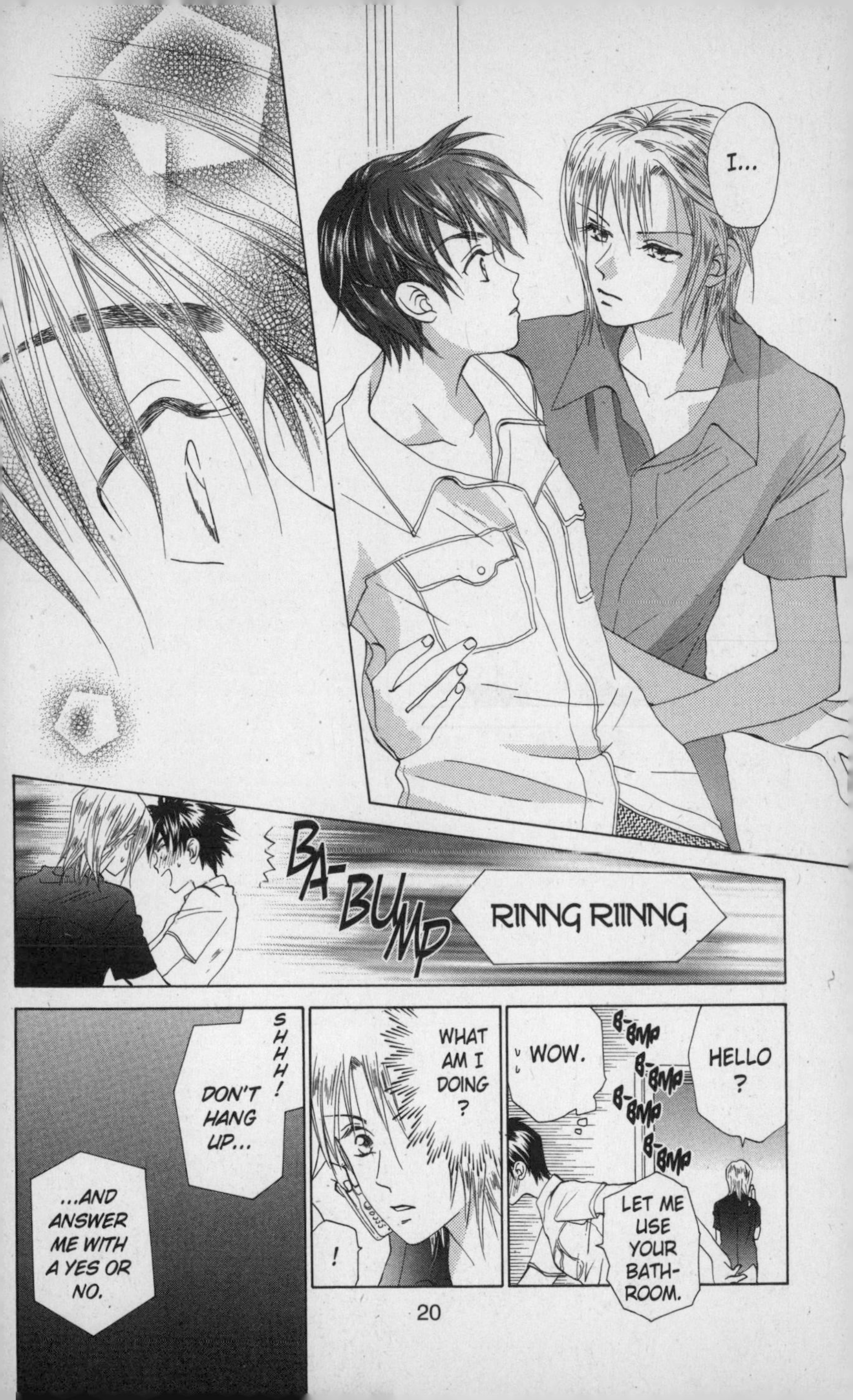

I...
RIINNG RIINNG
BA-BUMP
HELLO?
B-BMP B-BMP B-BMP B-BMP
WOW.
LET ME USE YOUR BATHROOM.
WHAT AM I DOING?
!
SHHH!
DON'T HANG UP...
...AND ANSWER ME WITH A YES OR NO.

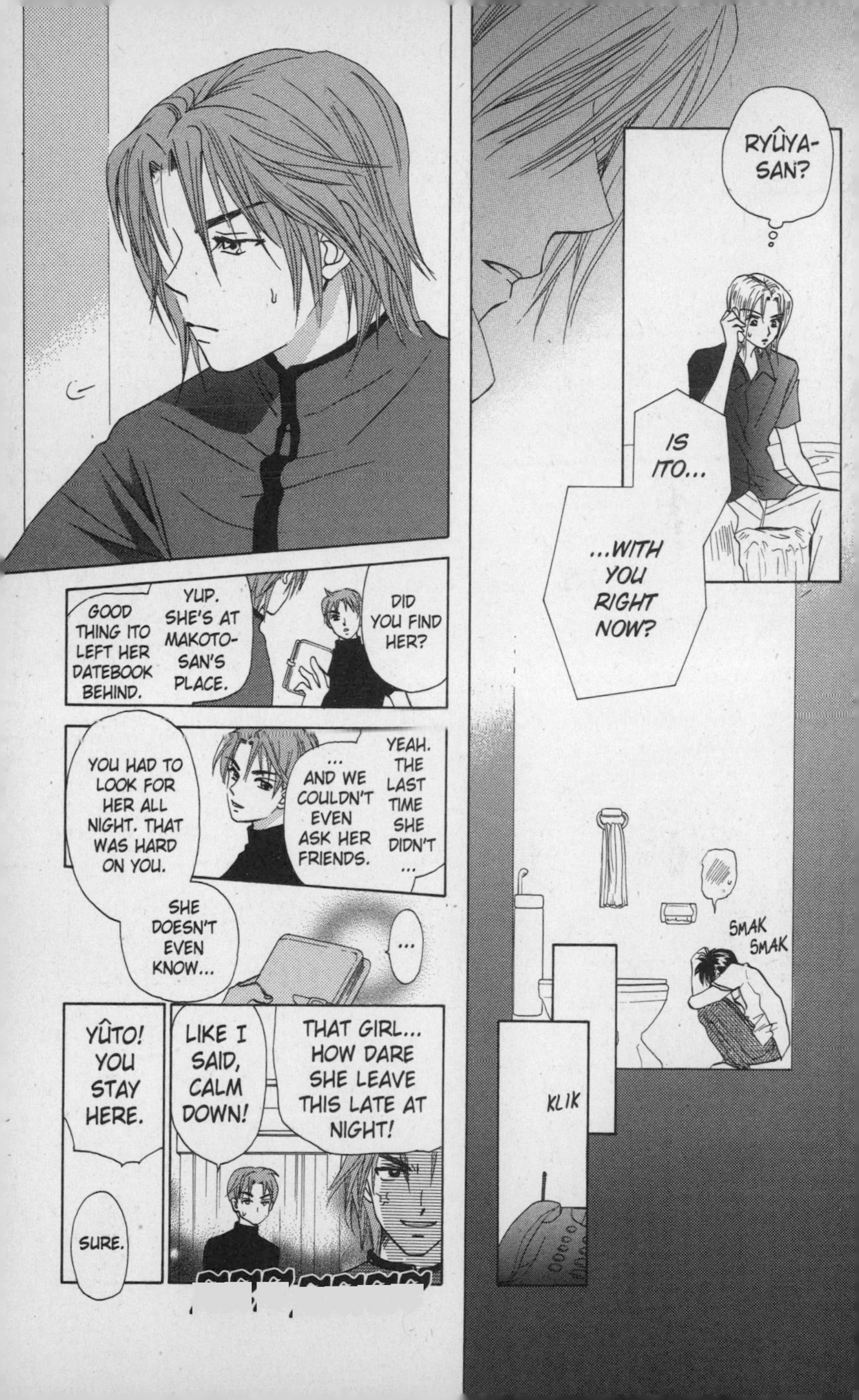
RYÛYA-SAN?
IS ITO...
...WITH YOU RIGHT NOW?
SMAK SMAK
KLIK
DID YOU FIND HER?
YUP. SHE'S AT MAKOTO-SAN'S PLACE.
GOOD THING ITO LEFT HER DATEBOOK BEHIND.
YEAH. THE LAST TIME SHE DIDN'T ...
... AND WE COULDN'T EVEN ASK HER FRIENDS.
YOU HAD TO LOOK FOR HER ALL NIGHT. THAT WAS HARD ON YOU.
SHE DOESN'T EVEN KNOW...
...
THAT GIRL... HOW DARE SHE LEAVE THIS LATE AT NIGHT!
LIKE I SAID, CALM DOWN!
YÛTO! YOU STAY HERE.
SURE.

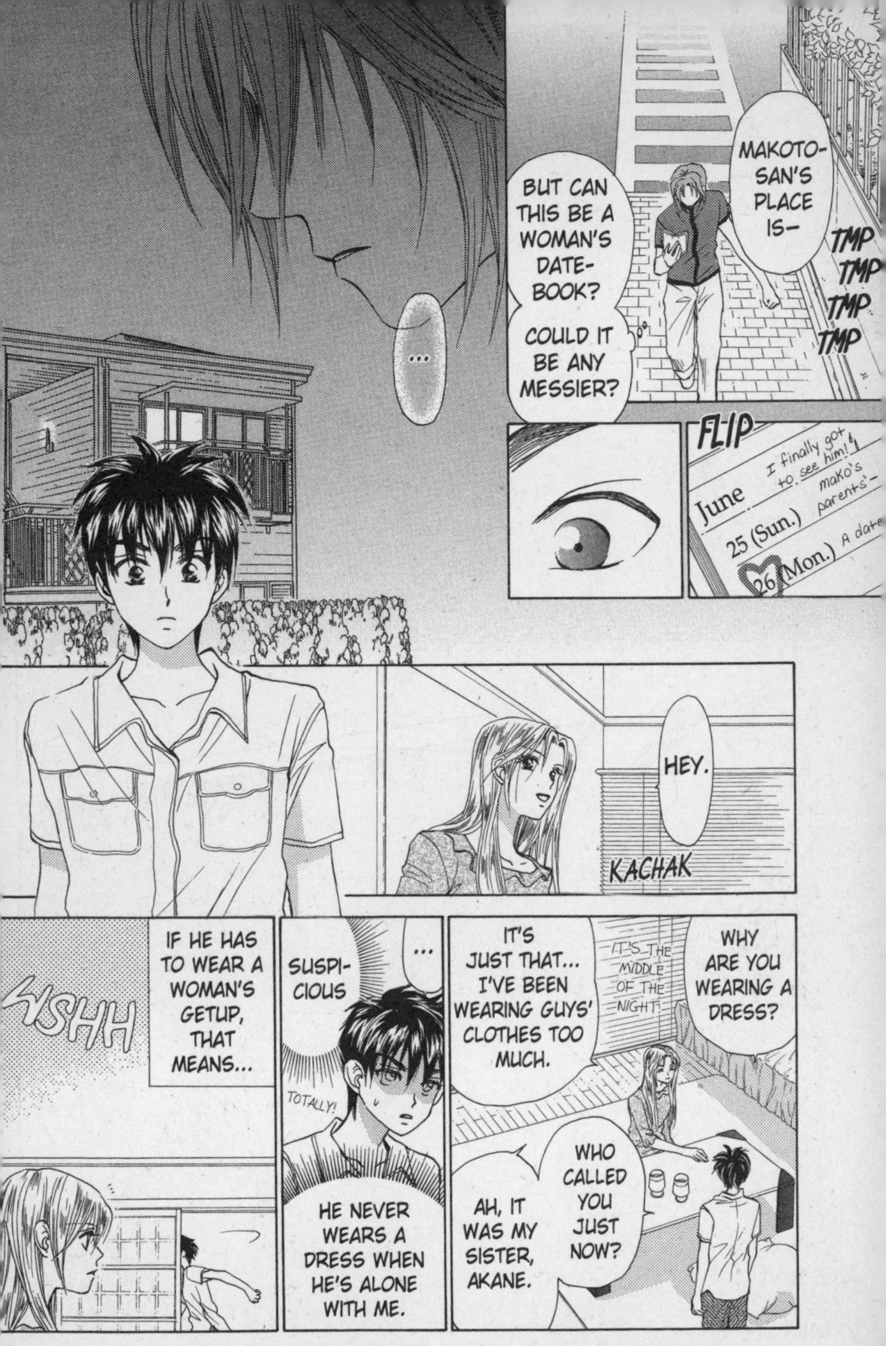
MAKOTO-SAN'S PLACE IS—
TMP TMP TMP TMP
BUT CAN THIS BE A WOMAN'S DATE-BOOK?
COULD IT BE ANY MESSIER?
FLIP
June
25 (Sun.) I finally got to see him!
mako's parents'—
26 (Mon.) A date
...
HEY.
KACHAK
WHY ARE YOU WEARING A DRESS?
IT'S THE MIDDLE OF THE NIGHT!
IT'S JUST THAT... I'VE BEEN WEARING GUYS' CLOTHES TOO MUCH.
WHO CALLED YOU JUST NOW?
AH, IT WAS MY SISTER, AKANE.
...
SUSPICIOUS
TOTALLY!
HE NEVER WEARS A DRESS WHEN HE'S ALONE WITH ME.
IF HE HAS TO WEAR A WOMAN'S GETUP, THAT MEANS...
WSHH

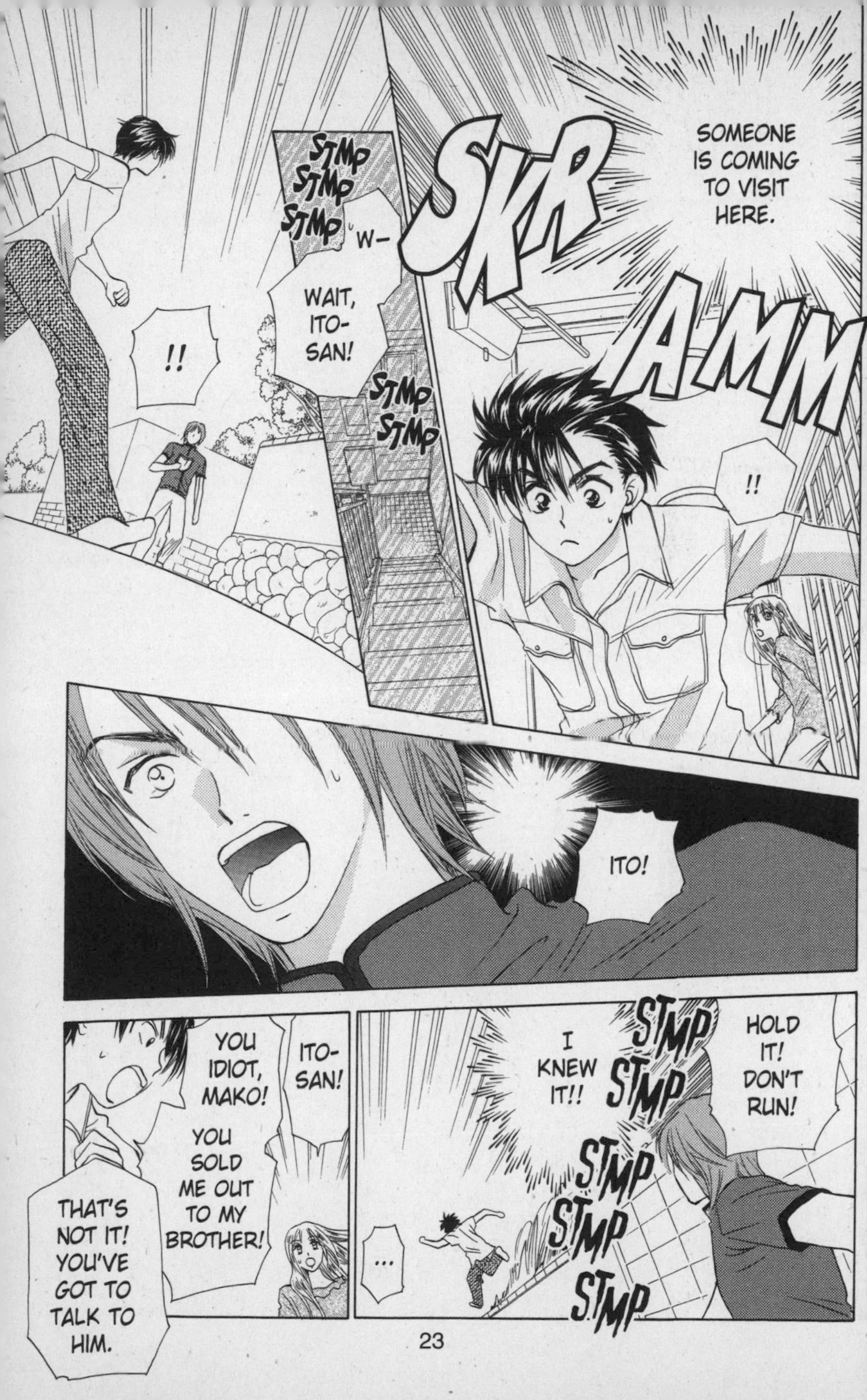
SOMEONE IS COMING TO VISIT HERE.
SKRAMM
!!
STMP STMP STMP
W-
WAIT, ITO-SAN!
STMP STMP
!!
ITO!
HOLD IT! DON'T RUN!
STMP STMP
I KNEW IT!!
STMP STMP STMP
...
ITO-SAN!
YOU IDIOT, MAKO!
YOU SOLD ME OUT TO MY BROTHER!
THAT'S NOT IT! YOU'VE GOT TO TALK TO HIM.

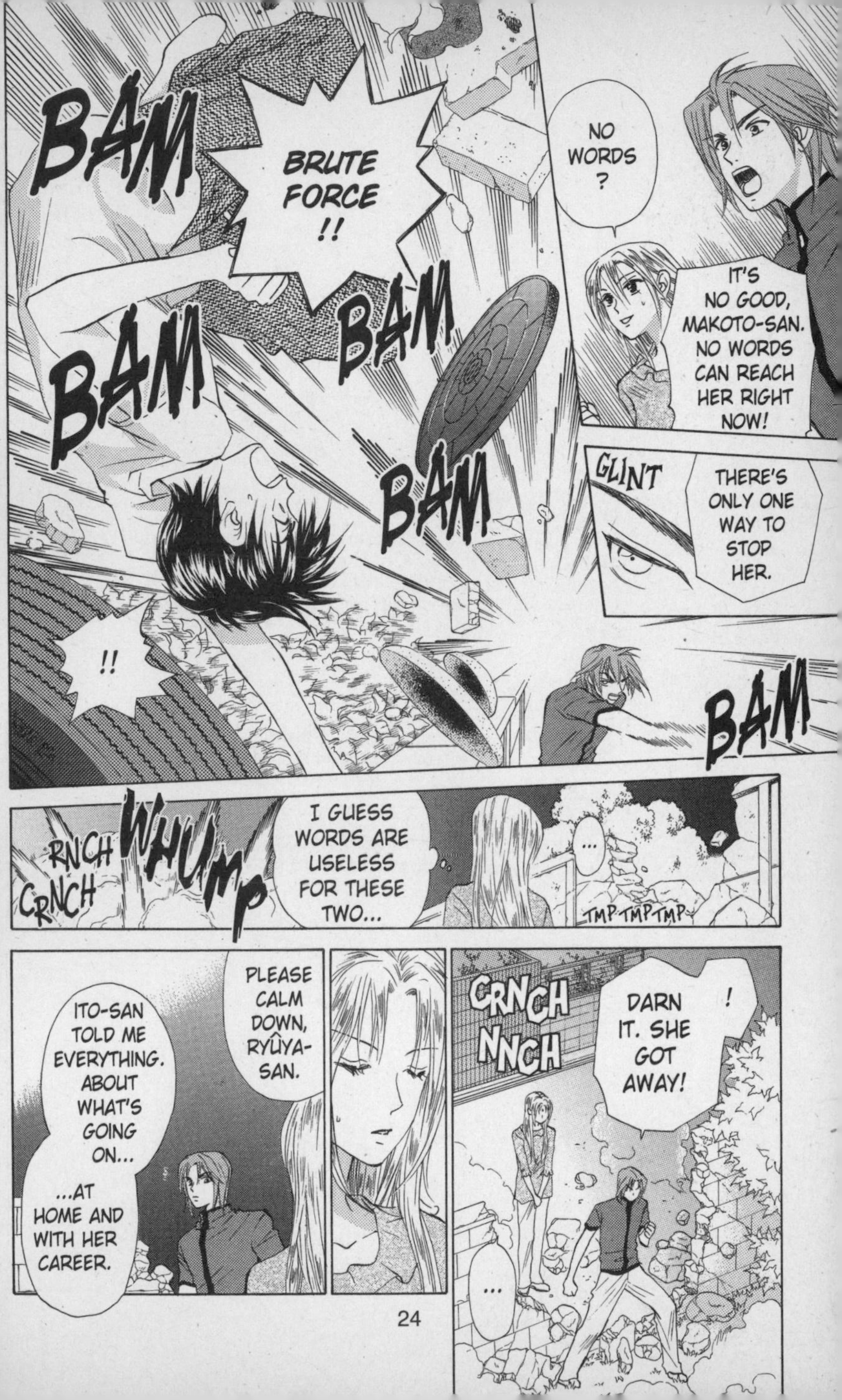
NO WORDS?
IT'S NO GOOD, MAKOTO-SAN. NO WORDS CAN REACH HER RIGHT NOW!
GLINT
THERE'S ONLY ONE WAY TO STOP HER.
BAM
BAM
BRUTE FORCE!!
BAM
BAM
BAM
!!
...
TMP TMP TMP
I GUESS WORDS ARE USELESS FOR THESE TWO...
WHUMP
RNCH
CRNCH
!
DARN IT. SHE GOT AWAY!
CRNCH
NNCH
...
PLEASE CALM DOWN, RYÛYA-SAN.
ITO-SAN TOLD ME EVERYTHING. ABOUT WHAT'S GOING ON...
...AT HOME AND WITH HER CAREER.

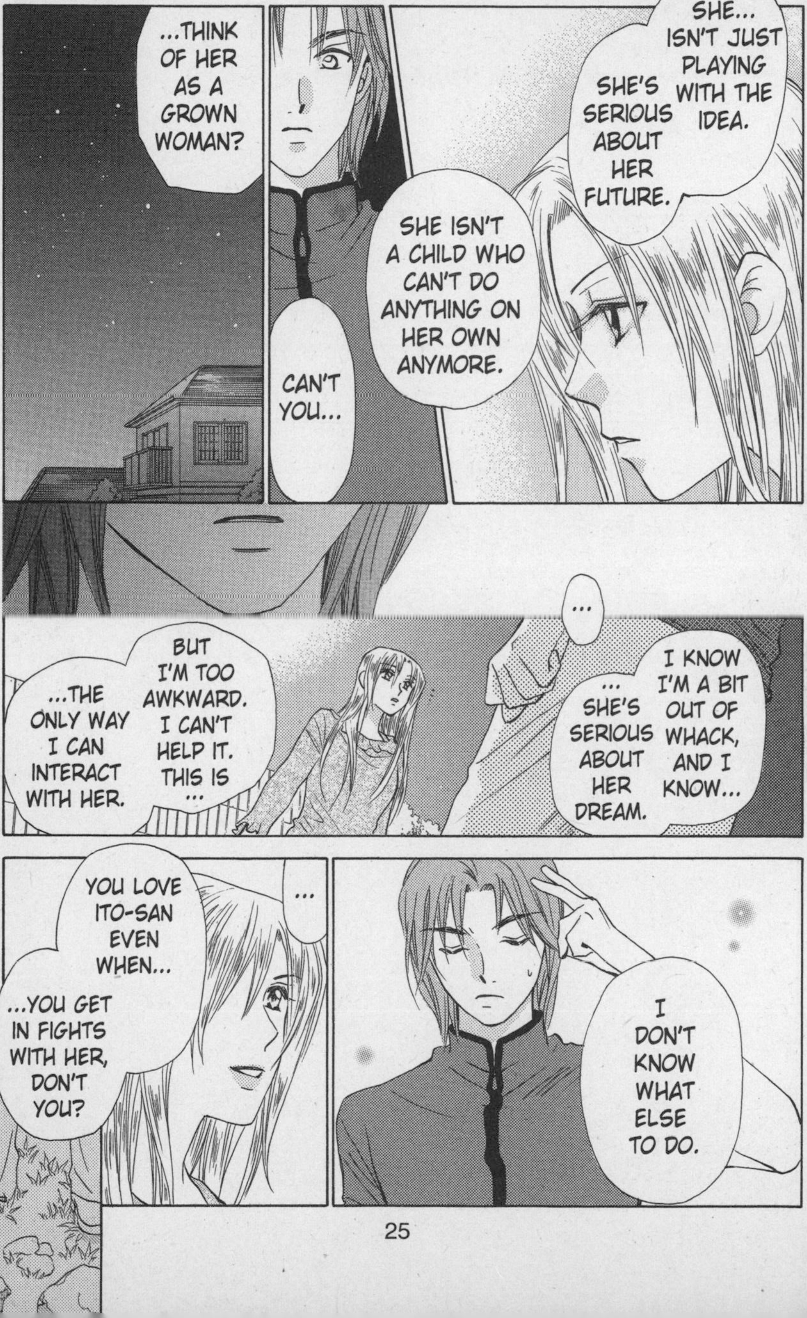
SHE... ISN'T JUST PLAYING WITH THE IDEA.
SHE'S SERIOUS ABOUT HER FUTURE.
SHE ISN'T A CHILD WHO CAN'T DO ANYTHING ON HER OWN ANYMORE.
CAN'T YOU...
...THINK OF HER AS A GROWN WOMAN?
...
I KNOW I'M A BIT OUT OF WHACK, AND I KNOW...
... SHE'S SERIOUS ABOUT HER DREAM.
BUT I'M TOO AWKWARD. I CAN'T HELP IT. THIS IS ...
...THE ONLY WAY I CAN INTERACT WITH HER.
I DON'T KNOW WHAT ELSE TO DO.
...
YOU LOVE ITO-SAN EVEN WHEN...
...YOU GET IN FIGHTS WITH HER, DON'T YOU?

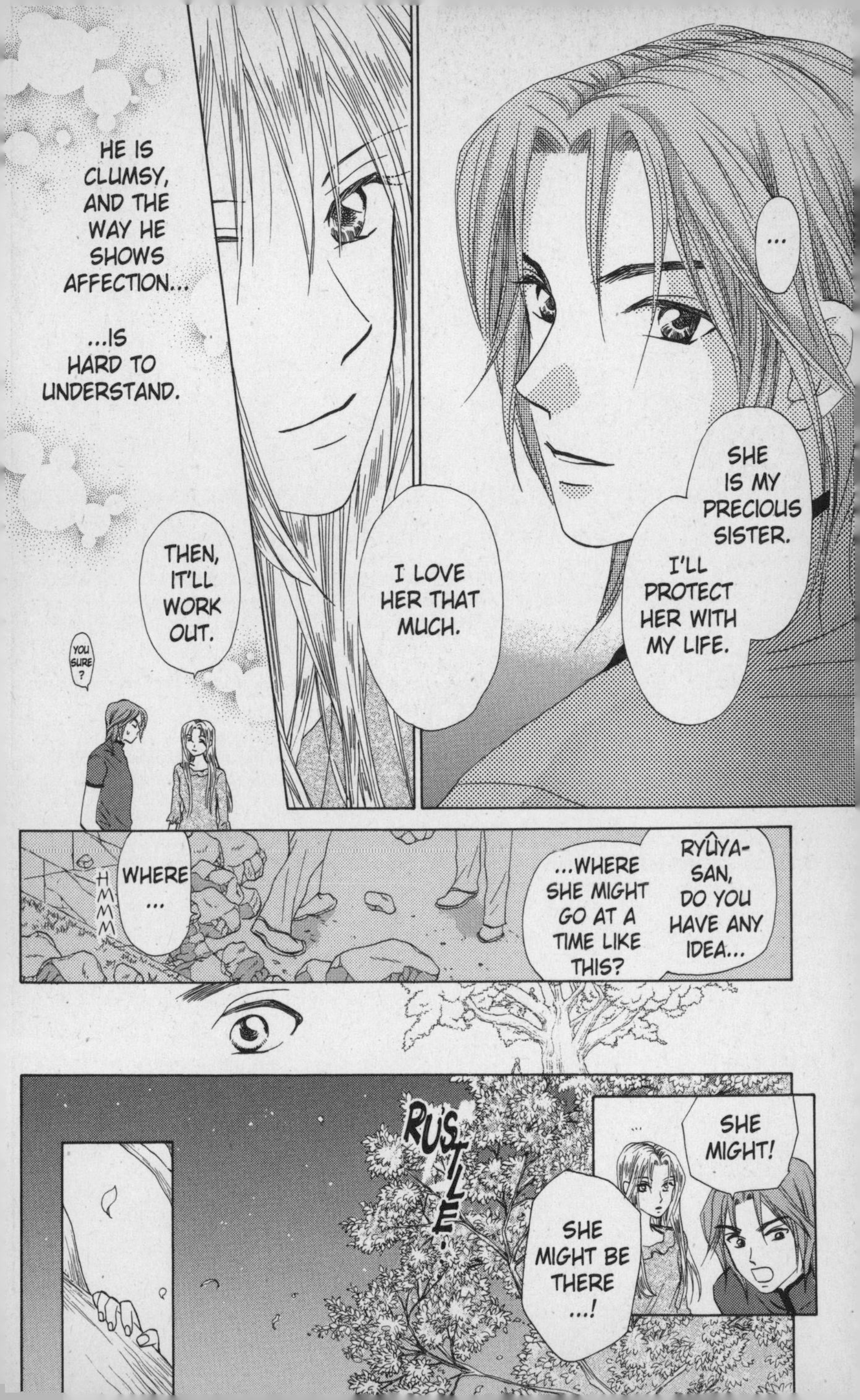
...
SHE IS MY PRECIOUS SISTER.
I'LL PROTECT HER WITH MY LIFE.
I LOVE HER THAT MUCH.
HE IS CLUMSY, AND THE WAY HE SHOWS AFFECTION...
...IS HARD TO UNDERSTAND.
THEN, IT'LL WORK OUT.
YOU SURE?
RYÛYA-SAN, DO YOU HAVE ANY IDEA...
...WHERE SHE MIGHT GO AT A TIME LIKE THIS?
WHERE ...
HMMM
SHE MIGHT!
...
SHE MIGHT BE THERE ...!
RUSTLE

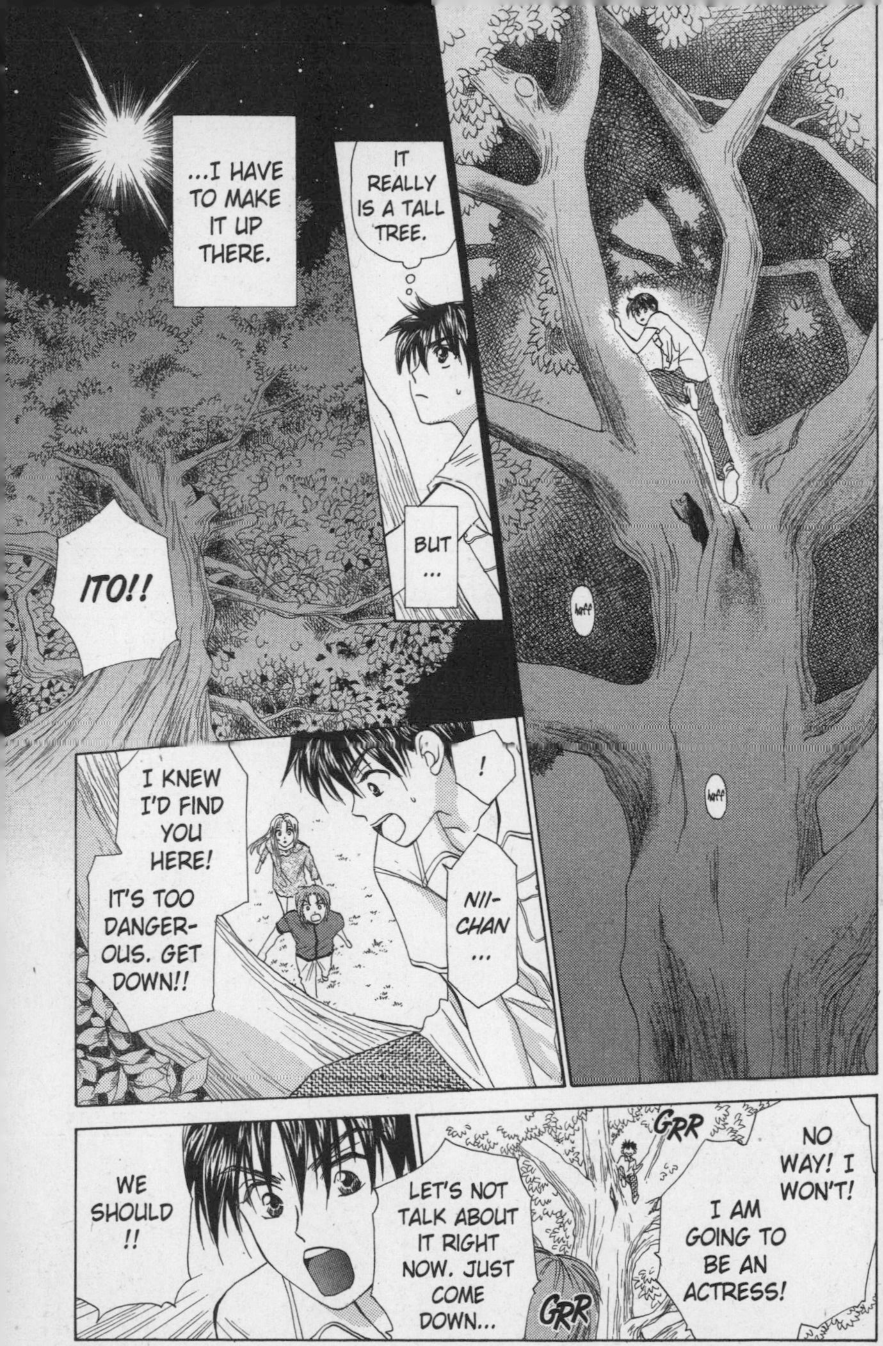

haff
haff
IT REALLY IS A TALL TREE.
BUT...
...I HAVE TO MAKE IT UP THERE.
ITO!!
!
NII-CHAN...
I KNEW I'D FIND YOU HERE!
IT'S TOO DANGER-OUS. GET DOWN!!
NO WAY! I WON'T!
I AM GOING TO BE AN ACTRESS!
GRR
GRR
LET'S NOT TALK ABOUT IT RIGHT NOW. JUST COME DOWN...
WE SHOULD!!

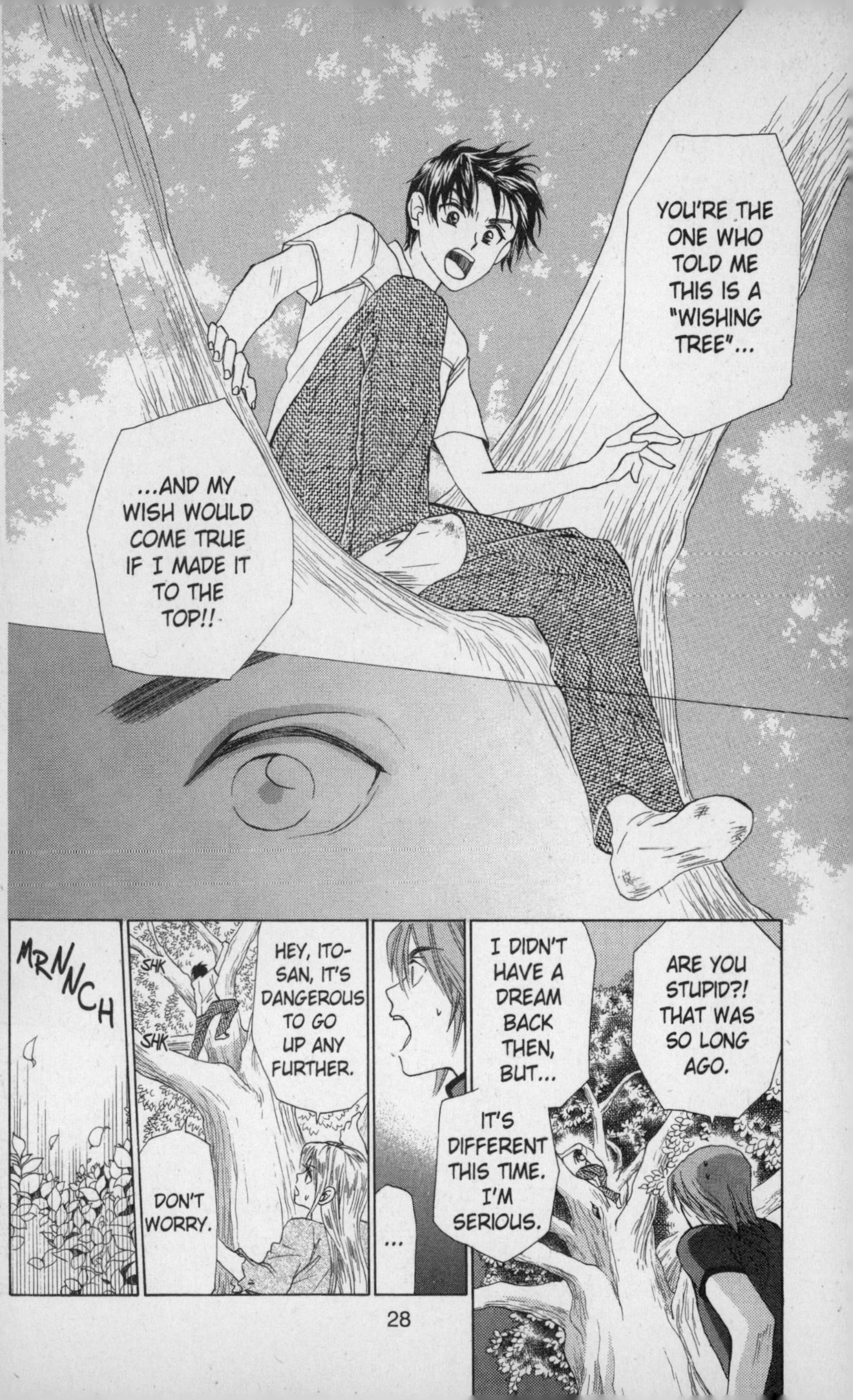
YOU'RE THE ONE WHO TOLD ME THIS IS A "WISHING TREE"...
...AND MY WISH WOULD COME TRUE IF I MADE IT TO THE TOP!!
ARE YOU STUPID?! THAT WAS SO LONG AGO.
I DIDN'T HAVE A DREAM BACK THEN, BUT...
IT'S DIFFERENT THIS TIME. I'M SERIOUS.
...
HEY, ITO-SAN, IT'S DANGEROUS TO GO UP ANY FURTHER.
SHK
SHK
DON'T WORRY.
MRNNCH

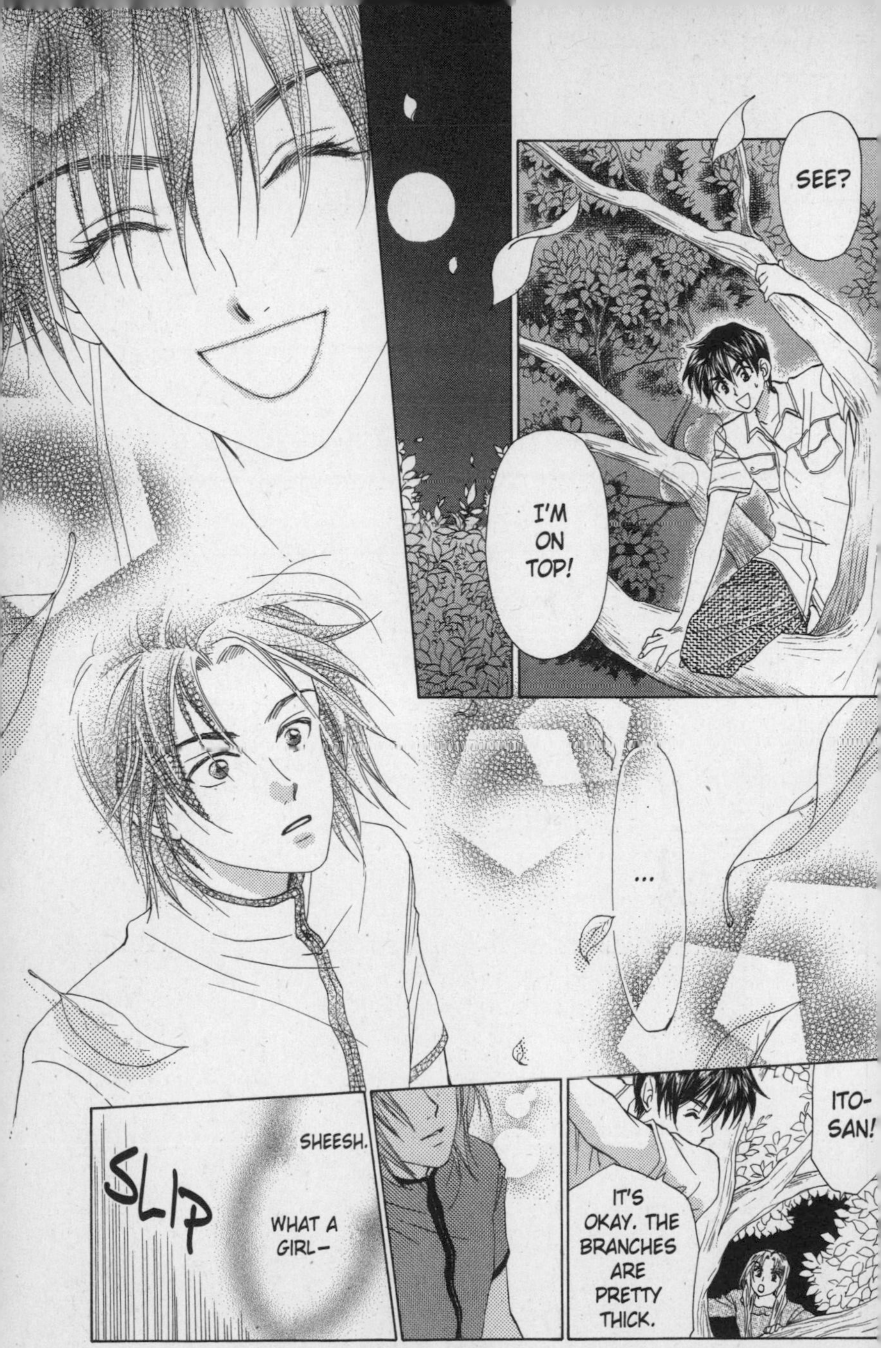
SEE?
I'M ON TOP!
...
ITO-SAN!
IT'S OKAY. THE BRANCHES ARE PRETTY THICK.
SHEESH.
WHAT A GIRL–
SLIP

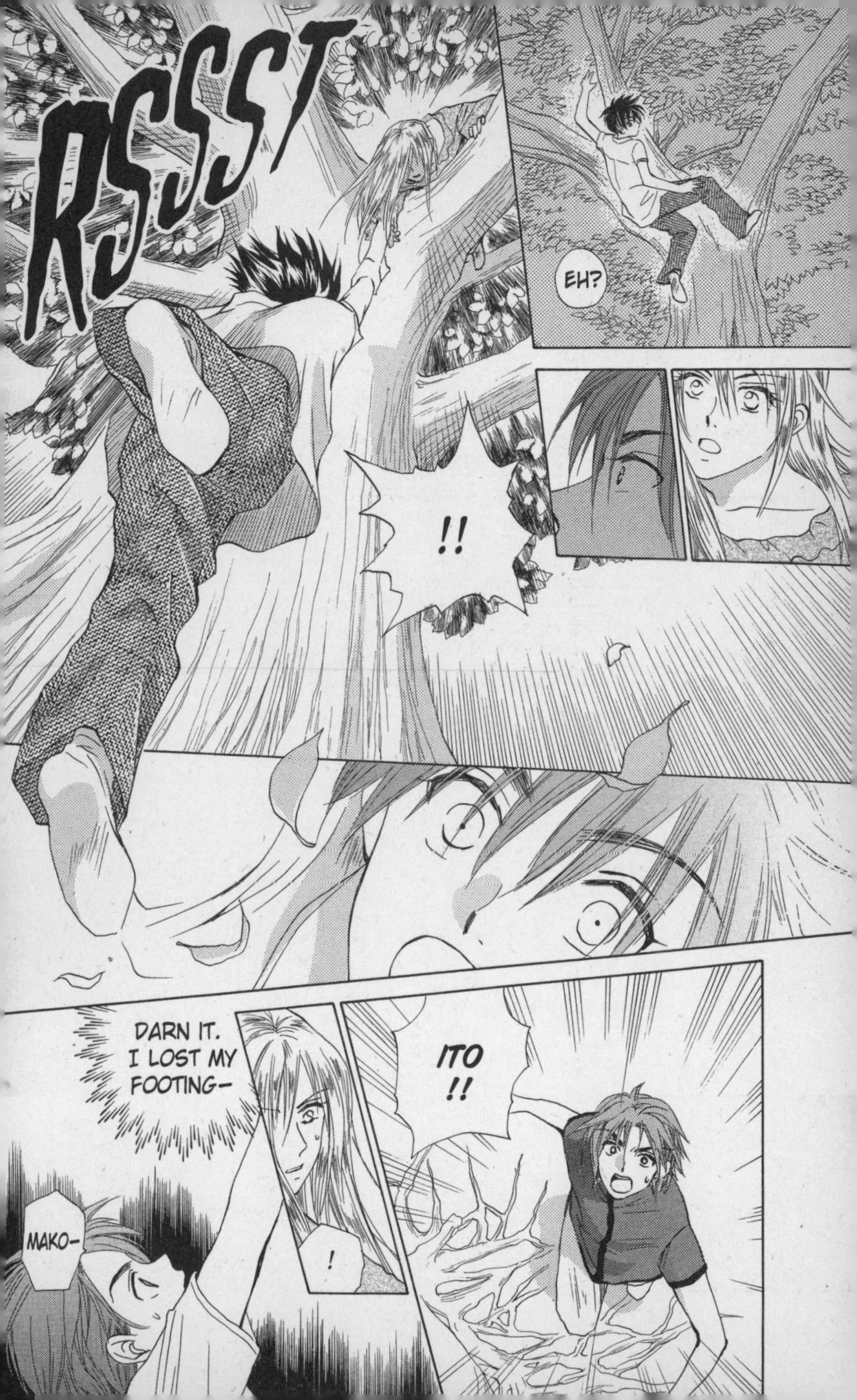
EH?
RSSST
!!
ITO !!
DARN IT. I LOST MY FOOTING-
!
MAKO-

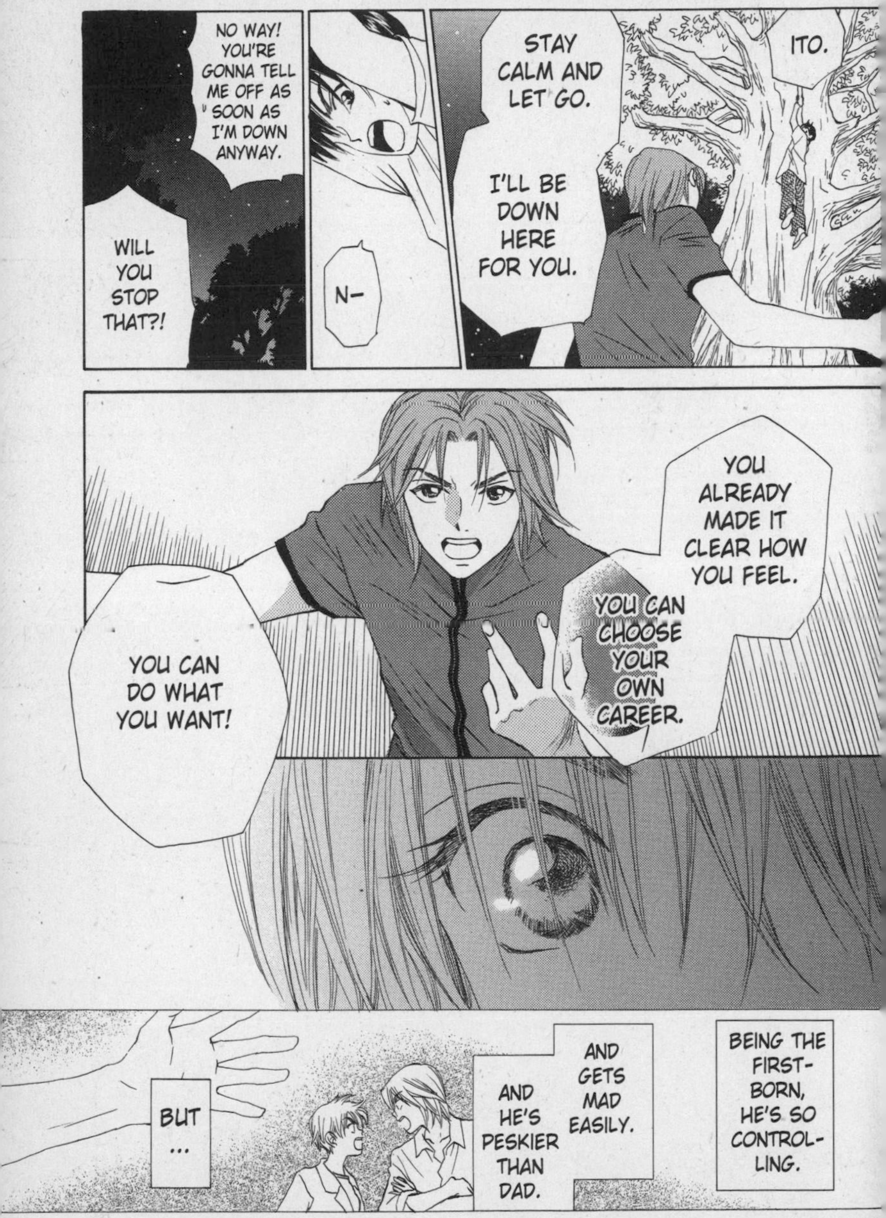
ITO.
STAY CALM AND LET GO.
I'LL BE DOWN HERE FOR YOU.
N–
NO WAY! YOU'RE GONNA TELL ME OFF AS SOON AS I'M DOWN ANYWAY.
WILL YOU STOP THAT?!
YOU ALREADY MADE IT CLEAR HOW YOU FEEL.
YOU CAN CHOOSE YOUR OWN CAREER.
YOU CAN DO WHAT YOU WANT!
BEING THE FIRST-BORN, HE'S SO CONTROL-LING.
AND GETS MAD EASILY.
AND HE'S PESKIER THAN DAD.
BUT ...

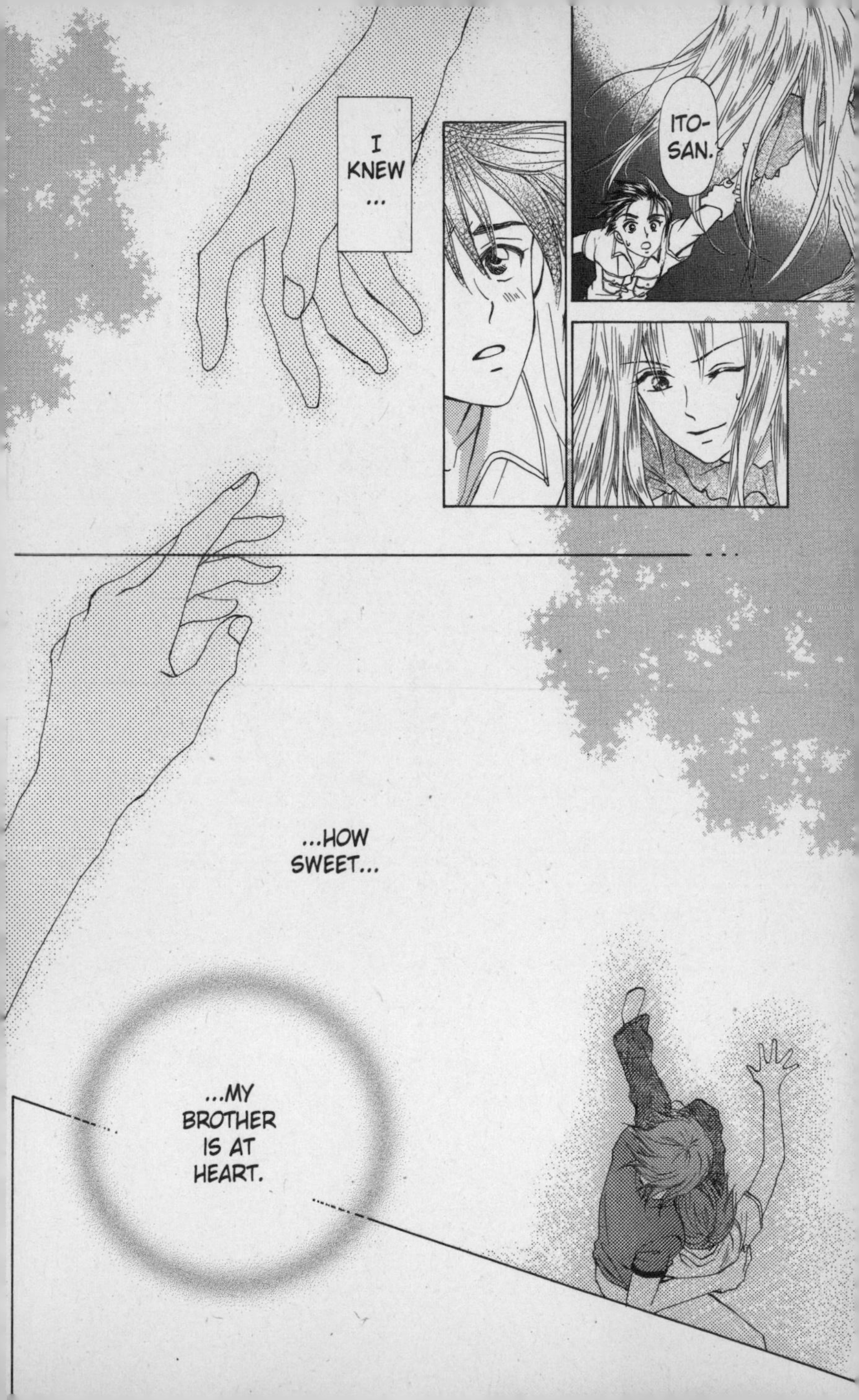
ITO-SAN.
I KNEW ...
...HOW SWEET...
...MY BROTHER IS AT HEART.

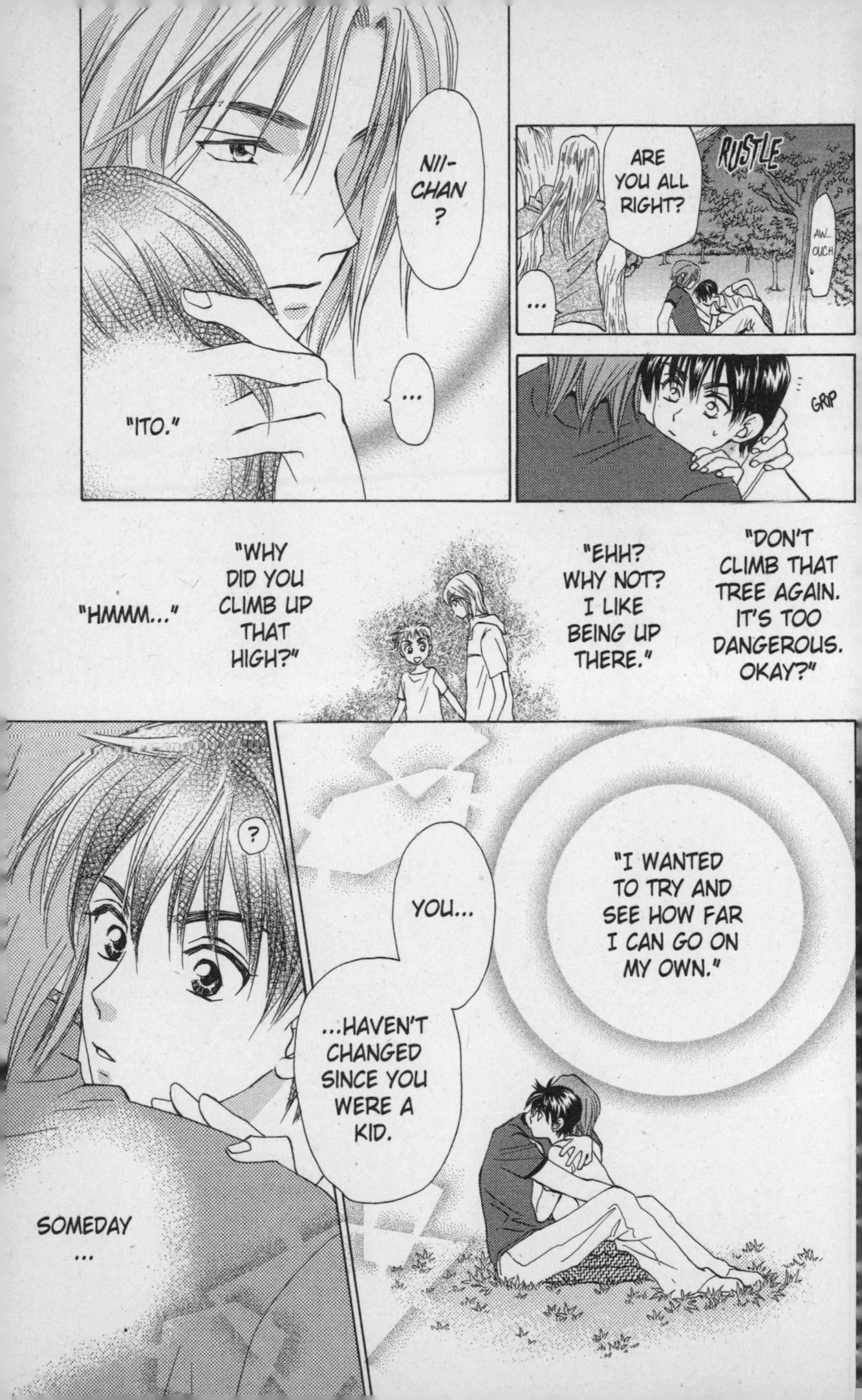
RUSTLE
AW... OUCH
ARE YOU ALL RIGHT?
...
GRIP
NII-CHAN?
...
"ITO."
"DON'T CLIMB THAT TREE AGAIN. IT'S TOO DANGEROUS. OKAY?"
"EHH? WHY NOT? I LIKE BEING UP THERE."
"WHY DID YOU CLIMB UP THAT HIGH?"
"HMMM..."
"I WANTED TO TRY AND SEE HOW FAR I CAN GO ON MY OWN."
YOU...
...HAVEN'T CHANGED SINCE YOU WERE A KID.
?
SOMEDAY ...

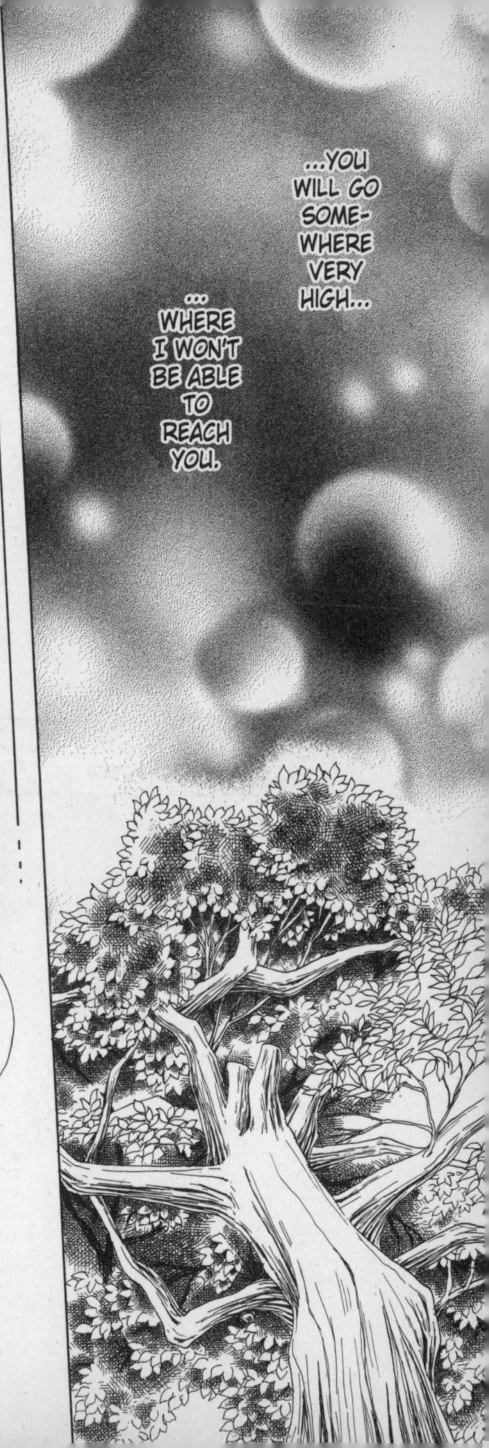
...YOU WILL GO SOME-WHERE VERY HIGH...
...WHERE I WON'T BE ABLE TO REACH YOU.

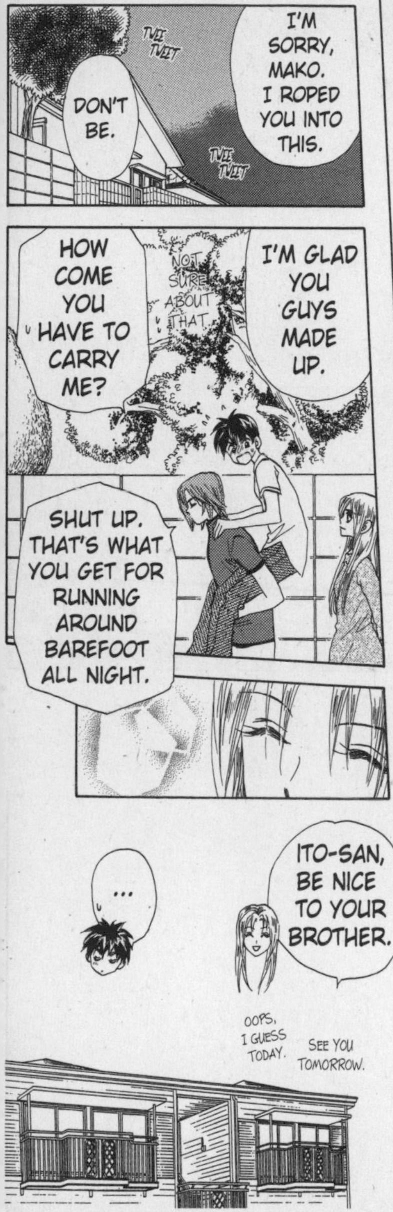
I'M SORRY, MAKO. I ROPED YOU INTO THIS.
TWEE TWEET
TWEE TWEET
DON'T BE.
I'M GLAD YOU GUYS MADE UP.
NOT SURE ABOUT THAT.
HOW COME YOU HAVE TO CARRY ME?
SHUT UP. THAT'S WHAT YOU GET FOR RUNNING AROUND BAREFOOT ALL NIGHT.
ITO-SAN, BE NICE TO YOUR BROTHER.
...
SEE YOU TOMORROW.
OOPS, I GUESS TODAY.

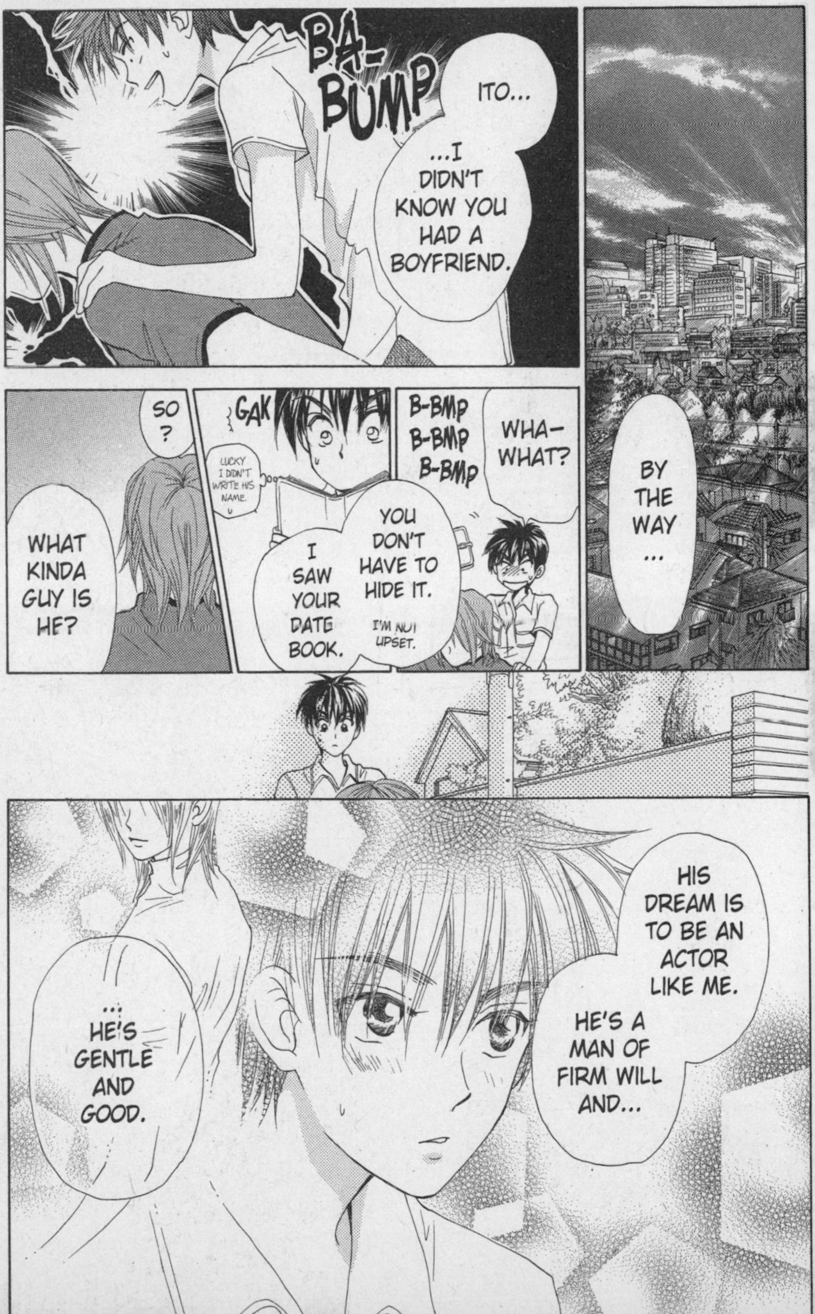
BY THE WAY...
BA-BUMP
ITO...
...I DIDN'T KNOW YOU HAD A BOYFRIEND.
B-BMP B-BMP B-BMP
WHA-WHAT?
YOU DON'T HAVE TO HIDE IT.
I'M NOT UPSET.
I SAW YOUR DATE BOOK.
GAK
LUCKY I DIDN'T WRITE HIS NAME.
SO?
WHAT KINDA GUY IS HE?
HIS DREAM IS TO BE AN ACTOR LIKE ME.
HE'S A MAN OF FIRM WILL AND...
...HE'S GENTLE AND GOOD.

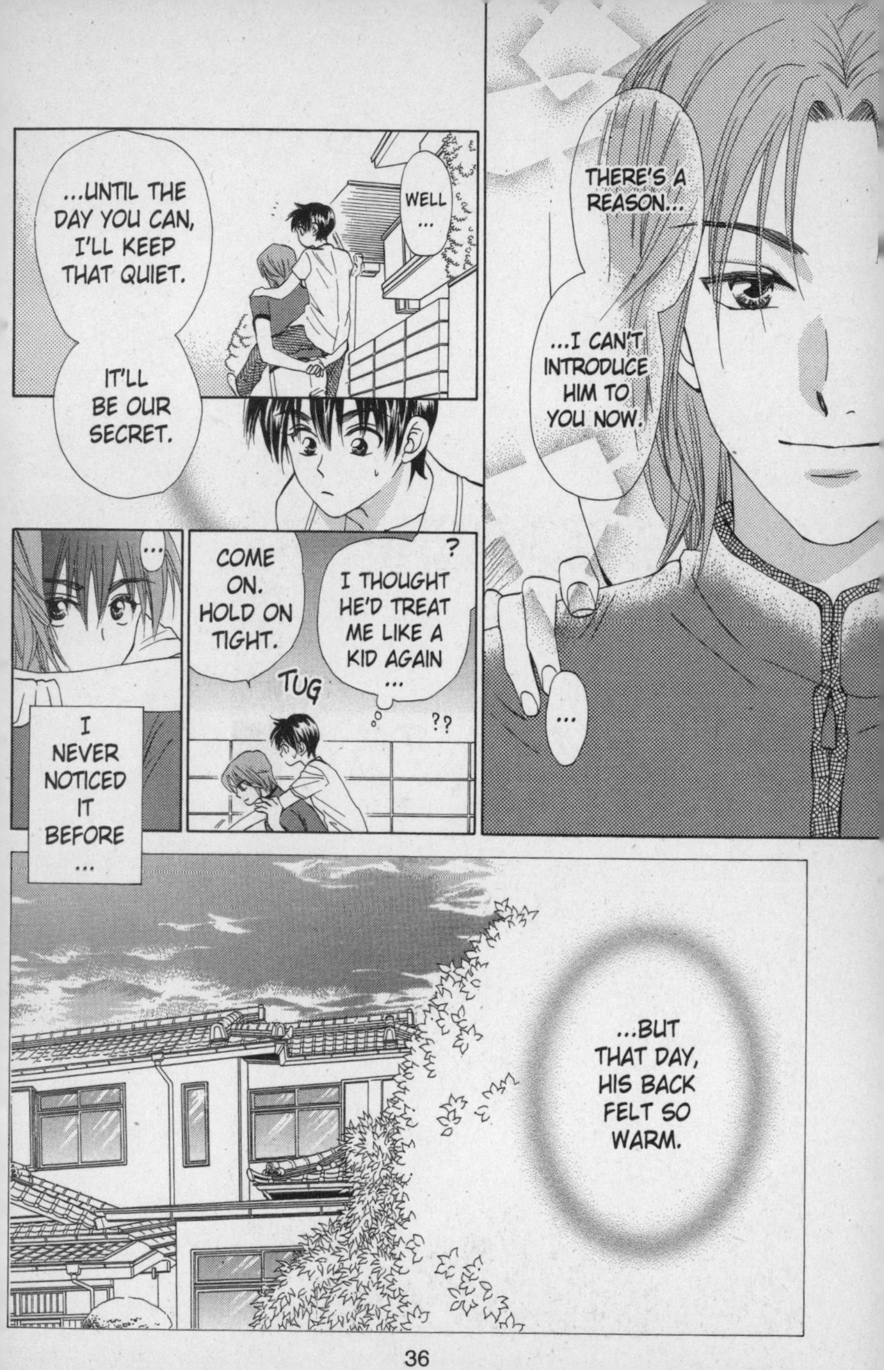
THERE'S A REASON...
...I CAN'T INTRODUCE HIM TO YOU NOW.
...
...UNTIL THE DAY YOU CAN, I'LL KEEP THAT QUIET.
WELL ...
IT'LL BE OUR SECRET.
?
COME ON. HOLD ON TIGHT.
I THOUGHT HE'D TREAT ME LIKE A KID AGAIN ...
TUG
??
...
I NEVER NOTICED IT BEFORE ...
...BUT THAT DAY, HIS BACK FELT SO WARM.

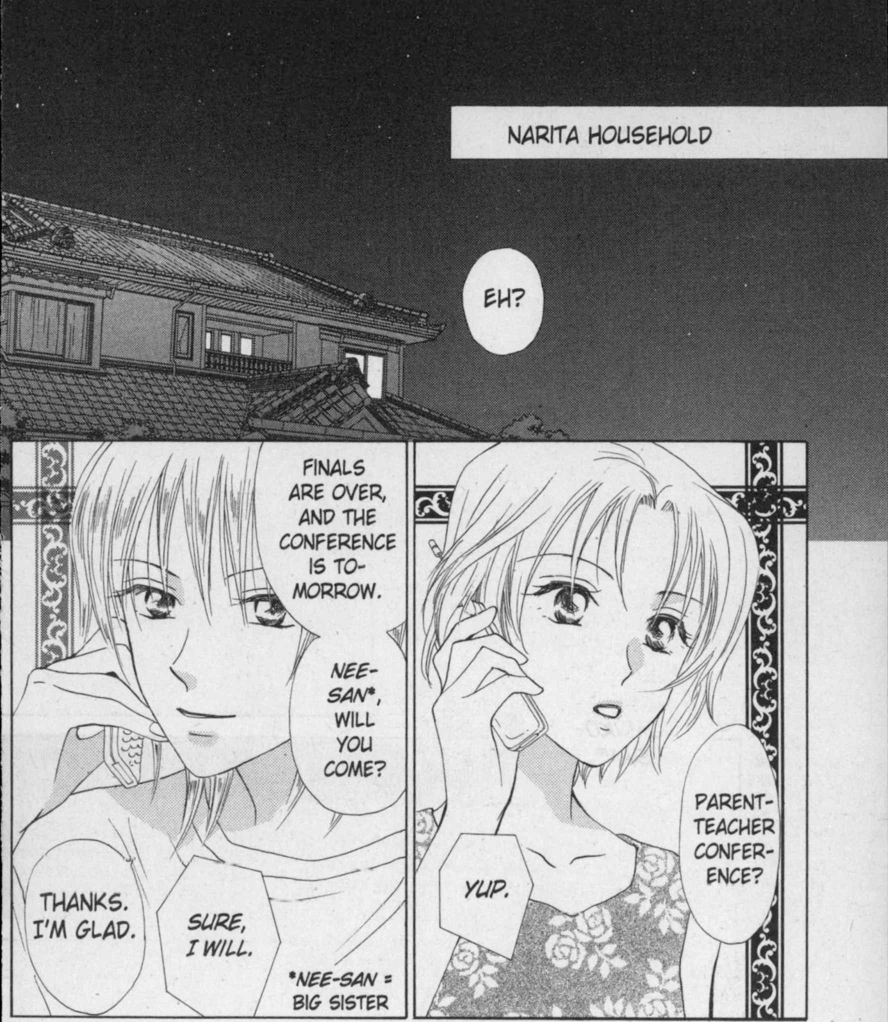
NARITA HOUSEHOLD
EH?
PARENT-TEACHER CONFERENCE?
YUP.
FINALS ARE OVER, AND THE CONFERENCE IS TO-MORROW.
NEE-SAN*, WILL YOU COME?
SURE, I WILL.
THANKS. I'M GLAD.
*NEE-SAN = BIG SISTER

-Behind the Scenes Story- ②

The *Omiai* (formally arranged date) episode for Akane is actually something I've warmed up to for quite some time, since around episode 5 or 6 of *WJ*. But at the time, Yûto was not involved in the plot, and Ito and Makoto were alone to rescue her. Besides, it had too few pages.
I am so happy that it could finally see the light of day.
But when I was working on the first half, my family and assistants started a big argument over Yûto.
Very explosive.

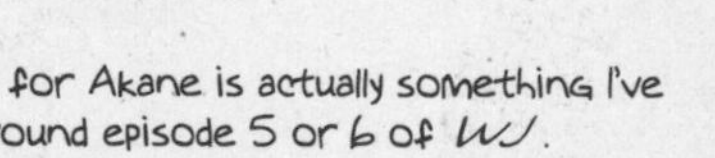
HOW COME YÛTO-SAN IS SO SMOOTH WITH WOMEN?
↑ Good point.
MAYBE HE FOOLS AROUND A LOT.
Mother
NOOO!!

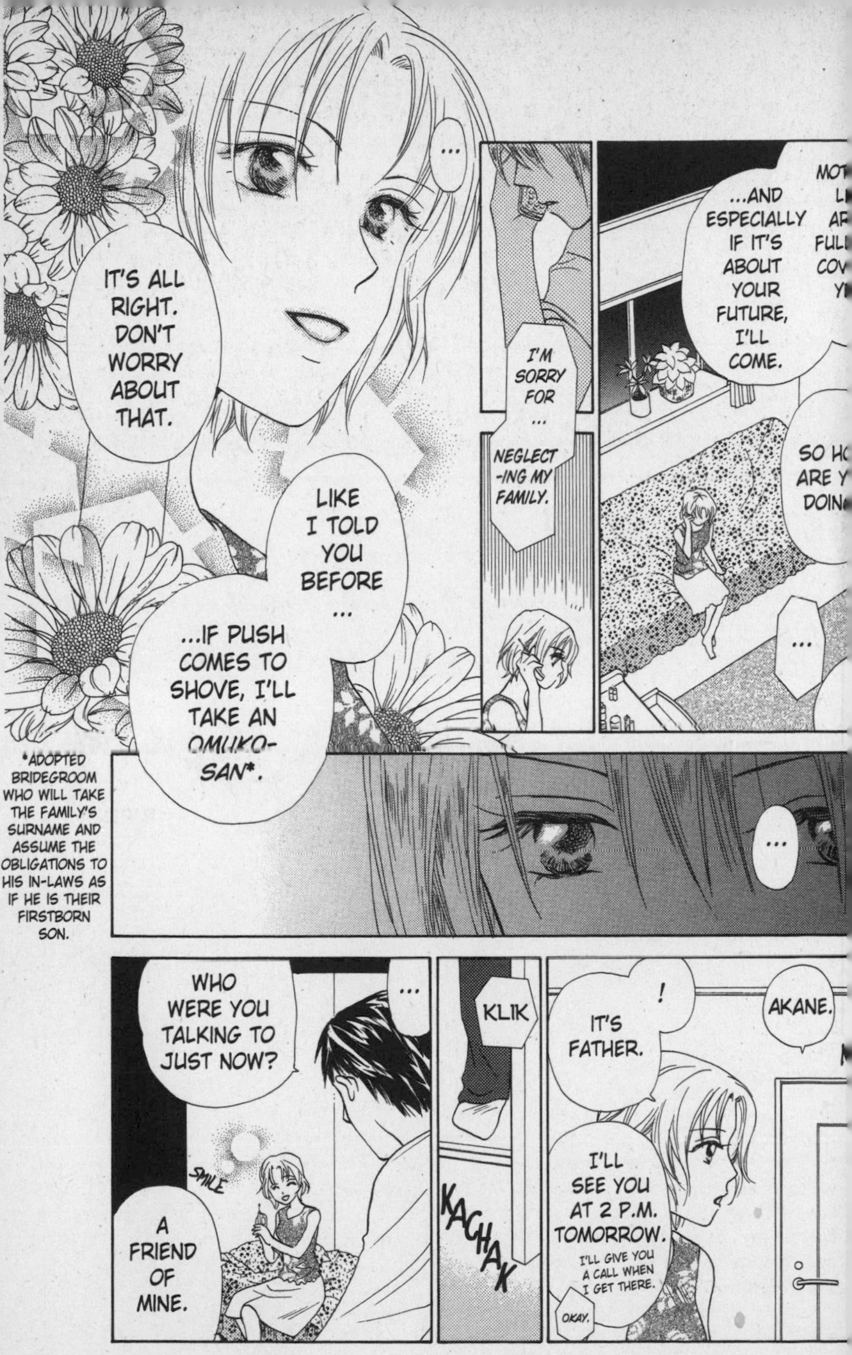
...AND ESPECIALLY IF IT'S ABOUT YOUR FUTURE, I'LL COME.
...
I'M SORRY FOR ...
NEGLECT-ING MY FAMILY.
...
...
IT'S ALL RIGHT. DON'T WORRY ABOUT THAT.
LIKE I TOLD YOU BEFORE ...
...IF PUSH COMES TO SHOVE, I'LL TAKE AN OMUKO-SAN*.
...
AKANE.
!
IT'S FATHER.
I'LL SEE YOU AT 2 P.M. TOMORROW.
I'LL GIVE YOU A CALL WHEN I GET THERE.
OKAY.
KLIK
KACHAK
...
WHO WERE YOU TALKING TO JUST NOW?
SMILE
A FRIEND OF MINE.

*ADOPTED BRIDEGROOM WHO WILL TAKE THE FAMILY'S SURNAME AND ASSUME THE OBLIGATIONS TO HIS IN-LAWS AS IF HE IS THEIR FIRSTBORN SON.

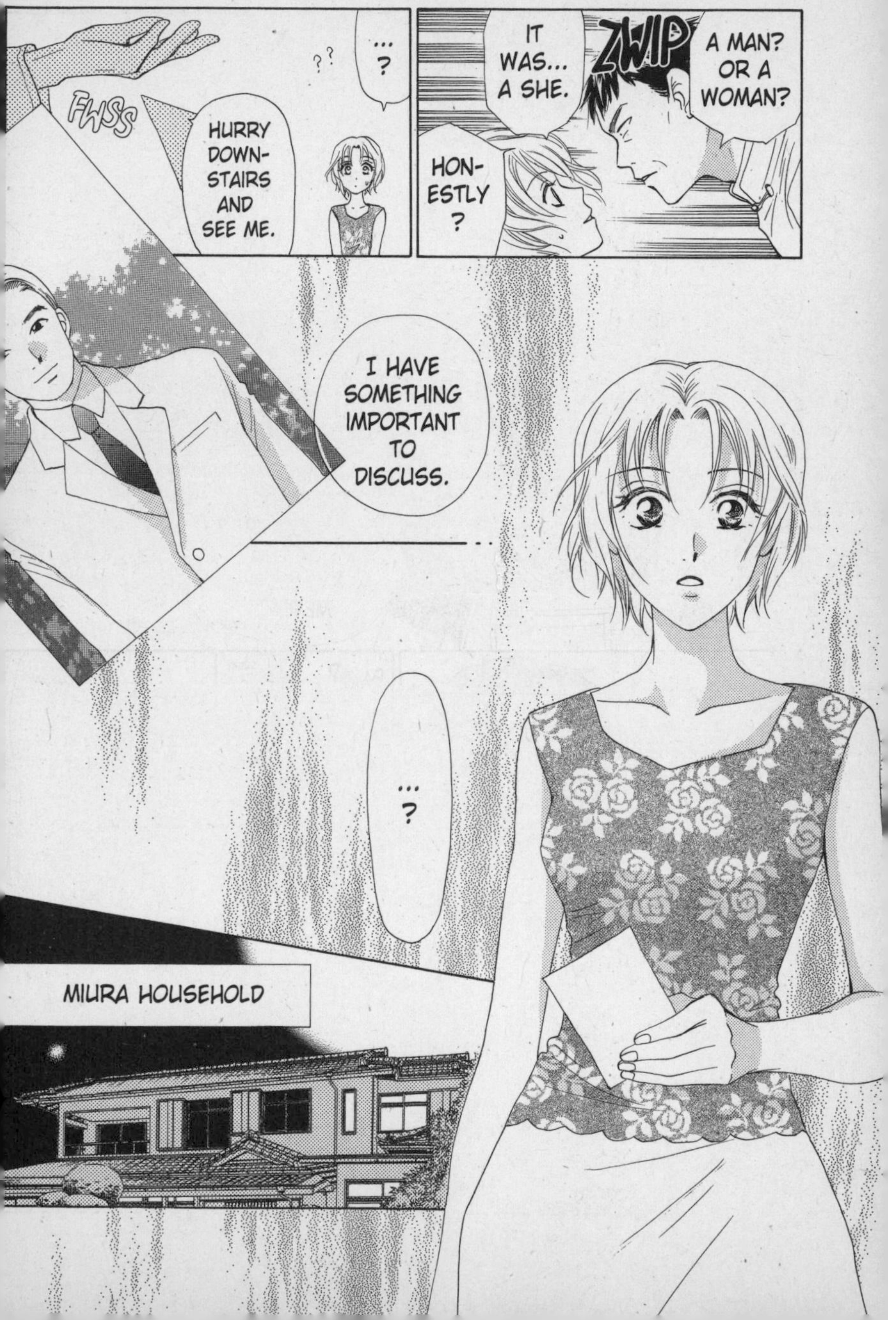

A MAN? OR A WOMAN?
ZWIP
IT WAS... A SHE.
HON-ESTLY?
...?
??
HURRY DOWN-STAIRS AND SEE ME.
FWSS
I HAVE SOMETHING IMPORTANT TO DISCUSS.
...?
MIURA HOUSEHOLD

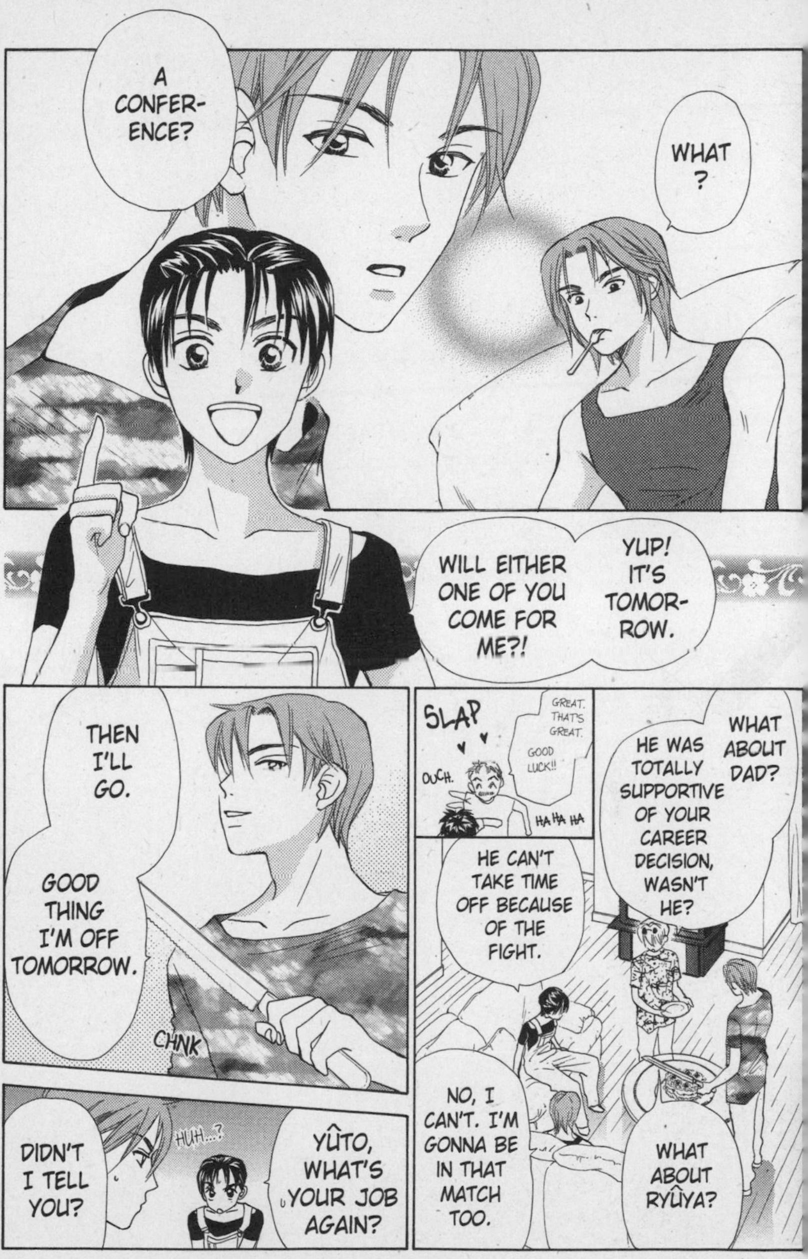
WHAT ?
A CONFERENCE?
YUP! IT'S TOMORROW.
WILL EITHER ONE OF YOU COME FOR ME?!
WHAT ABOUT DAD?
HE WAS TOTALLY SUPPORTIVE OF YOUR CAREER DECISION, WASN'T HE?
GREAT. THAT'S GREAT.
GOOD LUCK!!
SLAP
OUCH.
HA HA HA
HE CAN'T TAKE TIME OFF BECAUSE OF THE FIGHT.
WHAT ABOUT RYÛYA?
NO, I CAN'T. I'M GONNA BE IN THAT MATCH TOO.
THEN I'LL GO.
GOOD THING I'M OFF TOMORROW.
CHNK
YÛTO, WHAT'S YOUR JOB AGAIN?
HUH...?
DIDN'T I TELL YOU?

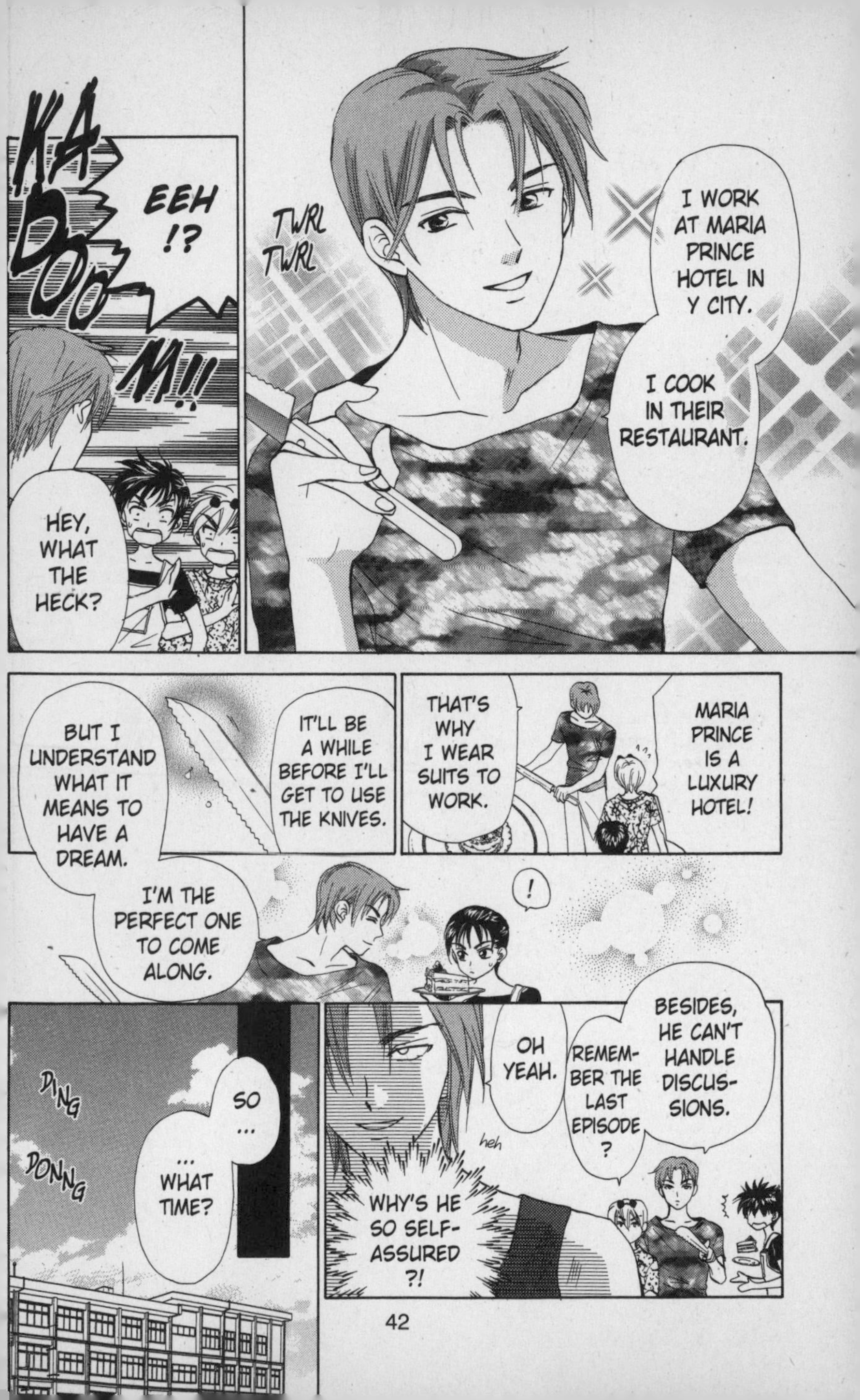
TWRL TWRL
I WORK AT MARIA PRINCE HOTEL IN Y CITY.
I COOK IN THEIR RESTAURANT.
KA BOOM!!
EEH !?
HEY, WHAT THE HECK?
MARIA PRINCE IS A LUXURY HOTEL!
THAT'S WHY I WEAR SUITS TO WORK.
IT'LL BE A WHILE BEFORE I'LL GET TO USE THE KNIVES.
BUT I UNDERSTAND WHAT IT MEANS TO HAVE A DREAM.
!
I'M THE PERFECT ONE TO COME ALONG.
BESIDES, HE CAN'T HANDLE DISCUS-SIONS.
REMEM-BER THE LAST EPISODE ?
OH YEAH.
heh
WHY'S HE SO SELF-ASSURED ?!
DING DONNG
SO ...
... WHAT TIME?

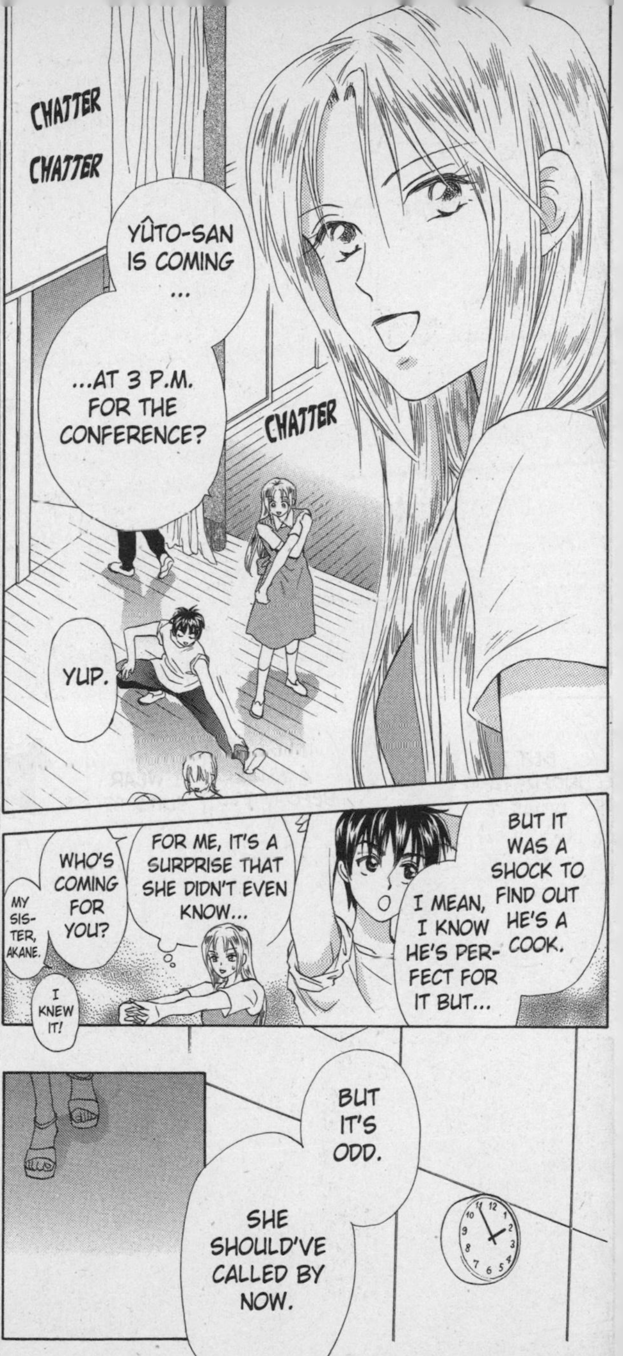
CHATTER
CHATTER
YÛTO-SAN IS COMING ...
...AT 3 P.M. FOR THE CONFERENCE?
CHATTER
YUP.
BUT IT WAS A SHOCK TO FIND OUT HE'S A COOK.
I MEAN, I KNOW HE'S PERFECT FOR IT BUT...
FOR ME, IT'S A SURPRISE THAT SHE DIDN'T EVEN KNOW...
WHO'S COMING FOR YOU?
MY SISTER, AKANE.
I KNEW IT!
BUT IT'S ODD.
SHE SHOULD'VE CALLED BY NOW.

COMMENT

It seems like I have a habit of writing about my work in spaces like this and in the comment section to be designated for "Please send us letters." Every now and then, I receive a letter asking about my private life. But what is my private life...? I mean, I'm always working--and there's nothing private about it. Oh no!! Making manga and drawing pictures was my hobby, and now that it turned into my job, I realize I don't have any hobbies. (Laugh) Ah ha ha ha! Oh well.

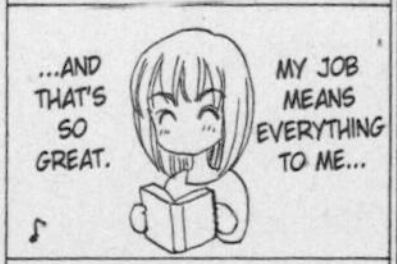
MY JOB MEANS EVERYTHING TO ME...
...AND THAT'S SO GREAT.

I'M TOTALLY HOOKED ON *HUNTER X HUNTER* AT THE MOMENT.

Other things I like to do are to wander about town, have long phone conversations with my friends, and go shopping. Darn normal, right? But in this time and era, I still don't have a game machine, a PC, or a cell phone. I'm not even interested in brand-name products. So I'm often told I'm weird.

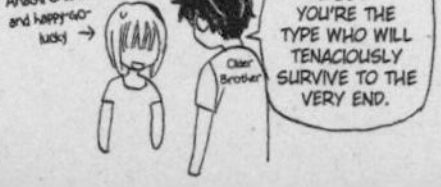
I BET YOU'RE THE TYPE WHO WILL TENACIOUSLY SURVIVE TO THE VERY END.
Older Brother
Anachronistic and happy-go-lucky →

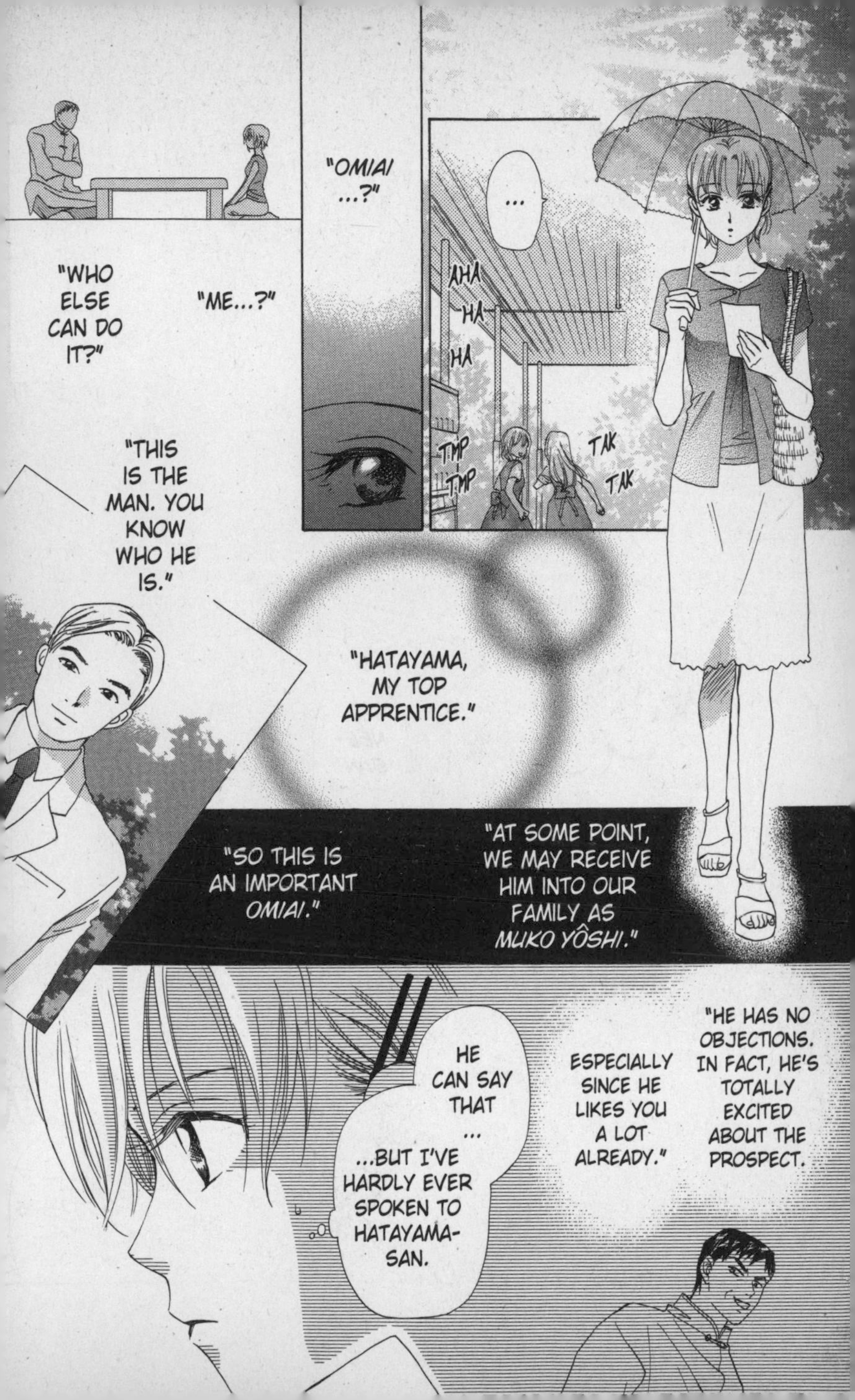
...
AHA HA HA
TMP TMP
TAK TAK
"OMIAI ...?"
"ME...?"
"WHO ELSE CAN DO IT?"
"HATAYAMA, MY TOP APPRENTICE."
"THIS IS THE MAN. YOU KNOW WHO HE IS."
"AT SOME POINT, WE MAY RECEIVE HIM INTO OUR FAMILY AS *MUKO YÔSHI*."
"SO THIS IS AN IMPORTANT *OMIAI*."
"HE HAS NO OBJECTIONS. IN FACT, HE'S TOTALLY EXCITED ABOUT THE PROSPECT.
ESPECIALLY SINCE HE LIKES YOU A LOT ALREADY."
HE CAN SAY THAT ...
...BUT I'VE HARDLY EVER SPOKEN TO HATAYAMA-SAN.

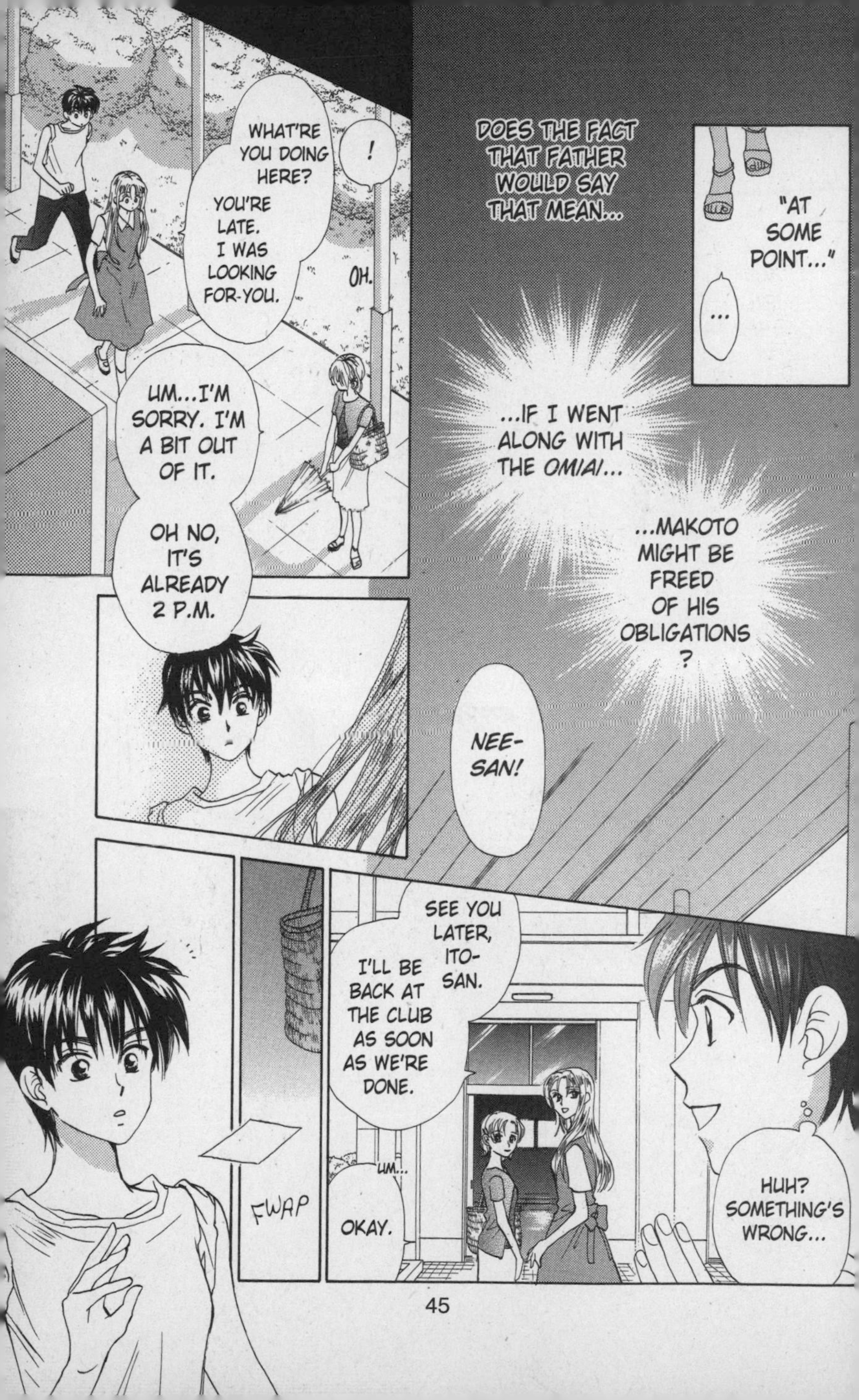
"AT SOME POINT..."
...
DOES THE FACT THAT FATHER WOULD SAY THAT MEAN...
...IF I WENT ALONG WITH THE OMIAI...
...MAKOTO MIGHT BE FREED OF HIS OBLIGATIONS?
NEE-SAN!
!
WHAT'RE YOU DOING HERE?
OH.
YOU'RE LATE. I WAS LOOKING FOR-YOU.
UM...I'M SORRY. I'M A BIT OUT OF IT.
OH NO, IT'S ALREADY 2 P.M.
HUH? SOMETHING'S WRONG...
SEE YOU LATER, ITO-SAN.
I'LL BE BACK AT THE CLUB AS SOON AS WE'RE DONE.
UM...
OKAY.
FWAP

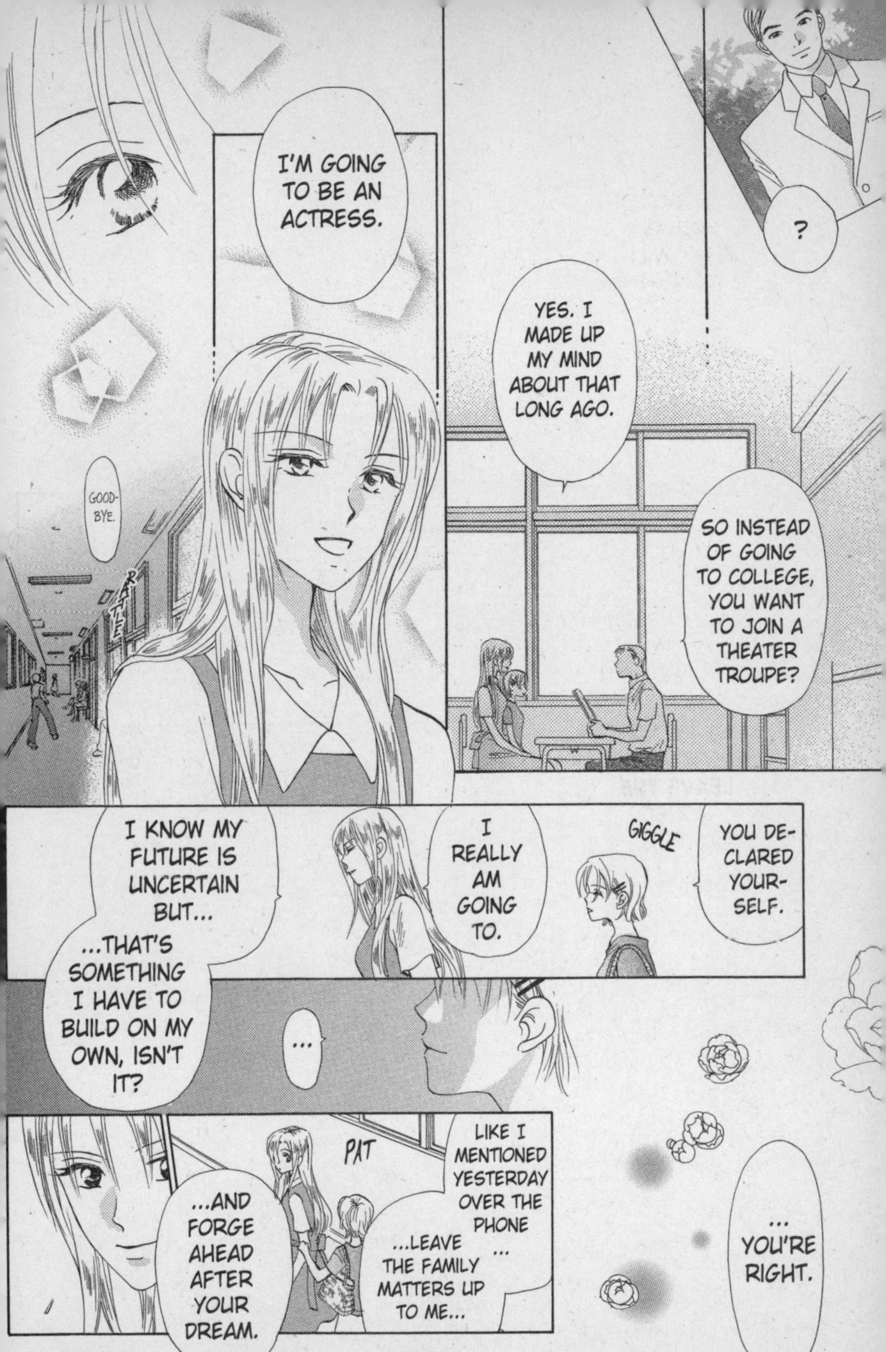
?
YES. I MADE UP MY MIND ABOUT THAT LONG AGO.
SO INSTEAD OF GOING TO COLLEGE, YOU WANT TO JOIN A THEATER TROUPE?
I'M GOING TO BE AN ACTRESS.
GOOD-BYE.
RATTLE
YOU DE-CLARED YOUR-SELF.
GIGGLE
I REALLY AM GOING TO.
I KNOW MY FUTURE IS UNCERTAIN BUT...
...THAT'S SOMETHING I HAVE TO BUILD ON MY OWN, ISN'T IT?
...
... YOU'RE RIGHT.
LIKE I MENTIONED YESTERDAY OVER THE PHONE ...
...LEAVE THE FAMILY MATTERS UP TO ME...
PAT
...AND FORGE AHEAD AFTER YOUR DREAM.

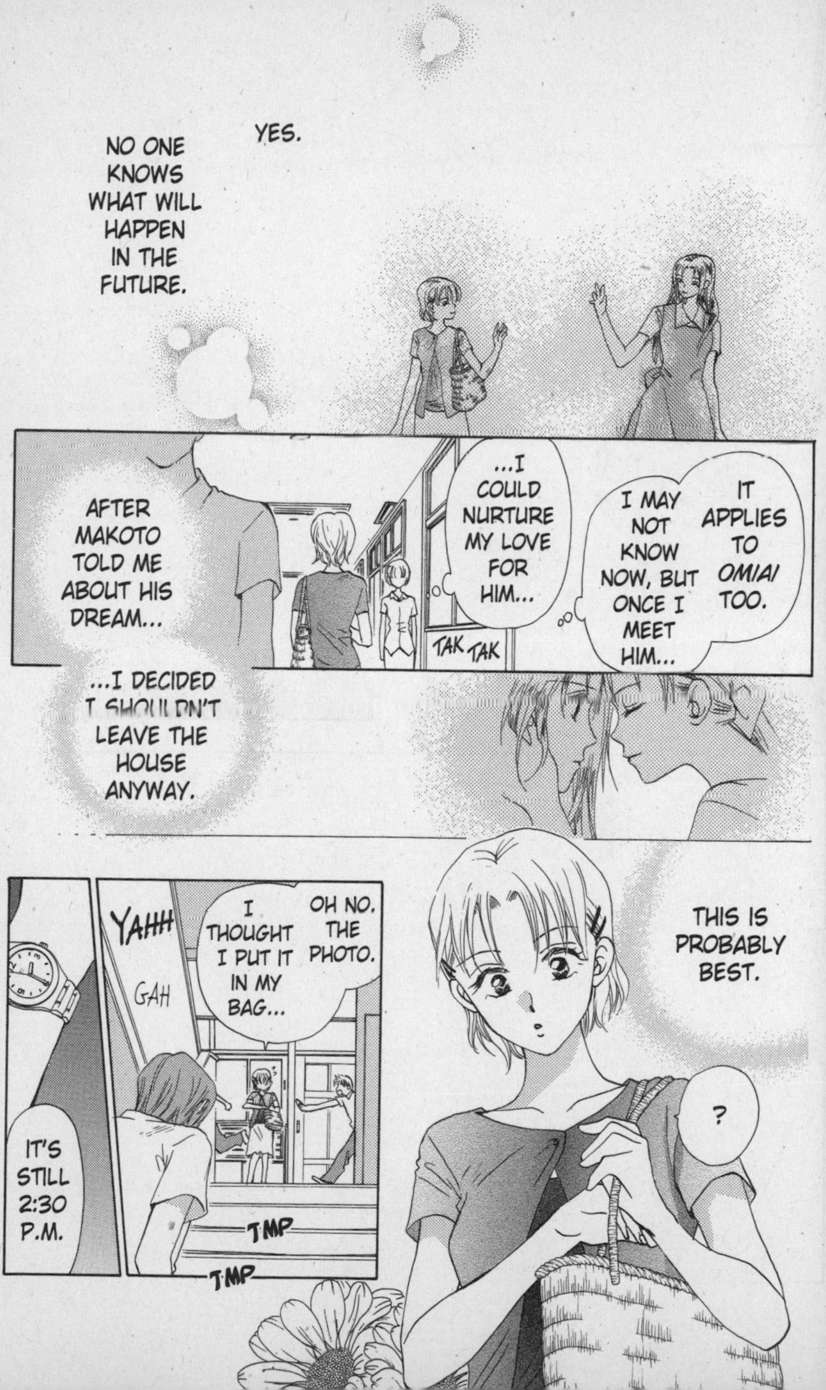
YES.
NO ONE KNOWS WHAT WILL HAPPEN IN THE FUTURE.
IT APPLIES TO *OMIAI* TOO.
I MAY NOT KNOW NOW, BUT ONCE I MEET HIM...
...I COULD NURTURE MY LOVE FOR HIM...
TAK TAK
AFTER MAKOTO TOLD ME ABOUT HIS DREAM...
...I DECIDED I SHOULDN'T LEAVE THE HOUSE ANYWAY.
THIS IS PROBABLY BEST.
?
OH NO. THE PHOTO.
I THOUGHT I PUT IT IN MY BAG...
YAHH
GAH
TMP
TMP
IT'S STILL 2:30 P.M.

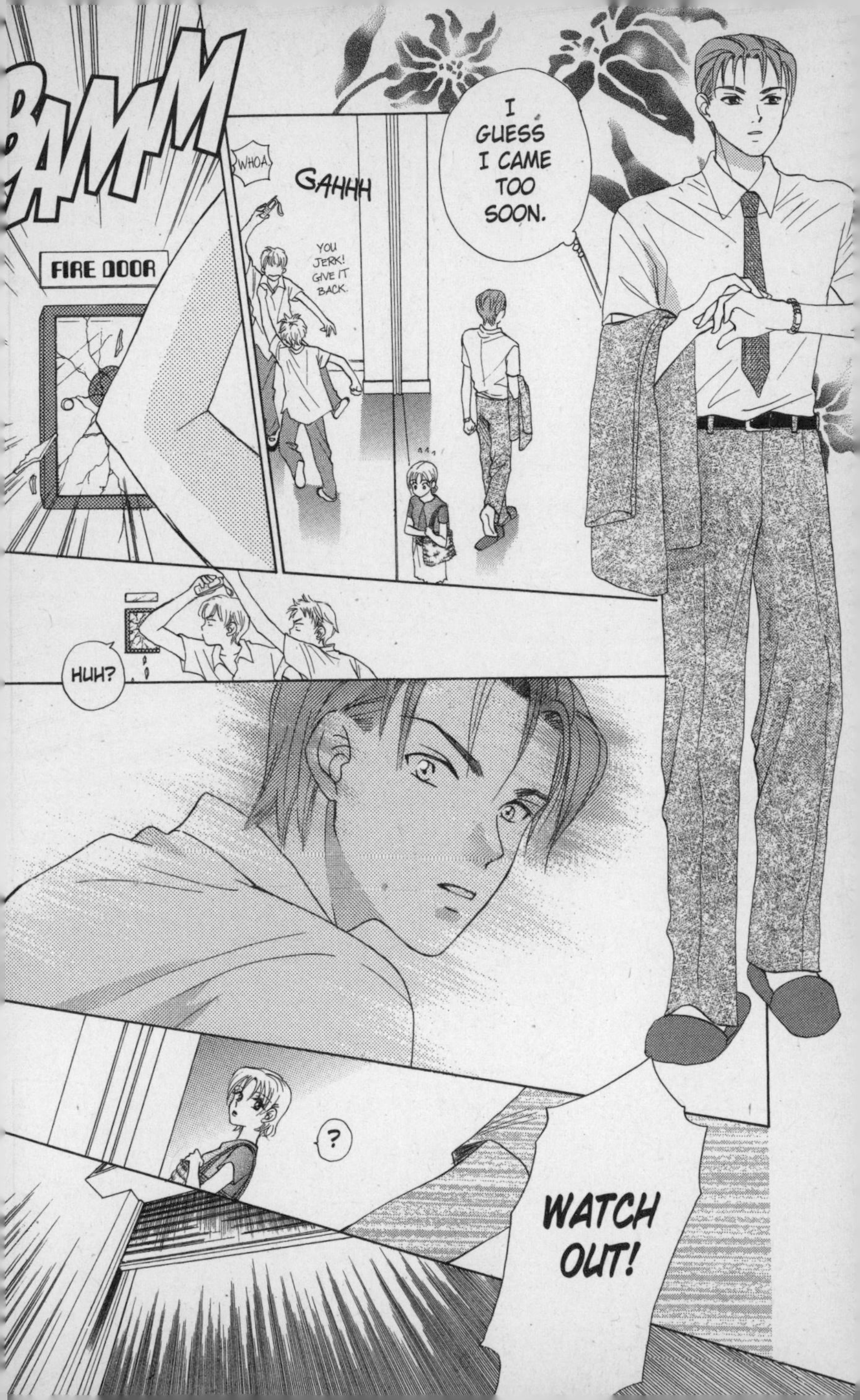
I GUESS I CAME TOO SOON.
WHOA
GAHHH
YOU JERK! GIVE IT BACK.
BAMM
FIRE DOOR
HUH?
WATCH OUT!
?

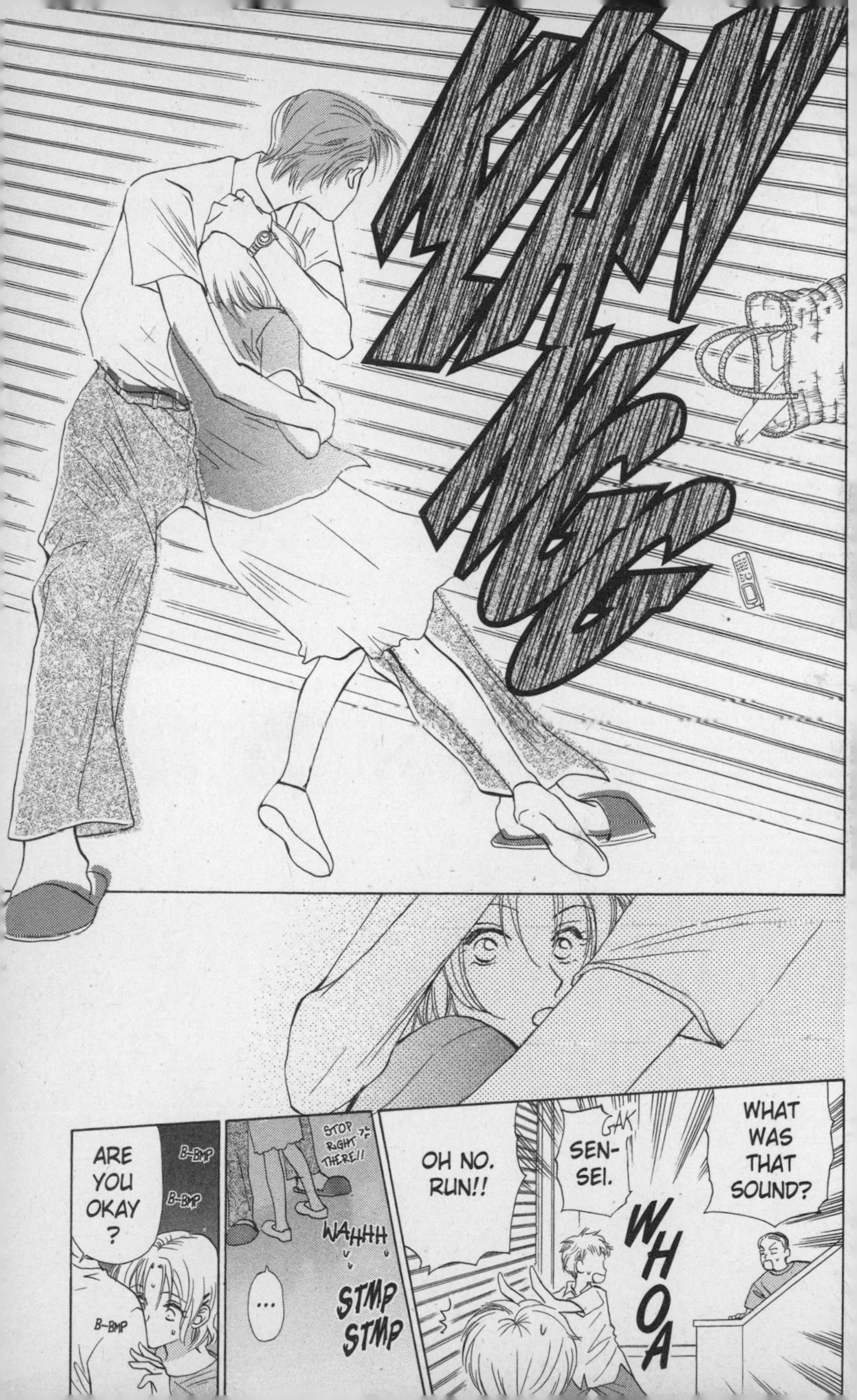
WHAT WAS THAT SOUND?
SEN-SEI.
GAK
WHOA
OH NO. RUN!!
STOP RIGHT THERE!!
WAHHH
...
STMP STMP
B-BMP
B-BMP
ARE YOU OKAY?
B-BMP

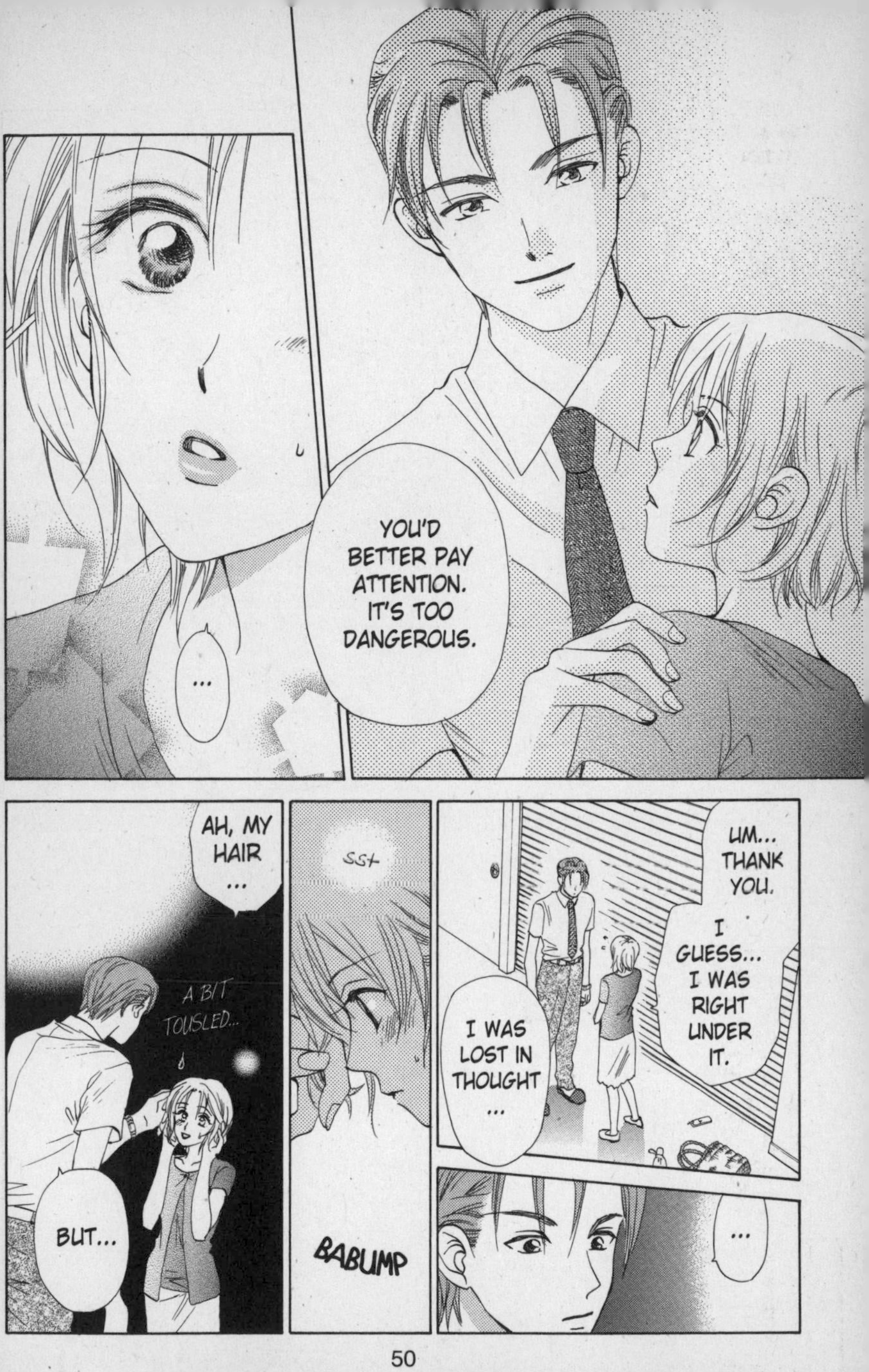
YOU'D BETTER PAY ATTENTION. IT'S TOO DANGEROUS.
...
UM... THANK YOU.
I GUESS... I WAS RIGHT UNDER IT.
I WAS LOST IN THOUGHT ...
...
SST
BABUMP
AH, MY HAIR ...
A BIT TOUSLED...
BUT...

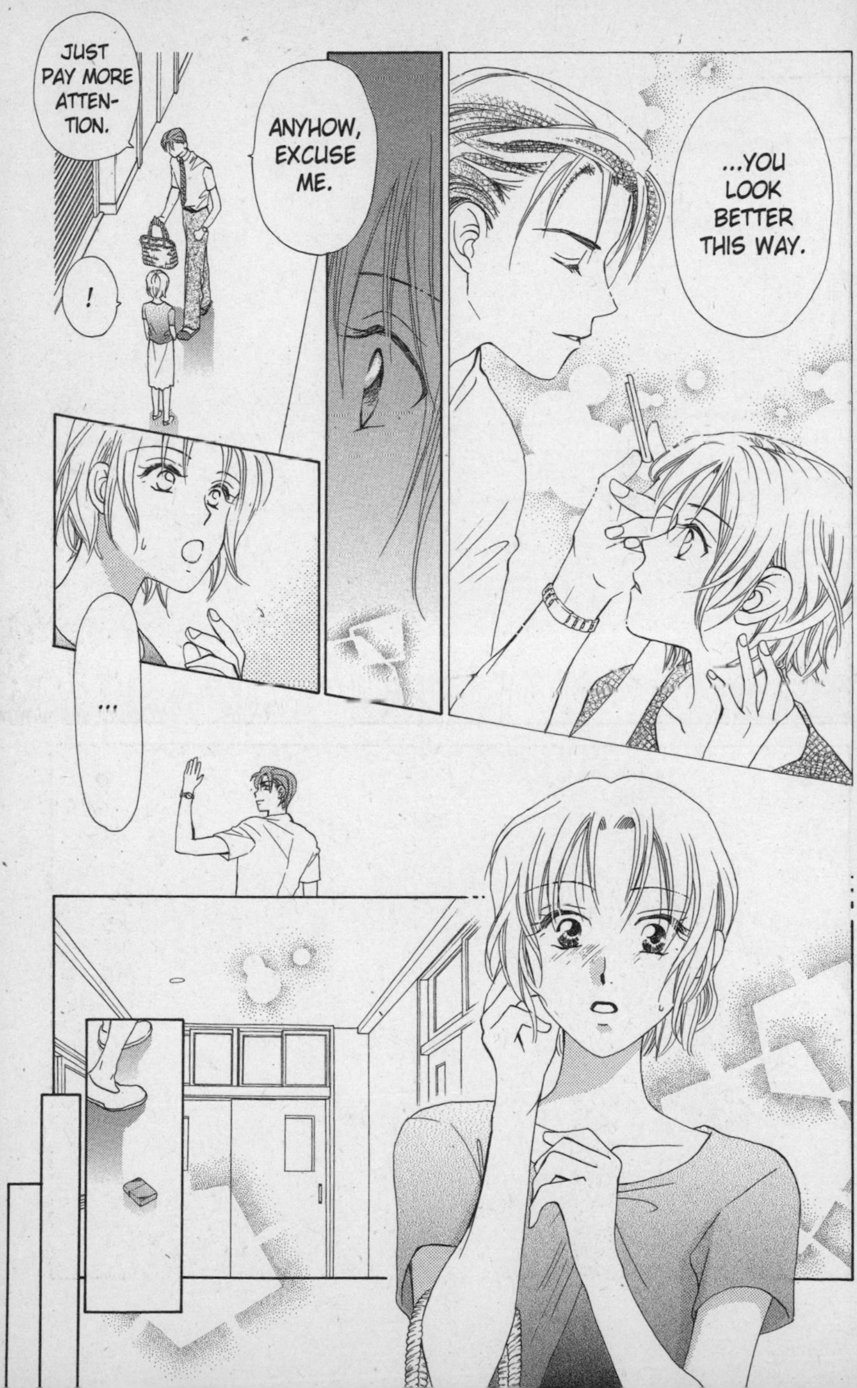
...YOU LOOK BETTER THIS WAY.
ANYHOW, EXCUSE ME.
JUST PAY MORE ATTENTION.
!
...

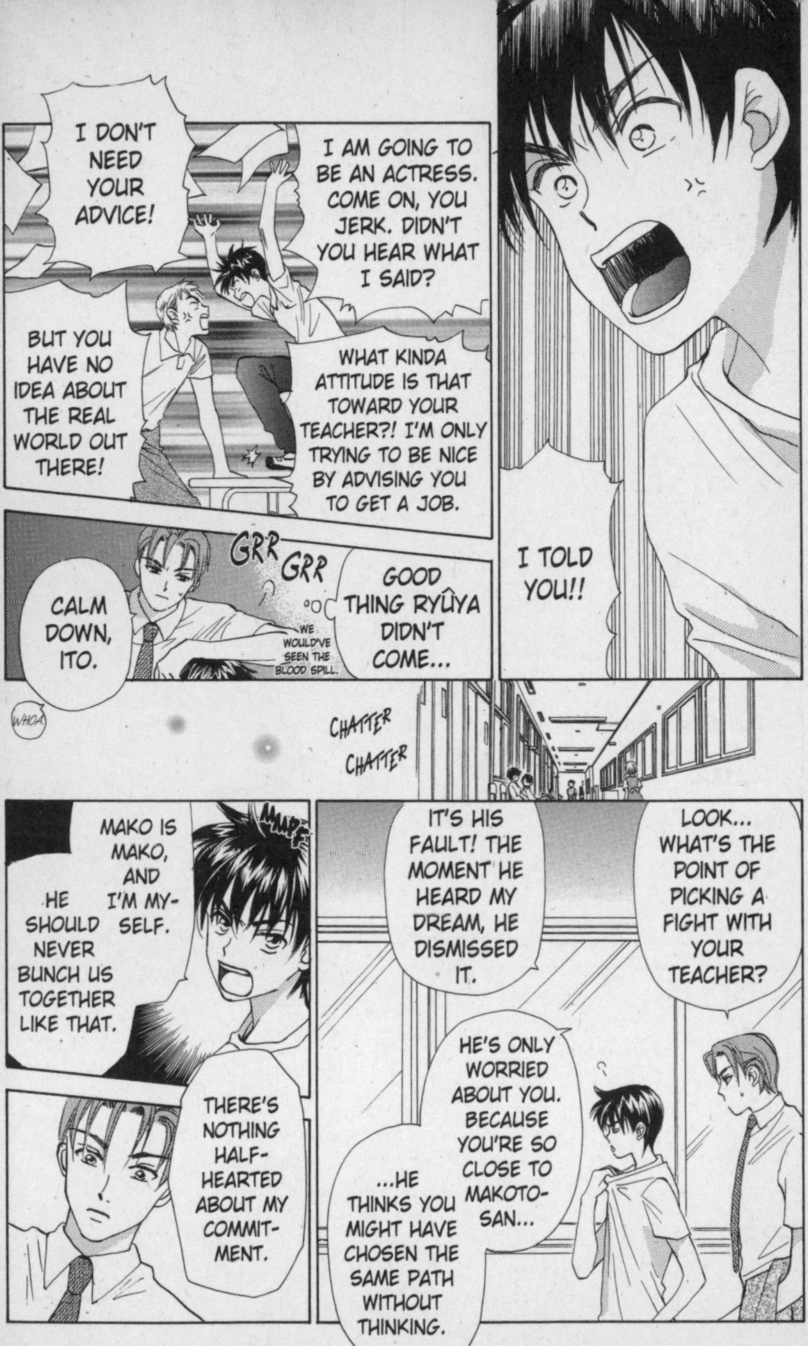
I TOLD YOU!!
I AM GOING TO BE AN ACTRESS. COME ON, YOU JERK. DIDN'T YOU HEAR WHAT I SAID?
I DON'T NEED YOUR ADVICE!
WHAT KINDA ATTITUDE IS THAT TOWARD YOUR TEACHER?! I'M ONLY TRYING TO BE NICE BY ADVISING YOU TO GET A JOB.
BUT YOU HAVE NO IDEA ABOUT THE REAL WORLD OUT THERE!
GRR
GRR
GOOD THING RYÛYA DIDN'T COME...
WE WOULD'VE SEEN THE BLOOD SPILL.
CALM DOWN, ITO.
WHOA
CHATTER
CHATTER
LOOK... WHAT'S THE POINT OF PICKING A FIGHT WITH YOUR TEACHER?
IT'S HIS FAULT! THE MOMENT HE HEARD MY DREAM, HE DISMISSED IT.
HE'S ONLY WORRIED ABOUT YOU. BECAUSE YOU'RE SO CLOSE TO MAKOTO-SAN...
...HE THINKS YOU MIGHT HAVE CHOSEN THE SAME PATH WITHOUT THINKING.
MAKO IS MAKO, AND I'M MY-SELF.
HE SHOULD NEVER BUNCH US TOGETHER LIKE THAT.
THERE'S NOTHING HALF-HEARTED ABOUT MY COMMIT-MENT.

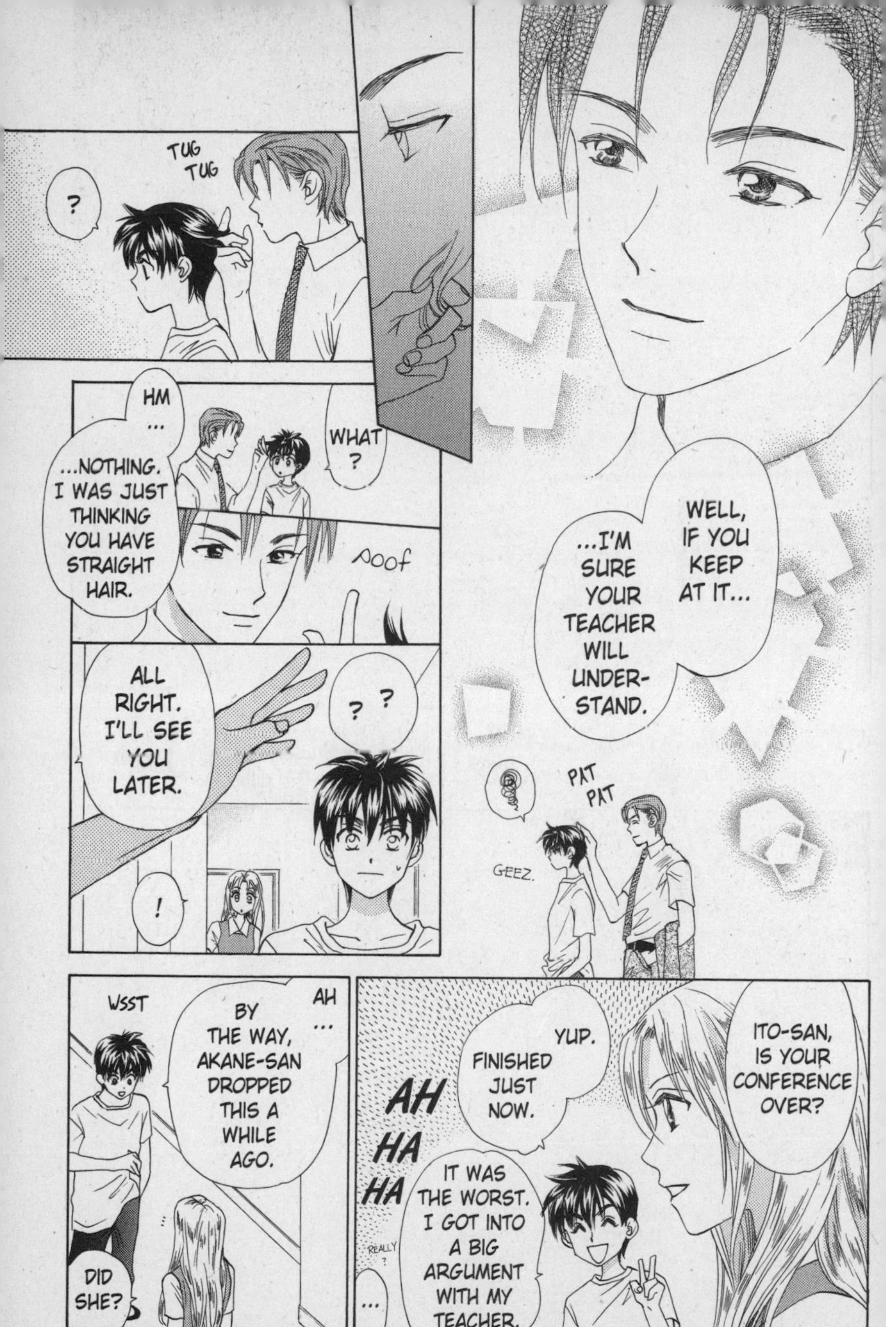
WELL, IF YOU KEEP AT IT...
...I'M SURE YOUR TEACHER WILL UNDERSTAND.
PAT PAT
GEEZ.
TUG TUG
?
WHAT?
HM...
...NOTHING. I WAS JUST THINKING YOU HAVE STRAIGHT HAIR.
poof
? ?
ALL RIGHT. I'LL SEE YOU LATER.
!
ITO-SAN, IS YOUR CONFERENCE OVER?
YUP. FINISHED JUST NOW.
AH HA HA
IT WAS THE WORST. I GOT INTO A BIG ARGUMENT WITH MY TEACHER.
REALLY?
...
AH...
BY THE WAY, AKANE-SAN DROPPED THIS A WHILE AGO.
WSST
DID SHE?

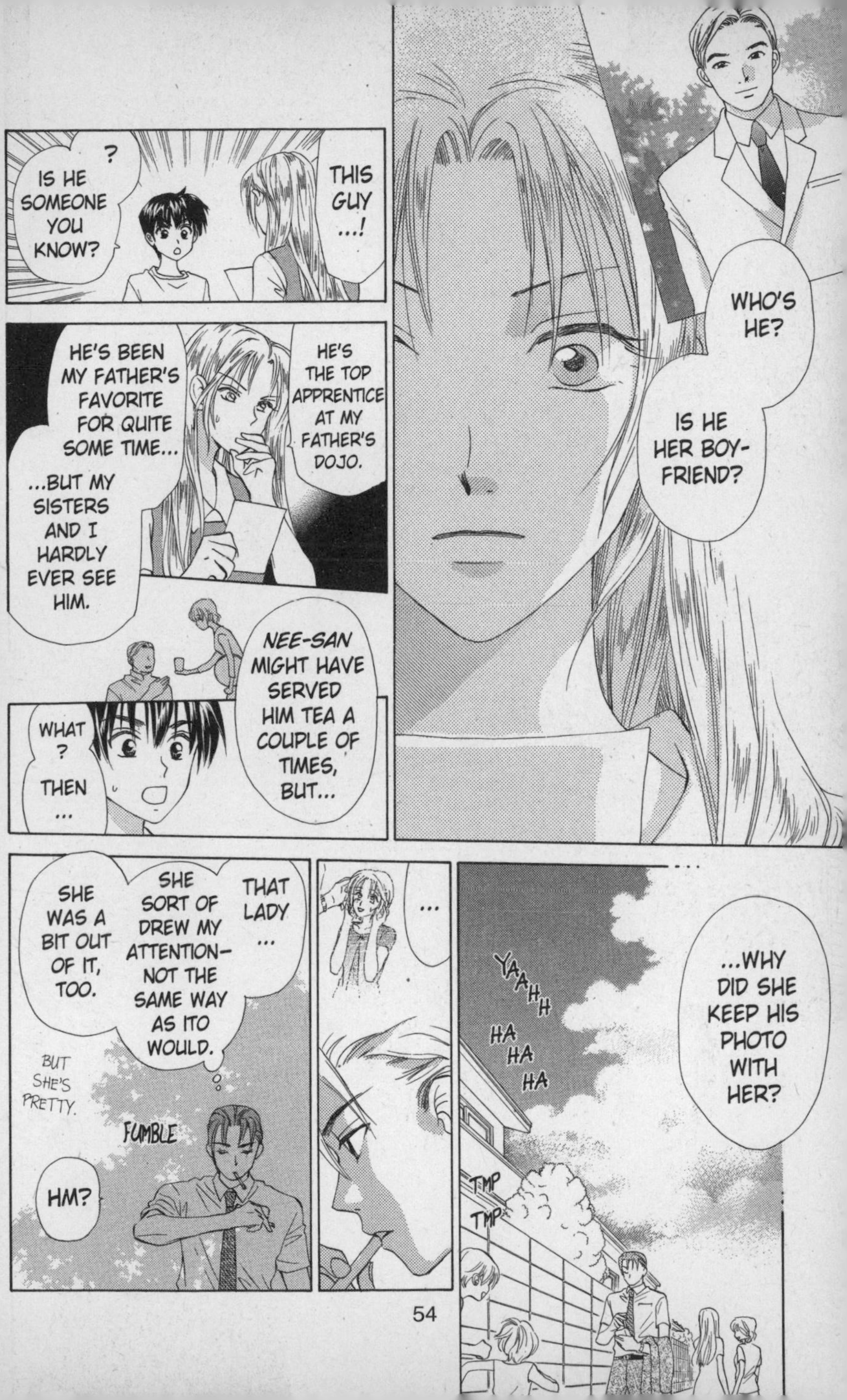
WHO'S HE?
IS HE HER BOY-FRIEND?
THIS GUY ...!
?
IS HE SOMEONE YOU KNOW?
HE'S THE TOP APPRENTICE AT MY FATHER'S DOJO.
HE'S BEEN MY FATHER'S FAVORITE FOR QUITE SOME TIME...
...BUT MY SISTERS AND I HARDLY EVER SEE HIM.
NEE-SAN MIGHT HAVE SERVED HIM TEA A COUPLE OF TIMES, BUT...
WHAT? THEN...
...WHY DID SHE KEEP HIS PHOTO WITH HER?
YAAHH
HA HA HA
TMP TMP
...
THAT LADY...
SHE SORT OF DREW MY ATTENTION—NOT THE SAME WAY AS ITO WOULD.
SHE WAS A BIT OUT OF IT, TOO.
BUT SHE'S PRETTY.
FUMBLE
HM?

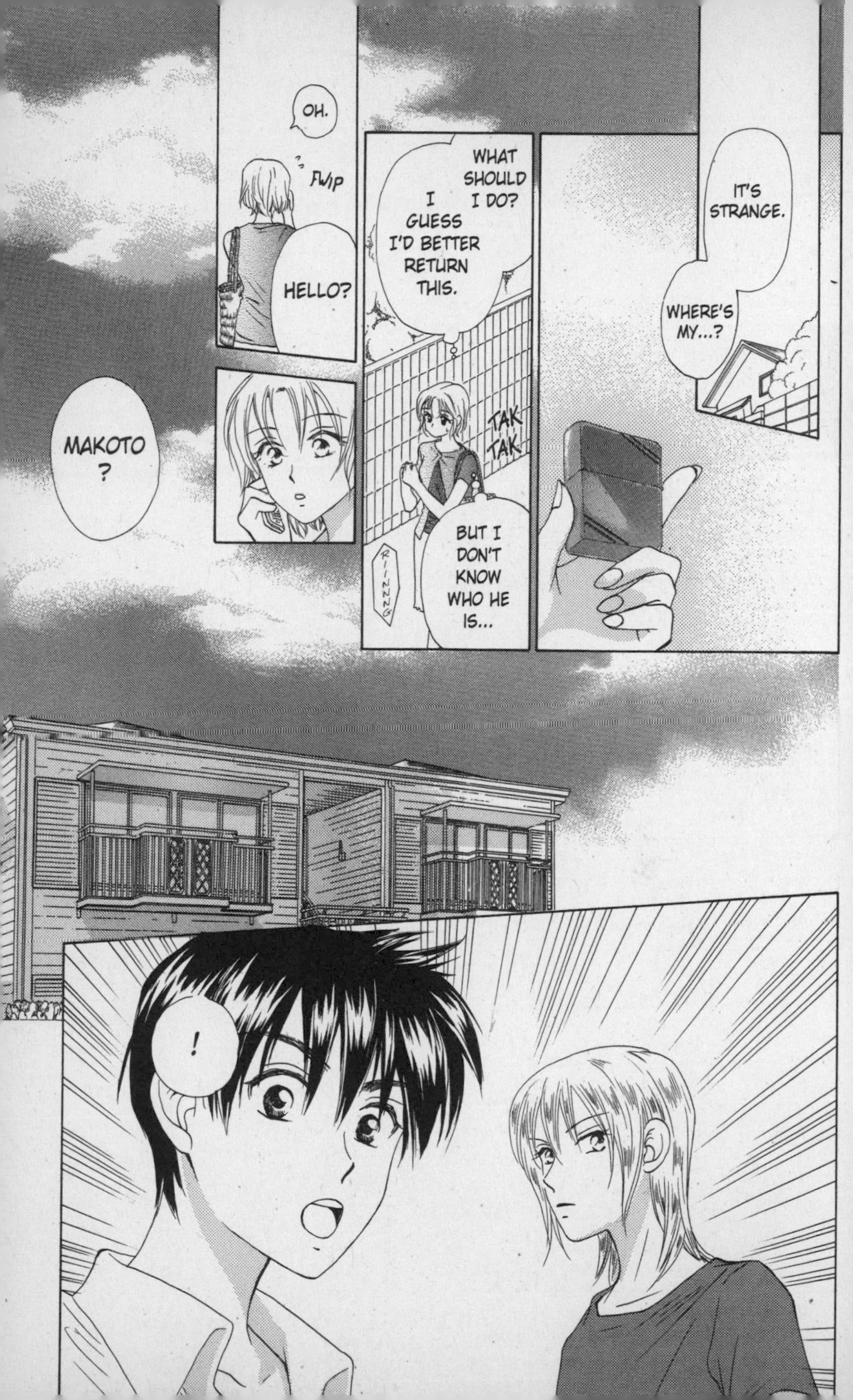
IT'S STRANGE.
WHERE'S MY...?
WHAT SHOULD I DO?
I GUESS I'D BETTER RETURN THIS.
TAK TAK
BUT I DON'T KNOW WHO HE IS...
RIINNG
OH.
FWIP
HELLO?
MAKOTO?
!

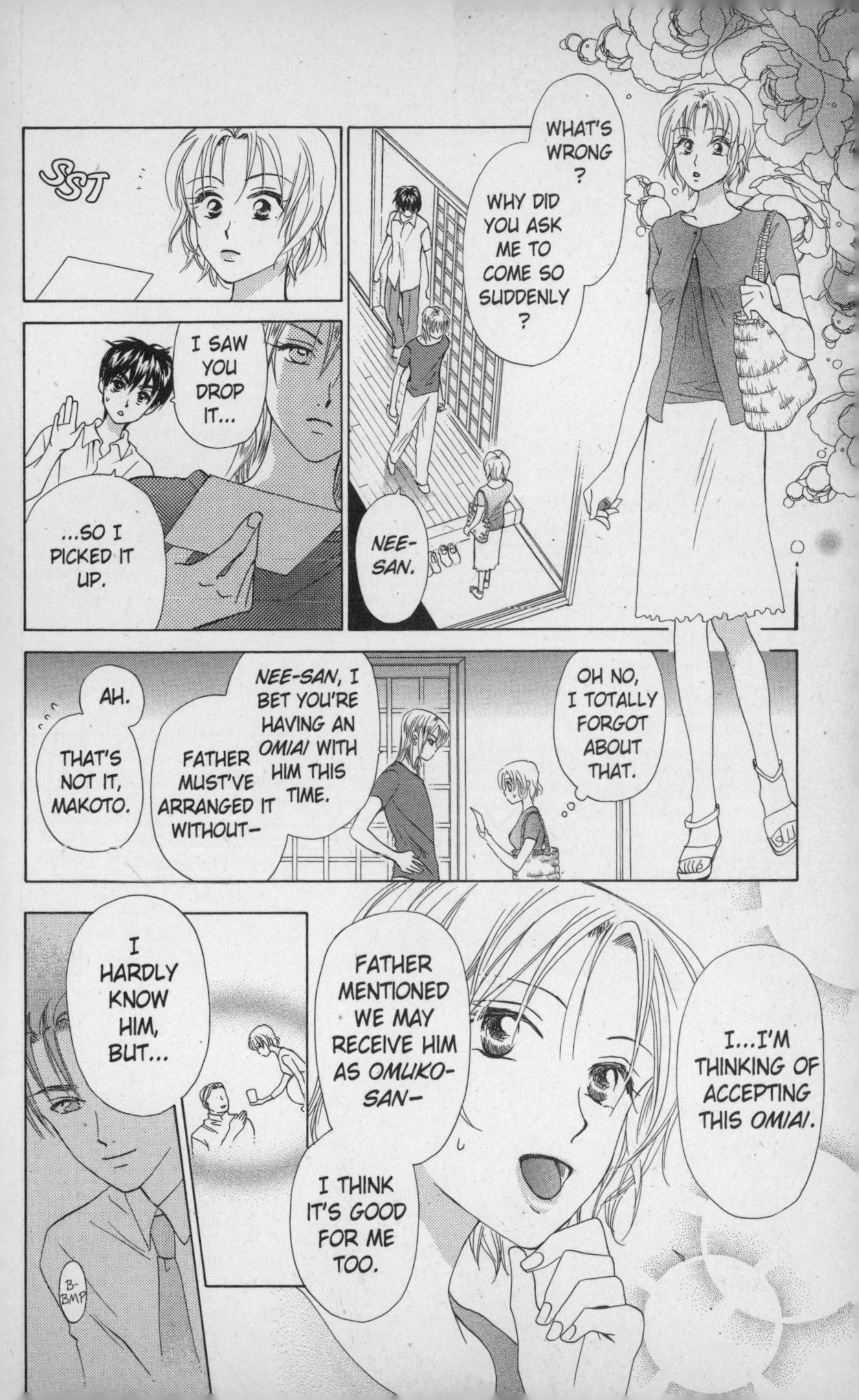
WHAT'S WRONG?
WHY DID YOU ASK ME TO COME SO SUDDENLY?
NEE-SAN.
SST
I SAW YOU DROP IT...
...SO I PICKED IT UP.
OH NO, I TOTALLY FORGOT ABOUT THAT.
NEE-SAN, I BET YOU'RE HAVING AN OMIAI WITH HIM THIS TIME.
FATHER MUST'VE ARRANGED IT WITHOUT–
AH.
THAT'S NOT IT, MAKOTO.
I...I'M THINKING OF ACCEPTING THIS OMIAI.
FATHER MENTIONED WE MAY RECEIVE HIM AS OMUKO-SAN–
I THINK IT'S GOOD FOR ME TOO.
I HARDLY KNOW HIM, BUT...
B-BMP

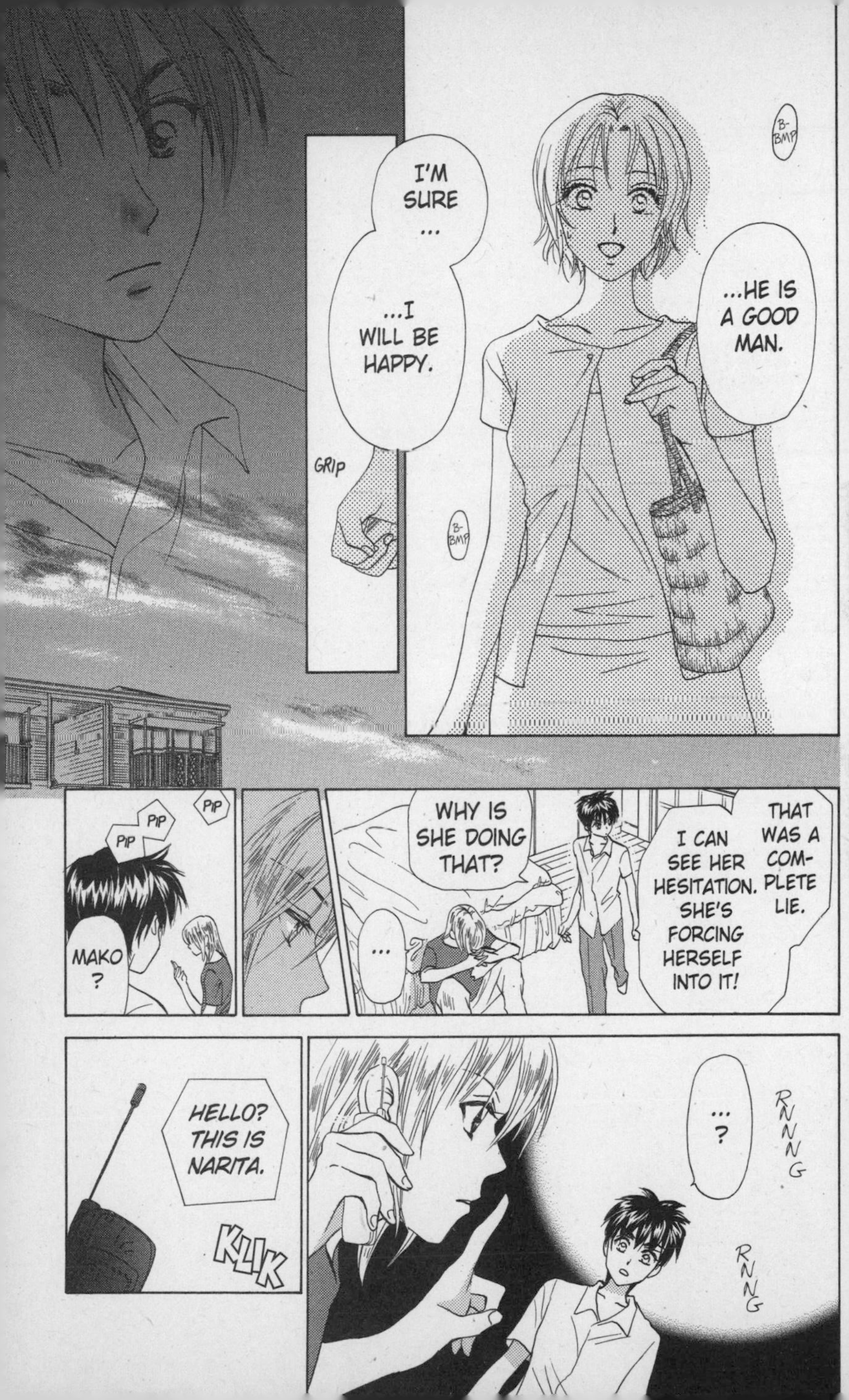
B-BMP
...HE IS A GOOD MAN.
I'M SURE ...
...I WILL BE HAPPY.
GRIP
B-BMP
THAT WAS A COMPLETE LIE.
I CAN SEE HER HESITATION. SHE'S FORCING HERSELF INTO IT!
WHY IS SHE DOING THAT?
...
PIP
PIP
PIP
MAKO?
RNNNG
...?
RNNG
HELLO? THIS IS NARITA.
KLIK

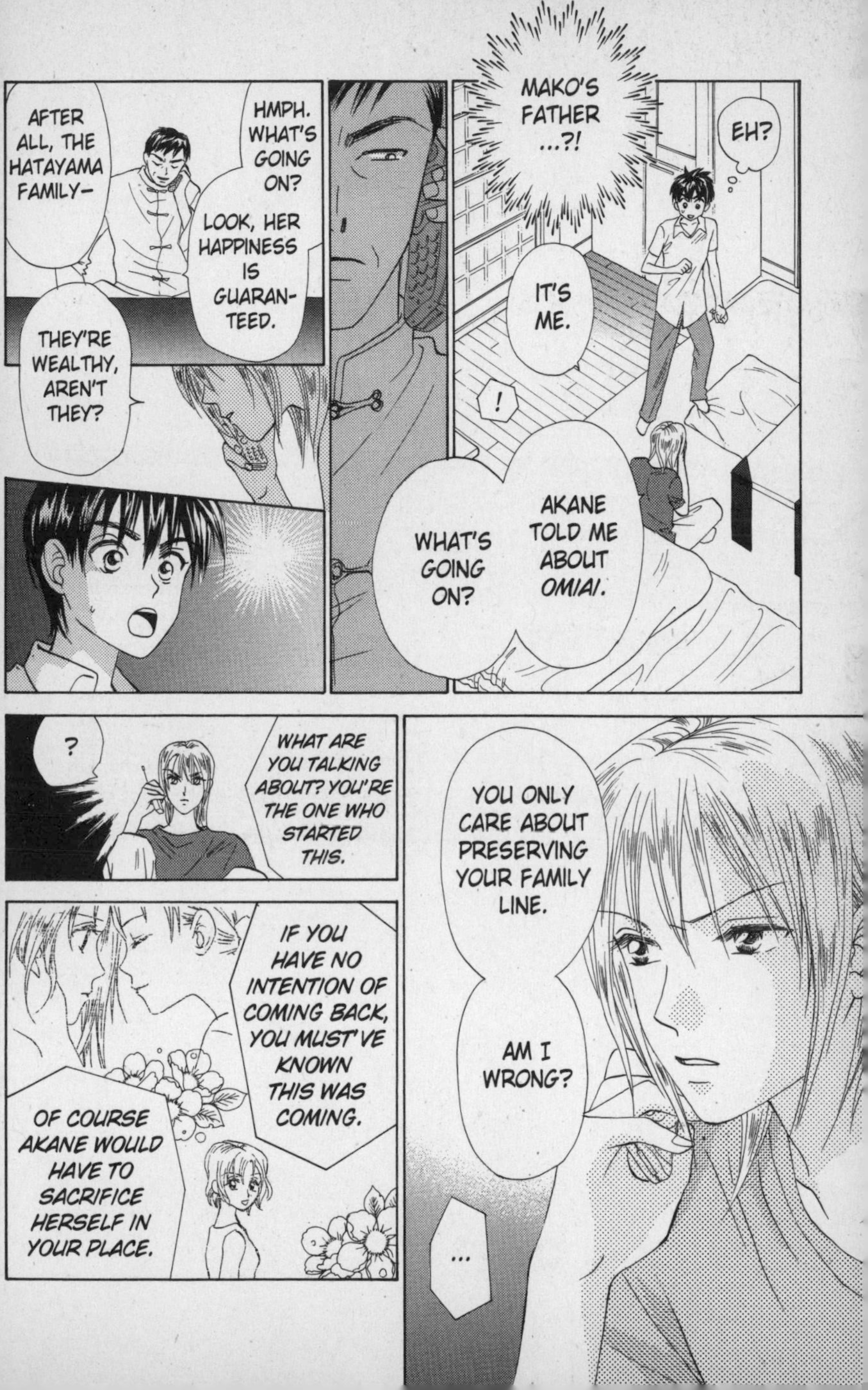
EH?
MAKO'S FATHER ...?!
IT'S ME.
!
AKANE TOLD ME ABOUT OMIAI.
WHAT'S GOING ON?
HMPH. WHAT'S GOING ON?
LOOK, HER HAPPINESS IS GUARAN-TEED.
AFTER ALL, THE HATAYAMA FAMILY—
THEY'RE WEALTHY, AREN'T THEY?
YOU ONLY CARE ABOUT PRESERVING YOUR FAMILY LINE.
AM I WRONG?
...
WHAT ARE YOU TALKING ABOUT? YOU'RE THE ONE WHO STARTED THIS.
?
IF YOU HAVE NO INTENTION OF COMING BACK, YOU MUST'VE KNOWN THIS WAS COMING.
OF COURSE AKANE WOULD HAVE TO SACRIFICE HERSELF IN YOUR PLACE.

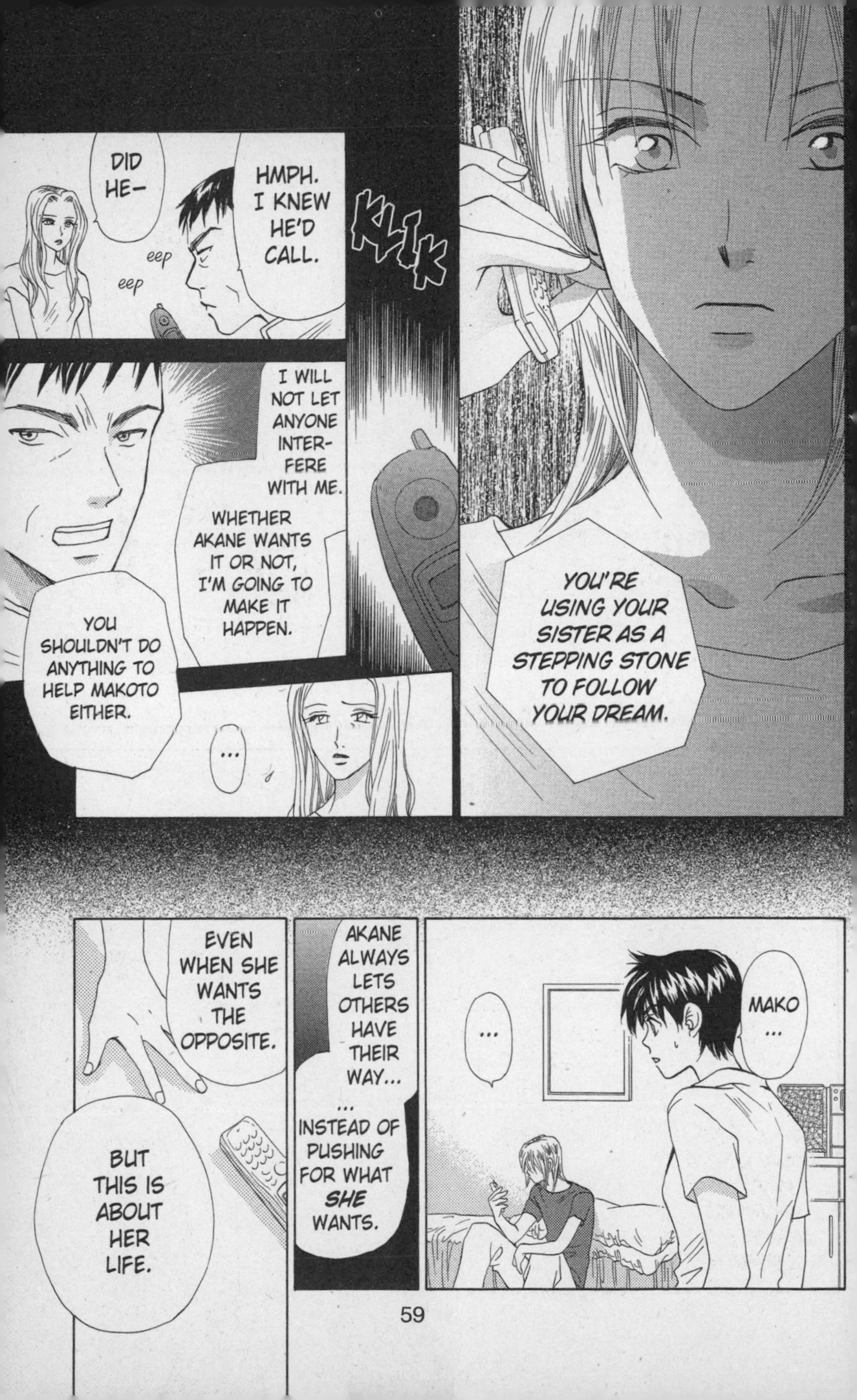
YOU'RE USING YOUR SISTER AS A STEPPING STONE TO FOLLOW YOUR DREAM.
KLIK
HMPH. I KNEW HE'D CALL.
DID HE–
eep
eep
I WILL NOT LET ANYONE INTER-FERE WITH ME.
WHETHER AKANE WANTS IT OR NOT, I'M GOING TO MAKE IT HAPPEN.
YOU SHOULDN'T DO ANYTHING TO HELP MAKOTO EITHER.
...
MAKO ...
...
AKANE ALWAYS LETS OTHERS HAVE THEIR WAY...
... INSTEAD OF PUSHING FOR WHAT SHE WANTS.
EVEN WHEN SHE WANTS THE OPPOSITE.
BUT THIS IS ABOUT HER LIFE.

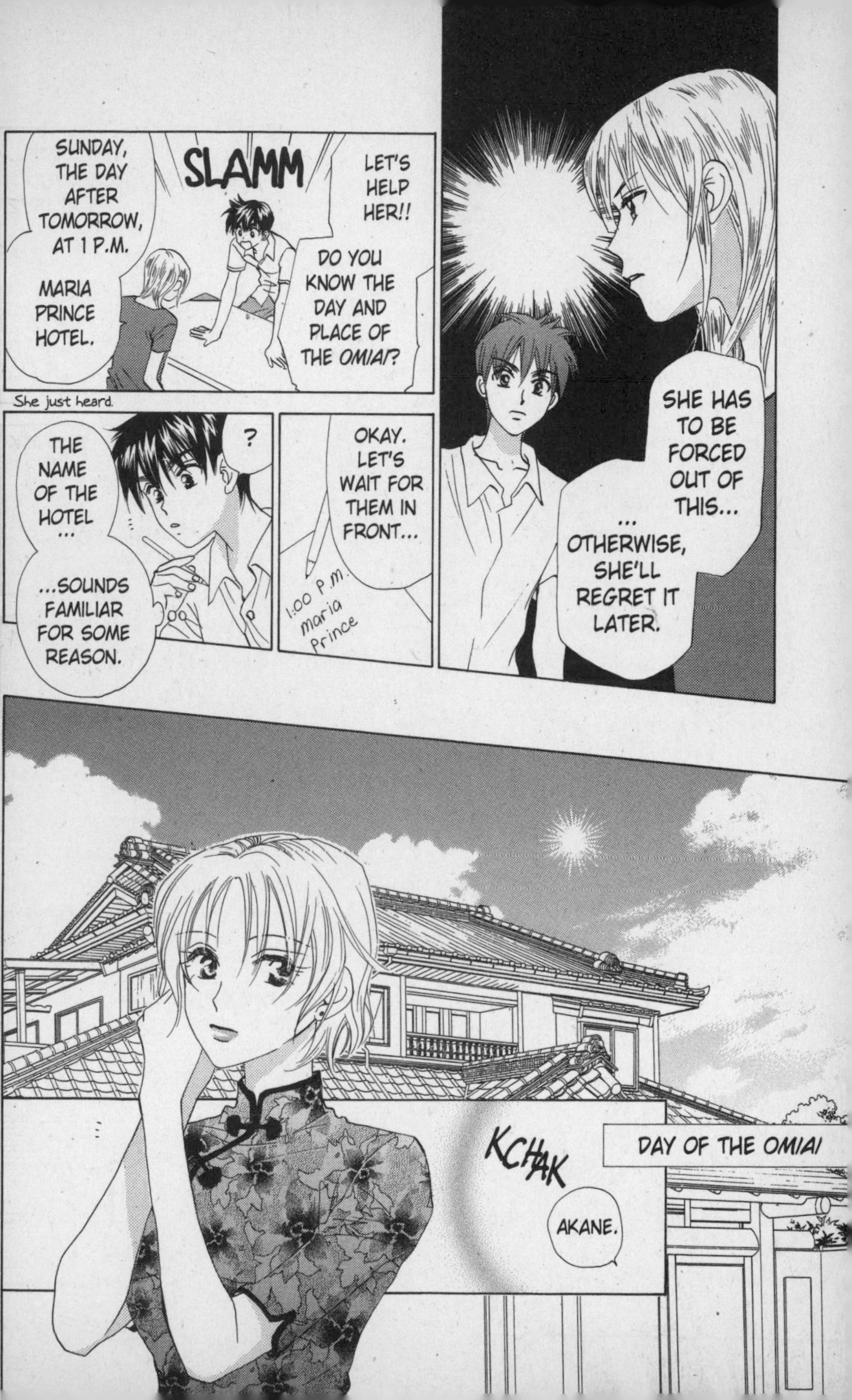
SHE HAS TO BE FORCED OUT OF THIS...
...OTHERWISE, SHE'LL REGRET IT LATER.
LET'S HELP HER!!
SLAMM
DO YOU KNOW THE DAY AND PLACE OF THE OMIAI?
SUNDAY, THE DAY AFTER TOMORROW, AT 1 P.M.
MARIA PRINCE HOTEL.
She just heard.
OKAY. LET'S WAIT FOR THEM IN FRONT...
1:00 P.M. maria Prince
?
THE NAME OF THE HOTEL ...
...SOUNDS FAMILIAR FOR SOME REASON.
DAY OF THE OMIAI
KCHAK
AKANE.

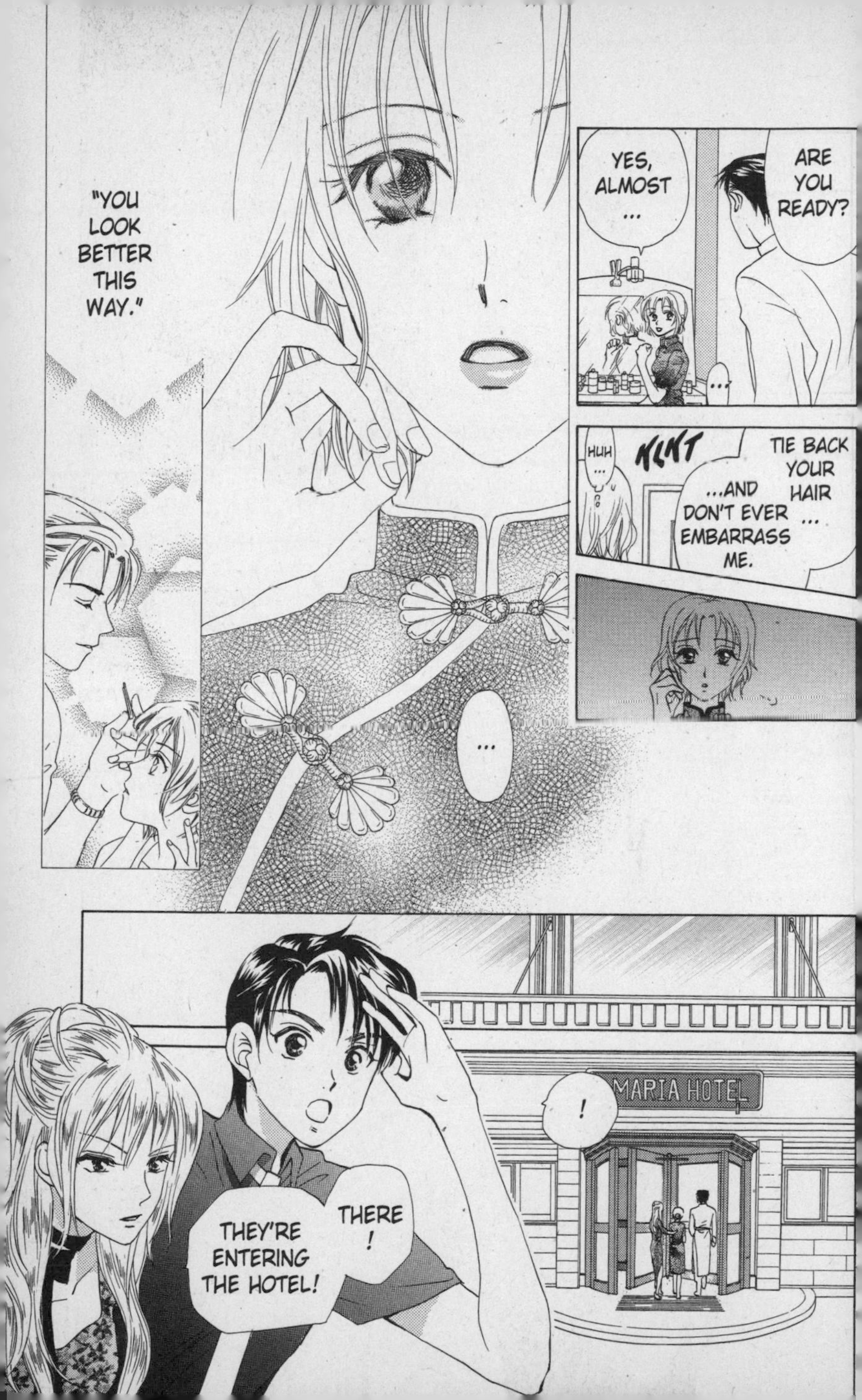
ARE YOU READY?
YES, ALMOST ...
...
TIE BACK YOUR HAIR ...
...AND DON'T EVER EMBARRASS ME.
KLNT
HUH ...
"YOU LOOK BETTER THIS WAY."
...
!
MARIA HOTEL
THERE!
THEY'RE ENTERING THE HOTEL!

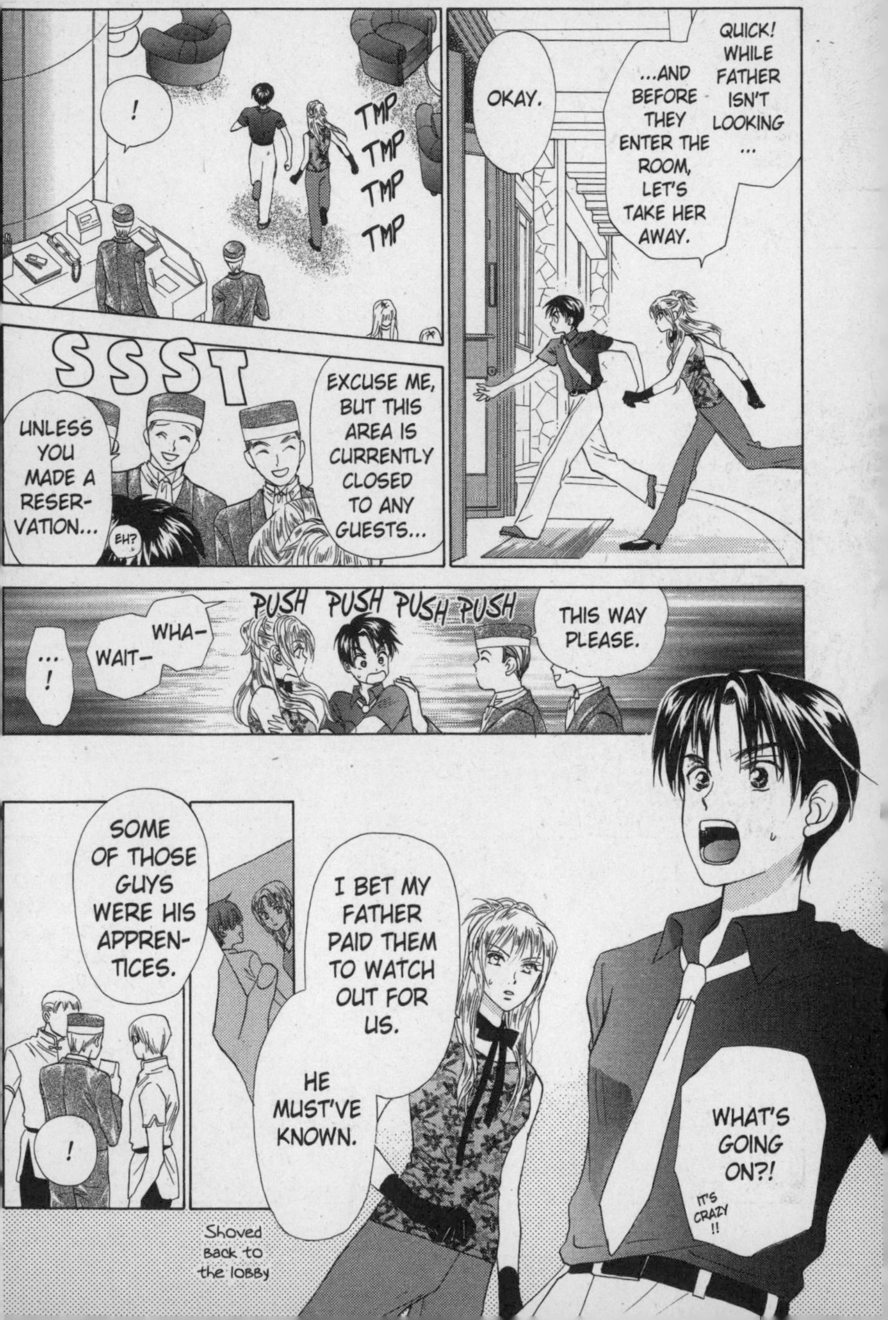
QUICK! WHILE FATHER ISN'T LOOKING...
...AND BEFORE THEY ENTER THE ROOM, LET'S TAKE HER AWAY.
OKAY.
!
TMP TMP TMP TMP
SSST
EXCUSE ME, BUT THIS AREA IS CURRENTLY CLOSED TO ANY GUESTS...
UNLESS YOU MADE A RESER-VATION...
EH?
THIS WAY PLEASE.
PUSH PUSH PUSH PUSH
WHA-
WAIT-
...!
WHAT'S GOING ON?!
IT'S CRAZY!!
I BET MY FATHER PAID THEM TO WATCH OUT FOR US.
HE MUST'VE KNOWN.
SOME OF THOSE GUYS WERE HIS APPREN-TICES.
!
Shoved back to the lobby

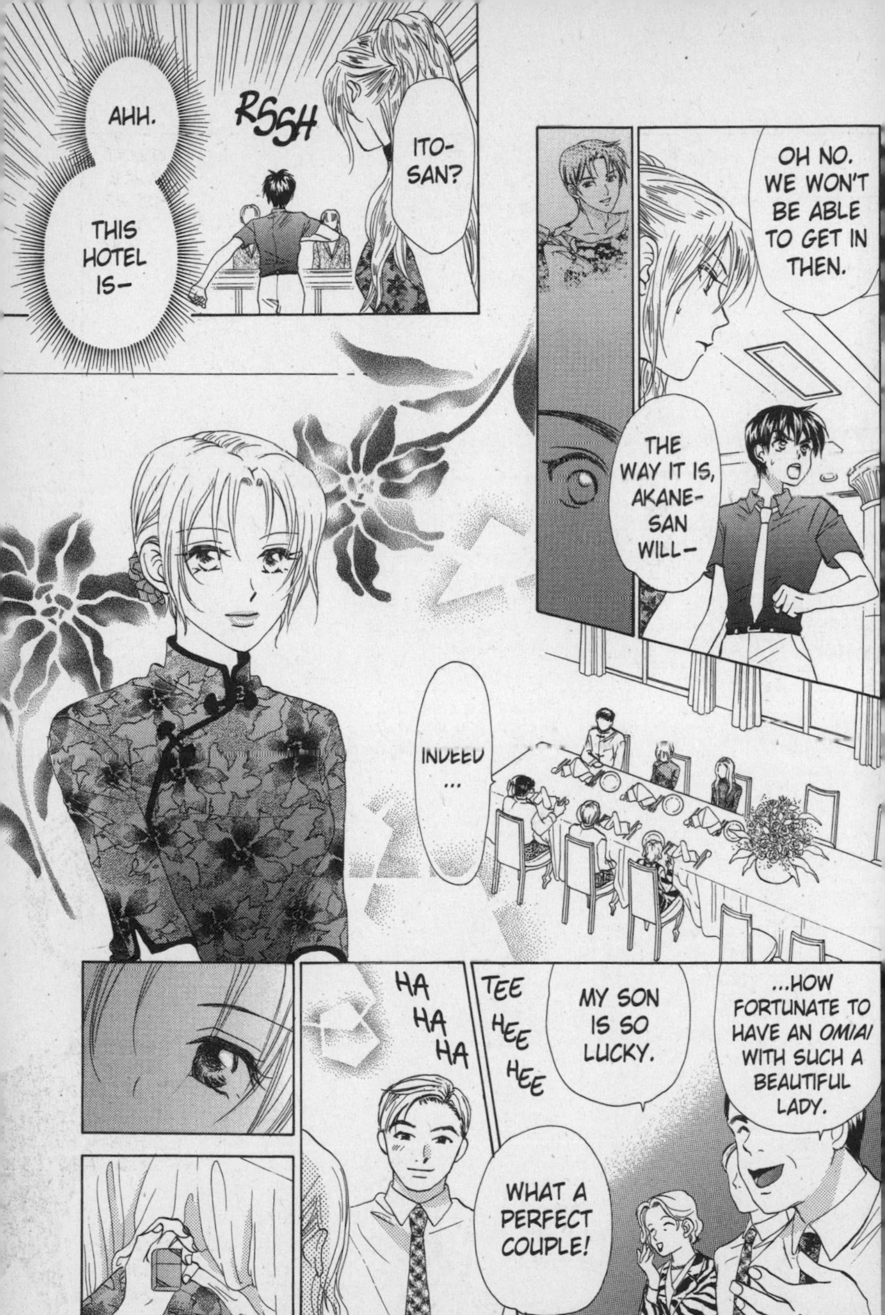
ITO-SAN?
RSSH
AHH.
THIS HOTEL IS-
OH NO. WE WON'T BE ABLE TO GET IN THEN.
THE WAY IT IS, AKANE-SAN WILL-
INDEED ...
...HOW FORTUNATE TO HAVE AN *OMIAI* WITH SUCH A BEAUTIFUL LADY.
MY SON IS SO LUCKY.
TEE HEE HEE
WHAT A PERFECT COUPLE!
HA HA HA

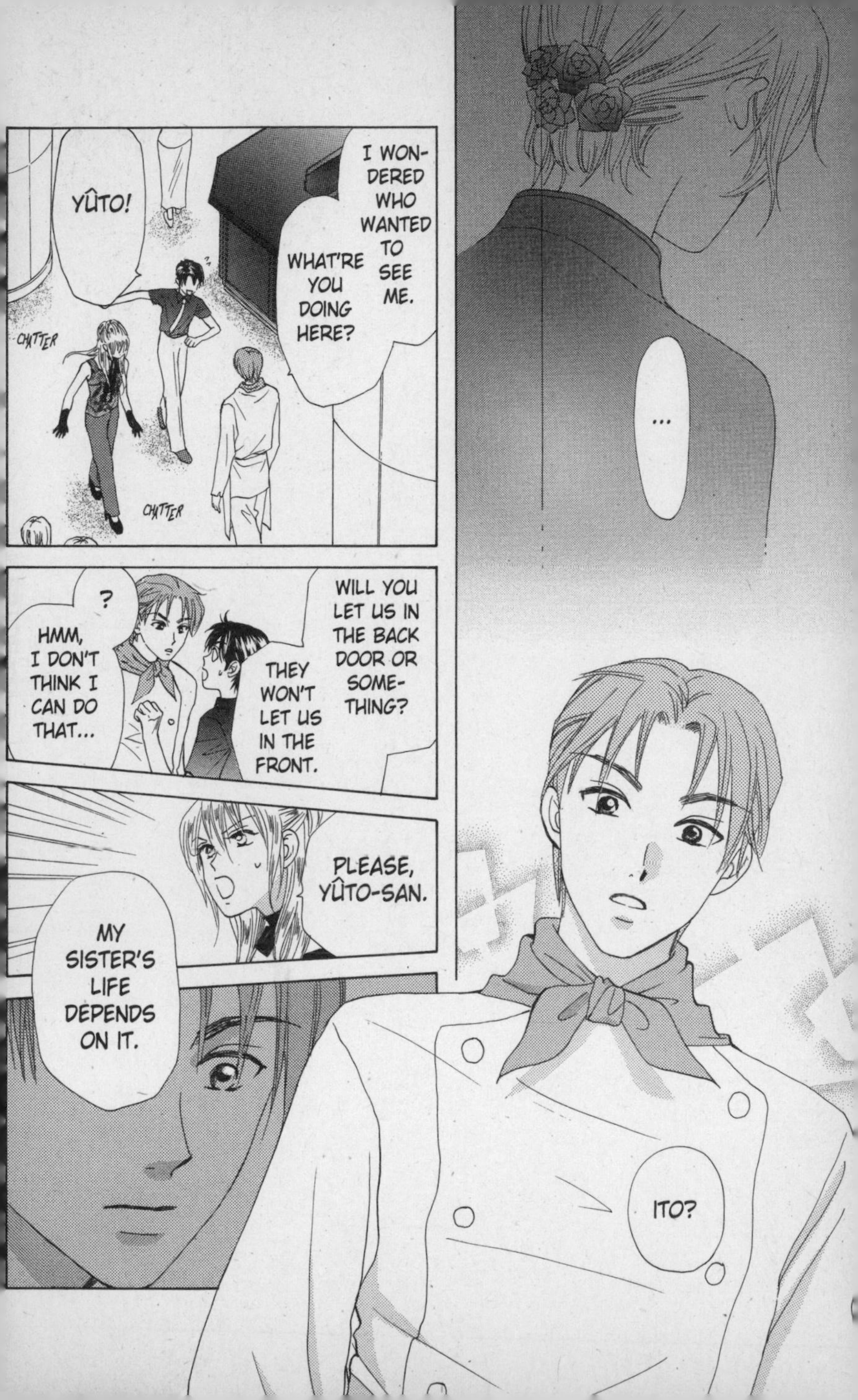
...
I WON-DERED WHO WANTED TO SEE ME.
WHAT'RE YOU DOING HERE?
YÛTO!
CHATTER
CHATTER
WILL YOU LET US IN THE BACK DOOR OR SOME-THING?
THEY WON'T LET US IN THE FRONT.
?
HMM, I DON'T THINK I CAN DO THAT...
PLEASE, YÛTO-SAN.
MY SISTER'S LIFE DEPENDS ON IT.
ITO?

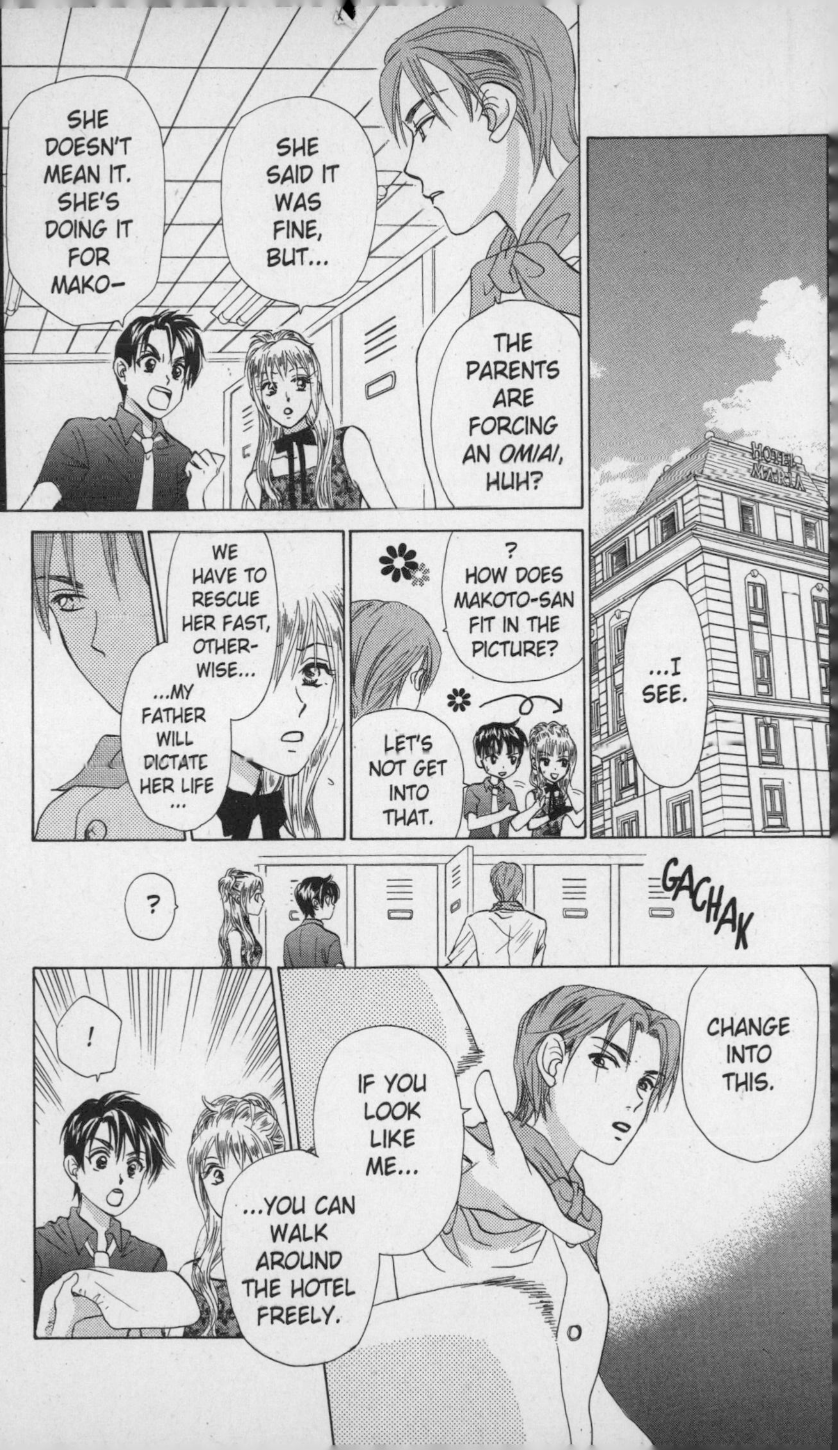
THE PARENTS ARE FORCING AN *OMIAI*, HUH?
SHE SAID IT WAS FINE, BUT...
SHE DOESN'T MEAN IT. SHE'S DOING IT FOR MAKO–
...I SEE.
? HOW DOES MAKOTO-SAN FIT IN THE PICTURE?
LET'S NOT GET INTO THAT.
WE HAVE TO RESCUE HER FAST, OTHERWISE...
...MY FATHER WILL DICTATE HER LIFE...
GACHAK
?
CHANGE INTO THIS.
IF YOU LOOK LIKE ME...
...YOU CAN WALK AROUND THE HOTEL FREELY.
!

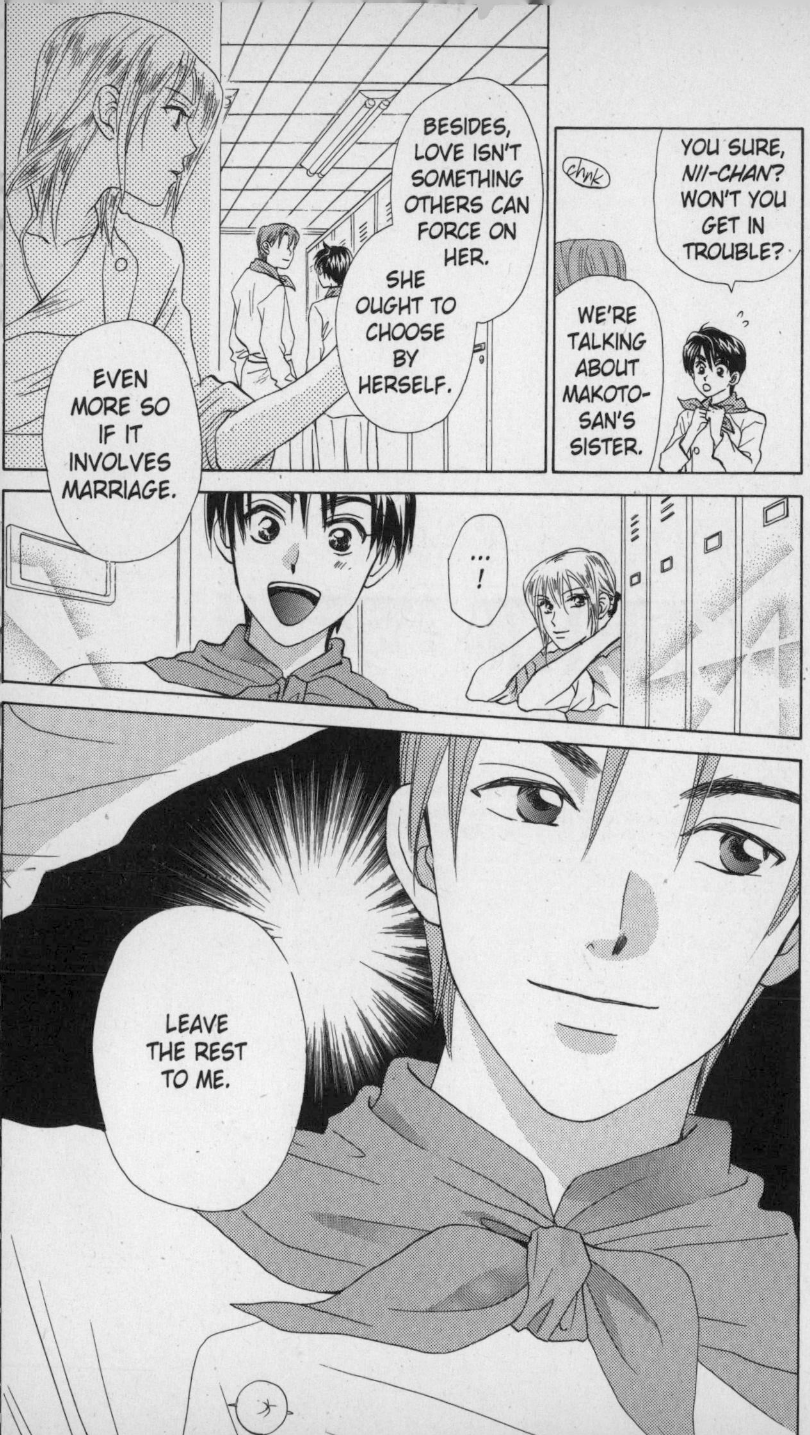
chnk
YOU SURE, *NII-CHAN*? WON'T YOU GET IN TROUBLE?
WE'RE TALKING ABOUT MAKOTO-SAN'S SISTER.
BESIDES, LOVE ISN'T SOMETHING OTHERS CAN FORCE ON HER.
SHE OUGHT TO CHOOSE BY HERSELF.
EVEN MORE SO IF IT INVOLVES MARRIAGE.
...!
LEAVE THE REST TO ME.

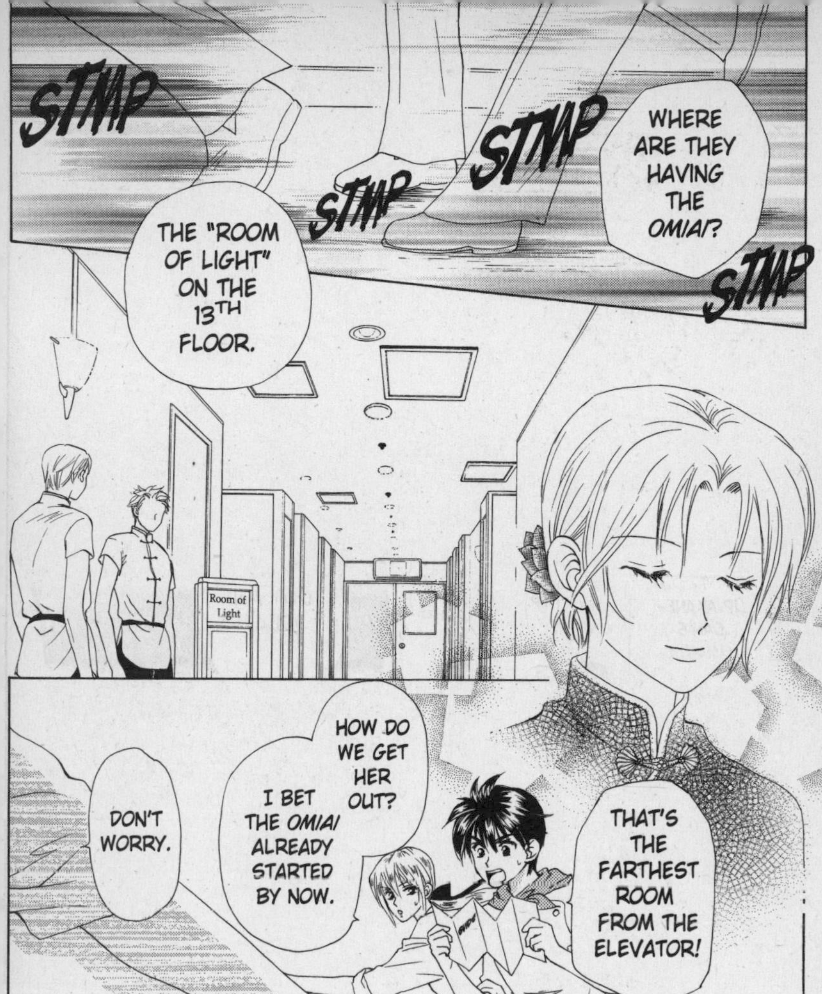
STMP
WHERE ARE THEY HAVING THE OMIAI?
STMP
STMP
STMP
THE "ROOM OF LIGHT" ON THE 13TH FLOOR.
Room of Light
THAT'S THE FARTHEST ROOM FROM THE ELEVATOR!
HOW DO WE GET HER OUT?
I BET THE OMIAI ALREADY STARTED BY NOW.
DON'T WORRY.

-Behind the Scenes Story- ③

I had no reference material for hotels!! It was only through a connection Mr. Editor-In-Charge used that I was able to interview T Hotel. "You may take pictures of the interiors, but do not photograph any of our guests." That was the condition, and it made it really hard... Since it was Christmas season, the place was filled with more people than usual and was decked out in Christmas decorations. But my story was to take place in the middle of summer. The most popular scene in this episode was the page in which Mako threw the cart down . He easily captured more attention than Akane or Yûto!

As expected, Makoto's popularity was sensational.

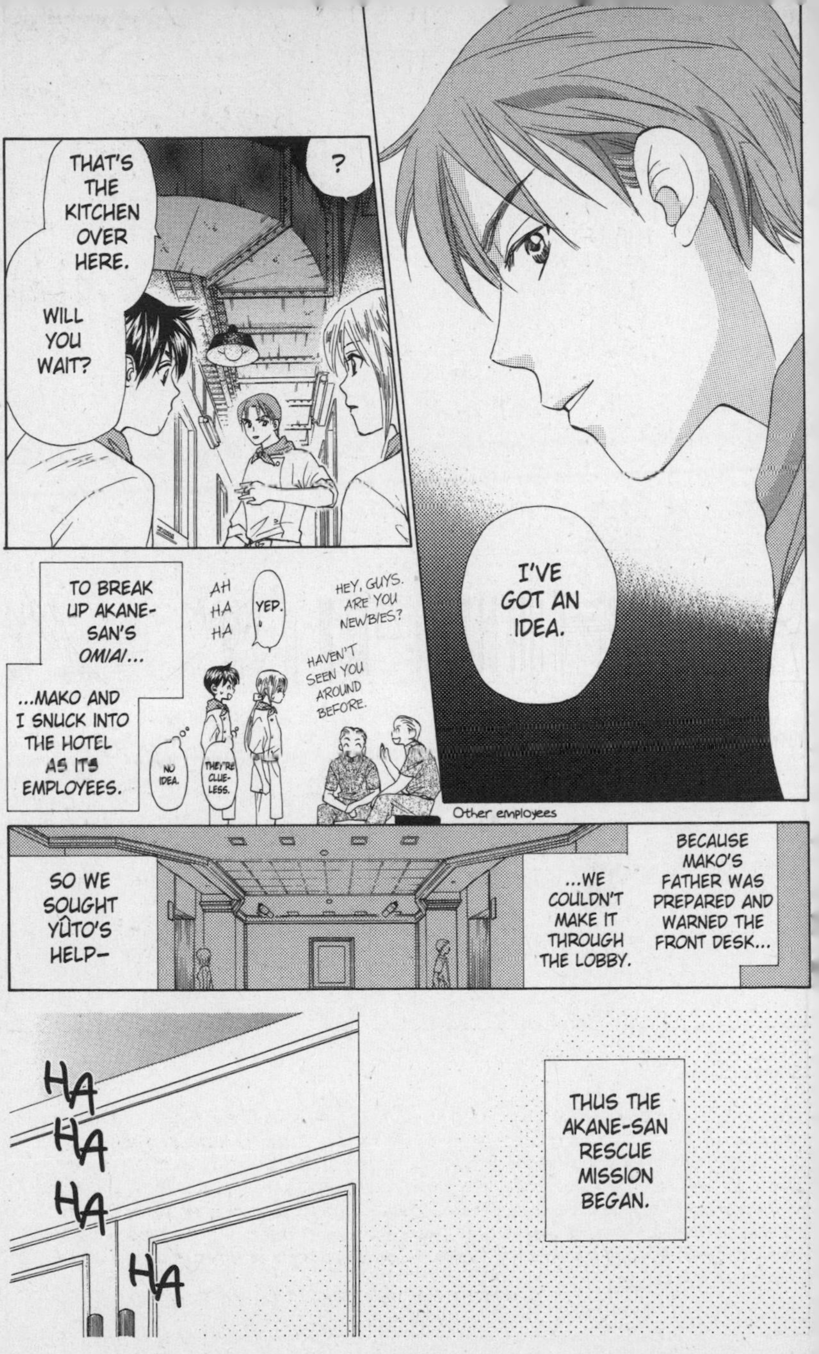
I'VE GOT AN IDEA.
?
THAT'S THE KITCHEN OVER HERE.
WILL YOU WAIT?
HEY, GUYS. ARE YOU NEWBIES?
HAVEN'T SEEN YOU AROUND BEFORE.
YEP.
AH HA HA
TO BREAK UP AKANE-SAN'S *OMIAI*...
...MAKO AND I SNUCK INTO THE HOTEL AS ITS EMPLOYEES.
THEY'RE CLUELESS.
NO IDEA.
Other employees
BECAUSE MAKO'S FATHER WAS PREPARED AND WARNED THE FRONT DESK...
...WE COULDN'T MAKE IT THROUGH THE LOBBY.
SO WE SOUGHT YÛTO'S HELP—
THUS THE AKANE-SAN RESCUE MISSION BEGAN.
HA HA HA HA

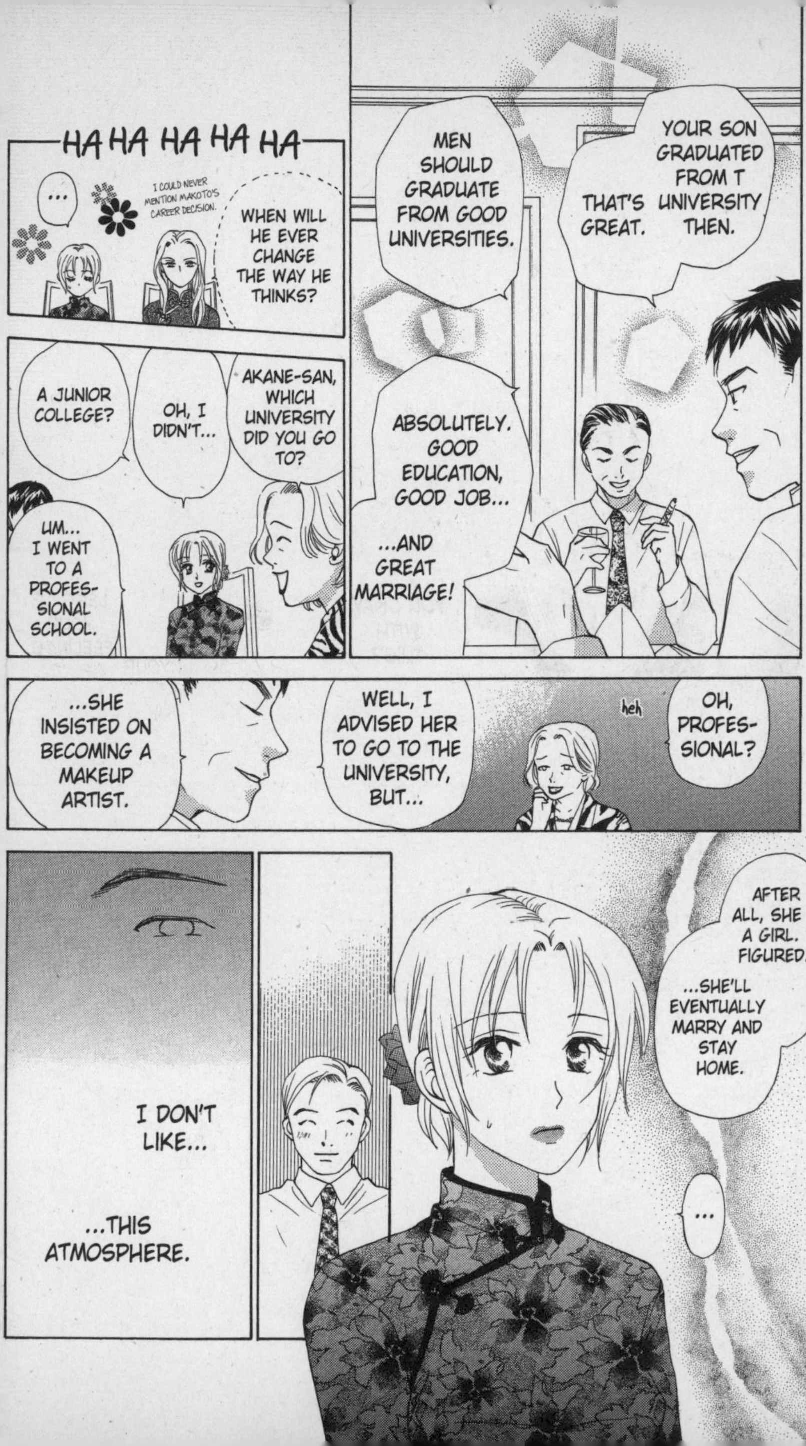
YOUR SON GRADUATED FROM T UNIVERSITY THEN.
THAT'S GREAT.
MEN SHOULD GRADUATE FROM GOOD UNIVERSITIES.
ABSOLUTELY. GOOD EDUCATION, GOOD JOB...
...AND GREAT MARRIAGE!
HA HA HA HA HA
WHEN WILL HE EVER CHANGE THE WAY HE THINKS?
I COULD NEVER MENTION MAKOTO'S CAREER DECISION.
...
AKANE-SAN, WHICH UNIVERSITY DID YOU GO TO?
OH, I DIDN'T...
A JUNIOR COLLEGE?
UM... I WENT TO A PROFESSIONAL SCHOOL.
OH, PROFESSIONAL?
heh
WELL, I ADVISED HER TO GO TO THE UNIVERSITY, BUT...
...SHE INSISTED ON BECOMING A MAKEUP ARTIST.
AFTER ALL, SHE IS A GIRL. I FIGURED...
...SHE'LL EVENTUALLY MARRY AND STAY HOME.
...
I DON'T LIKE...
...THIS ATMOSPHERE.

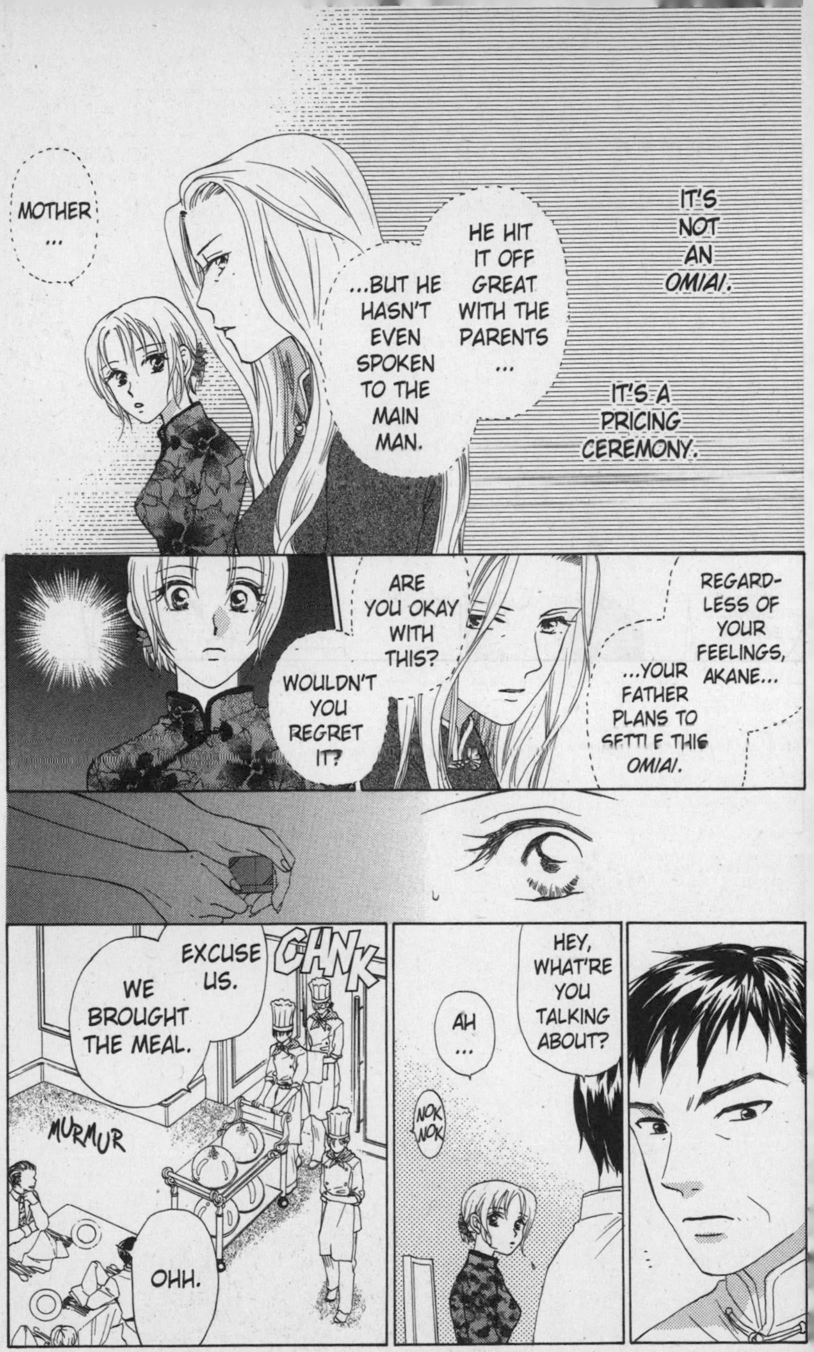
IT'S NOT AN OMIAI.
IT'S A PRICING CEREMONY.
HE HIT IT OFF GREAT WITH THE PARENTS ...
...BUT HE HASN'T EVEN SPOKEN TO THE MAIN MAN.
MOTHER ...
REGARD-LESS OF YOUR FEELINGS, AKANE...
...YOUR FATHER PLANS TO SETTLE THIS OMIAI.
ARE YOU OKAY WITH THIS?
WOULDN'T YOU REGRET IT?
HEY, WHAT'RE YOU TALKING ABOUT?
AH ...
NOK NOK
CHNK
EXCUSE US.
WE BROUGHT THE MEAL.
MURMUR
OHH.

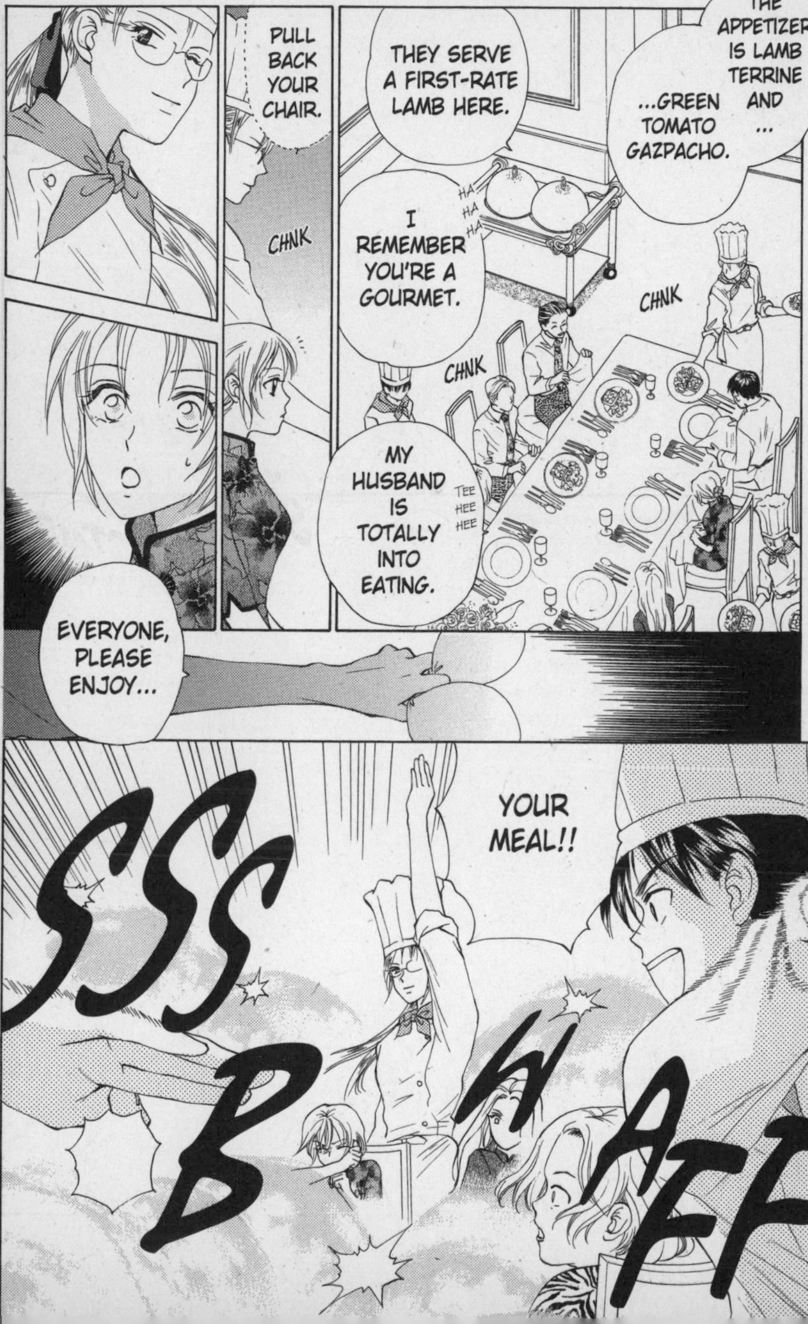
THE APPETIZER IS LAMB TERRINE AND ...
...GREEN TOMATO GAZPACHO.
THEY SERVE A FIRST-RATE LAMB HERE.
HA HA HA
I REMEMBER YOU'RE A GOURMET.
CHNK
CHNK
TEE HEE HEE
MY HUSBAND IS TOTALLY INTO EATING.
PULL BACK YOUR CHAIR.
CHNK
EVERYONE, PLEASE ENJOY...
YOUR MEAL!!
SSBWAFF

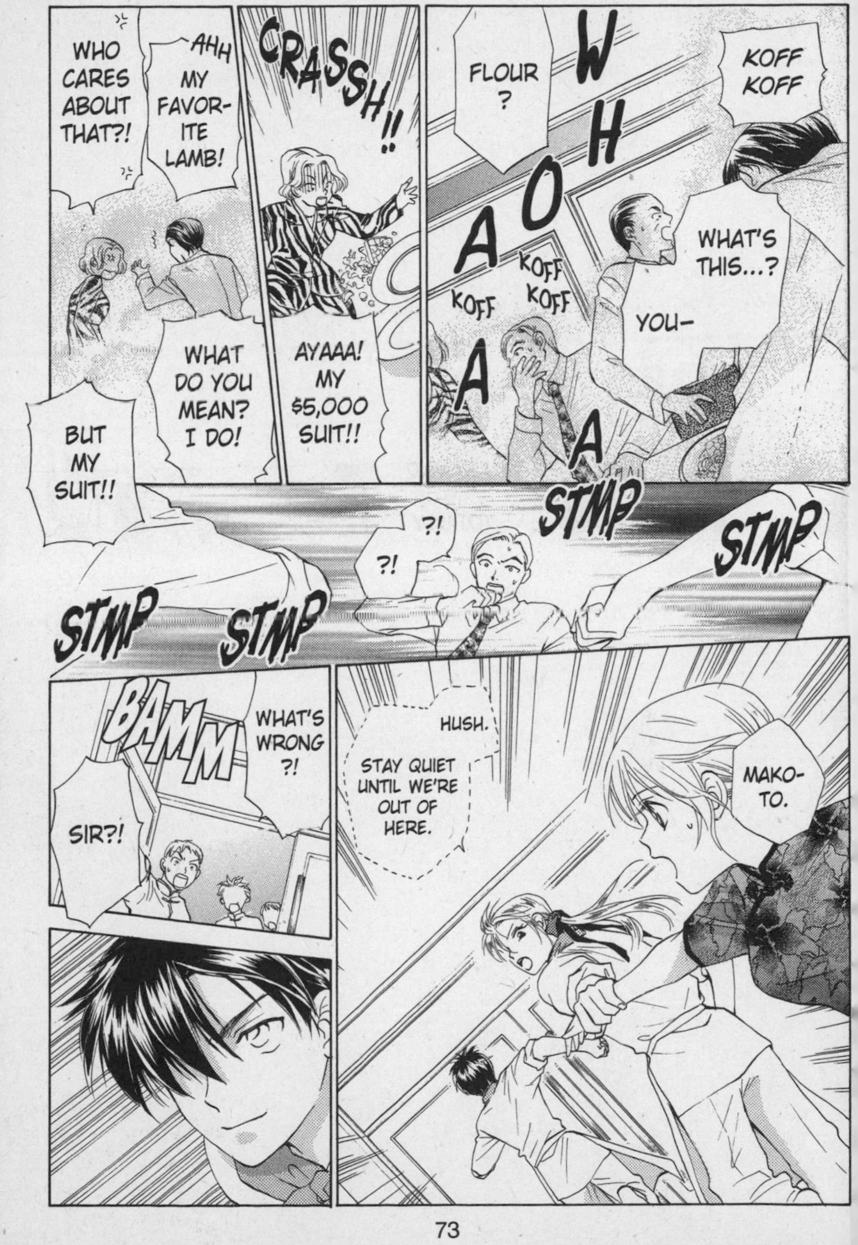
KOFF KOFF
FLOUR ?
WHAOAAA
WHAT'S THIS...?
KOFF KOFF
KOFF
YOU-
CRASSH!!
AYAAA! MY $5,000 SUIT!!
AHH MY FAVOR-ITE LAMB!
WHO CARES ABOUT THAT?!
WHAT DO YOU MEAN? I DO!
STMP
STMP
?!
?!
BUT MY SUIT!!
STMP
STMP
MAKO-TO.
HUSH.
STAY QUIET UNTIL WE'RE OUT OF HERE.
WHAT'S WRONG ?!
BAMM
SIR?!

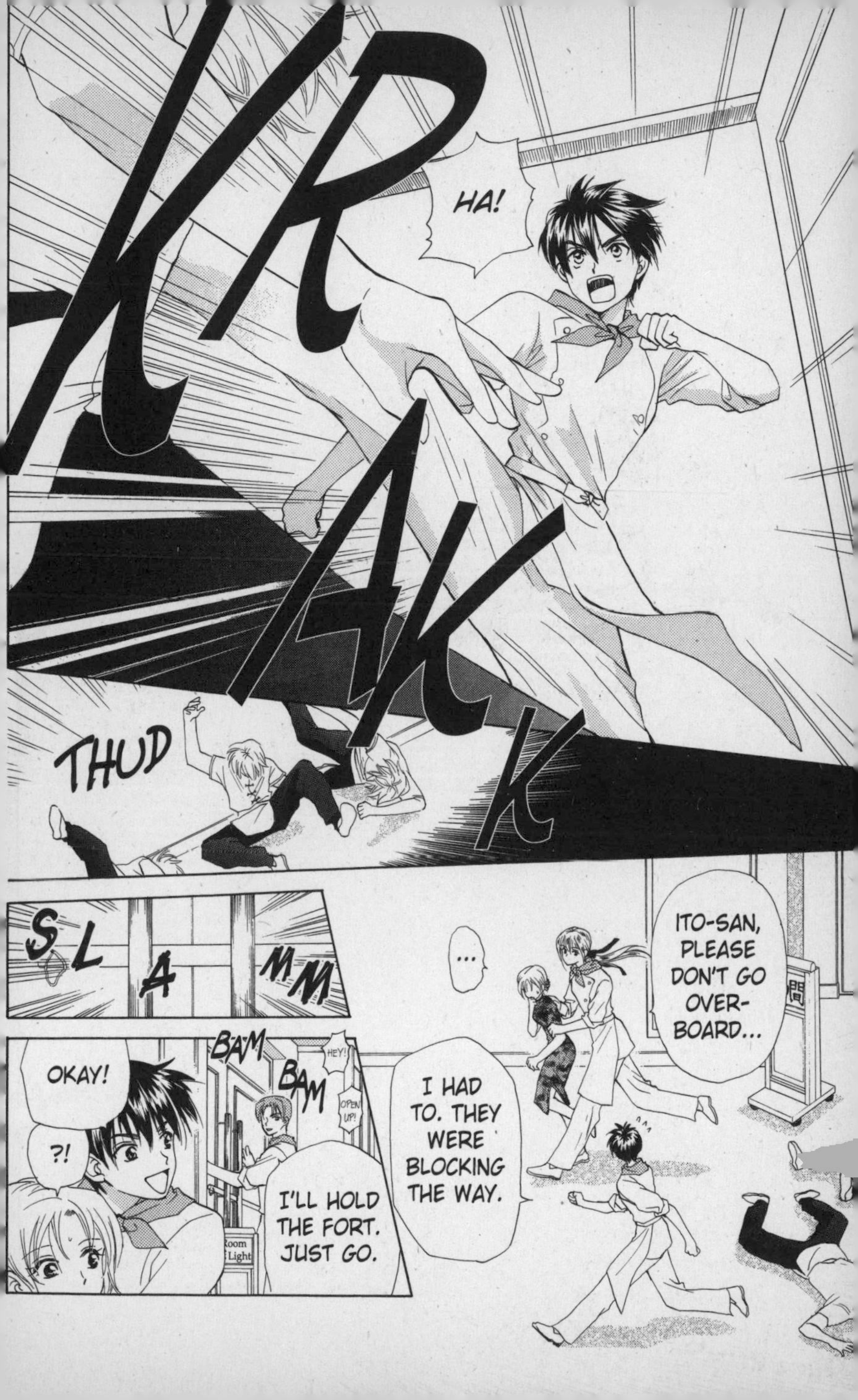
HA!
KRAKK
THUD
ITO-SAN, PLEASE DON'T GO OVERBOARD...
...
I HAD TO. THEY WERE BLOCKING THE WAY.
SLAMM
BAM BAM
HEY!
OPEN UP!
I'LL HOLD THE FORT. JUST GO.
OKAY!
?!
Room
Light

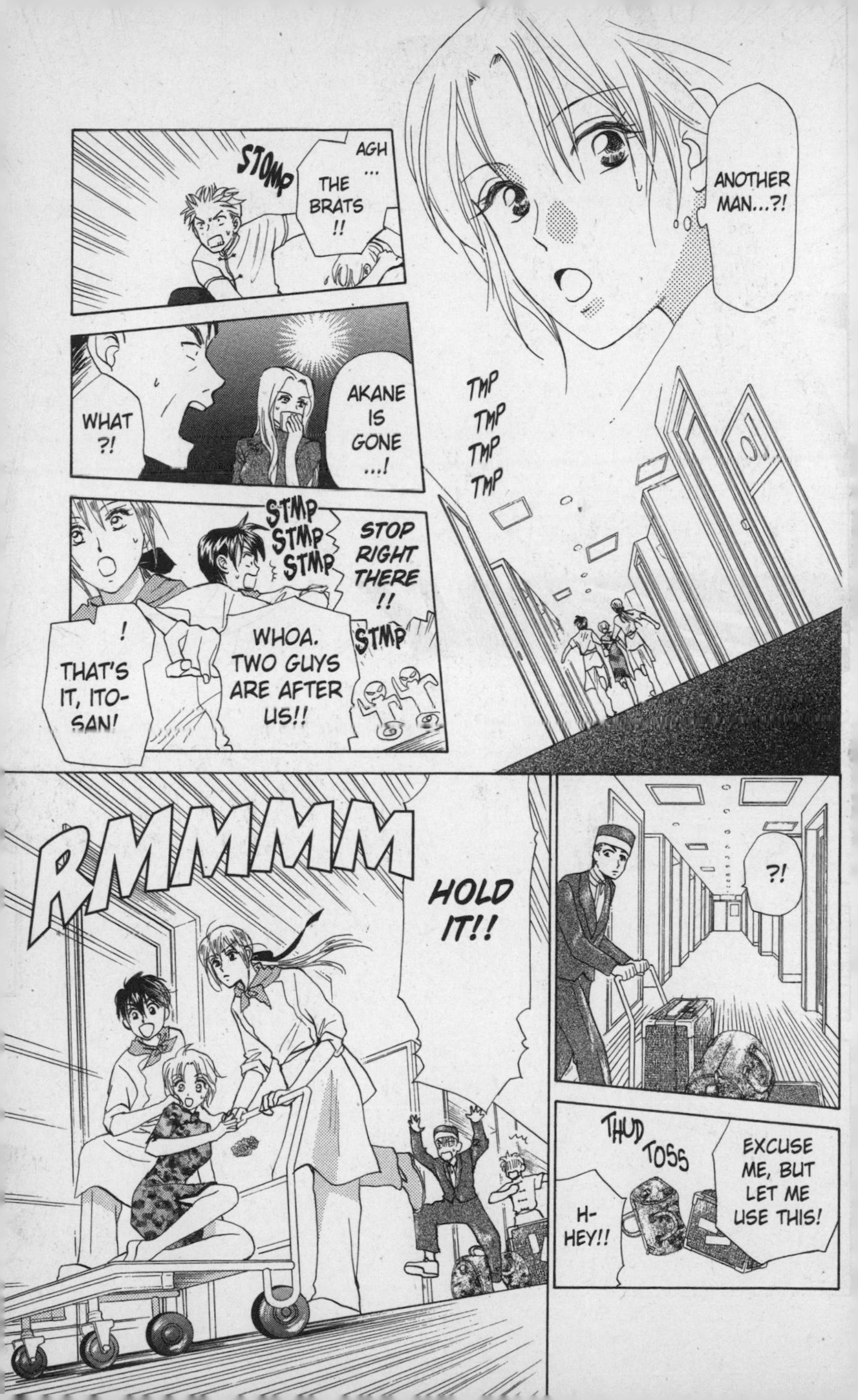
ANOTHER MAN...?!
TMP TMP TMP TMP
AGH ... THE BRATS !!
STOMP
AKANE IS GONE ...!
WHAT ?!
STOP RIGHT THERE !!
STMP STMP STMP
STMP
WHOA. TWO GUYS ARE AFTER US!!
! THAT'S IT, ITO-SAN!
?!
EXCUSE ME, BUT LET ME USE THIS!
THUD TOSS
H- HEY!!
HOLD IT!!
RMMMMM

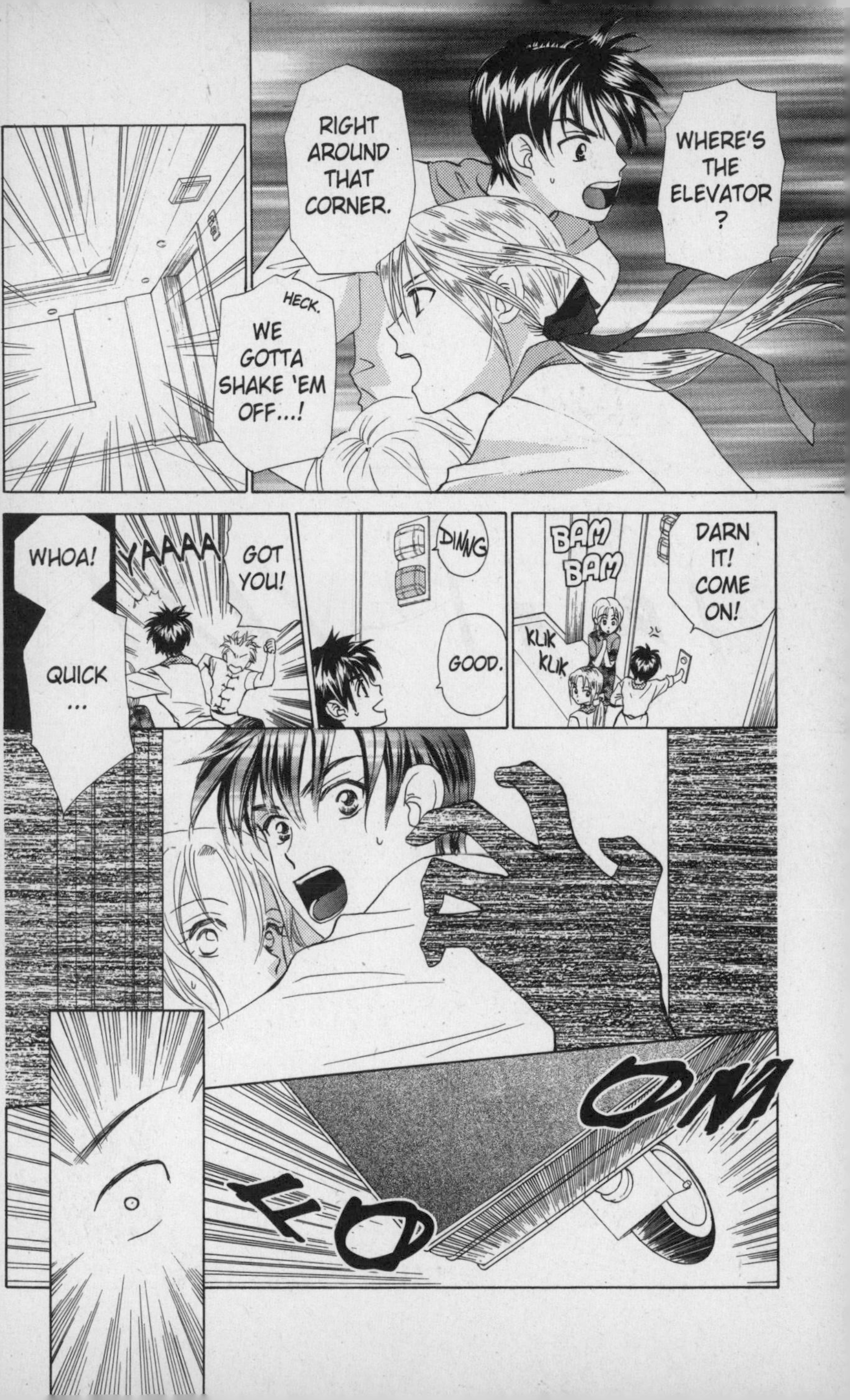
WHERE'S THE ELEVATOR ?
RIGHT AROUND THAT CORNER.
HECK.
WE GOTTA SHAKE 'EM OFF...!
BAM BAM
DARN IT! COME ON!
KLIK KLIK
DINNG
GOOD.
GOT YOU!
YAAAA
WHOA!
QUICK ...

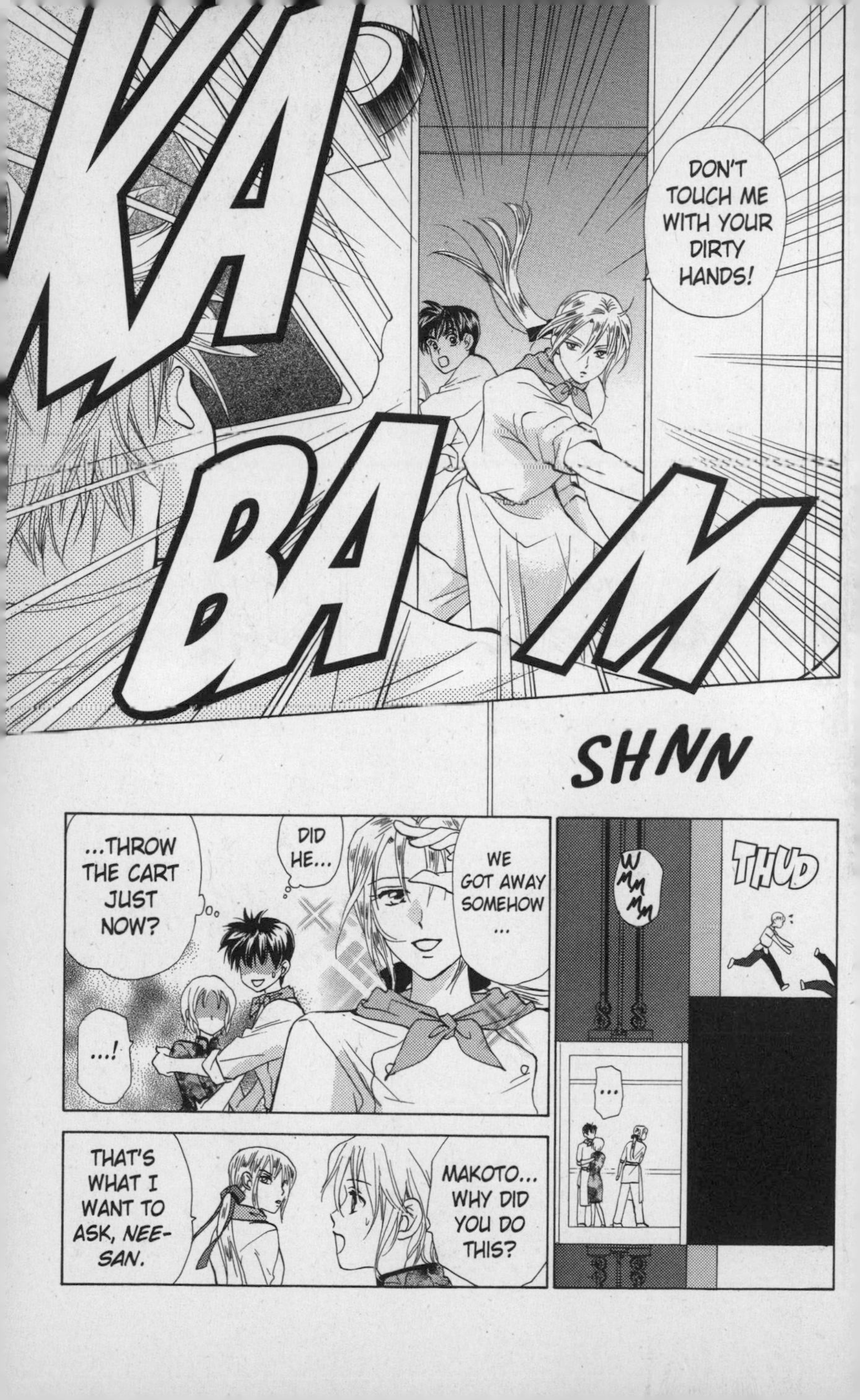
DON'T TOUCH ME WITH YOUR DIRTY HANDS!
VA
BAM
SHNN
THUD
WMMMMM
...
WE GOT AWAY SOMEHOW ...
DID HE...
...THROW THE CART JUST NOW?
...!
MAKOTO... WHY DID YOU DO THIS?
THAT'S WHAT I WANT TO ASK, NEE-SAN.

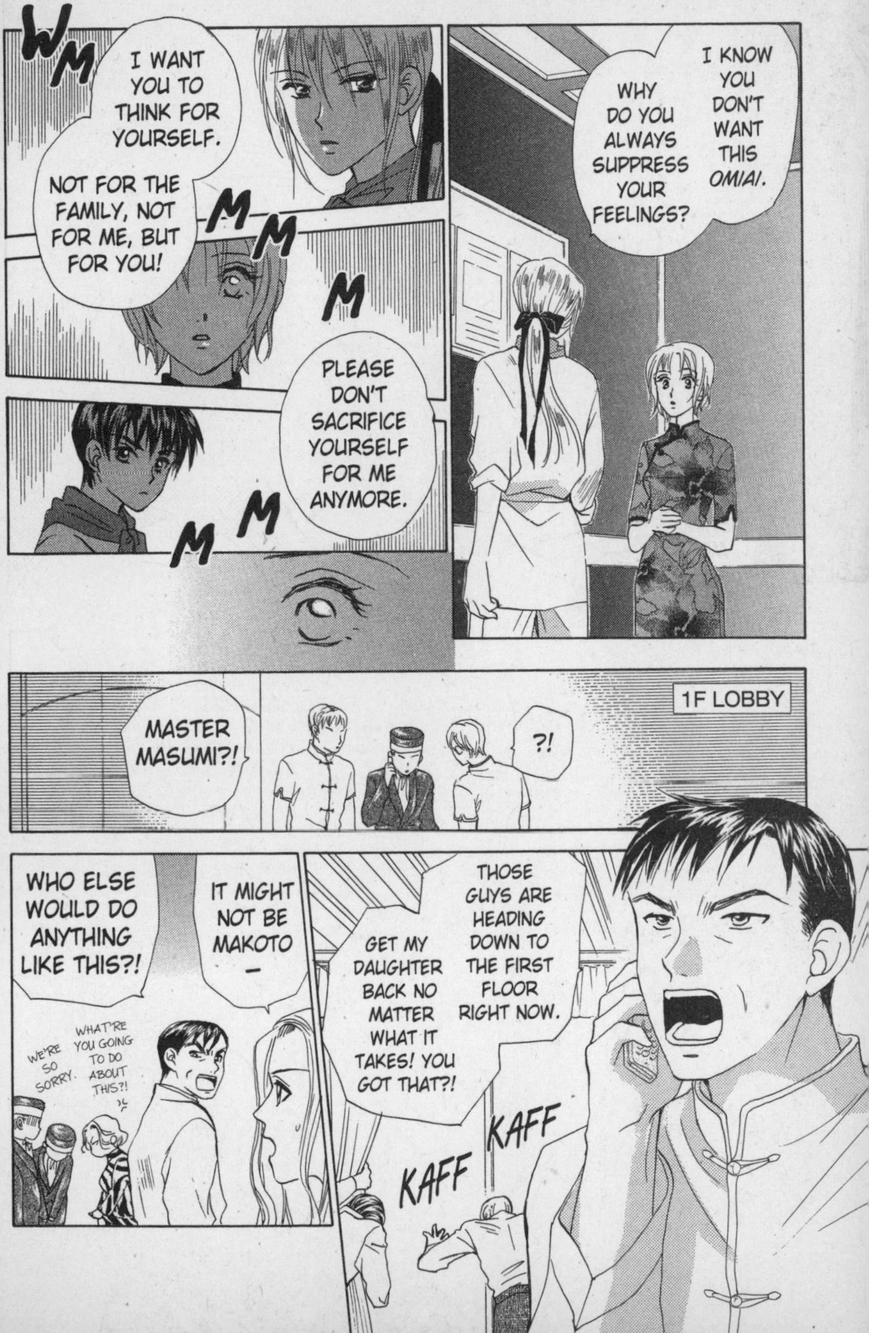
I KNOW YOU DON'T WANT THIS *OMIAI*.
WHY DO YOU ALWAYS SUPPRESS YOUR FEELINGS?
WM
I WANT YOU TO THINK FOR YOURSELF.
NOT FOR THE FAMILY, NOT FOR ME, BUT FOR YOU!
M M M
PLEASE DON'T SACRIFICE YOURSELF FOR ME ANYMORE.
M M
1F LOBBY
?!
MASTER MASUMI?!
THOSE GUYS ARE HEADING DOWN TO THE FIRST FLOOR RIGHT NOW.
GET MY DAUGHTER BACK NO MATTER WHAT IT TAKES! YOU GOT THAT?!
KAFF
KAFF
IT MIGHT NOT BE MAKOTO —
WHO ELSE WOULD DO ANYTHING LIKE THIS?!
WHAT'RE YOU GOING TO DO ABOUT THIS?!
WE'RE SO SORRY.

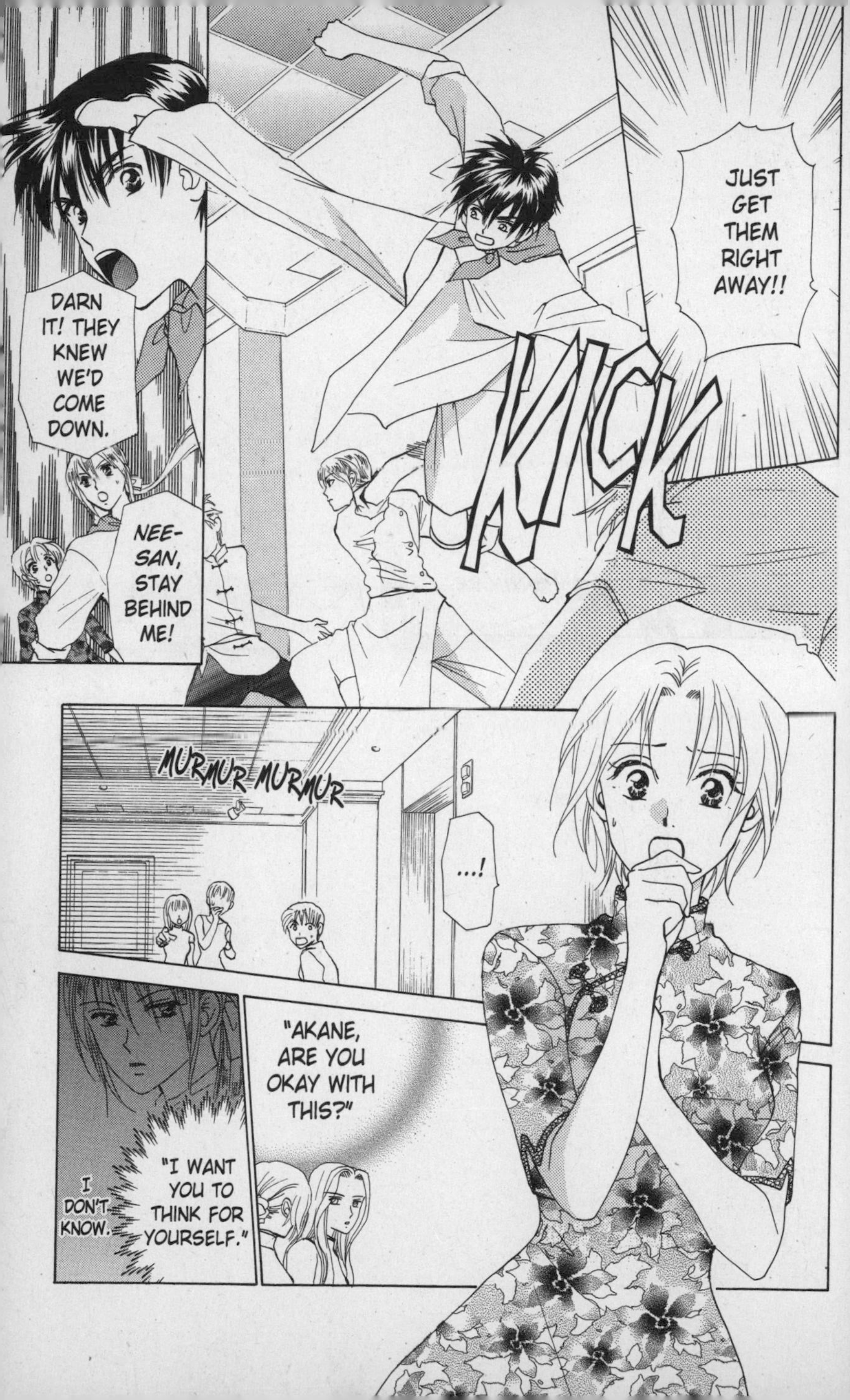
JUST GET THEM RIGHT AWAY!!
KICK
DARN IT! THEY KNEW WE'D COME DOWN.
NEE-SAN, STAY BEHIND ME!
MURMUR MURMUR
...!
"AKANE, ARE YOU OKAY WITH THIS?"
"I WANT YOU TO THINK FOR YOURSELF."
I DON'T KNOW.

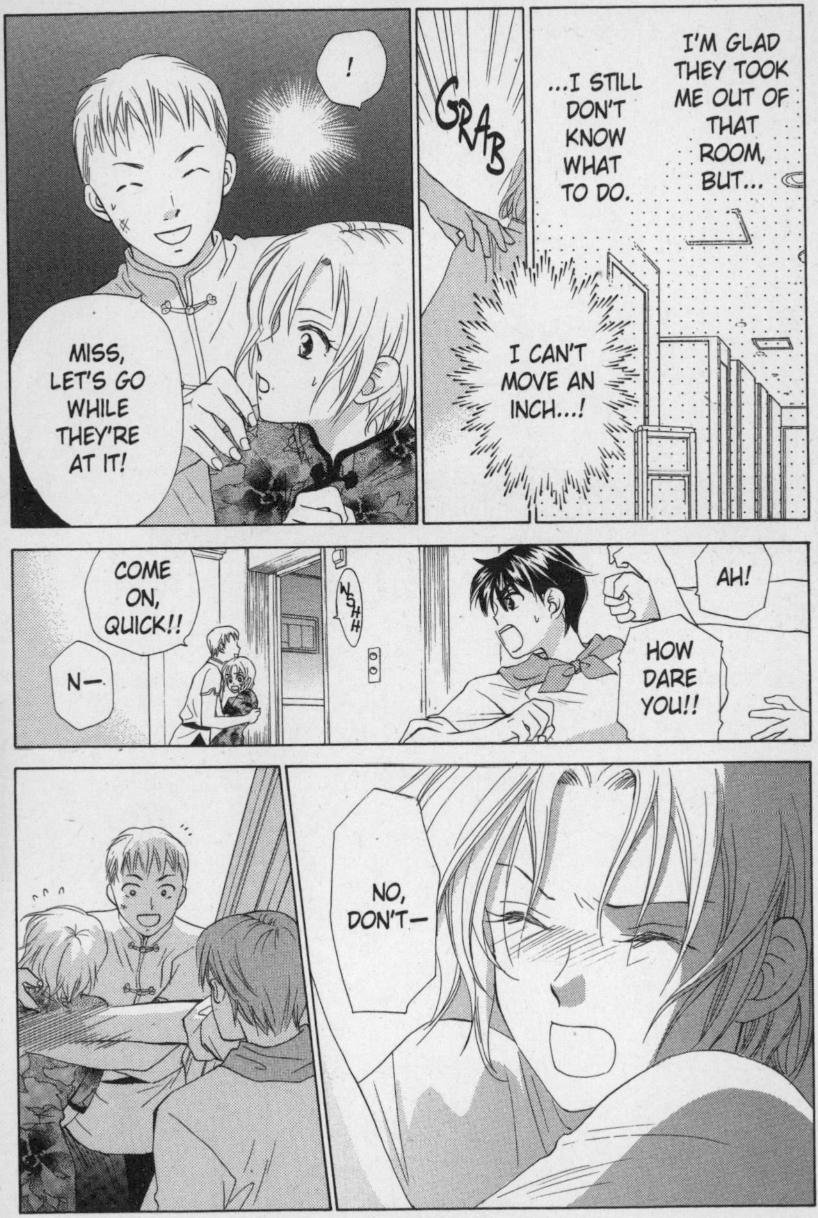
I'M GLAD THEY TOOK ME OUT OF THAT ROOM, BUT...
...I STILL DON'T KNOW WHAT TO DO.
I CAN'T MOVE AN INCH...!
GRAB
!
MISS, LET'S GO WHILE THEY'RE AT IT!
AH!
HOW DARE YOU!!
WSHH
COME ON, QUICK!!
N—.
NO, DON'T—

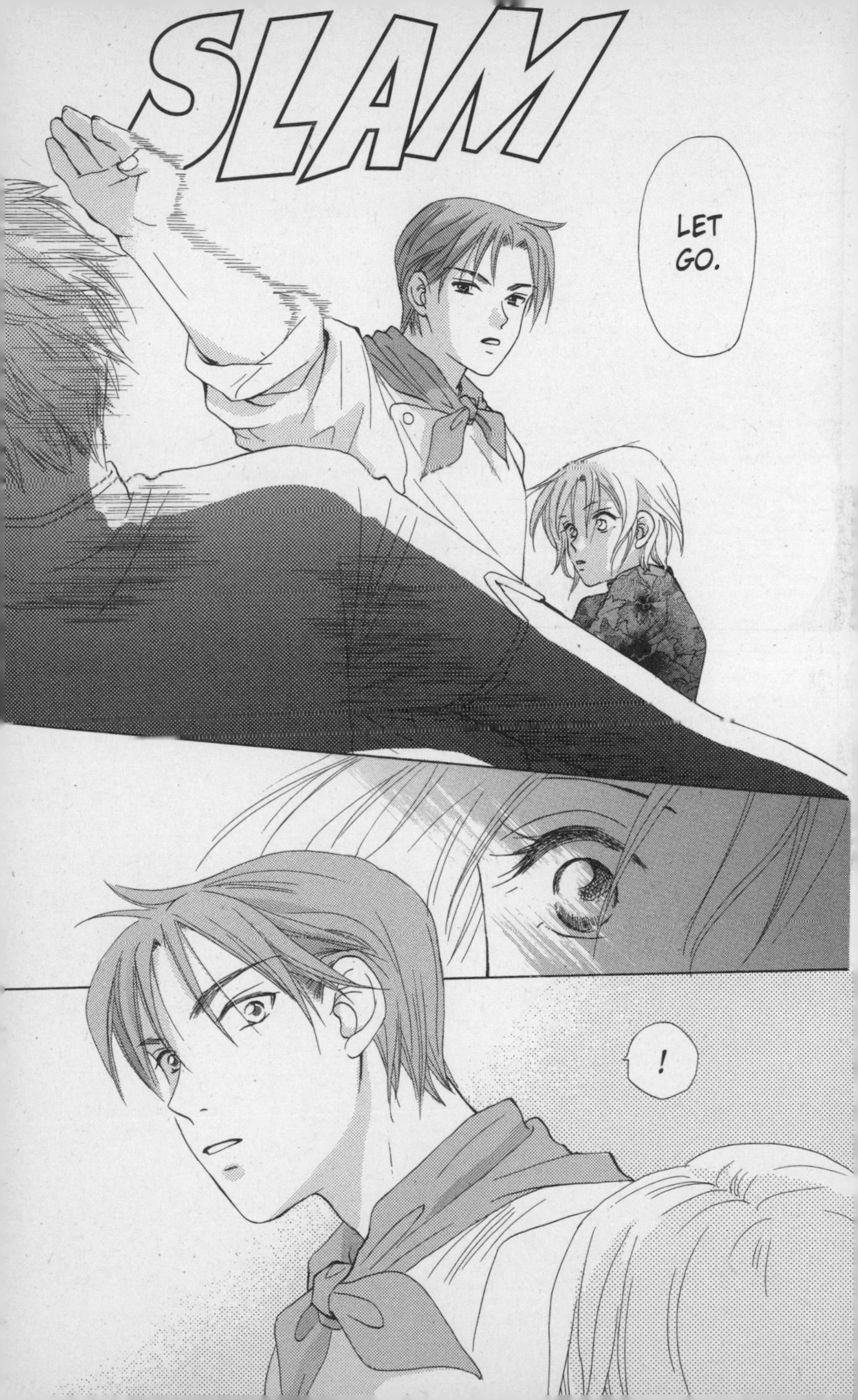
SLAM
LET GO.
!

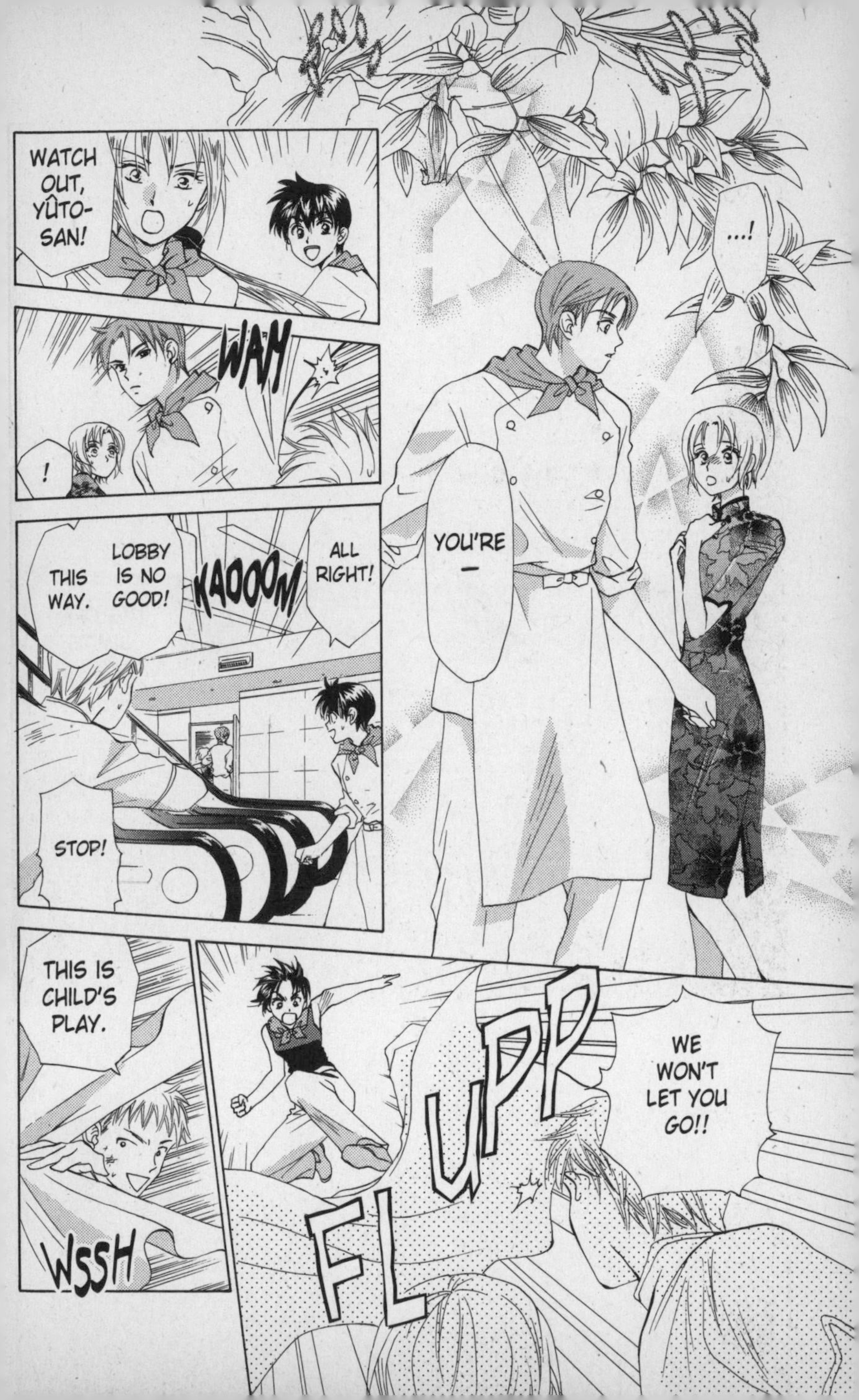
...!
YOU'RE —
WATCH OUT, YÛTO-SAN!
WAH
!
ALL RIGHT!
KAOOOM
LOBBY IS NO GOOD!
THIS WAY.
STOP!
WE WON'T LET YOU GO!!
FLUPP
THIS IS CHILD'S PLAY.
WSSH

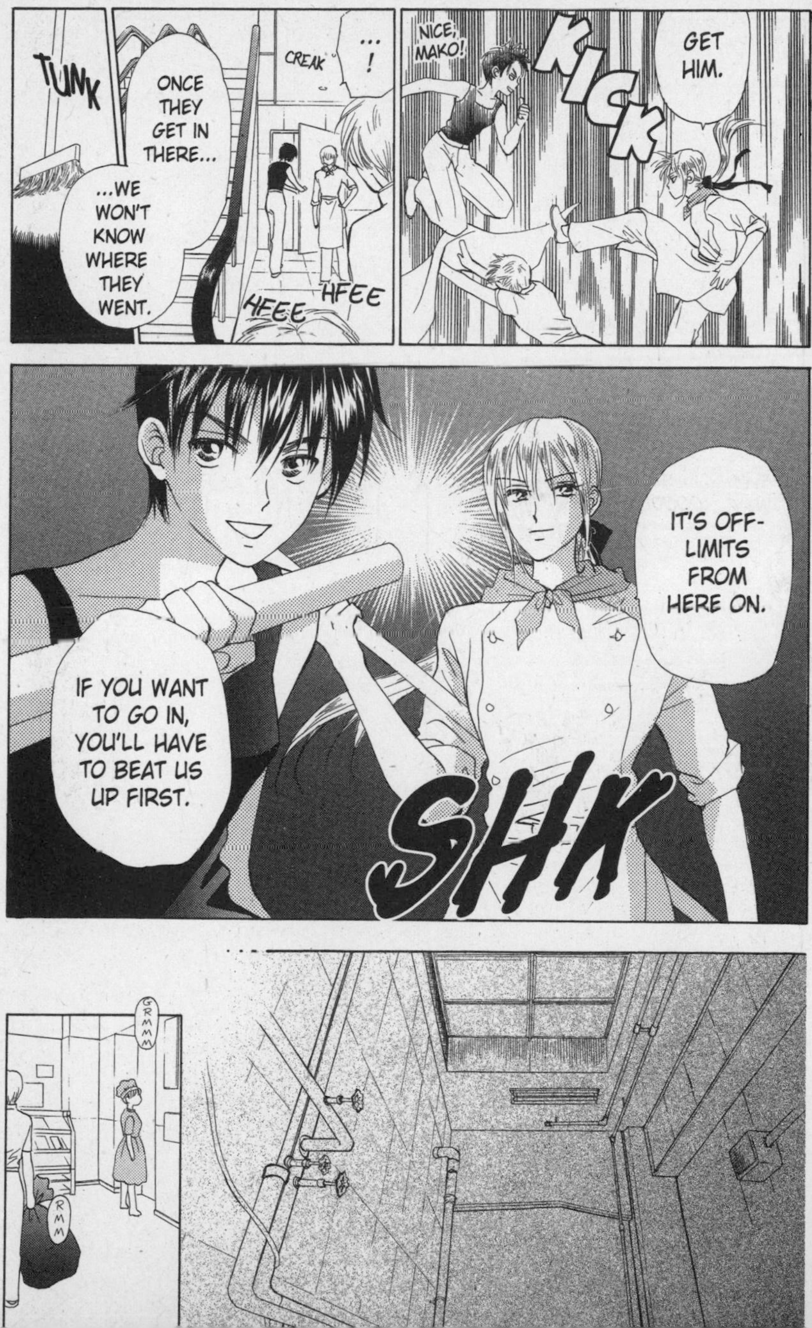
GET HIM.
KICK
NICE, MAKO!
...!
CREAK
ONCE THEY GET IN THERE...
...WE WON'T KNOW WHERE THEY WENT.
HFEE
HFEE
TUNK
IT'S OFF-LIMITS FROM HERE ON.
IF YOU WANT TO GO IN, YOU'LL HAVE TO BEAT US UP FIRST.
SHK
GRMMM
RMM

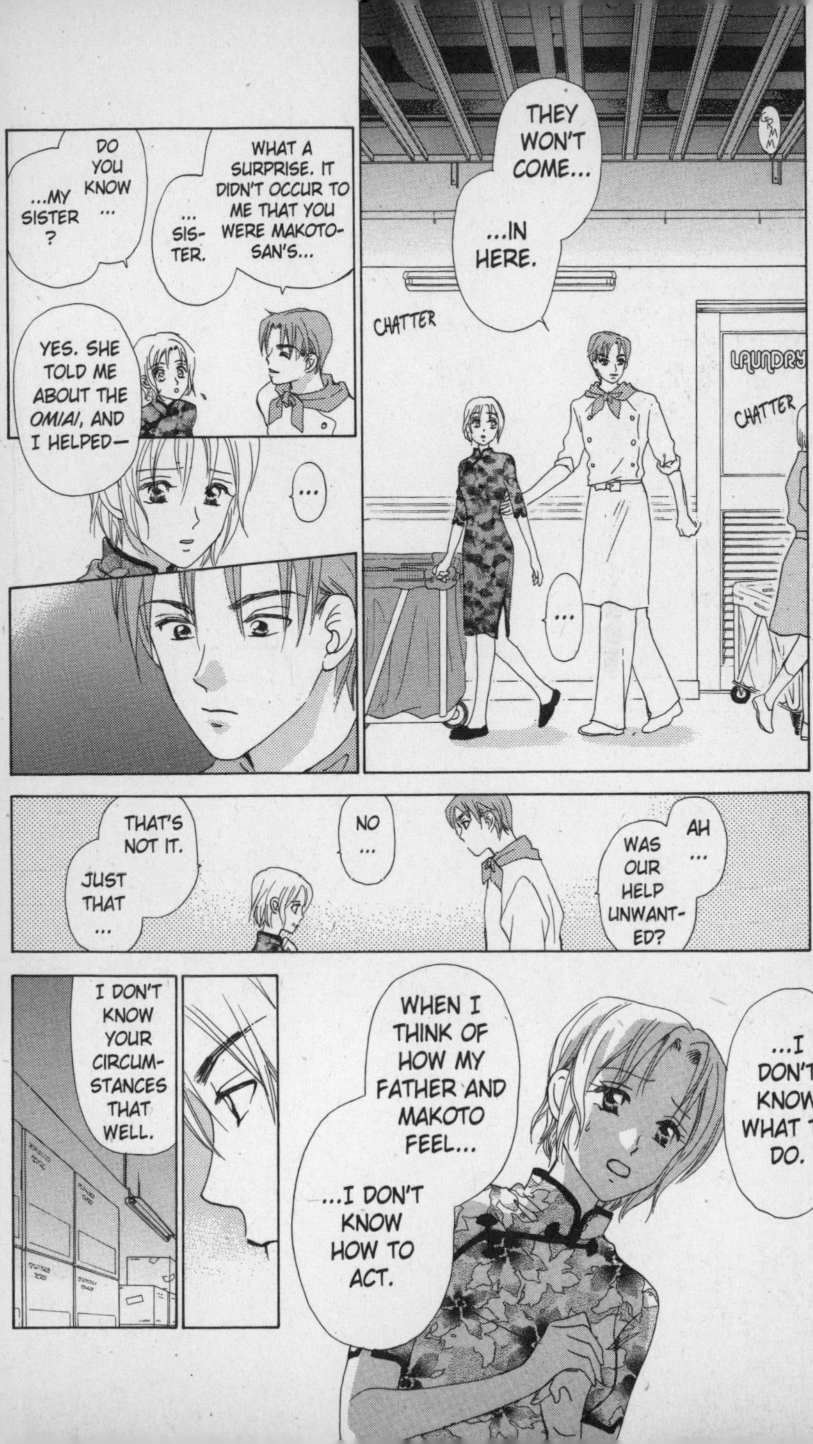
GRMM
THEY WON'T COME...
...IN HERE.
CHATTER
LAUNDRY
CHATTER
...
WHAT A SURPRISE. IT DIDN'T OCCUR TO ME THAT YOU WERE MAKOTO-SAN'S...
...SIS-TER.
DO YOU KNOW...
...MY SISTER?
YES. SHE TOLD ME ABOUT THE *OMIAI*, AND I HELPED—
...
AH...
WAS OUR HELP UNWANT-ED?
NO...
THAT'S NOT IT.
JUST THAT...
...I DON'T KNOW WHAT TO DO.
WHEN I THINK OF HOW MY FATHER AND MAKOTO FEEL...
...I DON'T KNOW HOW TO ACT.
I DON'T KNOW YOUR CIRCUM-STANCES THAT WELL.

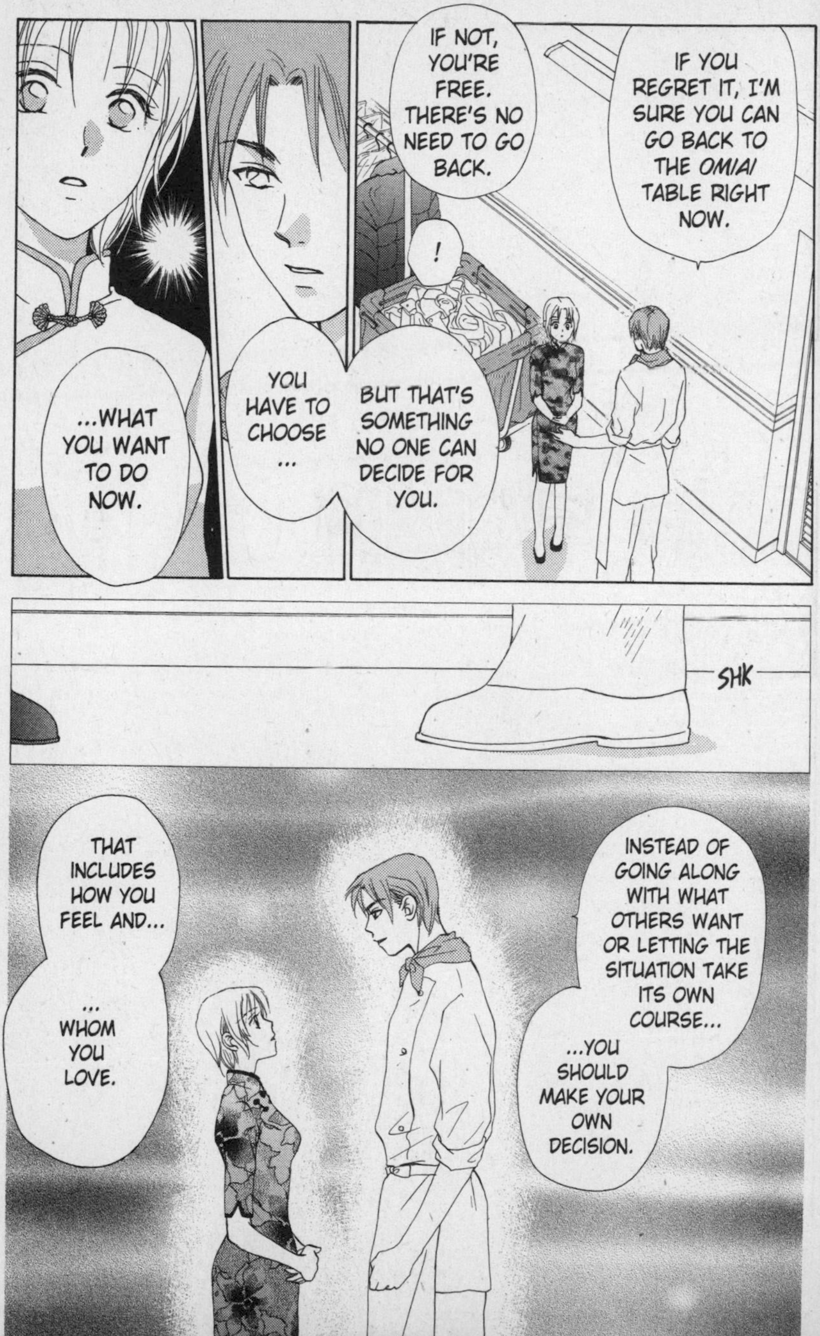
IF YOU REGRET IT, I'M SURE YOU CAN GO BACK TO THE *OMIAI* TABLE RIGHT NOW.
IF NOT, YOU'RE FREE. THERE'S NO NEED TO GO BACK.
!
BUT THAT'S SOMETHING NO ONE CAN DECIDE FOR YOU.
YOU HAVE TO CHOOSE ...
...WHAT YOU WANT TO DO NOW.
SHK
INSTEAD OF GOING ALONG WITH WHAT OTHERS WANT OR LETTING THE SITUATION TAKE ITS OWN COURSE...
...YOU SHOULD MAKE YOUR OWN DECISION.
THAT INCLUDES HOW YOU FEEL AND...
... WHOM YOU LOVE.

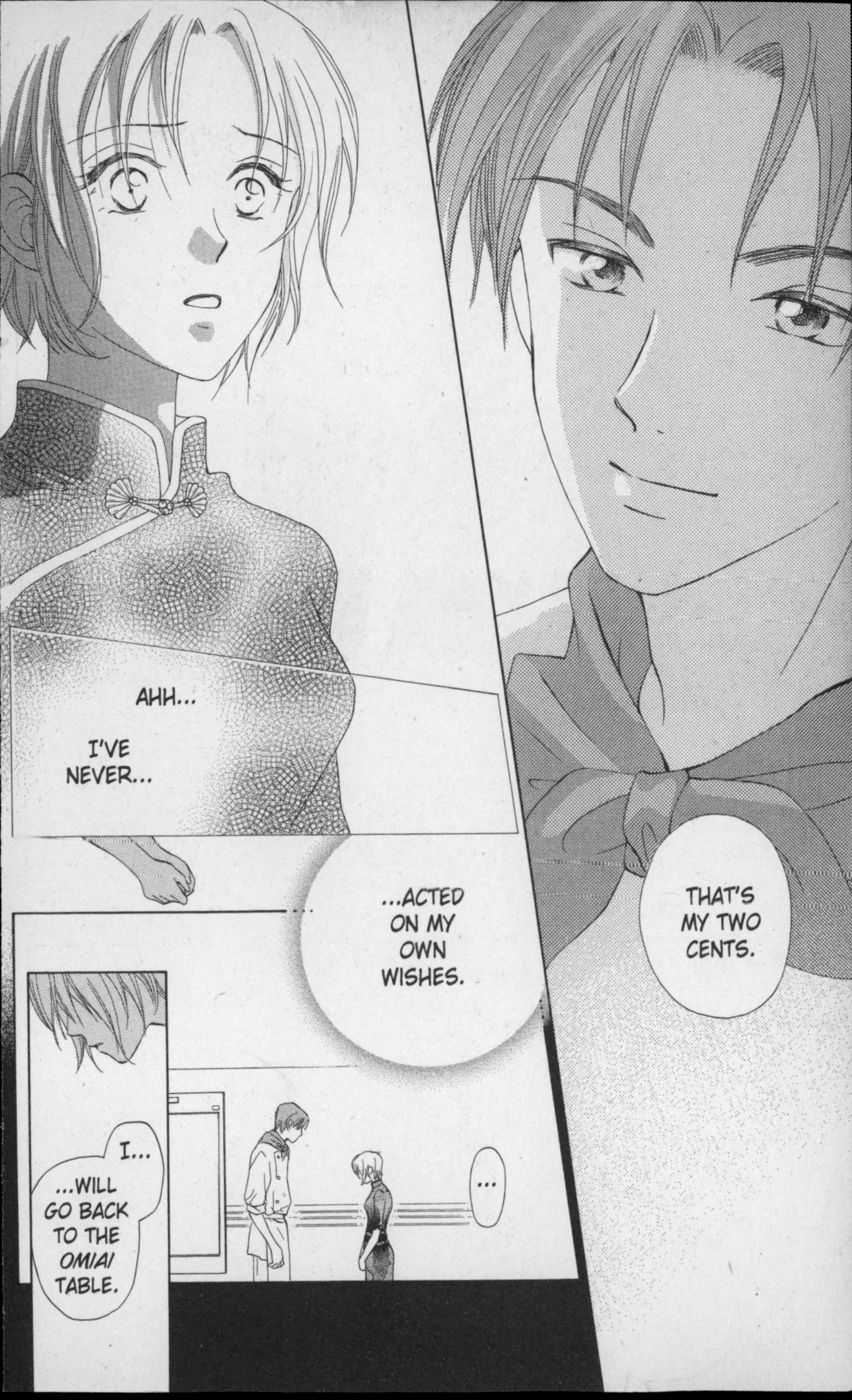
THAT'S MY TWO CENTS.
AHH...
I'VE NEVER...
...ACTED ON MY OWN WISHES.
...
I...
...WILL GO BACK TO THE *OMIAI* TABLE.

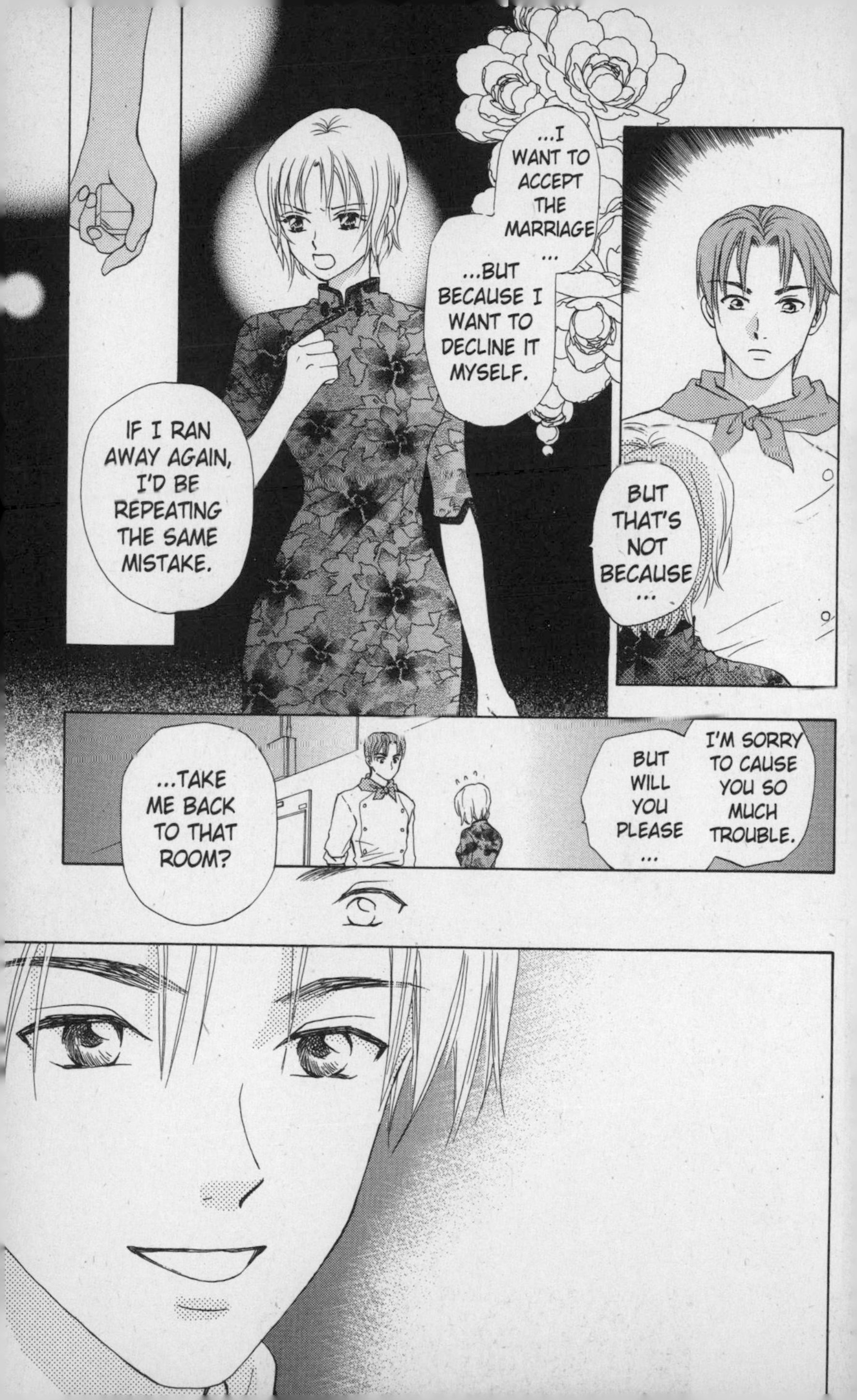
BUT THAT'S NOT BECAUSE ...
...I WANT TO ACCEPT THE MARRIAGE ...
...BUT BECAUSE I WANT TO DECLINE IT MYSELF.
IF I RAN AWAY AGAIN, I'D BE REPEATING THE SAME MISTAKE.
I'M SORRY TO CAUSE YOU SO MUCH TROUBLE.
BUT WILL YOU PLEASE ...
...TAKE ME BACK TO THAT ROOM?

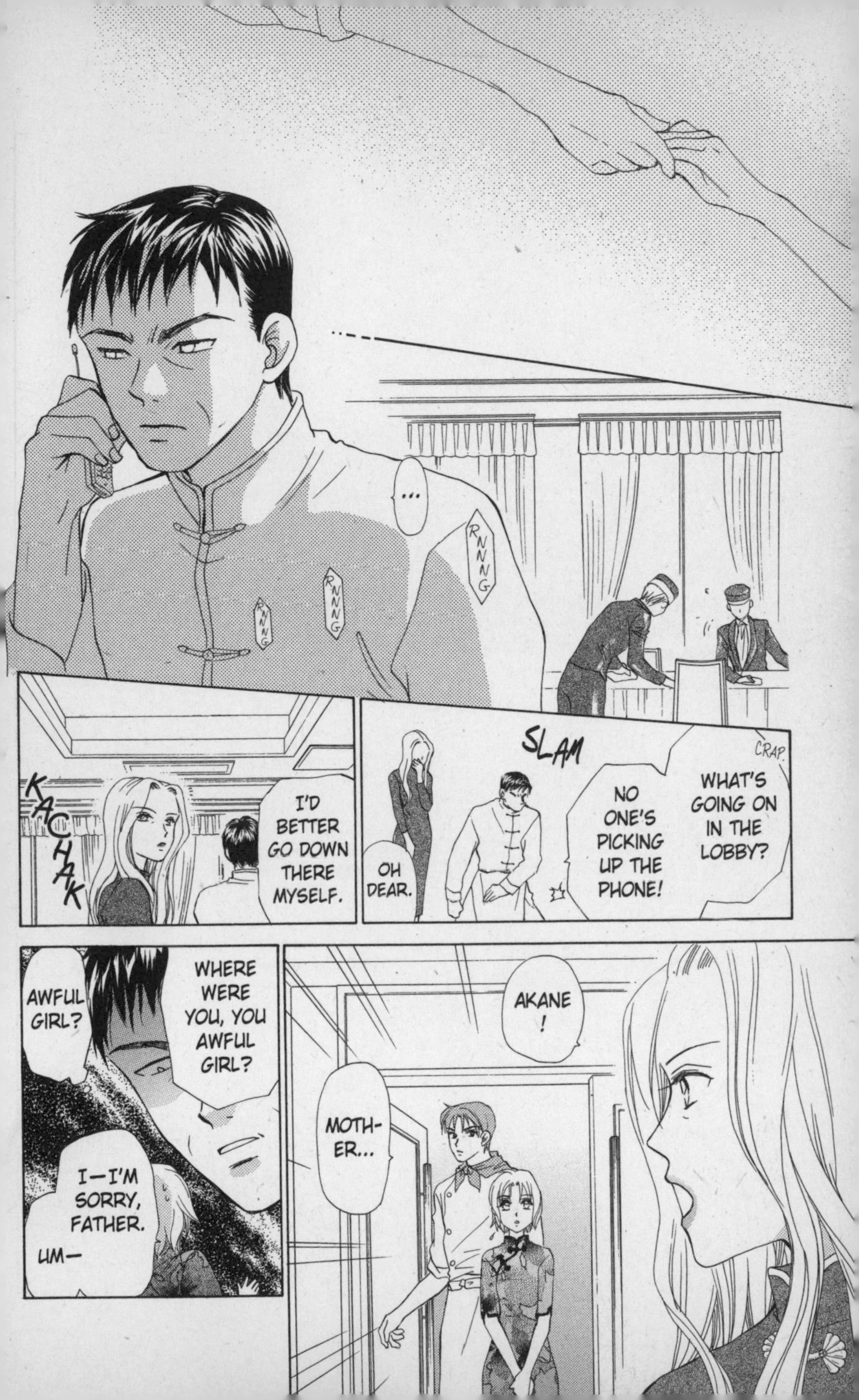
...
RNNG
RNNNG
RNNNG
CRAP.
WHAT'S GOING ON IN THE LOBBY?
NO ONE'S PICKING UP THE PHONE!
SLAM
OH DEAR.
I'D BETTER GO DOWN THERE MYSELF.
KACHAK
AKANE!
MOTHER...
WHERE WERE YOU, YOU AWFUL GIRL?
AWFUL GIRL?
I—I'M SORRY, FATHER.
UM—

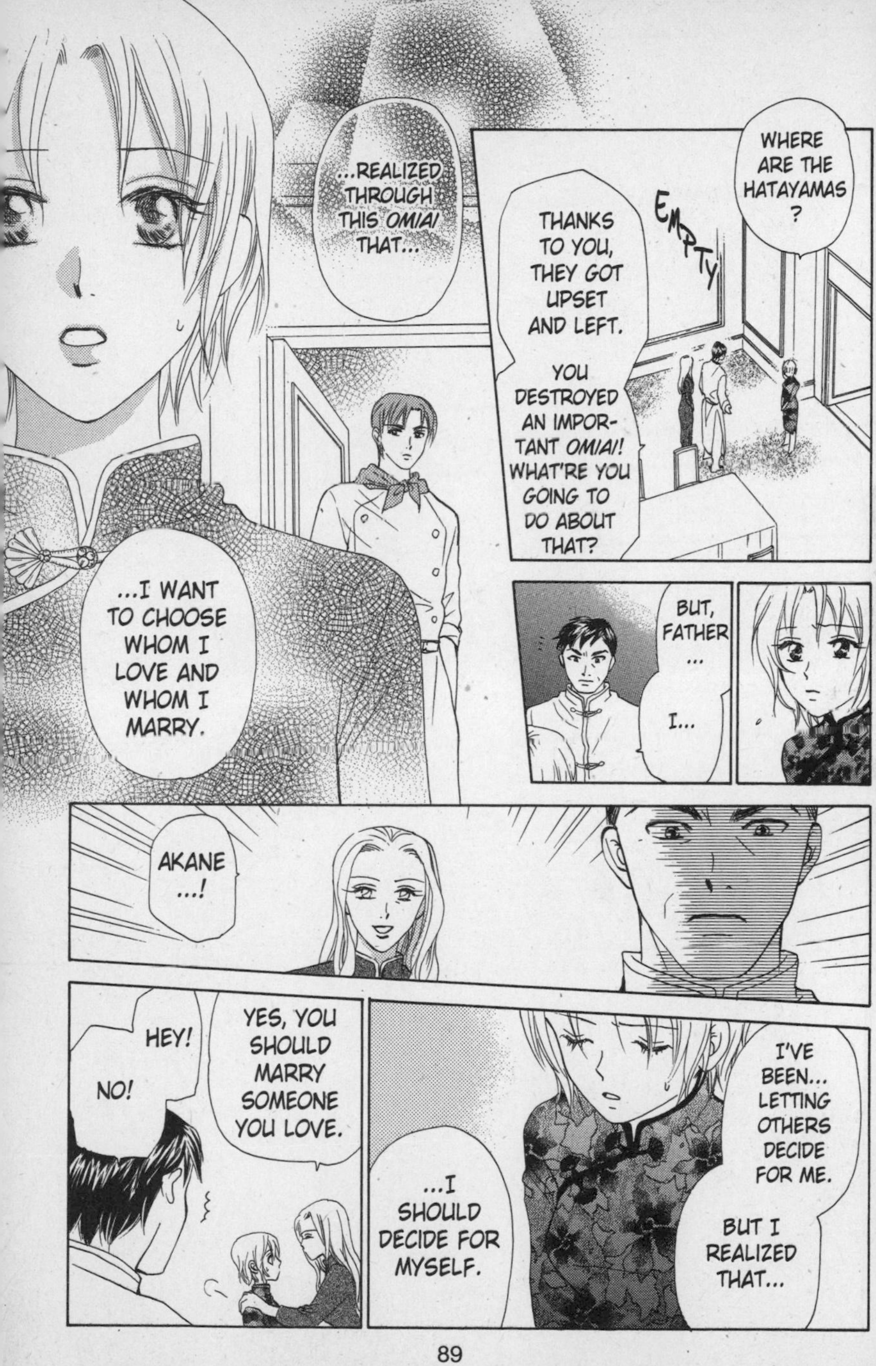
WHERE ARE THE HATAYAMAS ?
EMPTY
THANKS TO YOU, THEY GOT UPSET AND LEFT.
YOU DESTROYED AN IMPORTANT OMIAI! WHAT'RE YOU GOING TO DO ABOUT THAT?
BUT, FATHER ...
I...
...REALIZED THROUGH THIS OMIAI THAT...
...I WANT TO CHOOSE WHOM I LOVE AND WHOM I MARRY.
AKANE ...!
I'VE BEEN... LETTING OTHERS DECIDE FOR ME.
BUT I REALIZED THAT...
...I SHOULD DECIDE FOR MYSELF.
YES, YOU SHOULD MARRY SOMEONE YOU LOVE.
HEY!
NO!

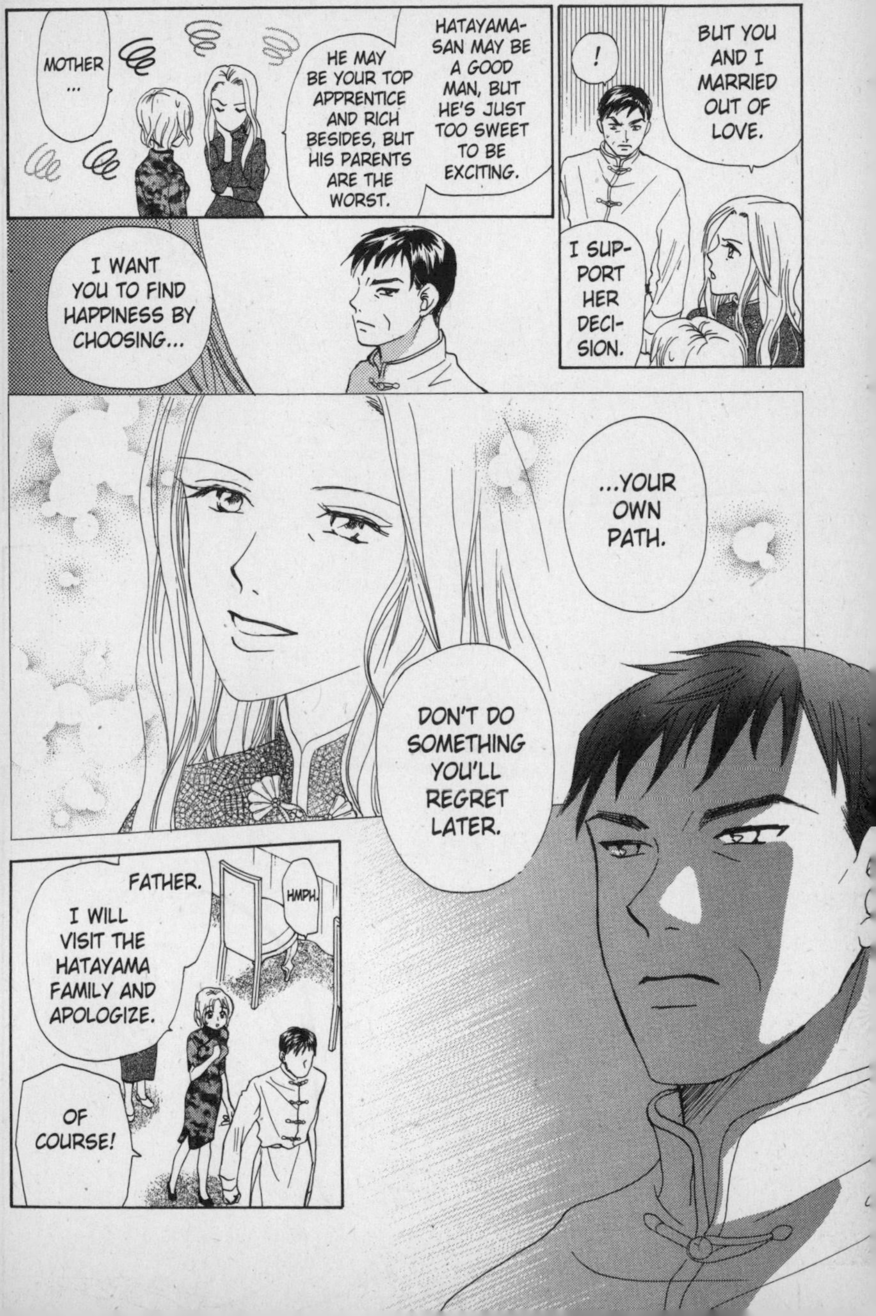
BUT YOU AND I MARRIED OUT OF LOVE.
!
I SUPPORT HER DECISION.
HATAYAMA-SAN MAY BE A GOOD MAN, BUT HE'S JUST TOO SWEET TO BE EXCITING.
HE MAY BE YOUR TOP APPRENTICE AND RICH BESIDES, BUT HIS PARENTS ARE THE WORST.
MOTHER ...
I WANT YOU TO FIND HAPPINESS BY CHOOSING...
...YOUR OWN PATH.
DON'T DO SOMETHING YOU'LL REGRET LATER.
HMPH.
FATHER.
I WILL VISIT THE HATAYAMA FAMILY AND APOLOGIZE.
OF COURSE!

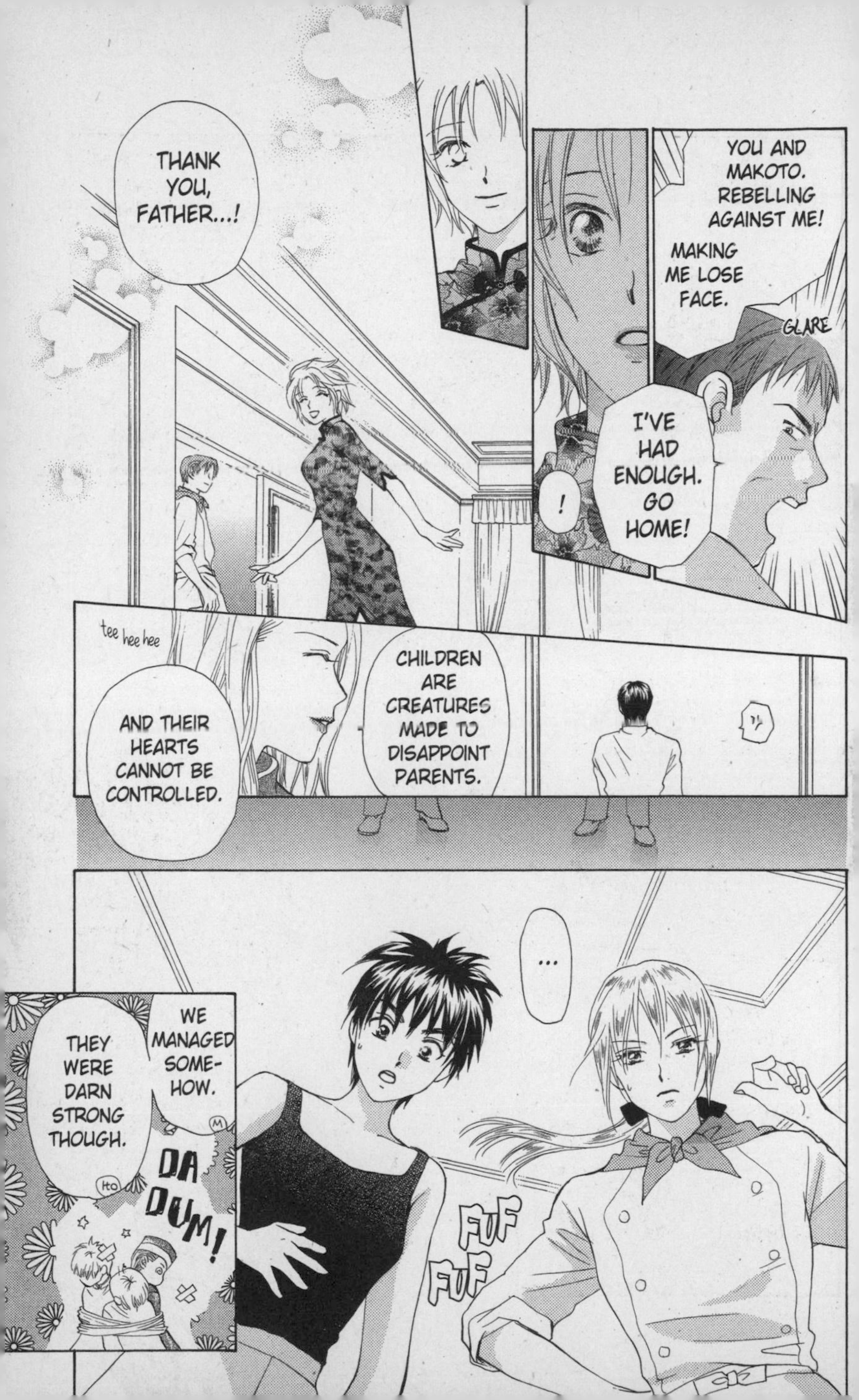
YOU AND MAKOTO. REBELLING AGAINST ME!
MAKING ME LOSE FACE.
GLARE
I'VE HAD ENOUGH. GO HOME!
!
THANK YOU, FATHER...!
ッ
CHILDREN ARE CREATURES MADE TO DISAPPOINT PARENTS.
tee hee hee
AND THEIR HEARTS CANNOT BE CONTROLLED.
...
FUF FUF
WE MANAGED SOME-HOW.
M
THEY WERE DARN STRONG THOUGH.
Ito
DA DUM!

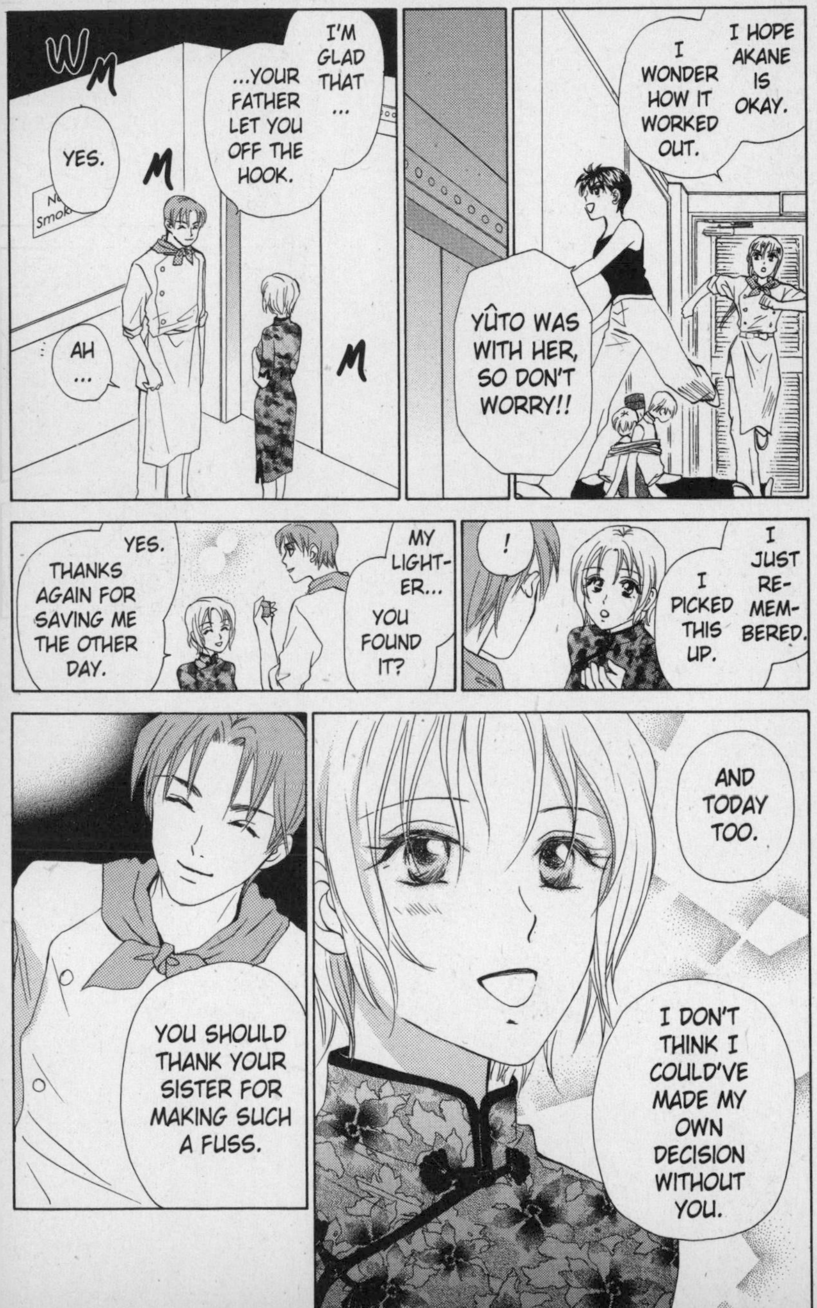
I HOPE AKANE IS OKAY.
I WONDER HOW IT WORKED OUT.
YÛTO WAS WITH HER, SO DON'T WORRY!!
I'M GLAD THAT ...
...YOUR FATHER LET YOU OFF THE HOOK.
YES.
WMM
M
AH ...
M
I JUST REMEMBERED.
I PICKED THIS UP.
!
MY LIGHTER... YOU FOUND IT?
YES. THANKS AGAIN FOR SAVING ME THE OTHER DAY.
AND TODAY TOO.
I DON'T THINK I COULD'VE MADE MY OWN DECISION WITHOUT YOU.
YOU SHOULD THANK YOUR SISTER FOR MAKING SUCH A FUSS.

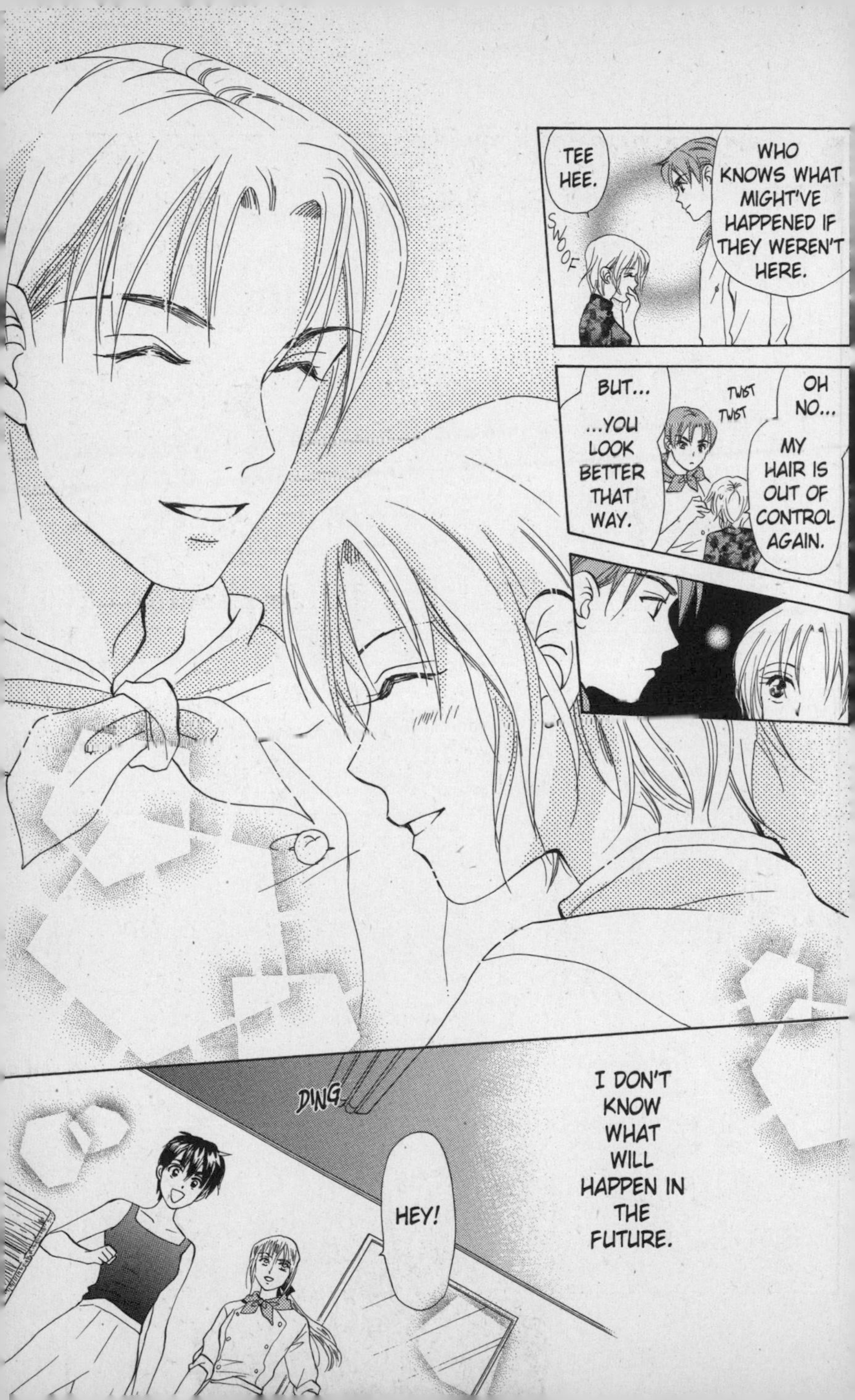
WHO KNOWS WHAT MIGHT'VE HAPPENED IF THEY WEREN'T HERE.
TEE HEE.
SWOOF
OH NO...
MY HAIR IS OUT OF CONTROL AGAIN.
TWIST TWIST
BUT...
...YOU LOOK BETTER THAT WAY.
I DON'T KNOW WHAT WILL HAPPEN IN THE FUTURE.
DING
HEY!

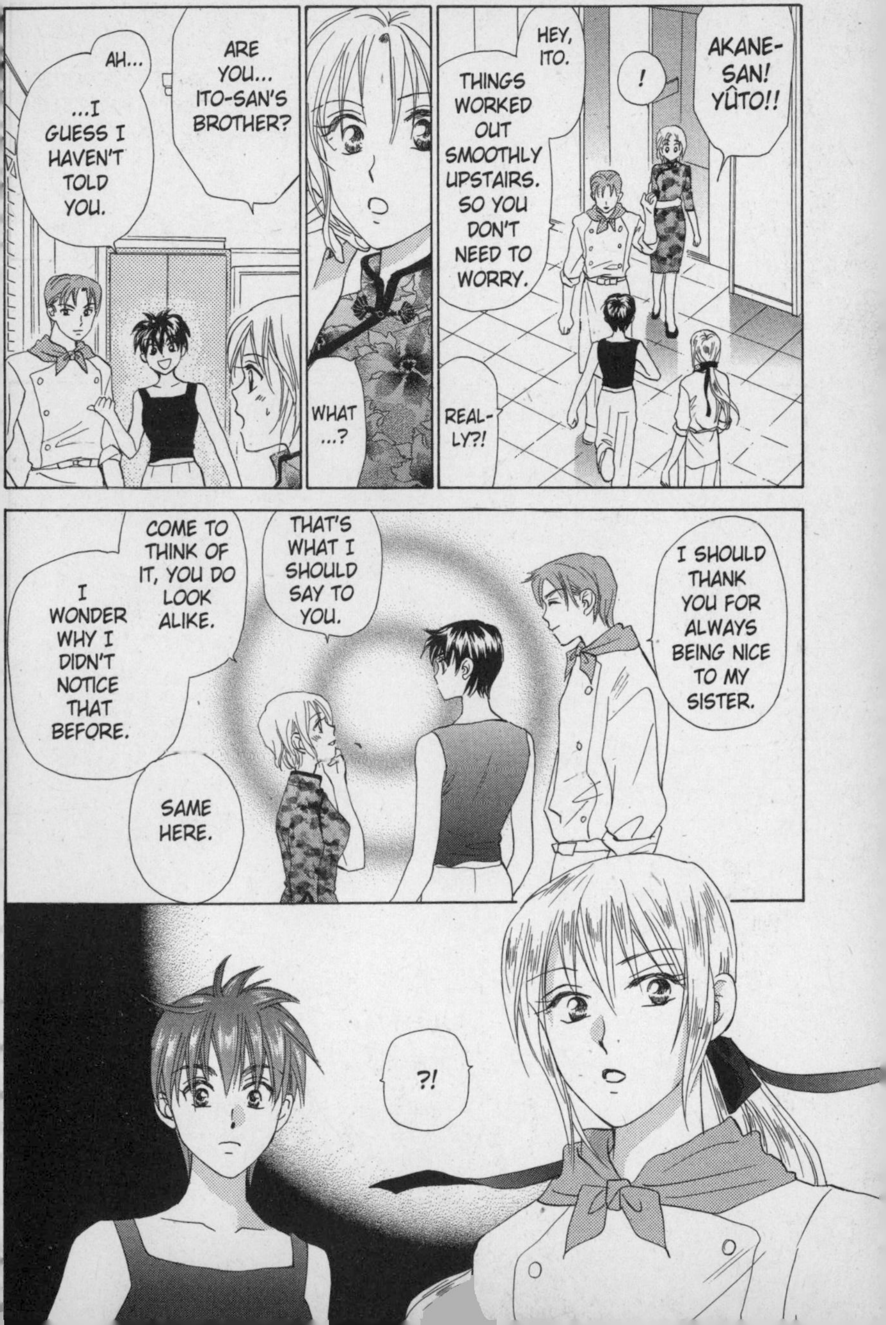
AKANE-SAN! YÛTO!!
!
HEY, ITO.
THINGS WORKED OUT SMOOTHLY UPSTAIRS. SO YOU DON'T NEED TO WORRY.
REALLY?!
WHAT ...?
ARE YOU... ITO-SAN'S BROTHER?
AH...
...I GUESS I HAVEN'T TOLD YOU.
I SHOULD THANK YOU FOR ALWAYS BEING NICE TO MY SISTER.
THAT'S WHAT I SHOULD SAY TO YOU.
COME TO THINK OF IT, YOU DO LOOK ALIKE.
I WONDER WHY I DIDN'T NOTICE THAT BEFORE.
SAME HERE.
?!

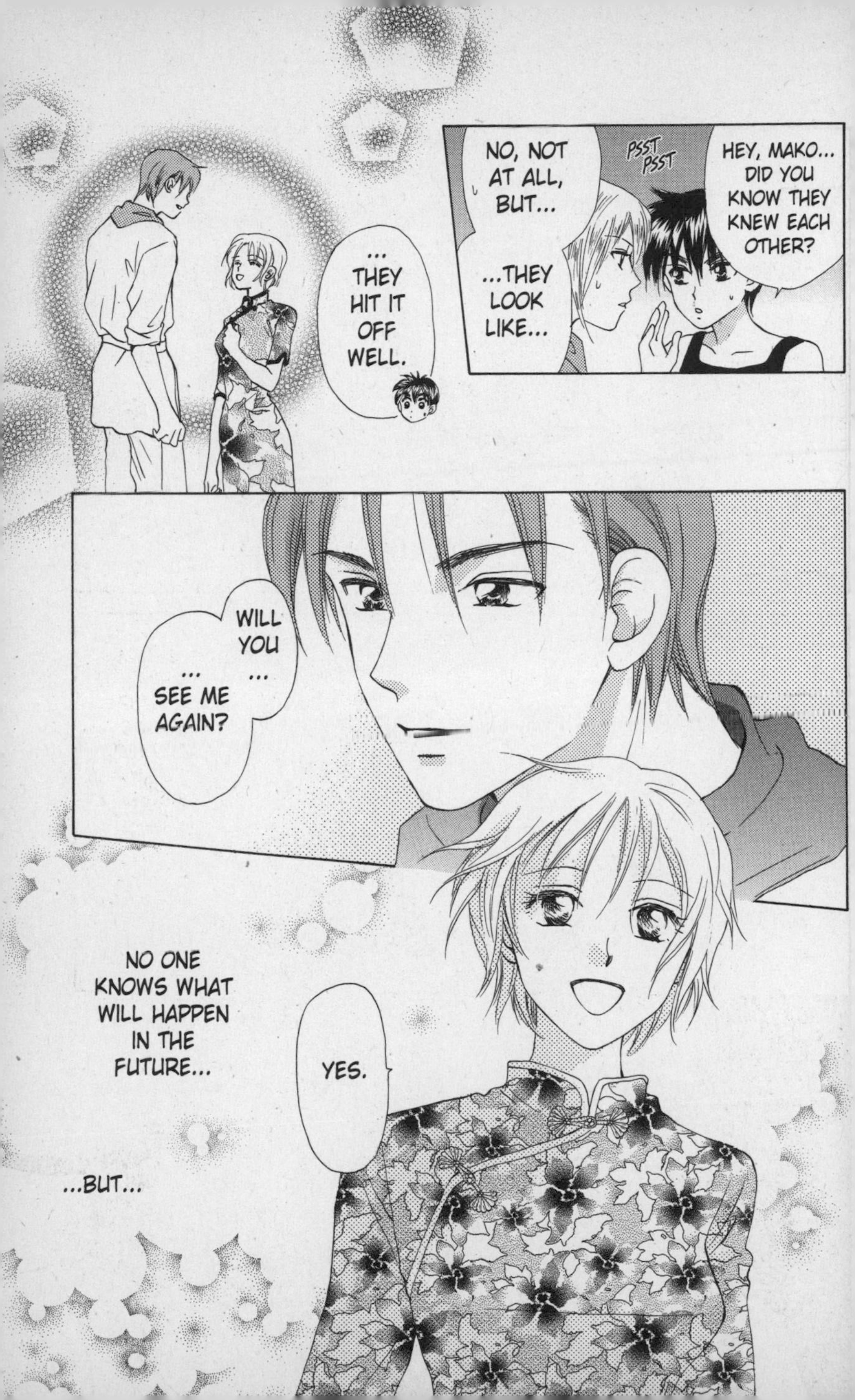

HEY, MAKO... DID YOU KNOW THEY KNEW EACH OTHER?
PSST PSST
NO, NOT AT ALL, BUT...
...THEY LOOK LIKE...
... THEY HIT IT OFF WELL.
WILL YOU ...
... SEE ME AGAIN?
YES.
NO ONE KNOWS WHAT WILL HAPPEN IN THE FUTURE...
...BUT...

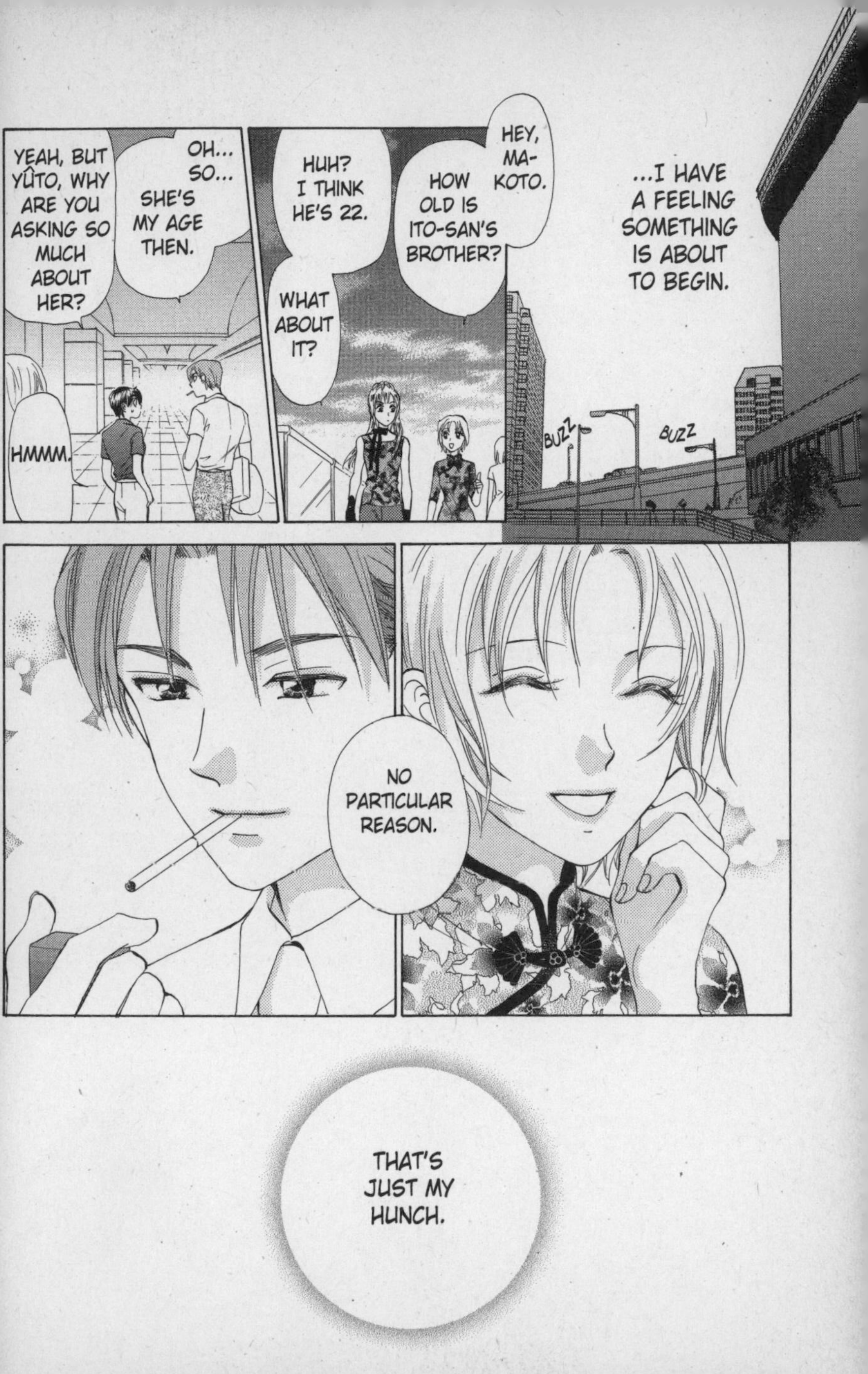
...I HAVE A FEELING SOMETHING IS ABOUT TO BEGIN.
BUZZ
BUZZ
HEY, MA-KOTO.
HOW OLD IS ITO-SAN'S BROTHER?
HUH? I THINK HE'S 22.
WHAT ABOUT IT?
OH... SO... SHE'S MY AGE THEN.
YEAH, BUT YÛTO, WHY ARE YOU ASKING SO MUCH ABOUT HER?
HMMM.
NO PARTICULAR REASON.
THAT'S JUST MY HUNCH.

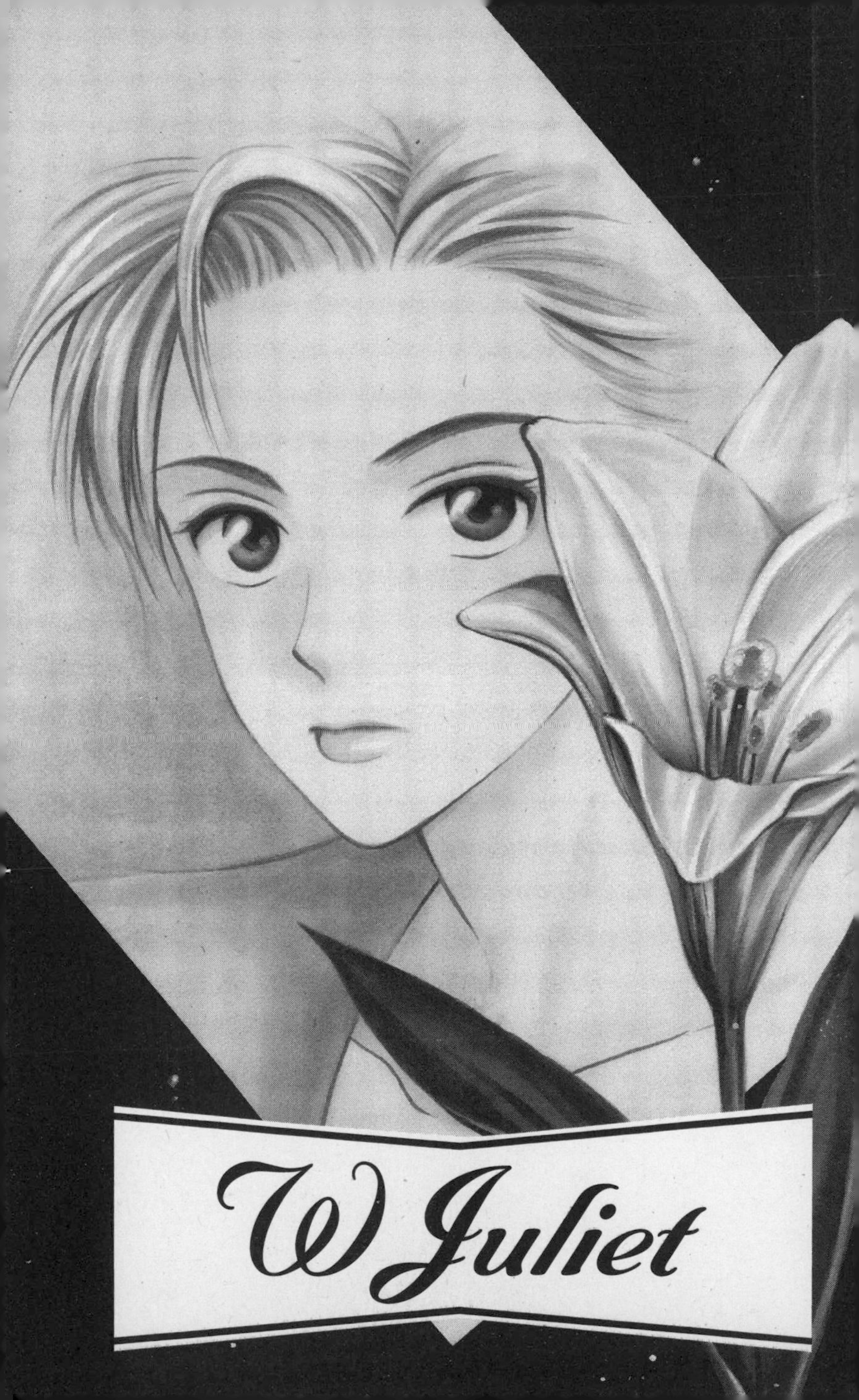
W Juliet

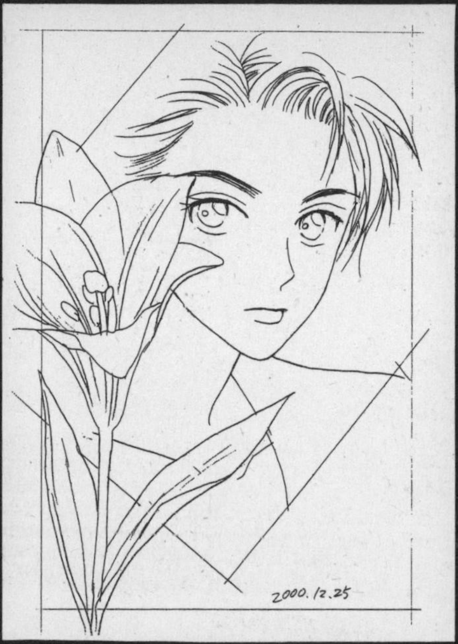
2000.12.25

← 2001, Hana to Yume No. 4, opening art, draft (B4 size)

2000, Hana to Yume No. 19, draft (B4 size)
↓ for Bonus Gift (B5 size notebook)

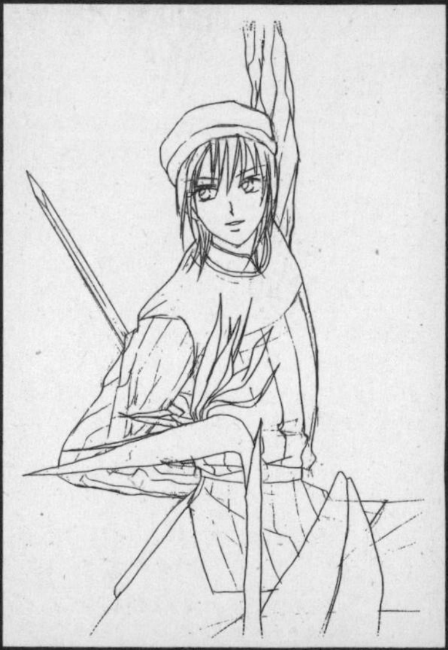

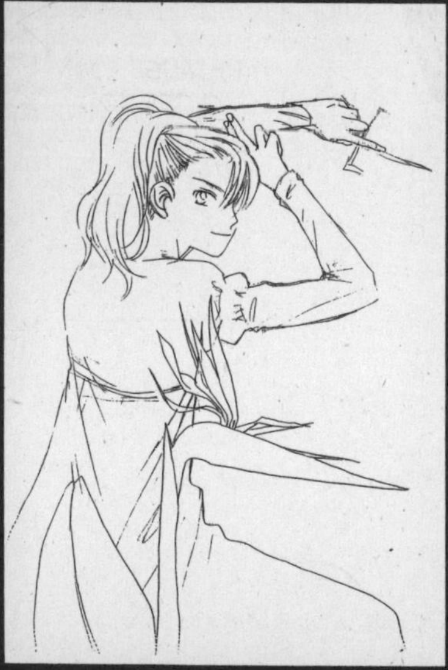

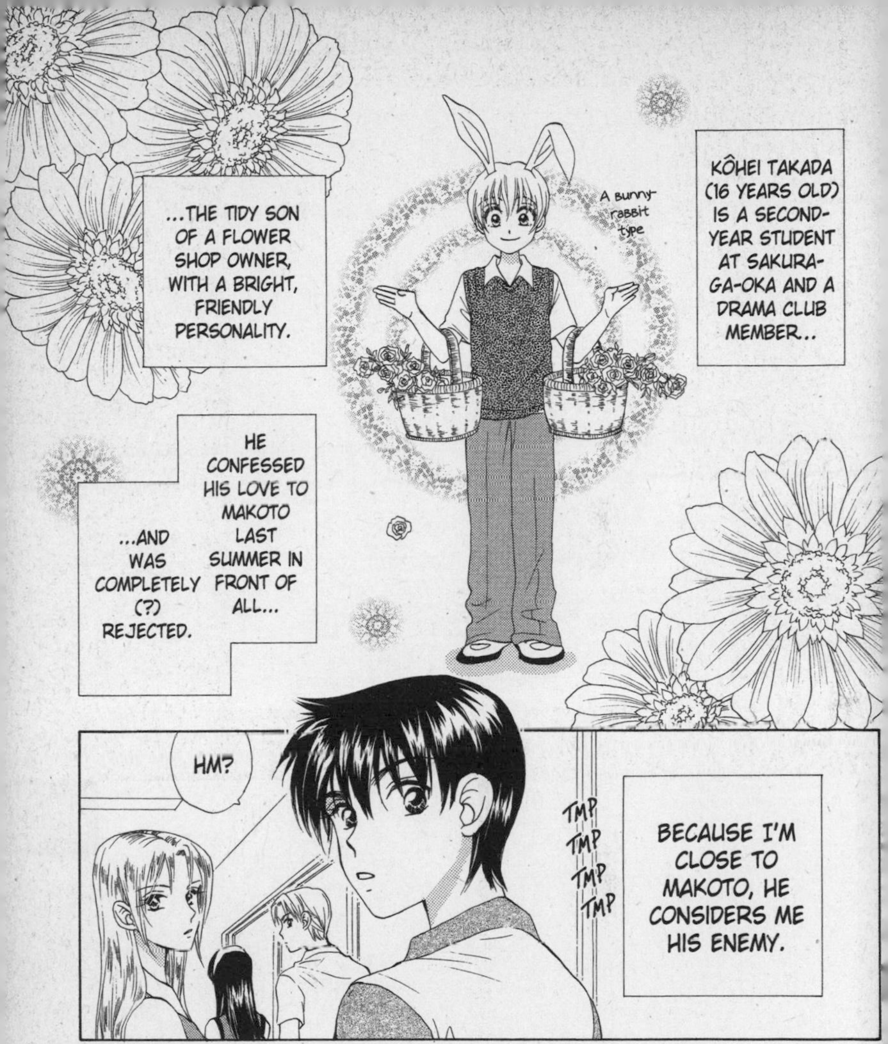
KÔHEI TAKADA (16 YEARS OLD) IS A SECOND-YEAR STUDENT AT SAKURA-GA-OKA AND A DRAMA CLUB MEMBER..
A bunny-rabbit type
...THE TIDY SON OF A FLOWER SHOP OWNER, WITH A BRIGHT, FRIENDLY PERSONALITY.
HE CONFESSED HIS LOVE TO MAKOTO LAST SUMMER IN FRONT OF ALL...
...AND WAS COMPLETELY (?) REJECTED.
BECAUSE I'M CLOSE TO MAKOTO, HE CONSIDERS ME HIS ENEMY.
TMP TMP TMP TMP
HM?

-Behind the Scenes Story- ④

Ko-chan is transferring schools?? This episode shocked everyone quite a bit. But when there is a meeting, there will be a parting too! (What was that about?)

But Kôhei should probably pursue a costume-related career instead of the flower shop... I couldn't help telling myself that as I drew this episode.

Anyhow, I totally agree with what Ito says on page 127 as well as with her last monologue. I should always keep that in mind.

Now, here's a question for you. What do you think Yoshirô's costume was meant for?

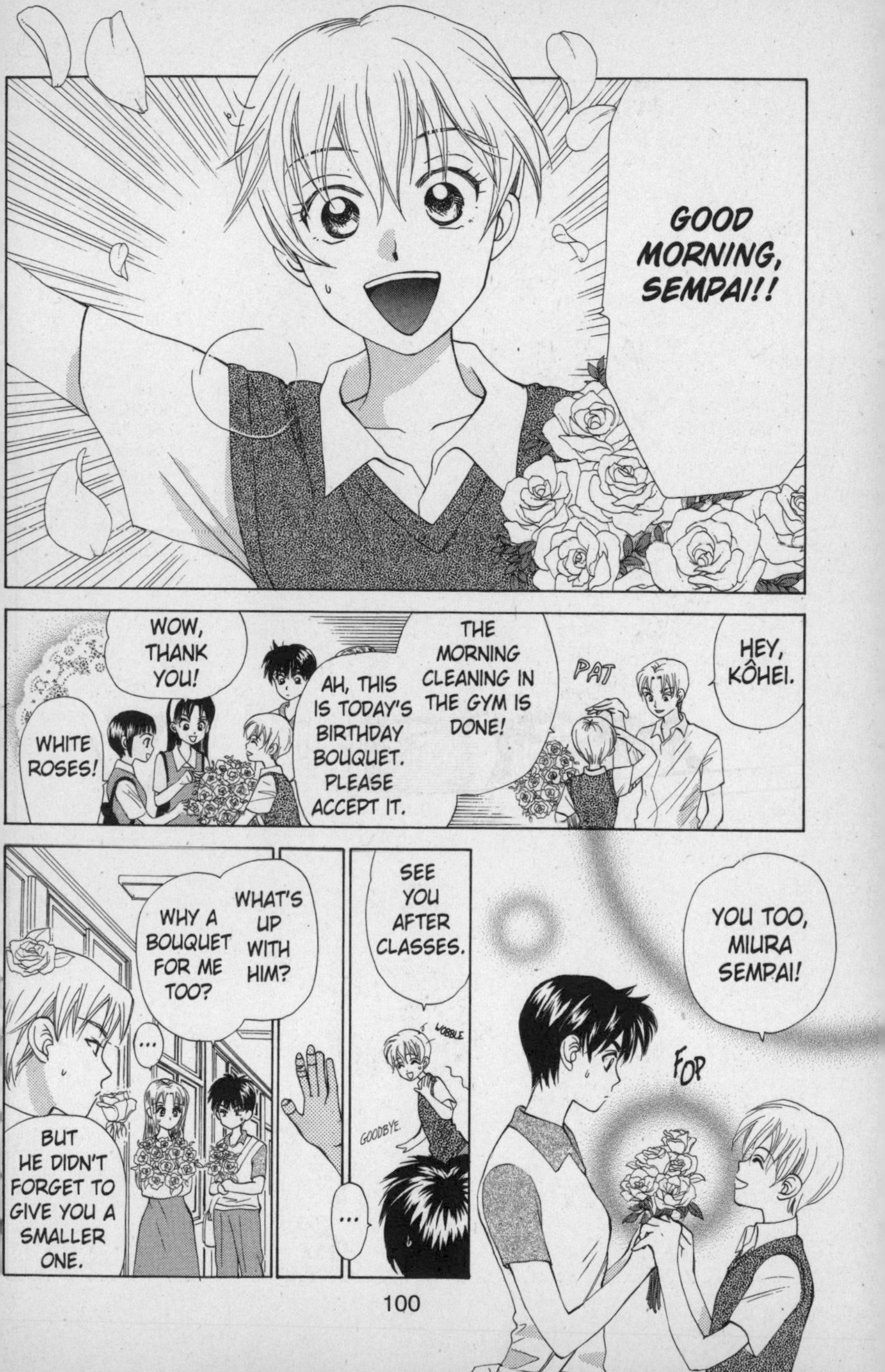
GOOD MORNING, SEMPAI!!
HEY, KÔHEI.
PAT
THE MORNING CLEANING IN THE GYM IS DONE!
AH, THIS IS TODAY'S BIRTHDAY BOUQUET. PLEASE ACCEPT IT.
WOW, THANK YOU!
WHITE ROSES!
YOU TOO, MIURA SEMPAI!
FOP
SEE YOU AFTER CLASSES.
WOBBLE
GOODBYE
...
WHAT'S UP WITH HIM?
WHY A BOUQUET FOR ME TOO?
...
BUT HE DIDN'T FORGET TO GIVE YOU A SMALLER ONE.

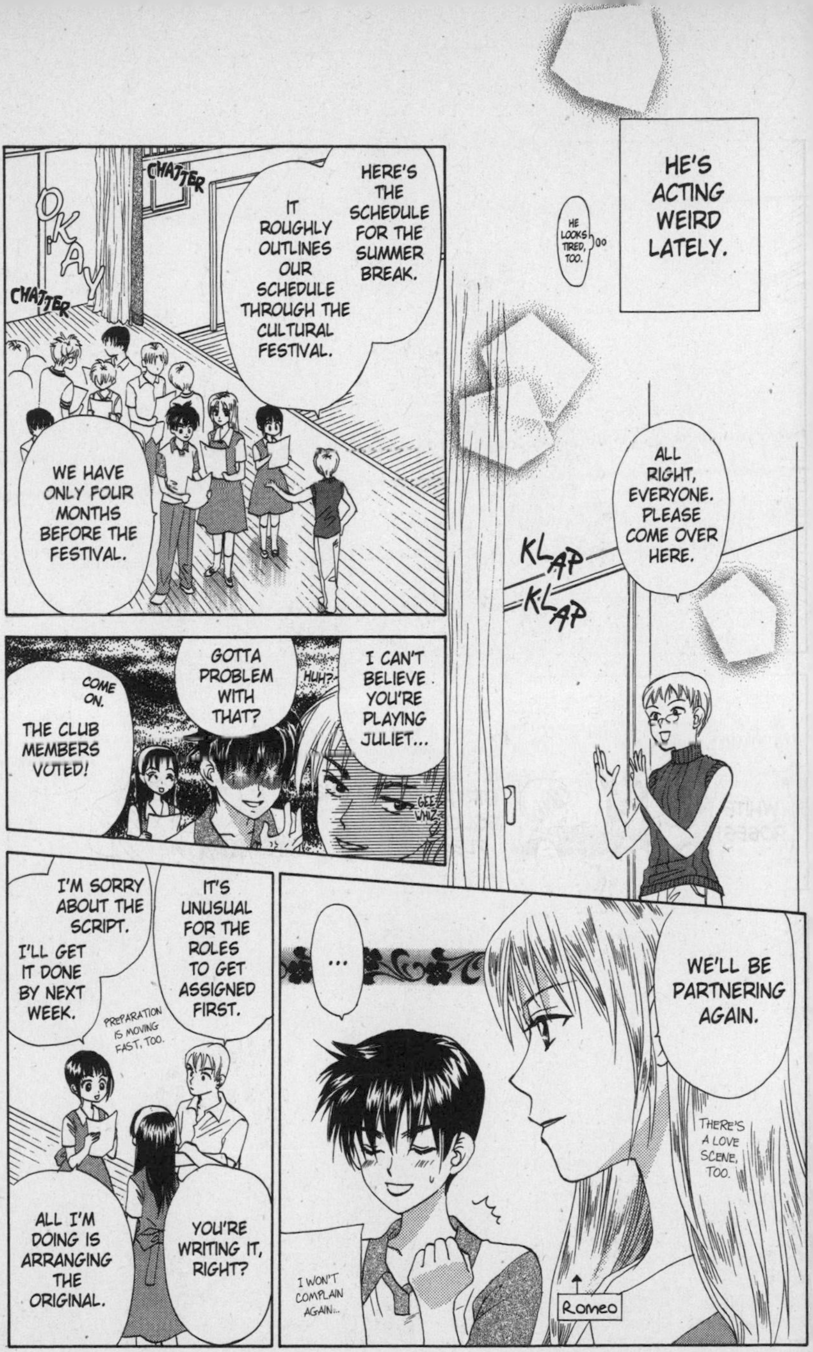

HE'S ACTING WEIRD LATELY.
HE LOOKS TIRED, TOO.
KLAP KLAP
ALL RIGHT, EVERYONE. PLEASE COME OVER HERE.
HERE'S THE SCHEDULE FOR THE SUMMER BREAK.
IT ROUGHLY OUTLINES OUR SCHEDULE THROUGH THE CULTURAL FESTIVAL.
CHATTER
OKAY
CHATTER
WE HAVE ONLY FOUR MONTHS BEFORE THE FESTIVAL.
I CAN'T BELIEVE YOU'RE PLAYING JULIET...
HUH?
GOTTA PROBLEM WITH THAT?
GEE WHIZ
COME ON.
THE CLUB MEMBERS VOTED!
WE'LL BE PARTNERING AGAIN.
...
THERE'S A LOVE SCENE, TOO.
Romeo
I WON'T COMPLAIN AGAIN...
IT'S UNUSUAL FOR THE ROLES TO GET ASSIGNED FIRST.
I'M SORRY ABOUT THE SCRIPT.
I'LL GET IT DONE BY NEXT WEEK.
PREPARATION IS MOVING FAST, TOO.
YOU'RE WRITING IT, RIGHT?
ALL I'M DOING IS ARRANGING THE ORIGINAL.

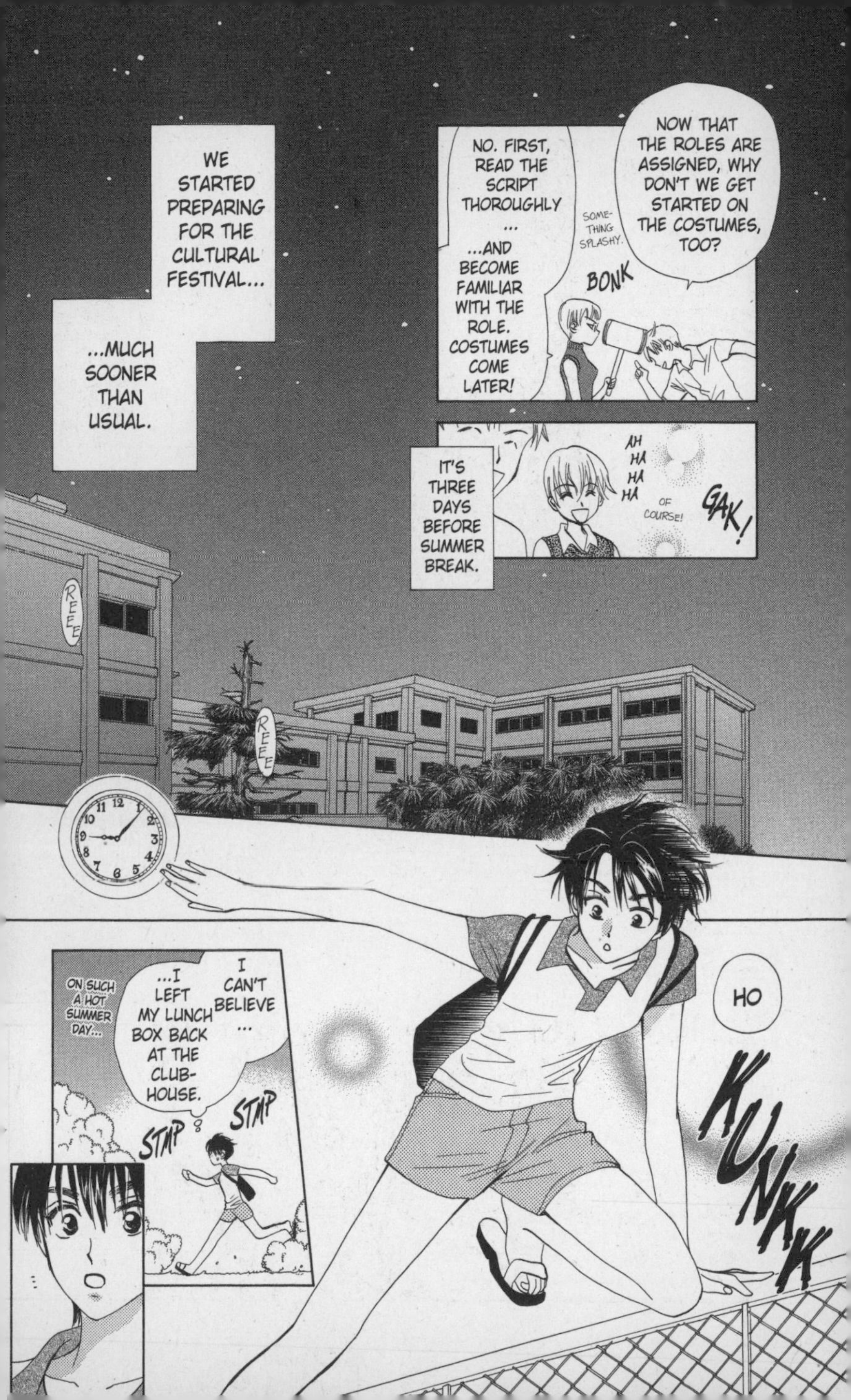
NOW THAT THE ROLES ARE ASSIGNED, WHY DON'T WE GET STARTED ON THE COSTUMES, TOO?
SOME-THING SPLASHY.
NO. FIRST, READ THE SCRIPT THOROUGHLY ...
...AND BECOME FAMILIAR WITH THE ROLE. COSTUMES COME LATER!
BONK
AH HA HA HA
OF COURSE!
GAK!
IT'S THREE DAYS BEFORE SUMMER BREAK.
WE STARTED PREPARING FOR THE CULTURAL FESTIVAL...
...MUCH SOONER THAN USUAL.
REEE
REEE
HO
KUNKK
I CAN'T BELIEVE ...
...I LEFT MY LUNCH BOX BACK AT THE CLUB-HOUSE.
ON SUCH A HOT SUMMER DAY...
STMP
STMP
...

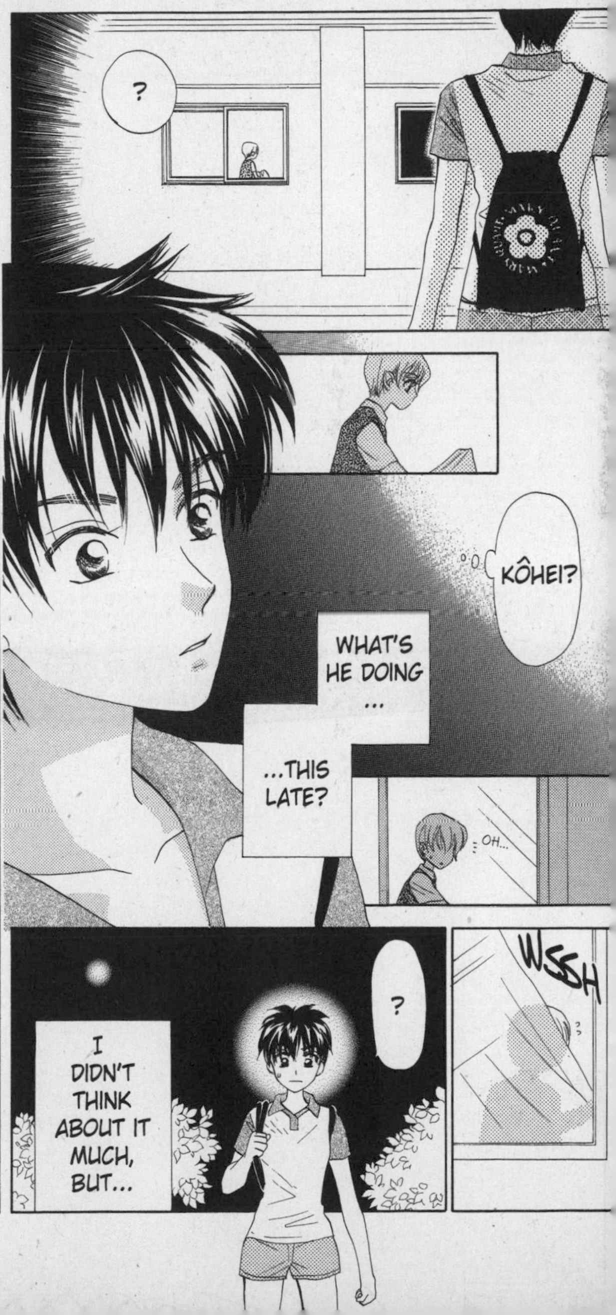
?
KÔHEI?
WHAT'S HE DOING ...
...THIS LATE?
OH...
WSSH
?
I DIDN'T THINK ABOUT IT MUCH, BUT...

STORY ON MANGA

I still love manga. Even though I am a manga-ka, I'm a reader too. I'm often asked who my favorite manga-ka are. So let me answer that question!

Shonen manga
↓

- Yoshihiro Togashi
- Rumiko Takahashi
- Naoki Urasawa
- Akira Toriyama
- Takehiko Inoue
- Tsukasa Hojo
- Yuzo Takada
- Kentaro Miura
- Eiichiro Oda
- Haruto Umezawa

Due to space limitations, I'll have to stop here. I've read every manga from the authors listed above.♥ There are a lot of fantasy stories for Shonen manga, and I get totally hooked. I guess I have a soft spot for friendship-type stories, and if a love element is added on top of it, I'm totally helpless. However, if it's only about love, unless I really get hooked, I won't read it. And I hear that's rather unusual.

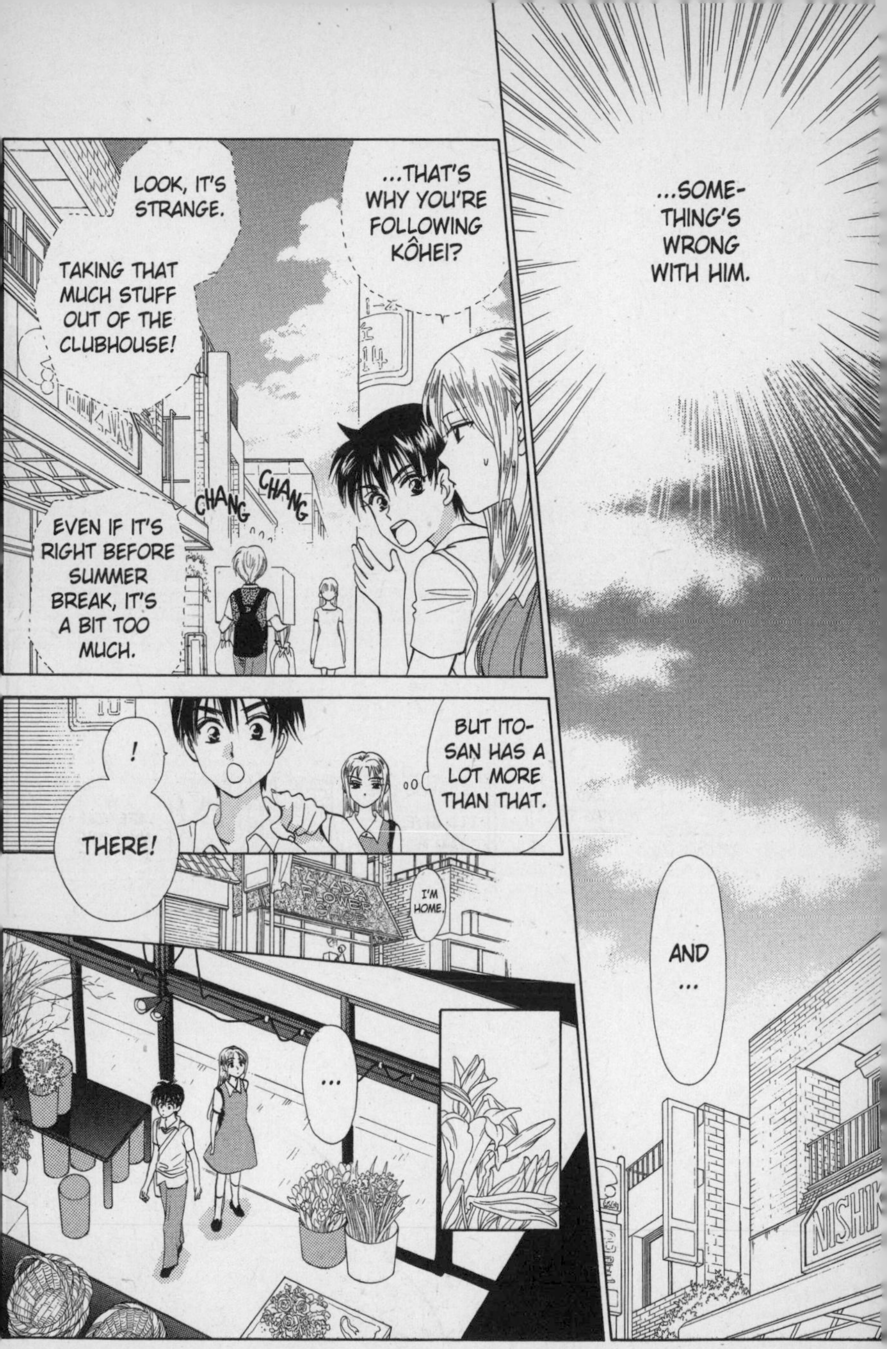

...SOME-THING'S WRONG WITH HIM.
AND ...
...THAT'S WHY YOU'RE FOLLOWING KÔHEI?
LOOK, IT'S STRANGE.
TAKING THAT MUCH STUFF OUT OF THE CLUBHOUSE!
CHANG CHANG
EVEN IF IT'S RIGHT BEFORE SUMMER BREAK, IT'S A BIT TOO MUCH.
BUT ITO-SAN HAS A LOT MORE THAN THAT.
!
THERE!
I'M HOME.
FLOWER SHOP
...
NISHIK

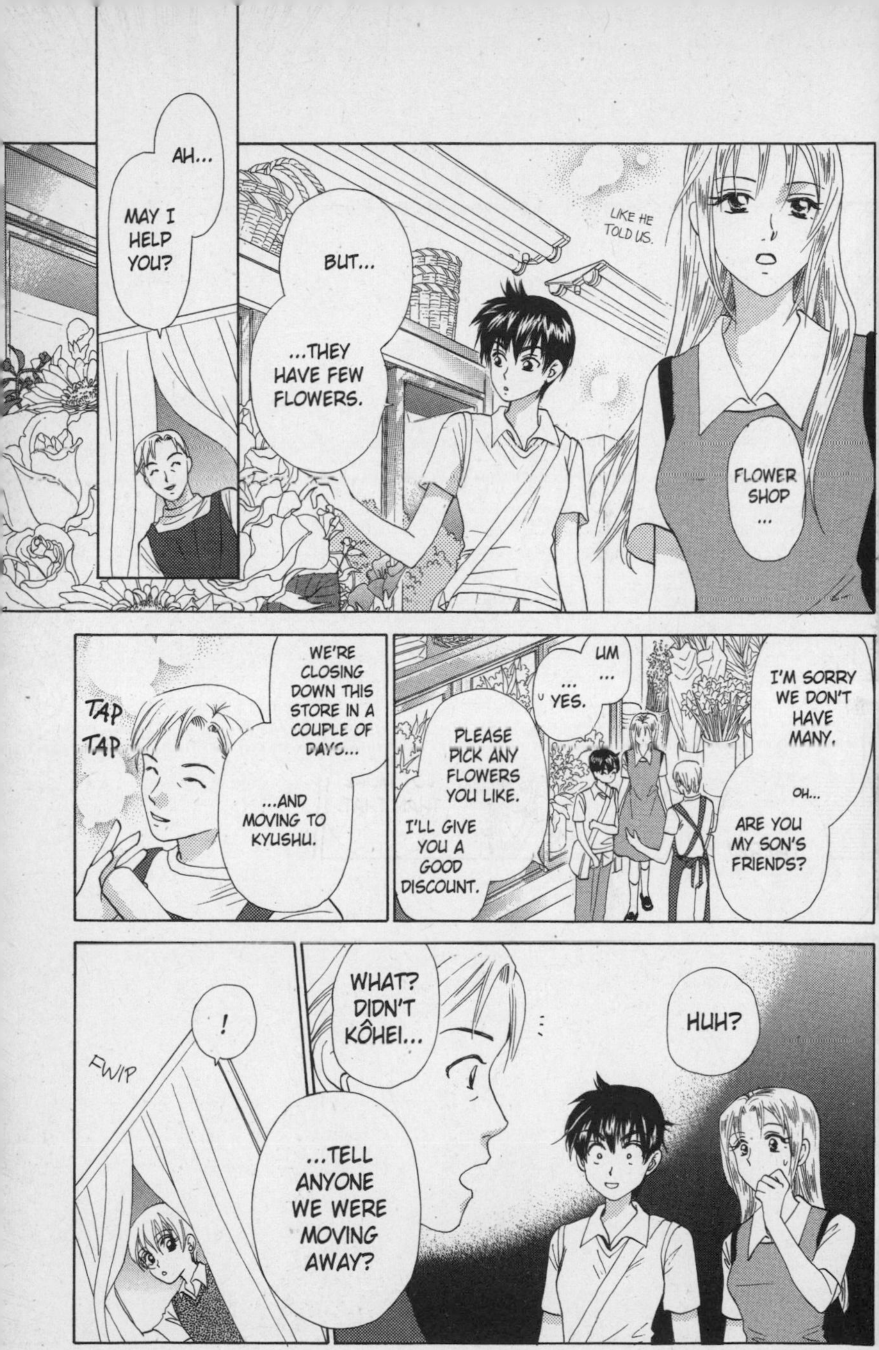
LIKE HE TOLD US.
FLOWER SHOP ...
BUT...
...THEY HAVE FEW FLOWERS.
AH...
MAY I HELP YOU?
I'M SORRY WE DON'T HAVE MANY.
OH...
ARE YOU MY SON'S FRIENDS?
UM ...
... YES.
PLEASE PICK ANY FLOWERS YOU LIKE.
I'LL GIVE YOU A GOOD DISCOUNT.
WE'RE CLOSING DOWN THIS STORE IN A COUPLE OF DAYS...
...AND MOVING TO KYUSHU.
TAP TAP
HUH?
WHAT? DIDN'T KÔHEI...
...TELL ANYONE WE WERE MOVING AWAY?
!
FWIP

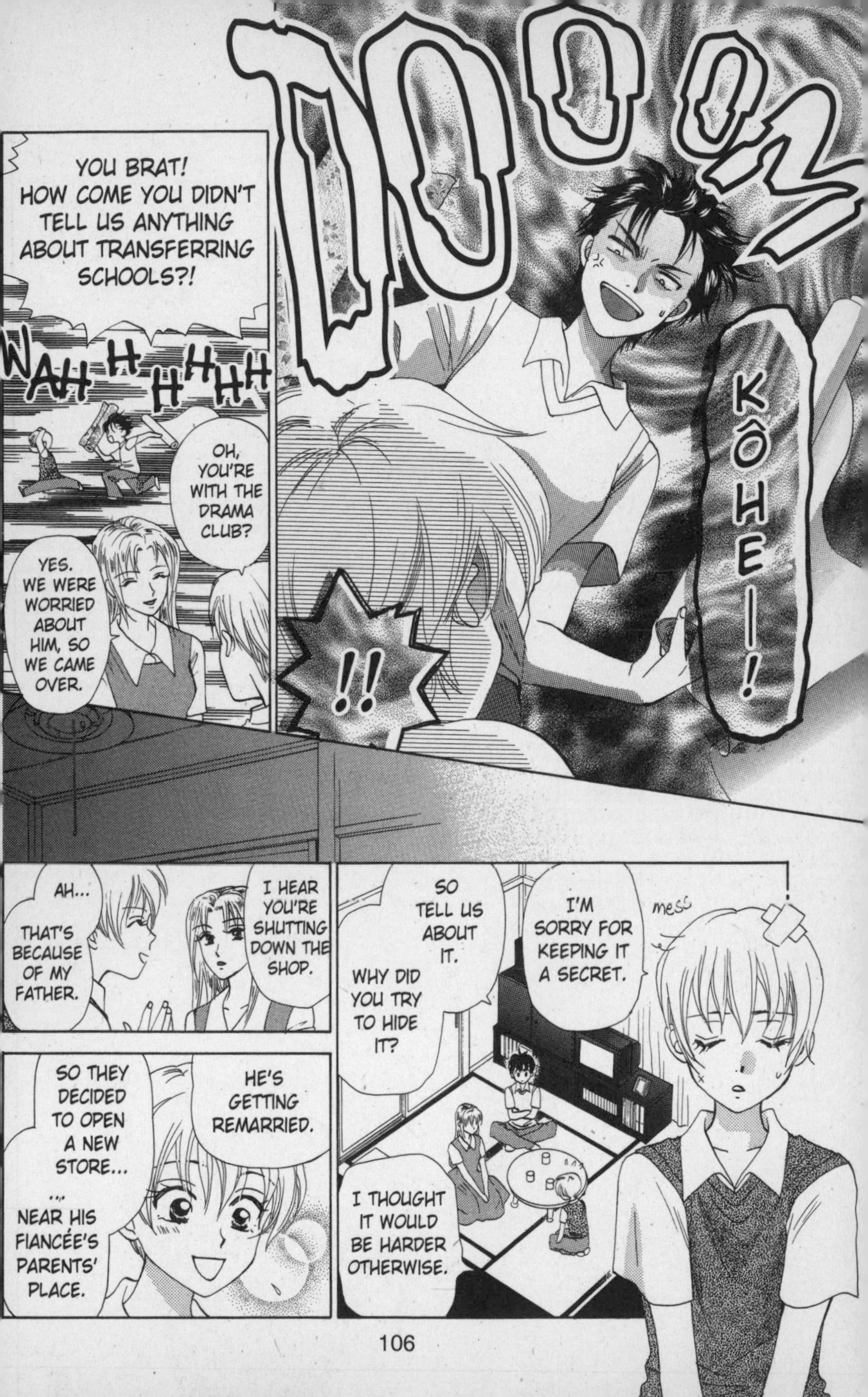
DOOOM
KÔHEI!
!!
YOU BRAT! HOW COME YOU DIDN'T TELL US ANYTHING ABOUT TRANSFERRING SCHOOLS?!
WAHHHHHH
OH, YOU'RE WITH THE DRAMA CLUB?
YES. WE WERE WORRIED ABOUT HIM, SO WE CAME OVER.
mess
I'M SORRY FOR KEEPING IT A SECRET.
SO TELL US ABOUT IT.
WHY DID YOU TRY TO HIDE IT?
I THOUGHT IT WOULD BE HARDER OTHERWISE.
I HEAR YOU'RE SHUTTING DOWN THE SHOP.
AH... THAT'S BECAUSE OF MY FATHER.
HE'S GETTING REMARRIED.
SO THEY DECIDED TO OPEN A NEW STORE...
... NEAR HIS FIANCÉE'S PARENTS' PLACE.

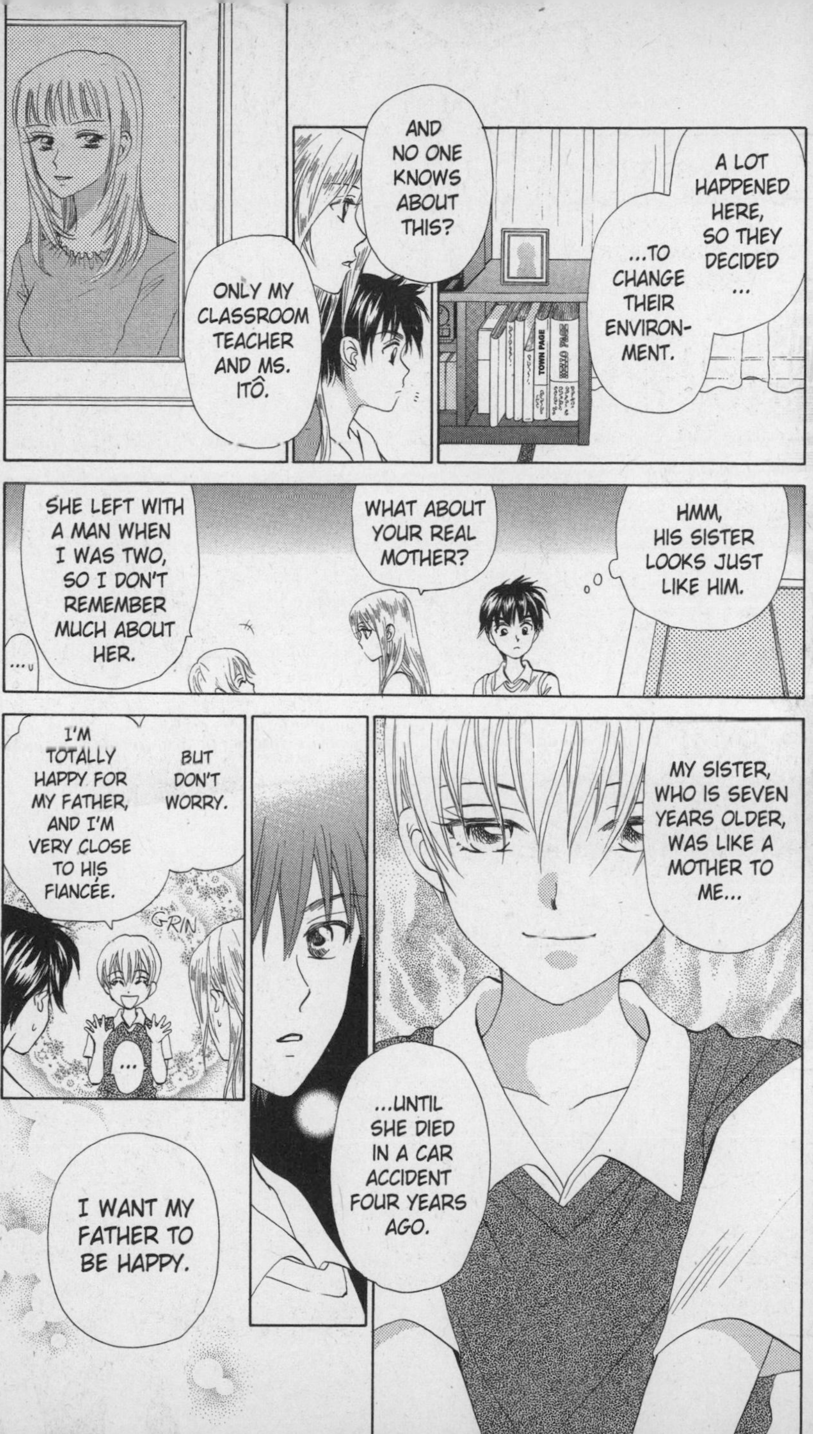
A LOT HAPPENED HERE, SO THEY DECIDED ...
...TO CHANGE THEIR ENVIRON-MENT.
TOWN PAGE
AND NO ONE KNOWS ABOUT THIS?
ONLY MY CLASSROOM TEACHER AND MS. ITÔ.
HMM, HIS SISTER LOOKS JUST LIKE HIM.
WHAT ABOUT YOUR REAL MOTHER?
SHE LEFT WITH A MAN WHEN I WAS TWO, SO I DON'T REMEMBER MUCH ABOUT HER.
...
MY SISTER, WHO IS SEVEN YEARS OLDER, WAS LIKE A MOTHER TO ME...
...UNTIL SHE DIED IN A CAR ACCIDENT FOUR YEARS AGO.
BUT DON'T WORRY.
I'M TOTALLY HAPPY FOR MY FATHER, AND I'M VERY CLOSE TO HIS FIANCÉE.
GRIN
...
I WANT MY FATHER TO BE HAPPY.

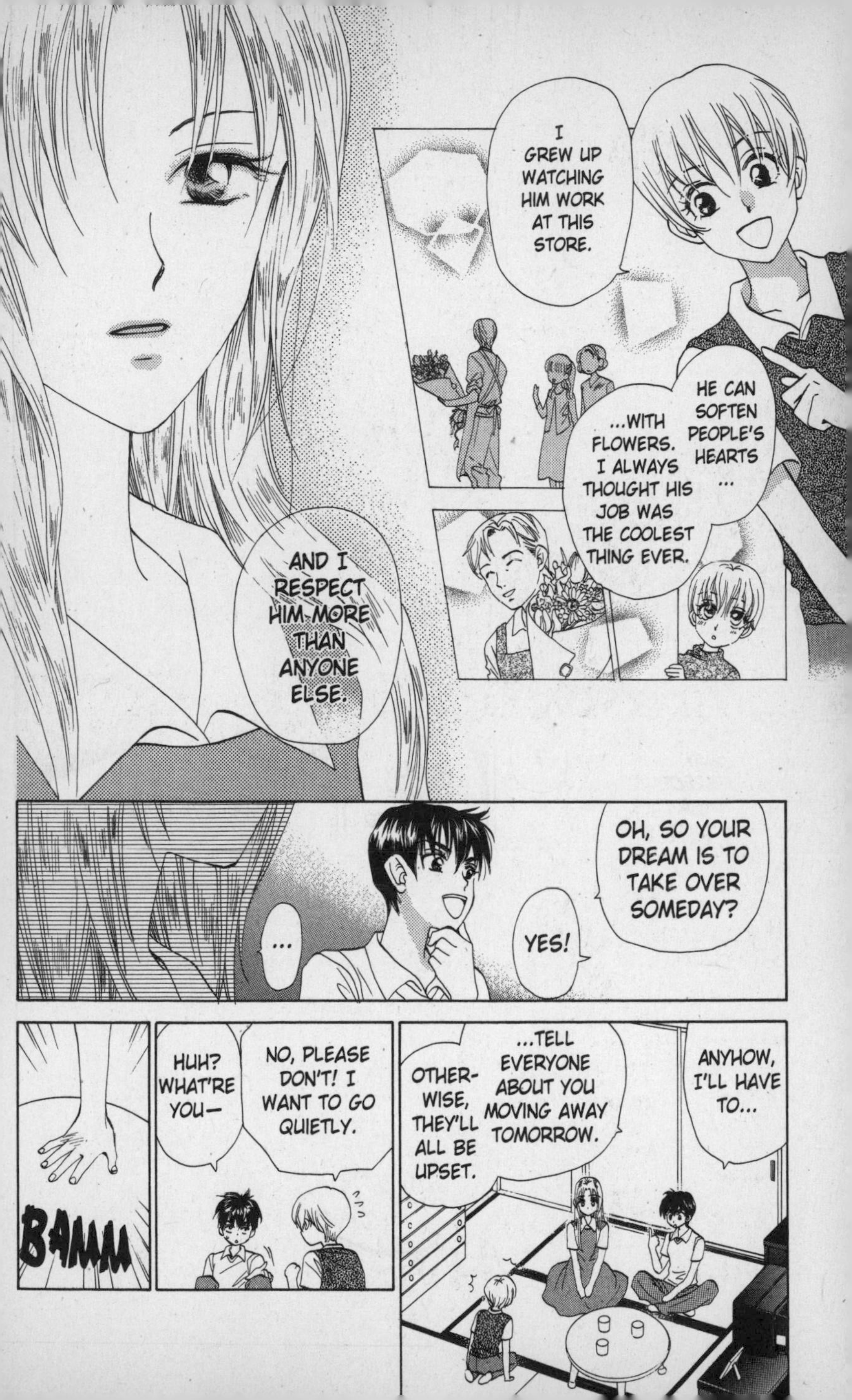
I GREW UP WATCHING HIM WORK AT THIS STORE.
HE CAN SOFTEN PEOPLE'S HEARTS ...
...WITH FLOWERS. I ALWAYS THOUGHT HIS JOB WAS THE COOLEST THING EVER.
AND I RESPECT HIM MORE THAN ANYONE ELSE.
OH, SO YOUR DREAM IS TO TAKE OVER SOMEDAY?
YES!
...
ANYHOW, I'LL HAVE TO...
...TELL EVERYONE ABOUT YOU MOVING AWAY TOMORROW.
OTHER-WISE, THEY'LL ALL BE UPSET.
NO, PLEASE DON'T! I WANT TO GO QUIETLY.
HUH? WHAT'RE YOU—
BAMM

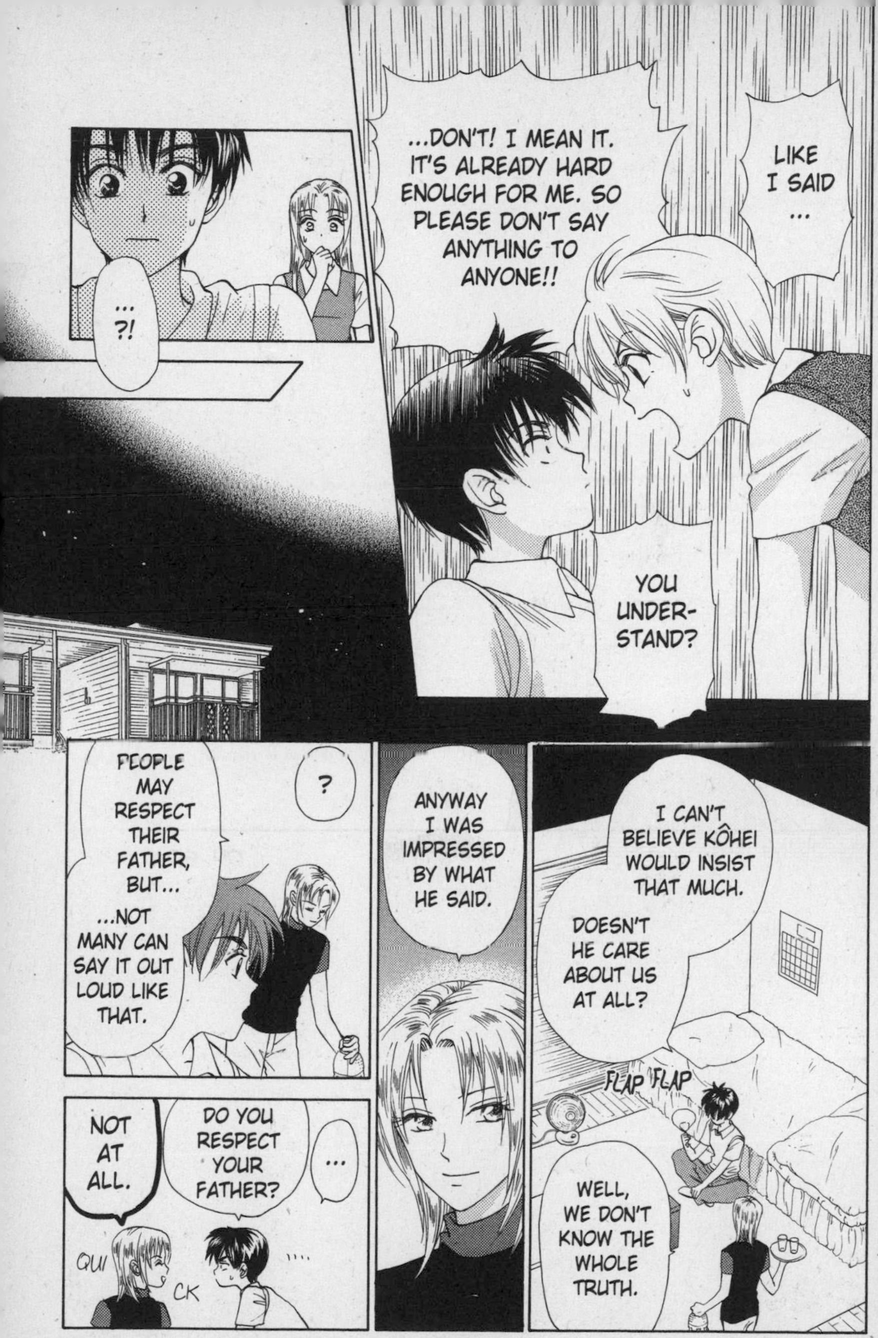
LIKE I SAID ...
...DON'T! I MEAN IT. IT'S ALREADY HARD ENOUGH FOR ME. SO PLEASE DON'T SAY ANYTHING TO ANYONE!!
YOU UNDER-STAND?
... ?!
I CAN'T BELIEVE KÔHEI WOULD INSIST THAT MUCH.
DOESN'T HE CARE ABOUT US AT ALL?
FLAP FLAP
WELL, WE DON'T KNOW THE WHOLE TRUTH.
ANYWAY I WAS IMPRESSED BY WHAT HE SAID.
?
PEOPLE MAY RESPECT THEIR FATHER, BUT...
...NOT MANY CAN SAY IT OUT LOUD LIKE THAT.
...
DO YOU RESPECT YOUR FATHER?
NOT AT ALL.
QUI
CK
....

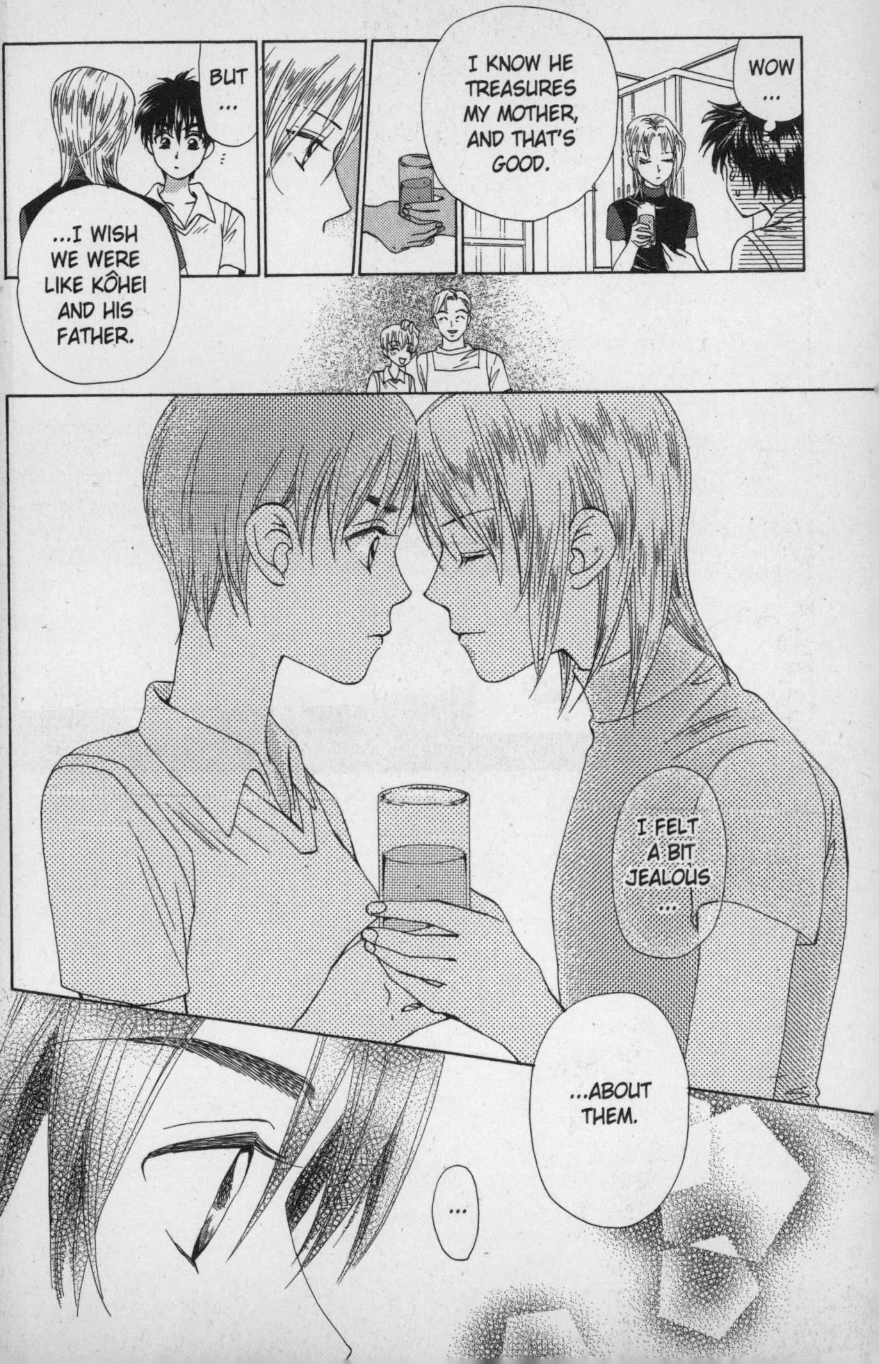
WOW ...
I KNOW HE TREASURES MY MOTHER, AND THAT'S GOOD.
BUT ...
...I WISH WE WERE LIKE KÔHEI AND HIS FATHER.
I FELT A BIT JEALOUS ...
...ABOUT THEM.
...

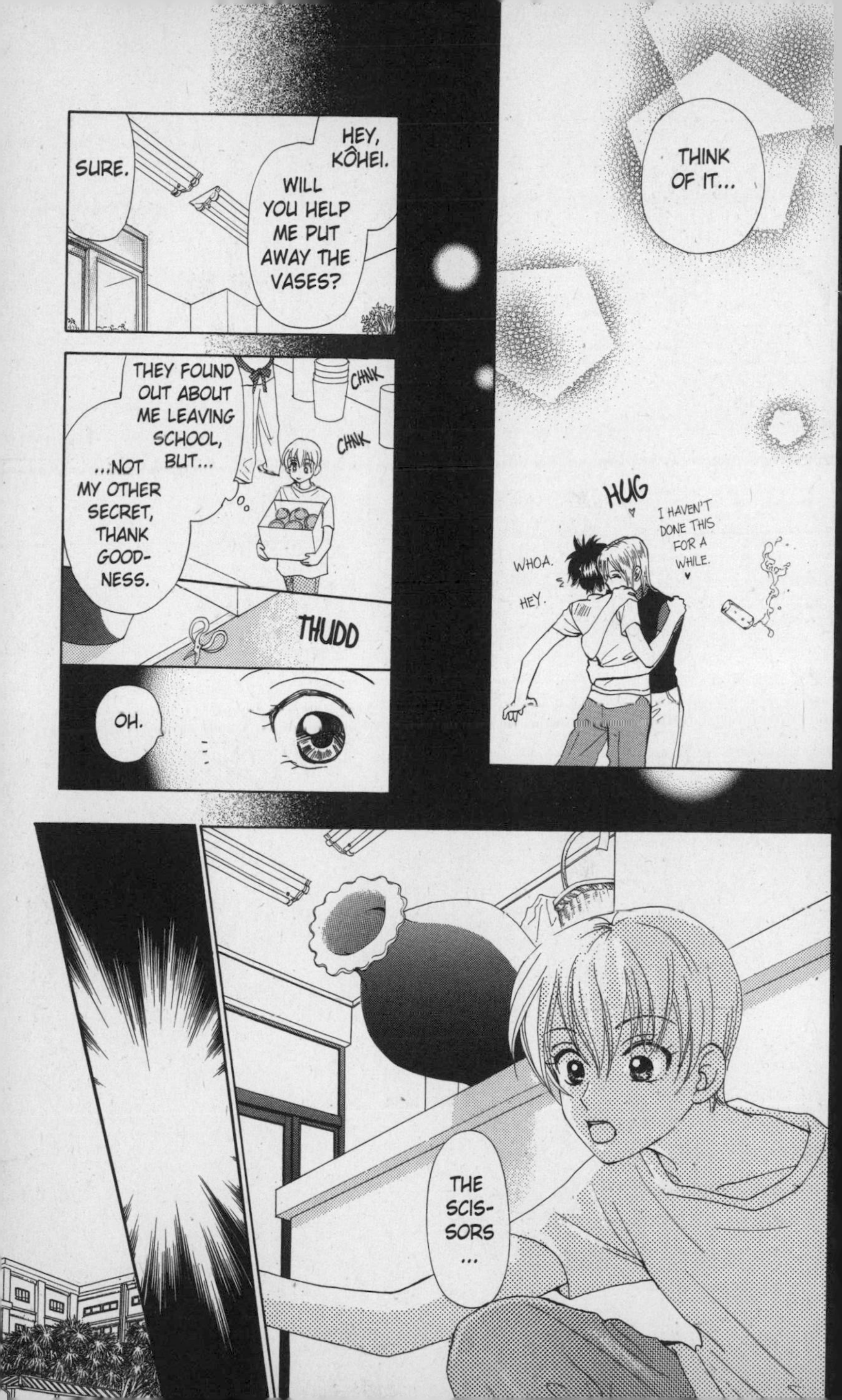
THINK OF IT...
HUG
I HAVEN'T DONE THIS FOR A WHILE.
WHOA.
HEY.
HEY, KÔHEI.
WILL YOU HELP ME PUT AWAY THE VASES?
SURE.
CHNK
CHNK
THEY FOUND OUT ABOUT ME LEAVING SCHOOL, BUT...
...NOT MY OTHER SECRET, THANK GOODNESS.
THUDD
OH.
THE SCIS-SORS...

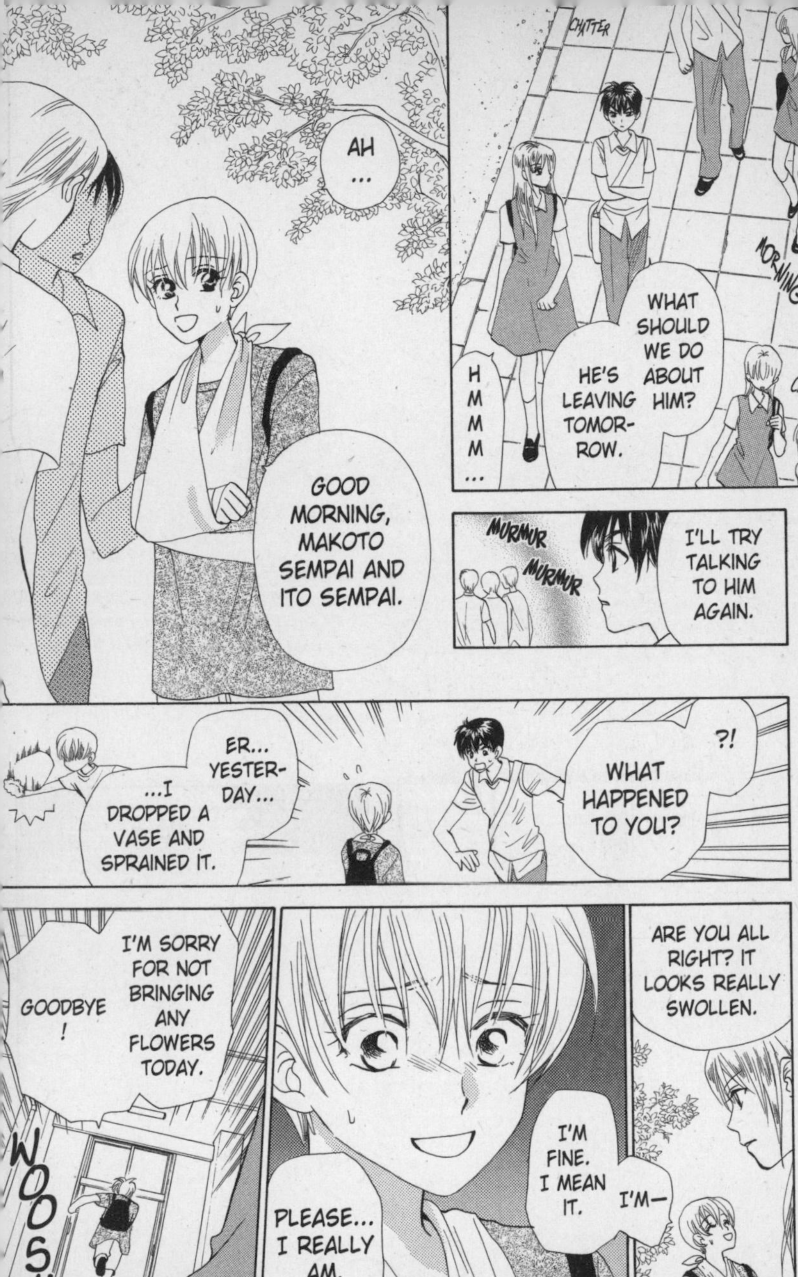
G'MORNING!
MORNING!
CHATTER
CHATTER
CHATTER
WHAT SHOULD WE DO ABOUT HIM?
HE'S LEAVING TOMORROW.
HMMM...
MURMUR
MURMUR
I'LL TRY TALKING TO HIM AGAIN.
AH ...
GOOD MORNING, MAKOTO SEMPAI AND ITO SEMPAI.
?!
WHAT HAPPENED TO YOU?
ER... YESTERDAY...
...I DROPPED A VASE AND SPRAINED IT.
ARE YOU ALL RIGHT? IT LOOKS REALLY SWOLLEN.
I'M—
I'M FINE. I MEAN IT.
PLEASE... I REALLY AM.
I'M SORRY FOR NOT BRINGING ANY FLOWERS TODAY.
GOODBYE!
WOOSH

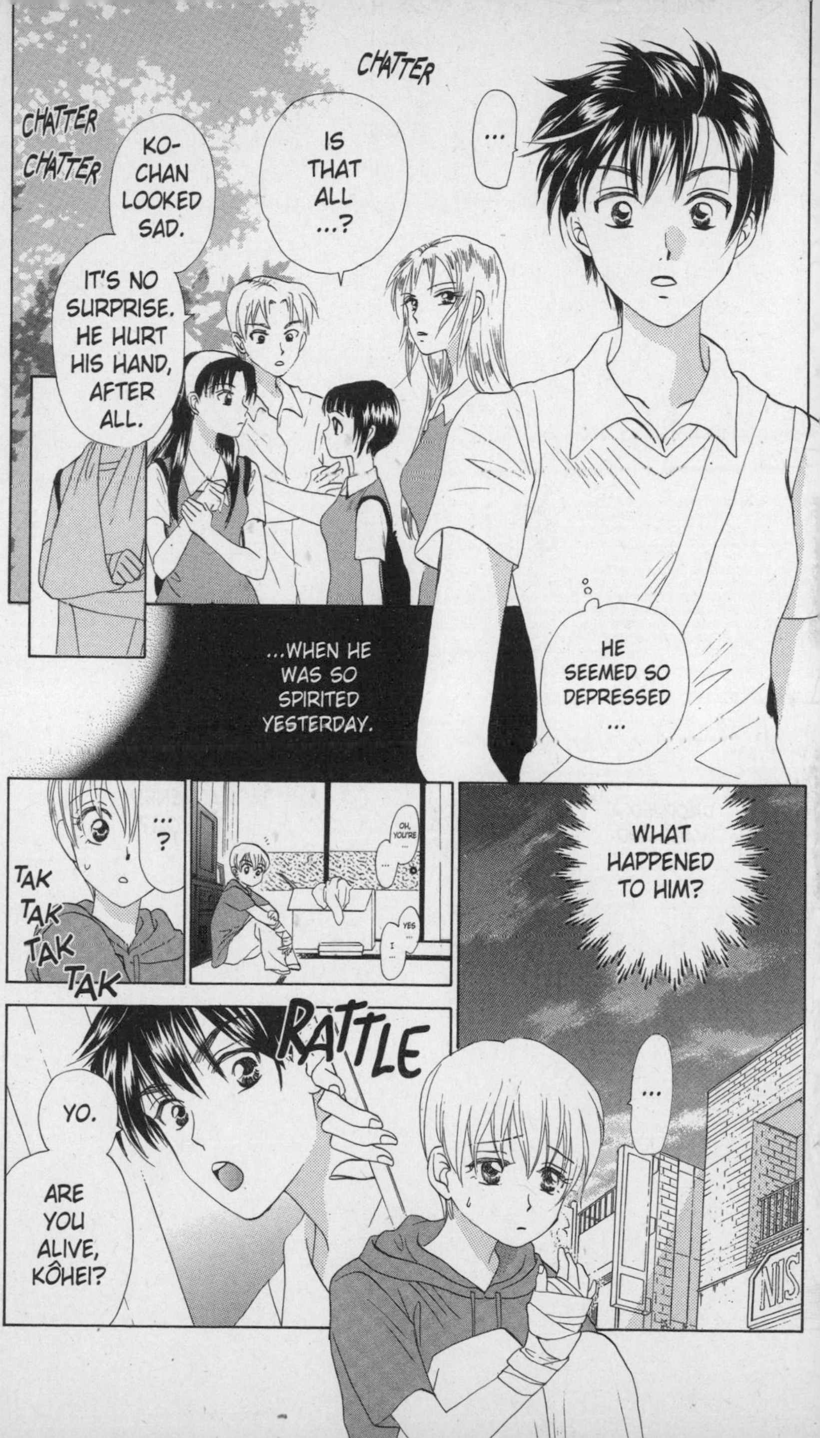
CHATTER
...
IS THAT ALL ...?
KO-CHAN LOOKED SAD.
CHATTER CHATTER
IT'S NO SURPRISE. HE HURT HIS HAND, AFTER ALL.
HE SEEMED SO DEPRESSED ...
...WHEN HE WAS SO SPIRITED YESTERDAY.
WHAT HAPPENED TO HIM?
OH, YOU'RE ...
...
YES ... I ...
... ?
TAK TAK TAK TAK
...
RATTLE
YO.
ARE YOU ALIVE, KÔHEI?

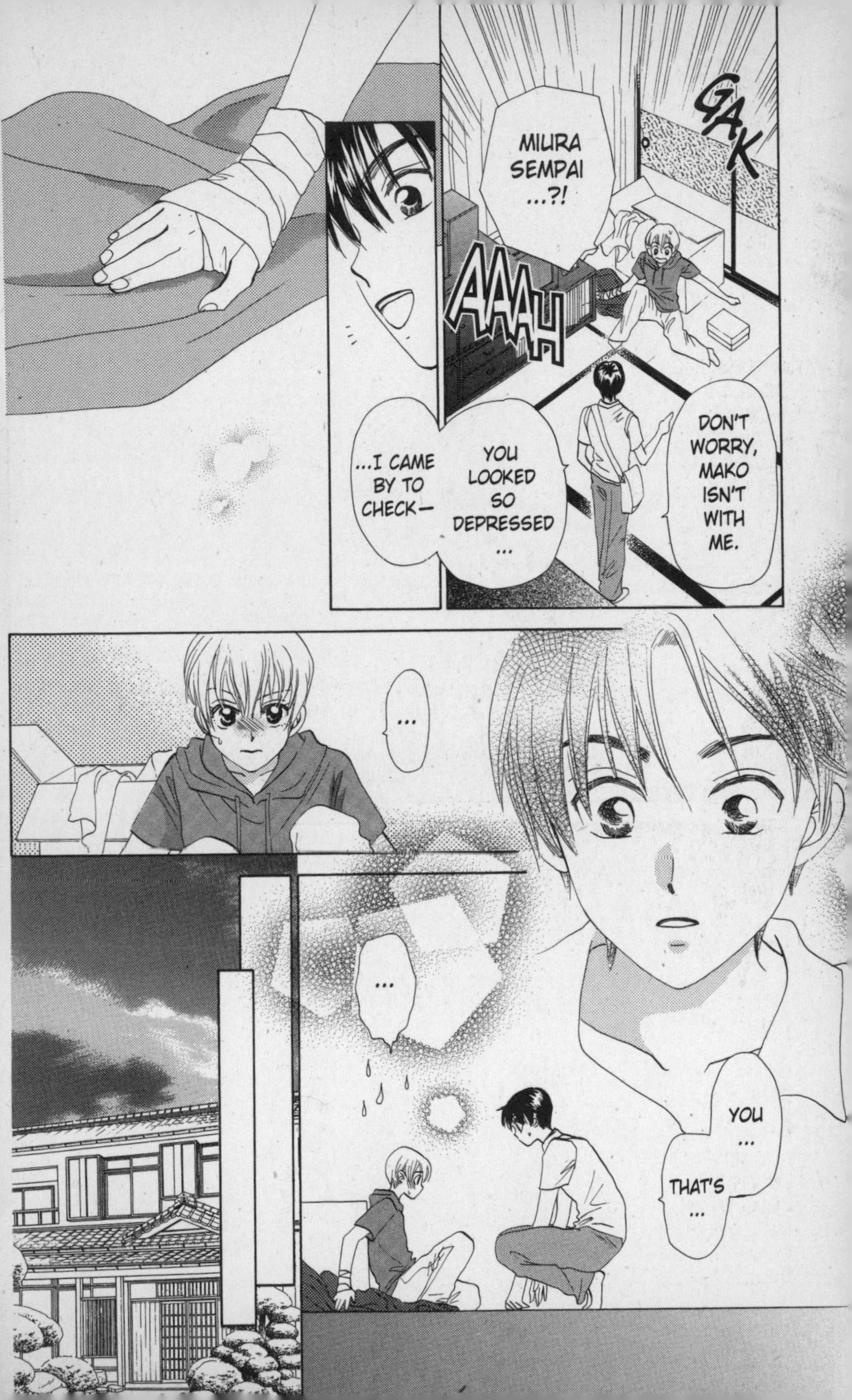
GAK
AAAH
MIURA SEMPAI ...?!
DON'T WORRY, MAKO ISN'T WITH ME.
YOU LOOKED SO DEPRESSED ...
...I CAME BY TO CHECK—
...
YOU ...
THAT'S ...
...

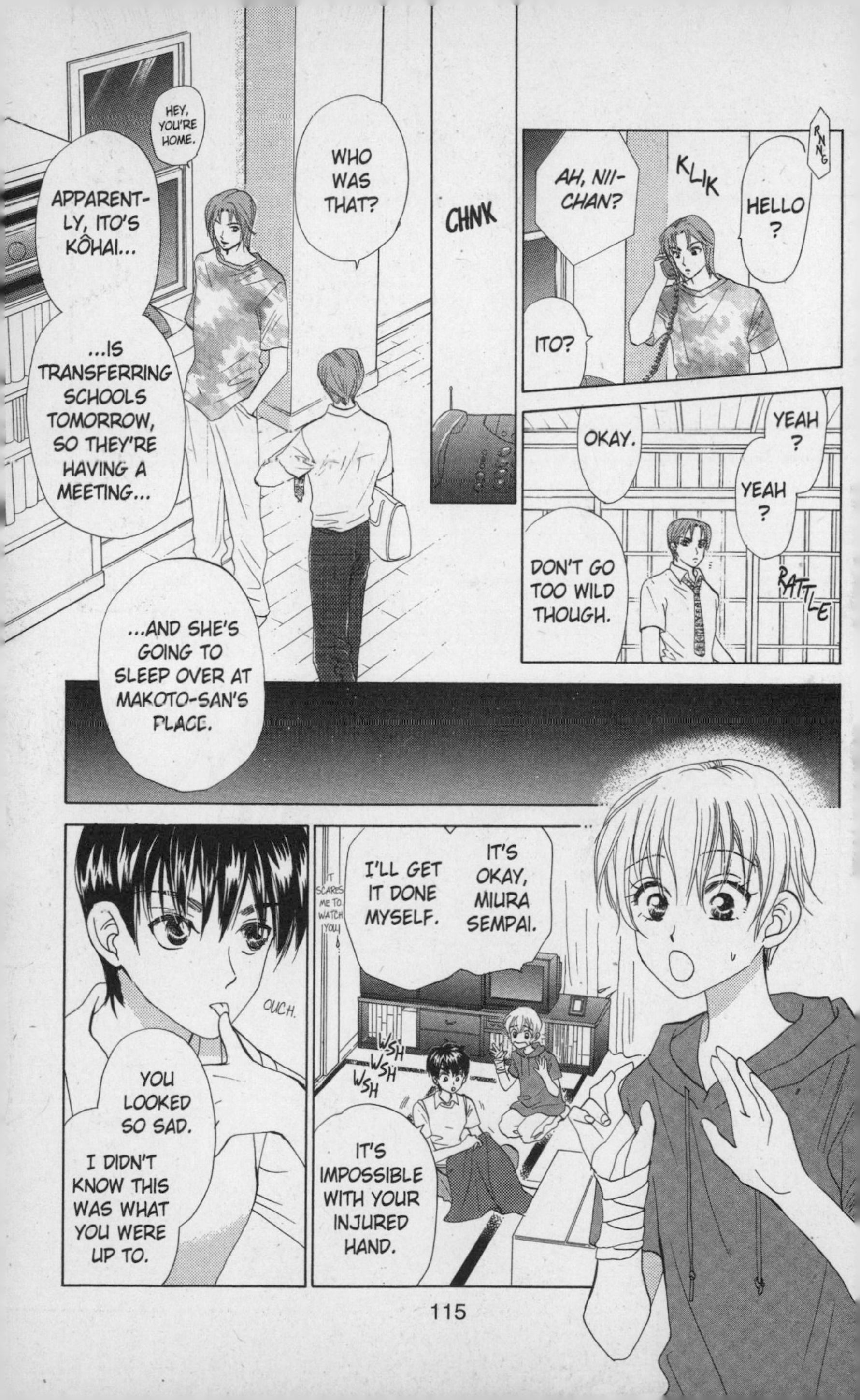
RNNG
HELLO?
KLIK
AH, NII-CHAN?
ITO?
YEAH?
YEAH?
OKAY.
RATTLE
DON'T GO TOO WILD THOUGH.
CHNK
HEY, YOU'RE HOME.
WHO WAS THAT?
APPARENTLY, ITO'S KÔHAI...
...IS TRANSFERRING SCHOOLS TOMORROW, SO THEY'RE HAVING A MEETING...
...AND SHE'S GOING TO SLEEP OVER AT MAKOTO-SAN'S PLACE.
IT'S OKAY, MIURA SEMPAI.
I'LL GET IT DONE MYSELF.
IT SCARES ME TO WATCH YOU
WSH WSH WSH
IT'S IMPOSSIBLE WITH YOUR INJURED HAND.
OUCH.
YOU LOOKED SO SAD.
I DIDN'T KNOW THIS WAS WHAT YOU WERE UP TO.

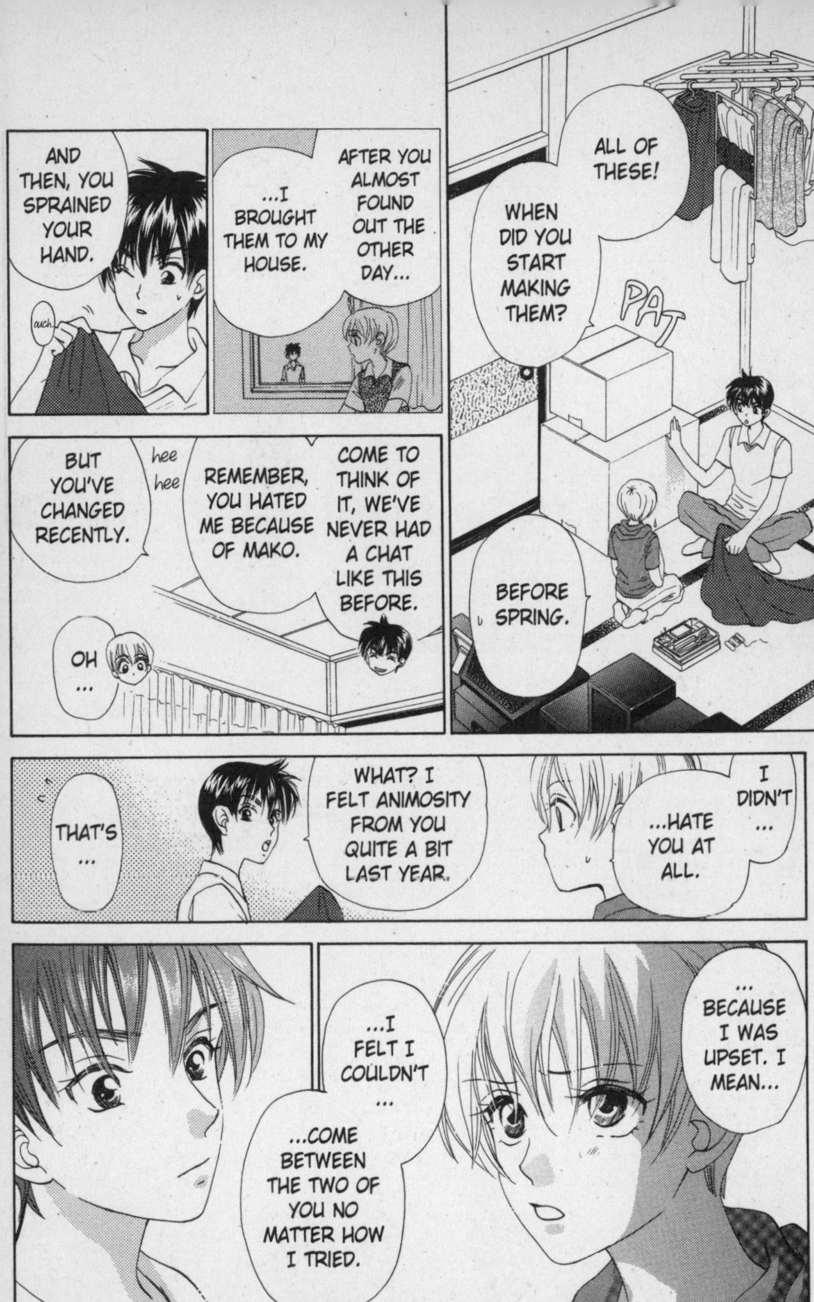
ALL OF THESE!
WHEN DID YOU START MAKING THEM?
PAT
BEFORE SPRING.
AFTER YOU ALMOST FOUND OUT THE OTHER DAY...
...I BROUGHT THEM TO MY HOUSE.
AND THEN, YOU SPRAINED YOUR HAND.
ouch.
COME TO THINK OF IT, WE'VE NEVER HAD A CHAT LIKE THIS BEFORE.
REMEMBER, YOU HATED ME BECAUSE OF MAKO.
hee hee
BUT YOU'VE CHANGED RECENTLY.
OH ...
I DIDN'T ...
...HATE YOU AT ALL.
WHAT? I FELT ANIMOSITY FROM YOU QUITE A BIT LAST YEAR.
THAT'S ...
... BECAUSE I WAS UPSET. I MEAN...
...I FELT I COULDN'T ...
...COME BETWEEN THE TWO OF YOU NO MATTER HOW I TRIED.

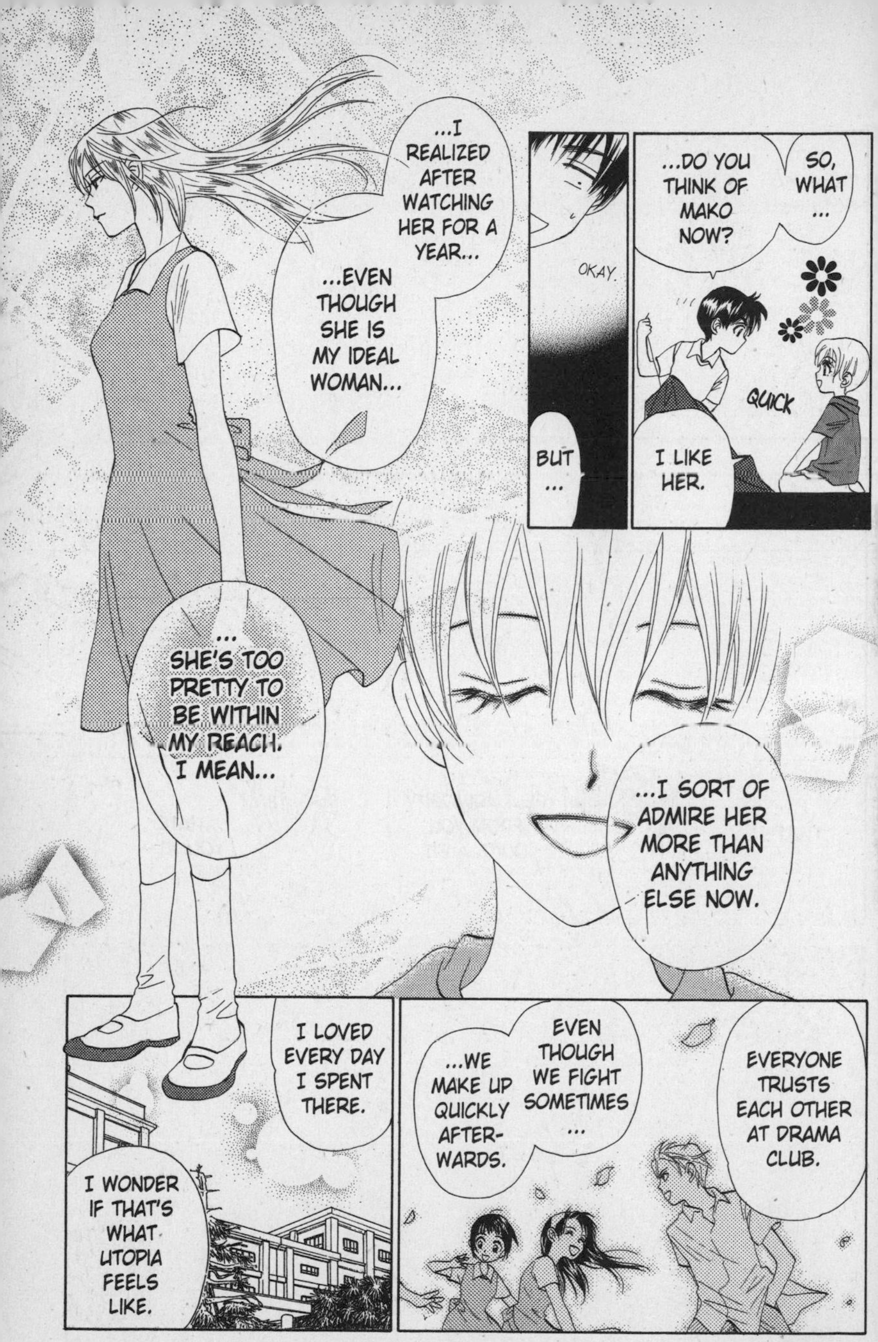
SO, WHAT ...
...DO YOU THINK OF MAKO NOW?
QUICK
I LIKE HER.
OKAY.
BUT ...
...I REALIZED AFTER WATCHING HER FOR A YEAR...
...EVEN THOUGH SHE IS MY IDEAL WOMAN...
... SHE'S TOO PRETTY TO BE WITHIN MY REACH. I MEAN...
...I SORT OF ADMIRE HER MORE THAN ANYTHING ELSE NOW.
EVERYONE TRUSTS EACH OTHER AT DRAMA CLUB.
EVEN THOUGH WE FIGHT SOMETIMES ...
...WE MAKE UP QUICKLY AFTER-WARDS.
I LOVED EVERY DAY I SPENT THERE.
I WONDER IF THAT'S WHAT UTOPIA FEELS LIKE.

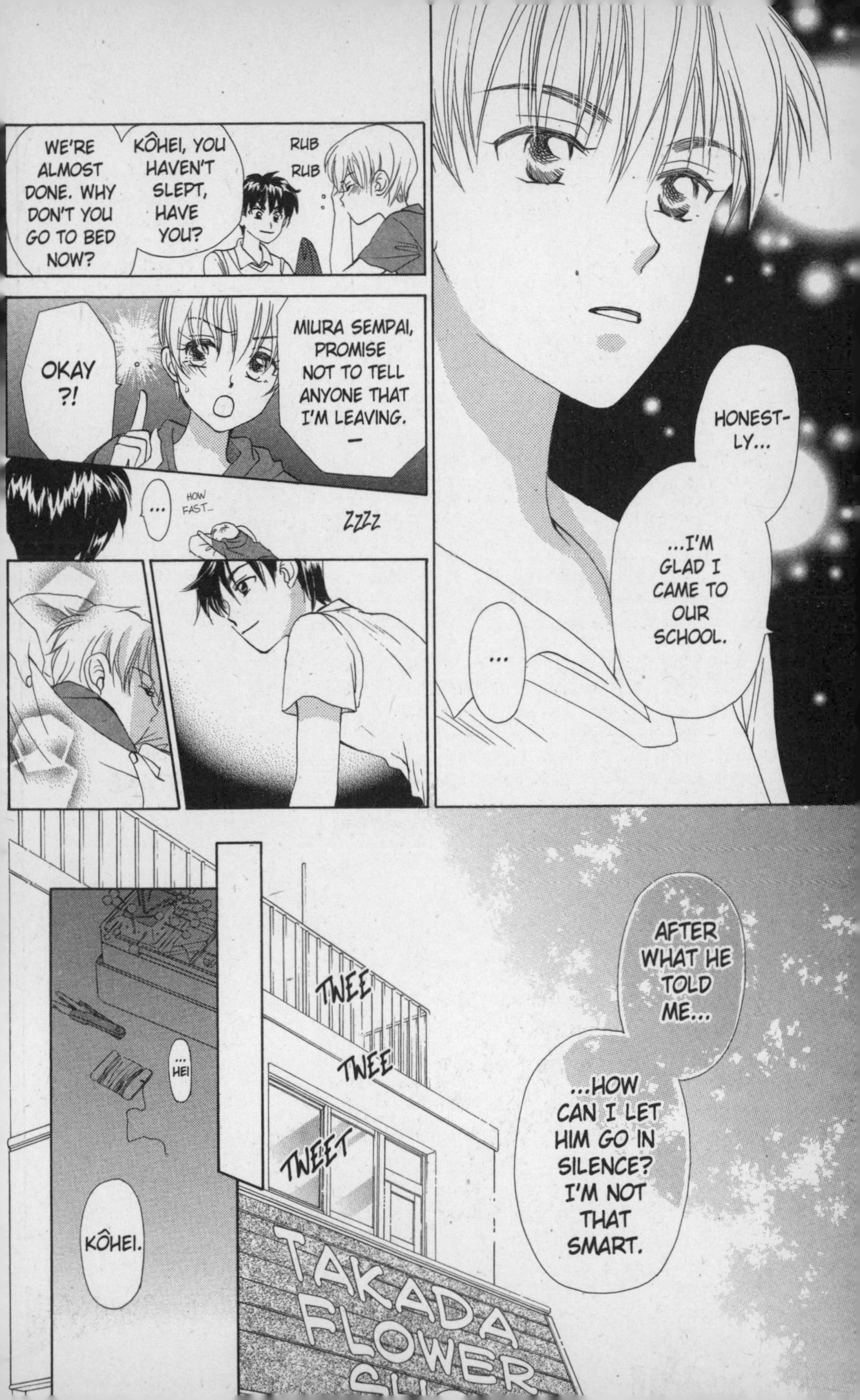
HONESTLY...
...I'M GLAD I CAME TO OUR SCHOOL.
...
RUB RUB
KÔHEI, YOU HAVEN'T SLEPT, HAVE YOU?
WE'RE ALMOST DONE. WHY DON'T YOU GO TO BED NOW?
MIURA SEMPAI, PROMISE NOT TO TELL ANYONE THAT I'M LEAVING. —
OKAY ?!
ZZZZ
HOW FAST...
...
AFTER WHAT HE TOLD ME...
...HOW CAN I LET HIM GO IN SILENCE? I'M NOT THAT SMART.
TWEE
TWEE
TWEET
TAKADA FLOWER
...HEI
KÔHEI.

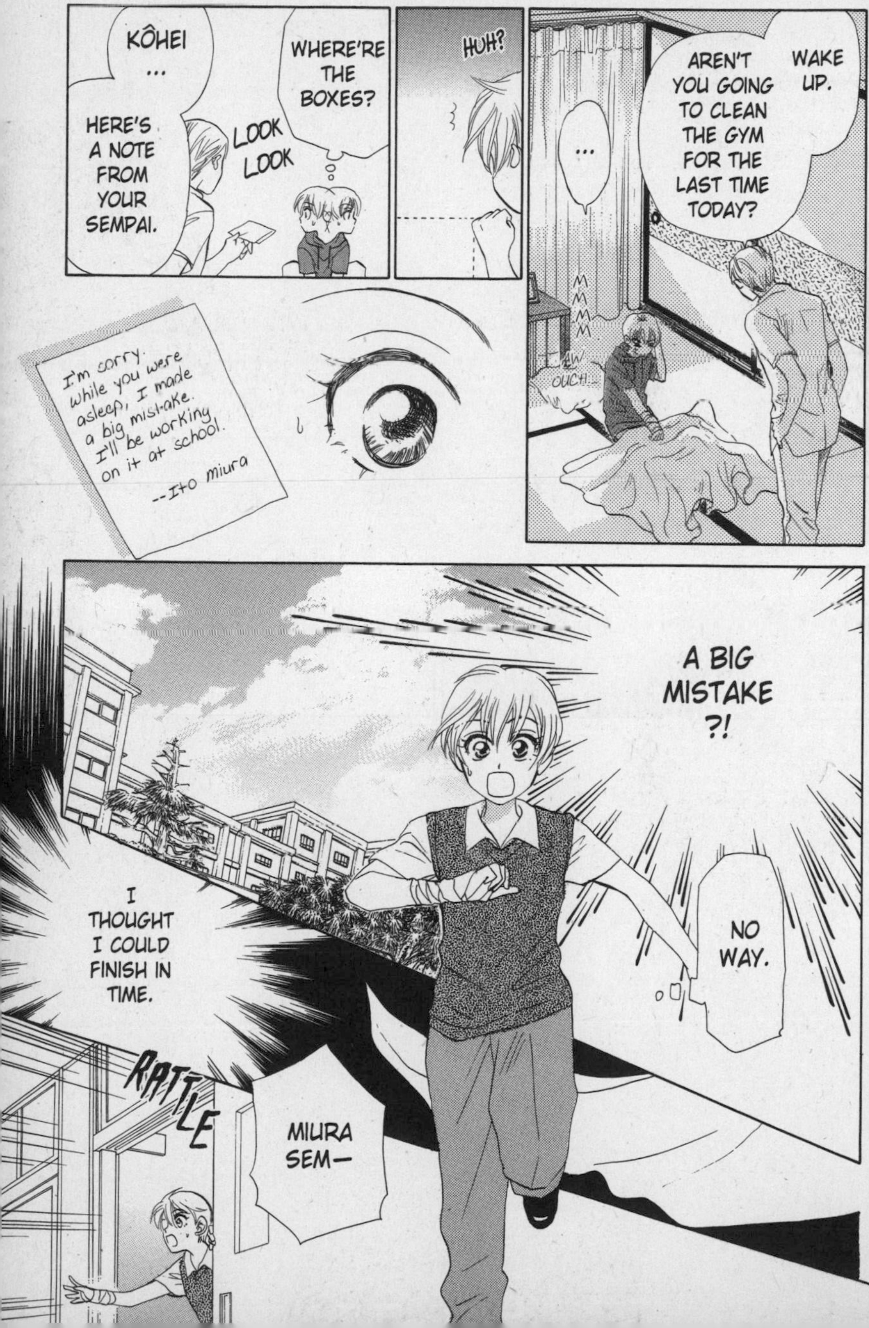
WAKE UP.
AREN'T YOU GOING TO CLEAN THE GYM FOR THE LAST TIME TODAY?
...
MMMMM
AW
OUCH...
HUH?
WHERE'RE THE BOXES?
KÔHEI ...
HERE'S A NOTE FROM YOUR SEMPAI.
LOOK LOOK
I'm sorry.
while you were asleep, I made a big mistake.
I'll be working on it at school.
--Ito miura
A BIG MISTAKE ?!
NO WAY.
I THOUGHT I COULD FINISH IN TIME.
RATTLE
MIURA SEM—

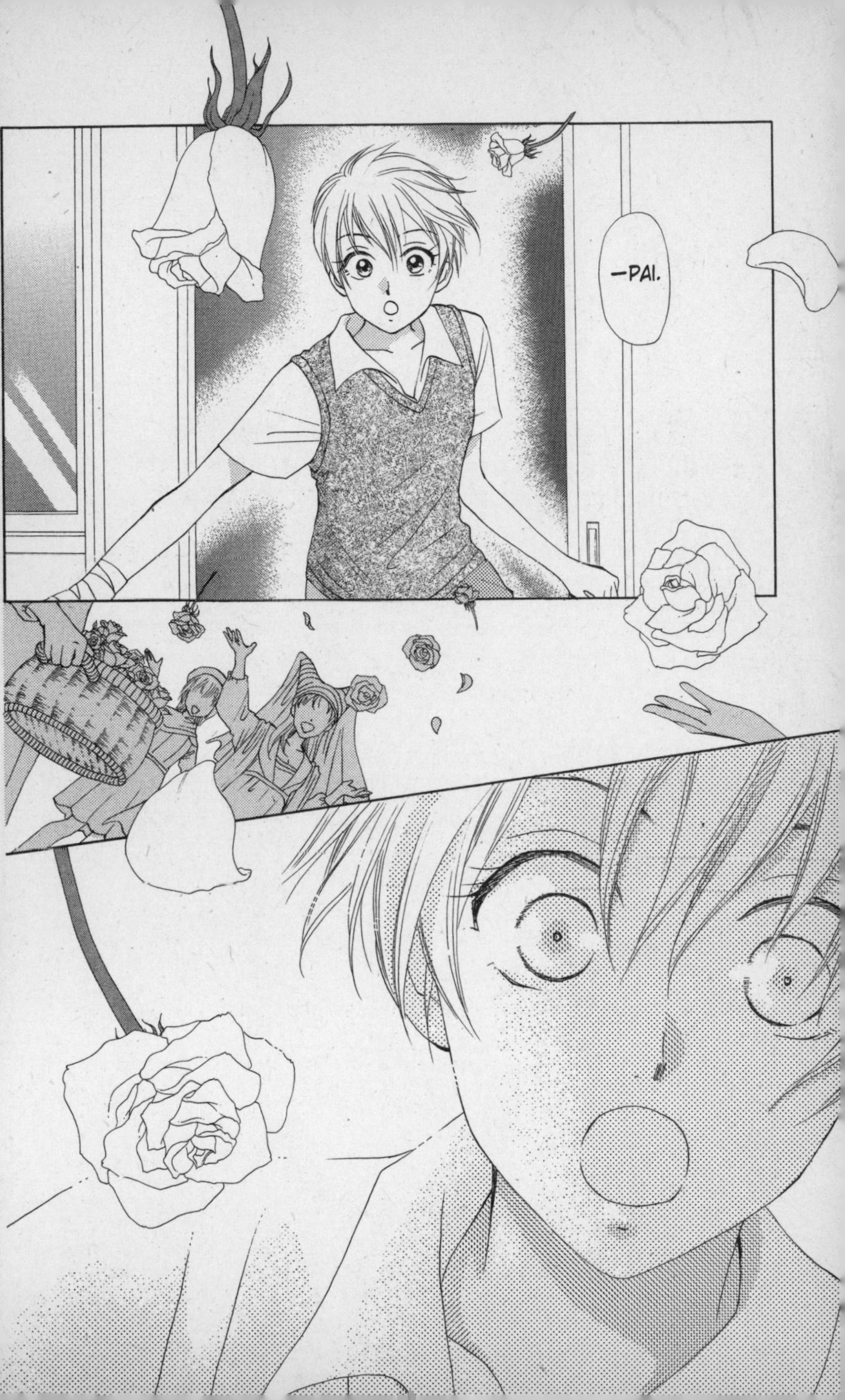
–PAI.

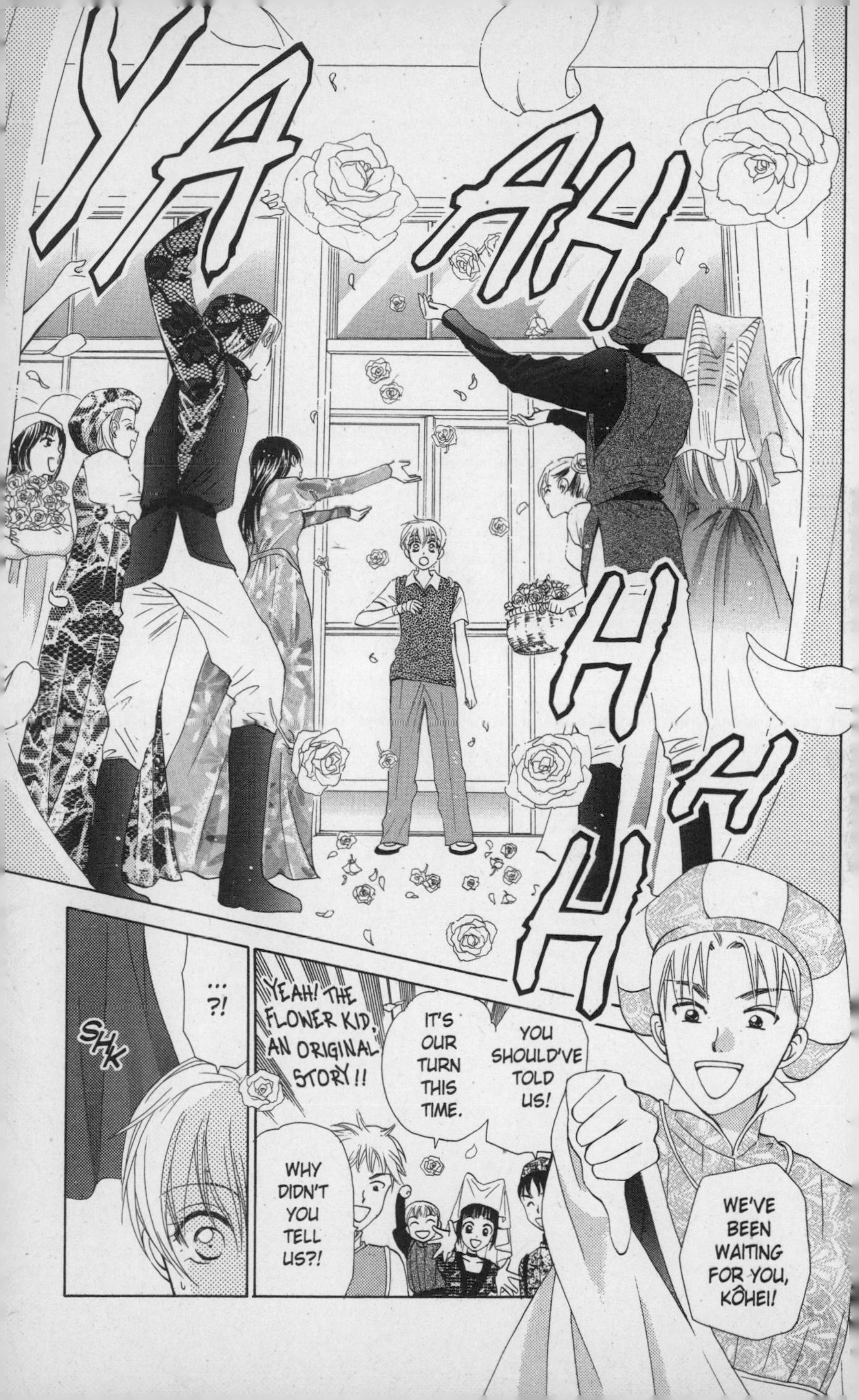
YAAHHHH
WE'VE BEEN WAITING FOR YOU, KÔHEI!
YOU SHOULD'VE TOLD US!
IT'S OUR TURN THIS TIME.
YEAH! THE FLOWER KID, AN ORIGINAL STORY!!
WHY DIDN'T YOU TELL US?!
...?!
SHK

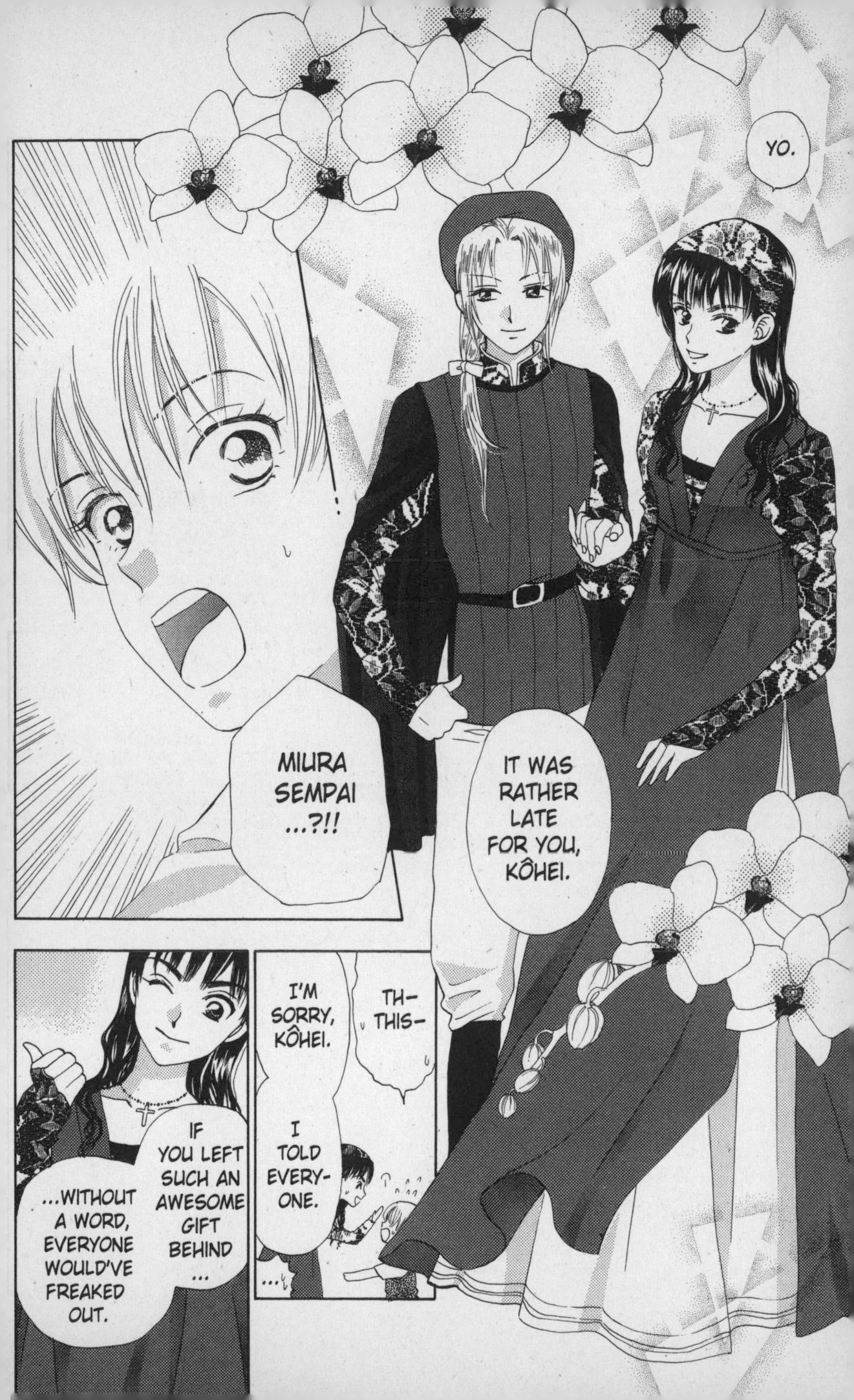

YO.
IT WAS RATHER LATE FOR YOU, KÔHEI.
MIURA SEMPAI ...?!!
TH- THIS-
I'M SORRY, KÔHEI.
I TOLD EVERY-ONE.
IF YOU LEFT SUCH AN AWESOME GIFT BEHIND ...
...WITHOUT A WORD, EVERYONE WOULD'VE FREAKED OUT.

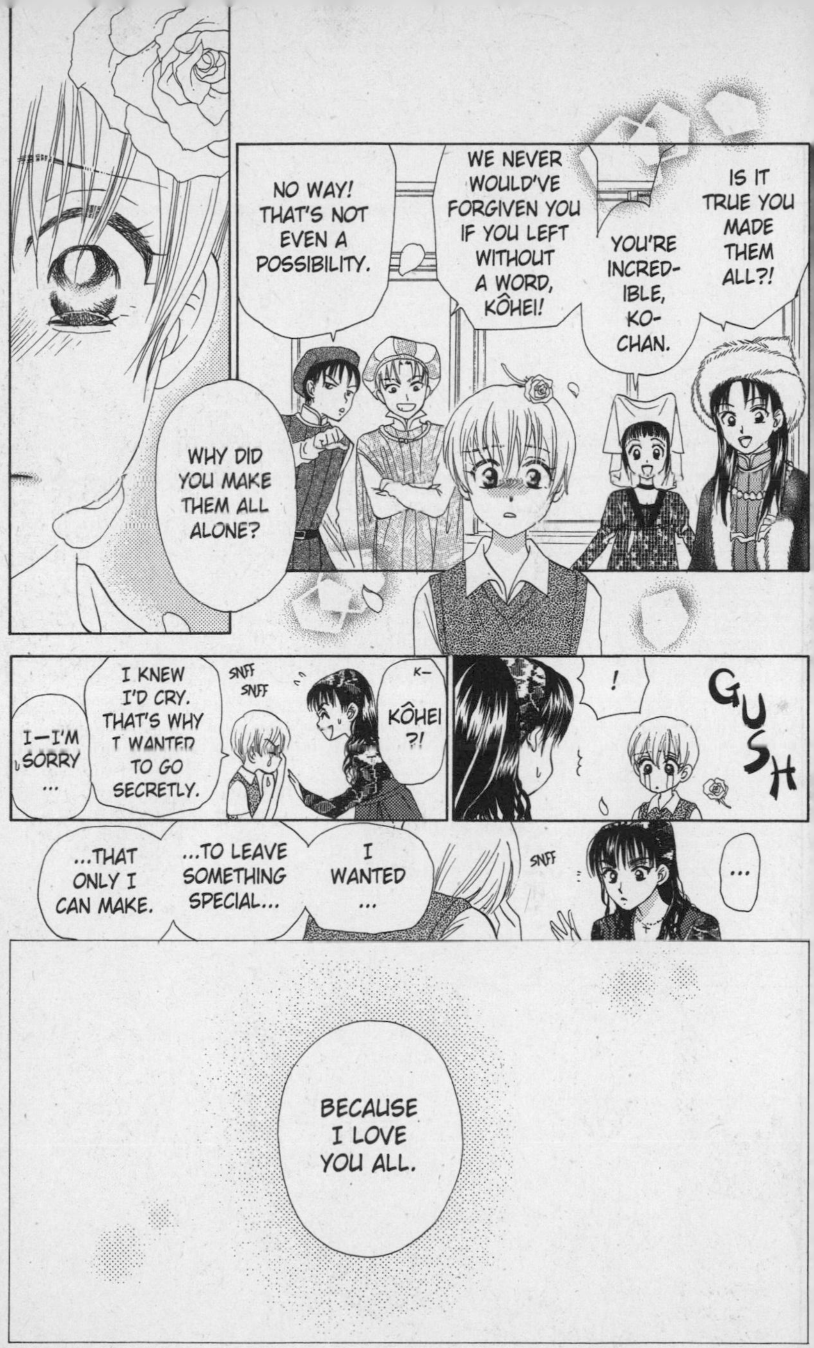
IS IT TRUE YOU MADE THEM ALL?!
YOU'RE INCRED-IBLE, KO-CHAN.
WE NEVER WOULD'VE FORGIVEN YOU IF YOU LEFT WITHOUT A WORD, KÔHEI!
NO WAY! THAT'S NOT EVEN A POSSIBILITY.
WHY DID YOU MAKE THEM ALL ALONE?
GUSH
!
K—KÔHEI?!
SNFF SNFF
I KNEW I'D CRY. THAT'S WHY I WANTED TO GO SECRETLY.
I—I'M SORRY...
...
SNFF
I WANTED...
...TO LEAVE SOMETHING SPECIAL...
...THAT ONLY I CAN MAKE.
BECAUSE I LOVE YOU ALL.

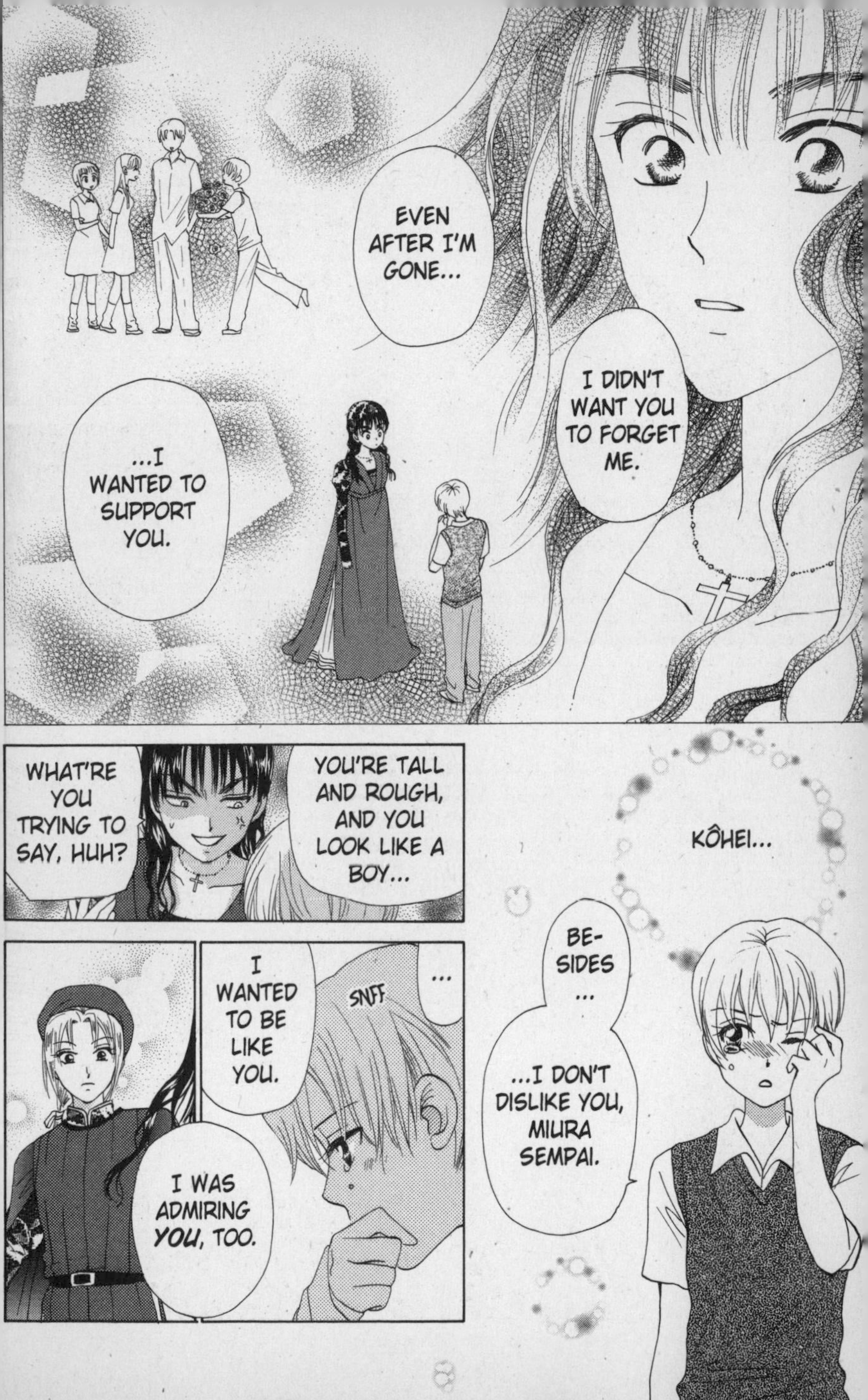
EVEN AFTER I'M GONE...
I DIDN'T WANT YOU TO FORGET ME.
...I WANTED TO SUPPORT YOU.
KÔHEI...
BE-SIDES...
...I DON'T DISLIKE YOU, MIURA SEMPAI.
YOU'RE TALL AND ROUGH, AND YOU LOOK LIKE A BOY...
WHAT'RE YOU TRYING TO SAY, HUH?
...
SNFF
I WANTED TO BE LIKE YOU.
I WAS ADMIRING *YOU*, TOO.

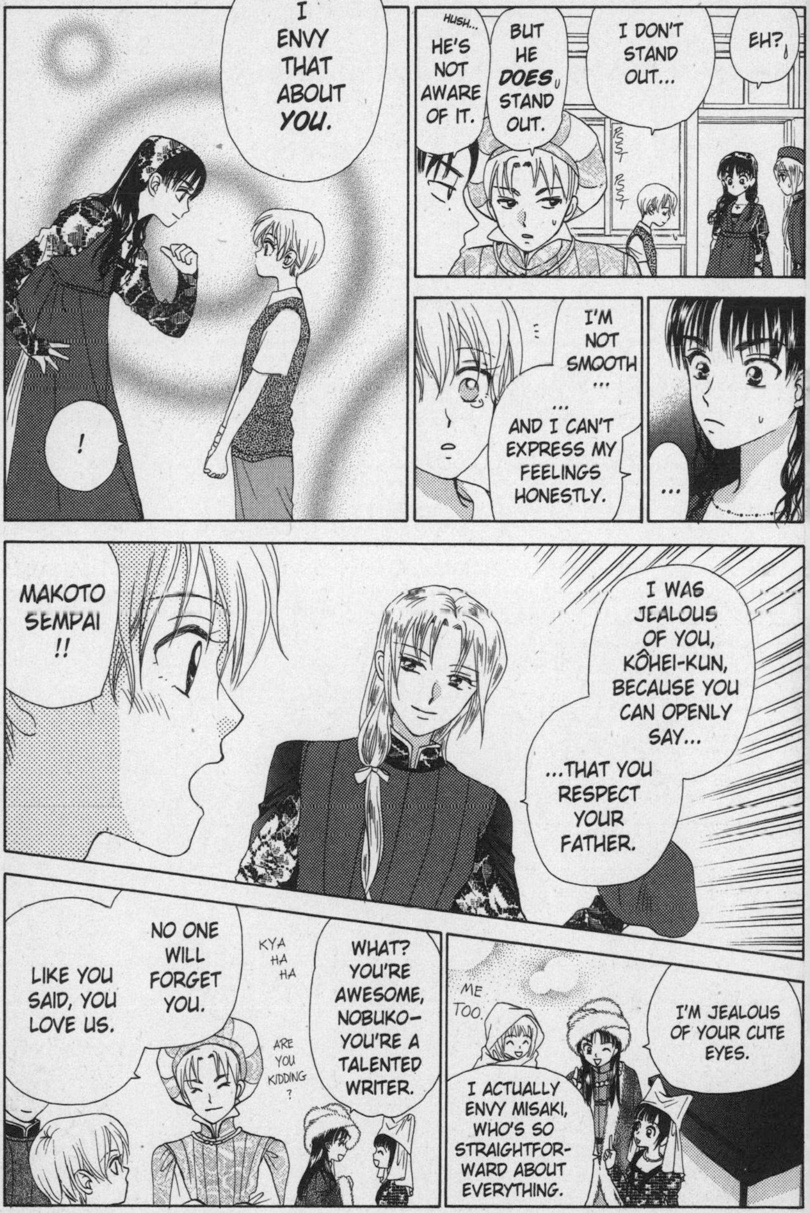
EH?
I DON'T STAND OUT...
BUT HE ***DOES*** STAND OUT.
HUSH...
HE'S NOT AWARE OF IT.
RSST RSST
...
I'M NOT SMOOTH...
... AND I CAN'T EXPRESS MY FEELINGS HONESTLY.
I ENVY THAT ABOUT ***YOU***.
!
I WAS JEALOUS OF YOU, KÔHEI-KUN, BECAUSE YOU CAN OPENLY SAY...
...THAT YOU RESPECT YOUR FATHER.
MAKOTO SEMPAI!!
I'M JEALOUS OF YOUR CUTE EYES.
ME TOO.
I ACTUALLY ENVY MISAKI, WHO'S SO STRAIGHTFORWARD ABOUT EVERYTHING.
WHAT? YOU'RE AWESOME, NOBUKO-YOU'RE A TALENTED WRITER.
KYA HA HA
ARE YOU KIDDING?
NO ONE WILL FORGET YOU.
LIKE YOU SAID, YOU LOVE US.

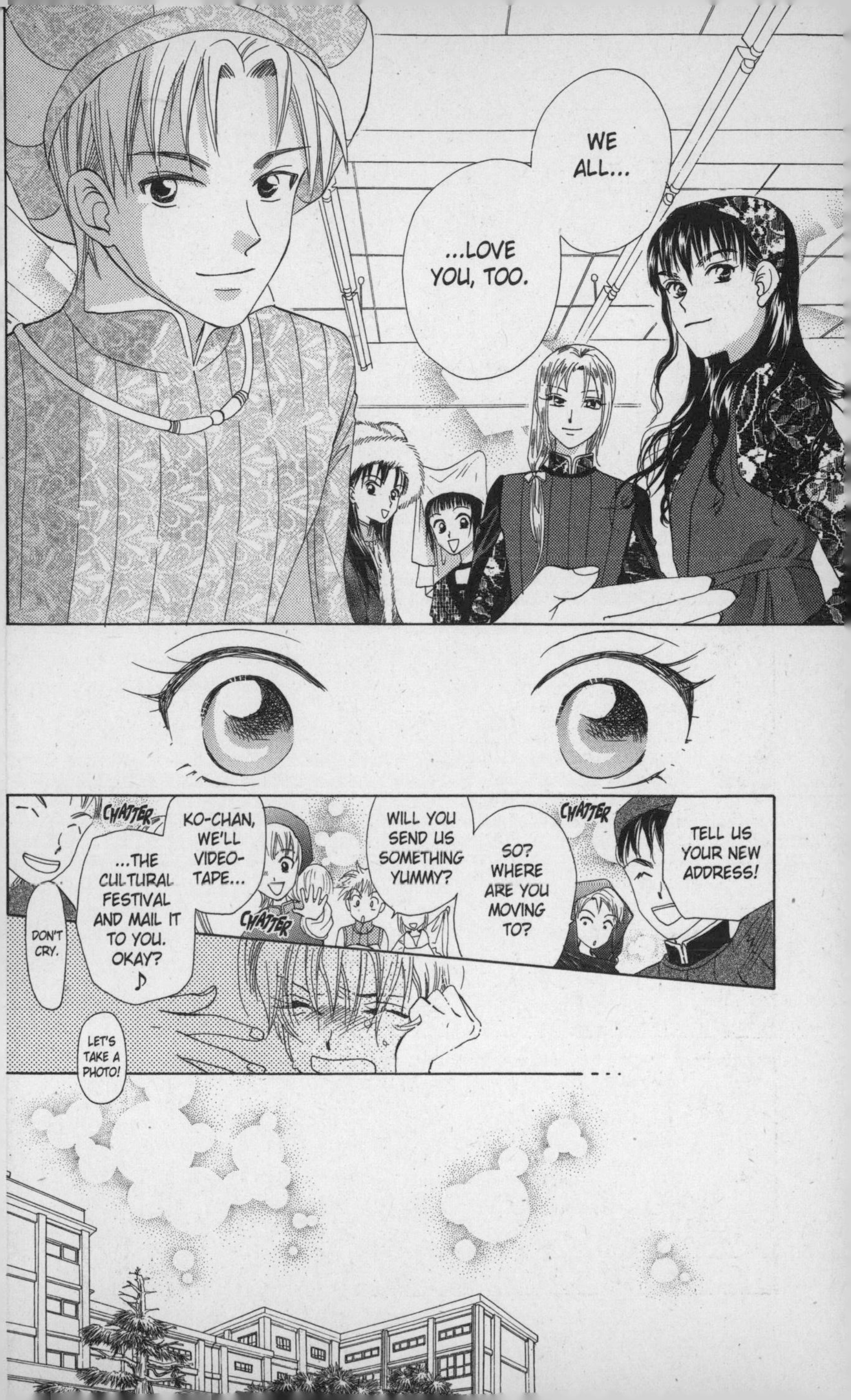
WE ALL...
...LOVE YOU, TOO.
TELL US YOUR NEW ADDRESS!
CHATTER
SO? WHERE ARE YOU MOVING TO?
WILL YOU SEND US SOMETHING YUMMY?
KO-CHAN, WE'LL VIDEO-TAPE...
CHATTER
...THE CULTURAL FESTIVAL AND MAIL IT TO YOU. OKAY? ♪
CHATTER
DON'T CRY.
LET'S TAKE A PHOTO!

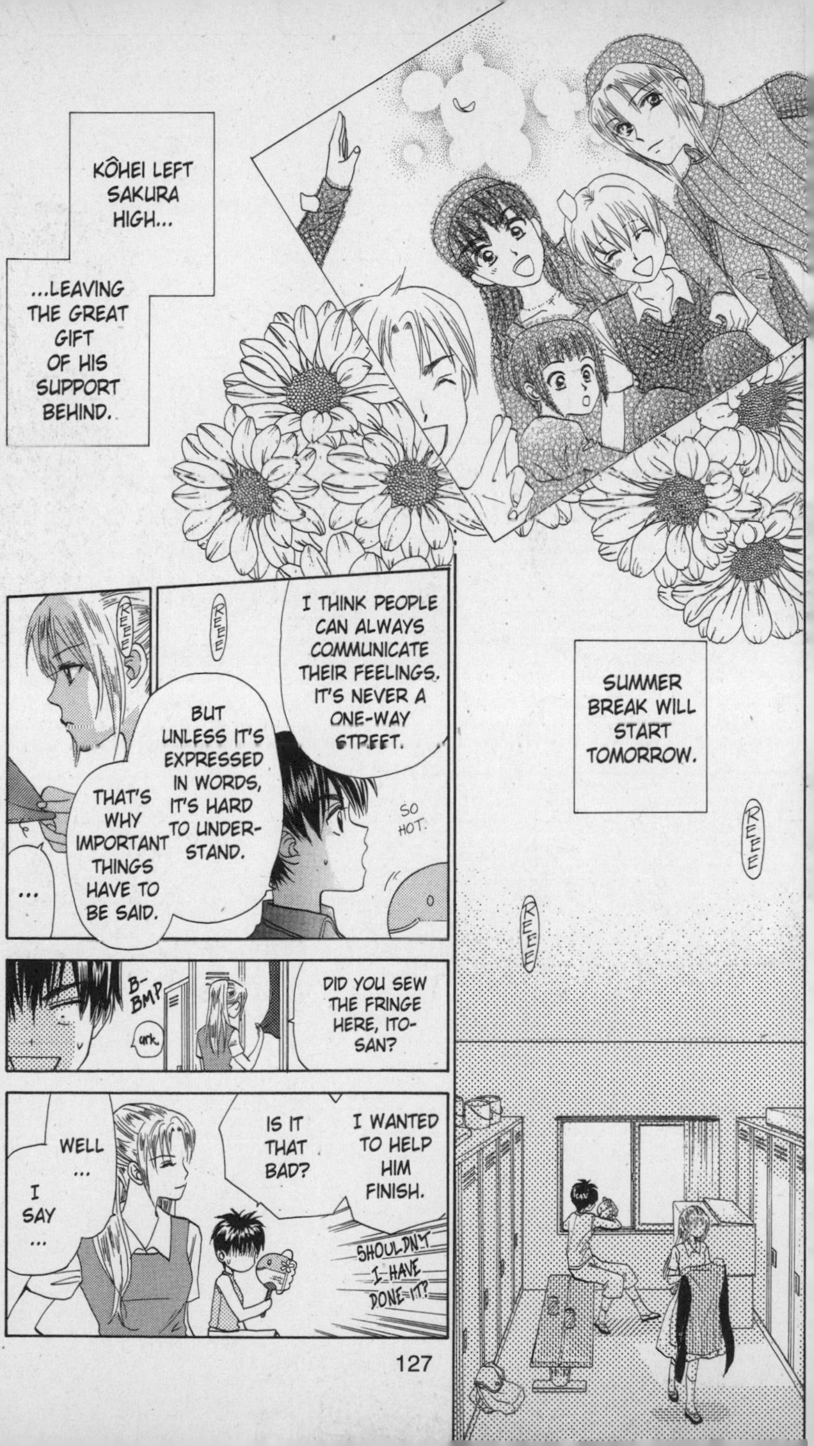
KÔHEI LEFT SAKURA HIGH...
...LEAVING THE GREAT GIFT OF HIS SUPPORT BEHIND.
SUMMER BREAK WILL START TOMORROW.
REEE
REEE
REEE
REEE
I THINK PEOPLE CAN ALWAYS COMMUNICATE THEIR FEELINGS. IT'S NEVER A ONE-WAY STREET.
SO HOT.
BUT UNLESS IT'S EXPRESSED IN WORDS, IT'S HARD TO UNDERSTAND.
THAT'S WHY IMPORTANT THINGS HAVE TO BE SAID.
...
DID YOU SEW THE FRINGE HERE, ITO-SAN?
B-BMP
urk.
I WANTED TO HELP HIM FINISH.
IS IT THAT BAD?
SHOULDN'T I HAVE DONE IT?
WELL... I SAY...

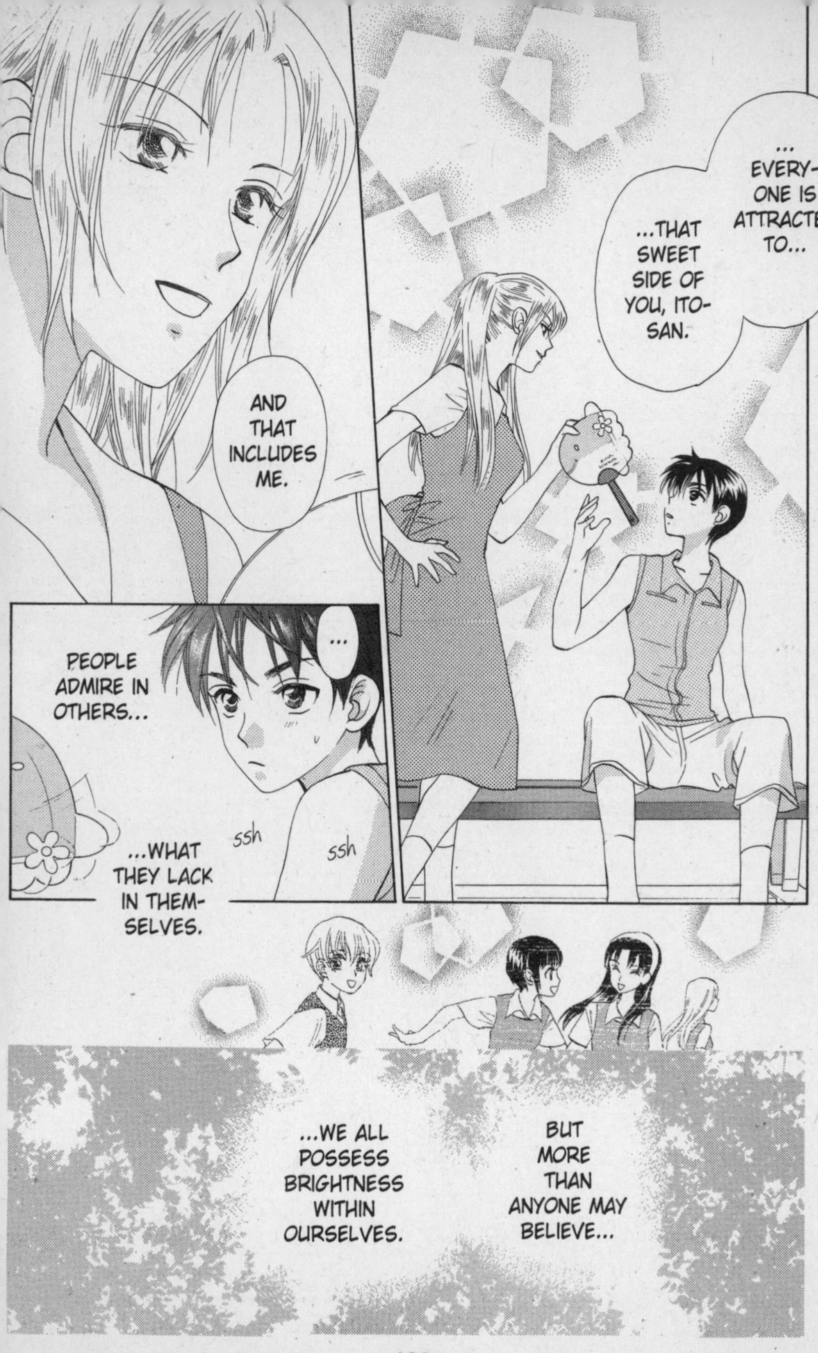
...EVERY-ONE IS ATTRACTED TO...
...THAT SWEET SIDE OF YOU, ITO-SAN.
AND THAT INCLUDES ME.
...
PEOPLE ADMIRE IN OTHERS...
ssh
ssh
...WHAT THEY LACK IN THEM-SELVES.
BUT MORE THAN ANYONE MAY BELIEVE...
...WE ALL POSSESS BRIGHTNESS WITHIN OURSELVES.

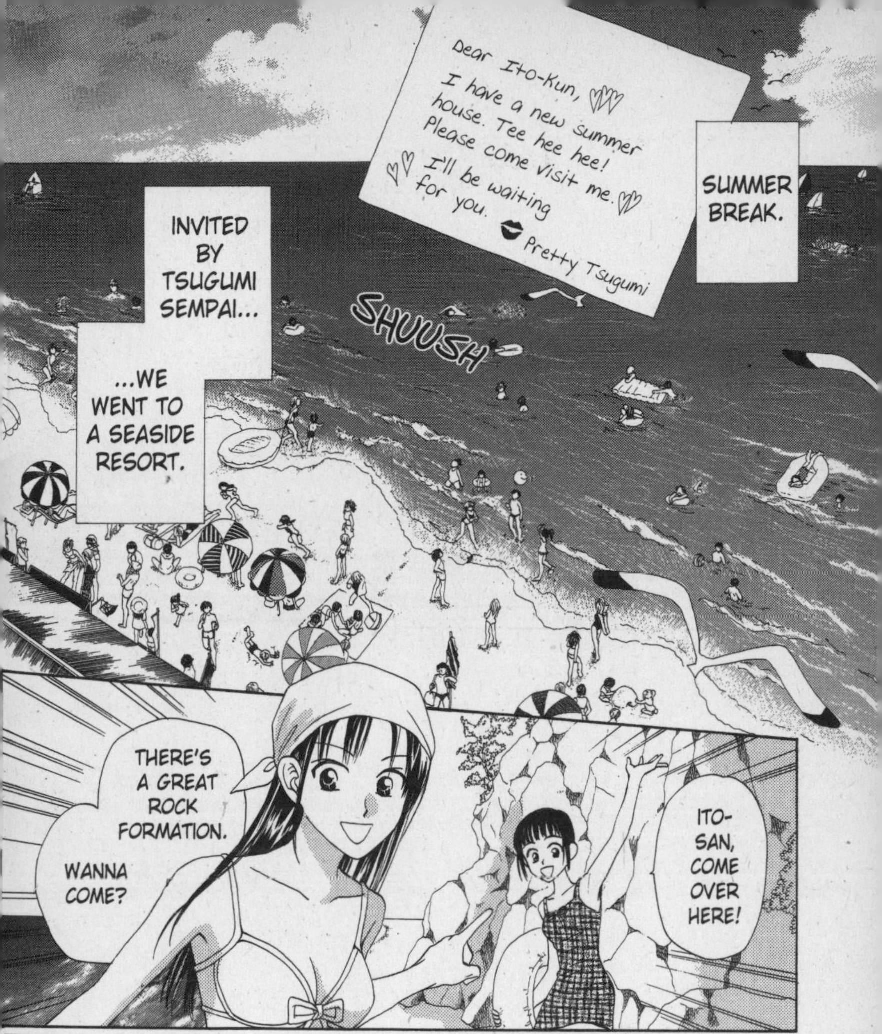
SUMMER BREAK.
Dear Ito-Kun,
I have a new summer house. Tee hee hee!
Please come visit me.
I'll be waiting for you.
Pretty Tsugumi
INVITED BY TSUGUMI SEMPAI...
...WE WENT TO A SEASIDE RESORT.
SHUUSH
ITO-SAN, COME OVER HERE!
THERE'S A GREAT ROCK FORMATION.
WANNA COME?

-Behind the Scenes Story- ⑤

I wanted to put together a story about "Yoshirô & Misaki," but before I knew it, it took an unbelievable turn. Seeing the Lady Mermaid's head poking out of the water, lots of you wrote "how scary!!" I did it! (Laugh) Oh well, the fact is, I think I got more letters asking "What is that monk's head about...?!" Ah ha ha. "Who is he?" "I'm surprised Hakusen-sha* permitted that." ←?! My sister was also darn shocked.

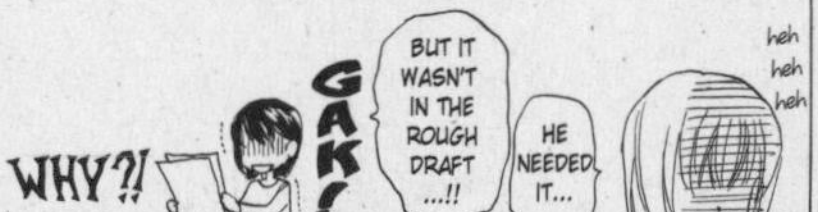
heh heh heh
HE NEEDED IT...
BUT IT WASN'T IN THE ROUGH DRAFT ...!!
GAK!
WHY?!

*Emura's publisher in Japan

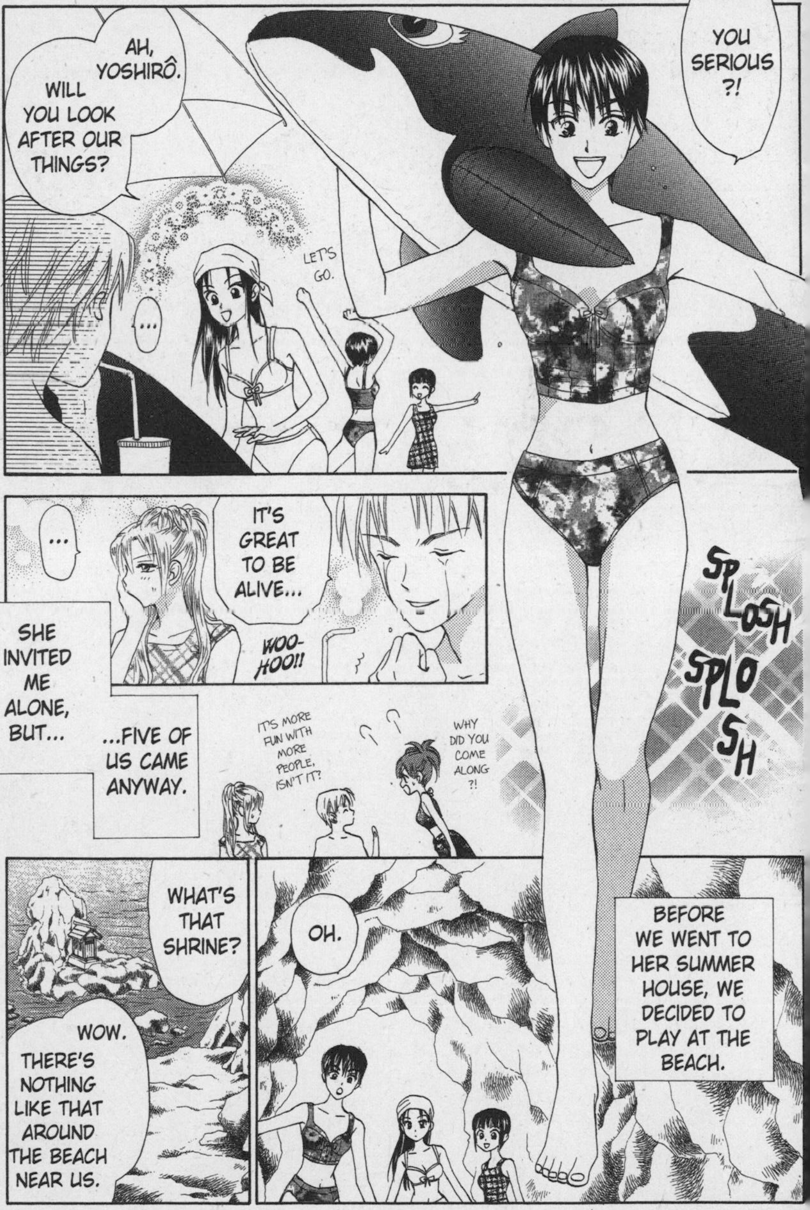
YOU SERIOUS ?!
AH, YOSHIRÔ. WILL YOU LOOK AFTER OUR THINGS?
LET'S GO.
...
SPLOSH SPLOSH SPLOSH
BEFORE WE WENT TO HER SUMMER HOUSE, WE DECIDED TO PLAY AT THE BEACH.
IT'S GREAT TO BE ALIVE...
WOO-HOO!!
...
SHE INVITED ME ALONE, BUT...
...FIVE OF US CAME ANYWAY.
WHY DID YOU COME ALONG ?!
IT'S MORE FUN WITH MORE PEOPLE, ISN'T IT?
OH.
WHAT'S THAT SHRINE?
WOW. THERE'S NOTHING LIKE THAT AROUND THE BEACH NEAR US.

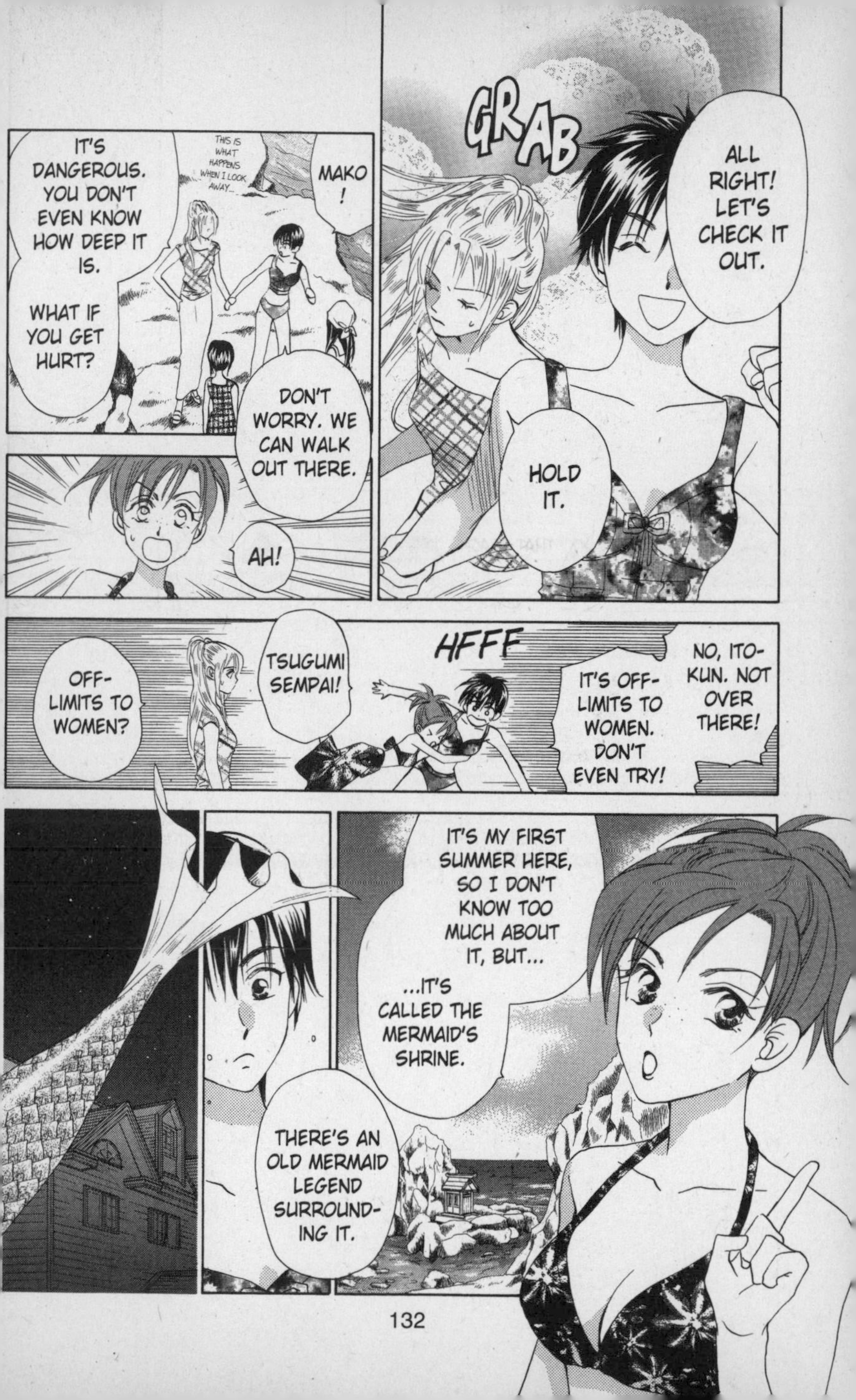
GRAB
ALL RIGHT! LET'S CHECK IT OUT.
HOLD IT.
MAKO!
THIS IS WHAT HAPPENS WHEN I LOOK AWAY...
IT'S DANGEROUS. YOU DON'T EVEN KNOW HOW DEEP IT IS.
WHAT IF YOU GET HURT?
DON'T WORRY. WE CAN WALK OUT THERE.
AH!
NO, ITO-KUN. NOT OVER THERE!
IT'S OFF-LIMITS TO WOMEN. DON'T EVEN TRY!
HFFF
TSUGUMI SEMPAI!
OFF-LIMITS TO WOMEN?
IT'S MY FIRST SUMMER HERE, SO I DON'T KNOW TOO MUCH ABOUT IT, BUT...
...IT'S CALLED THE MERMAID'S SHRINE.
THERE'S AN OLD MERMAID LEGEND SURROUNDING IT.

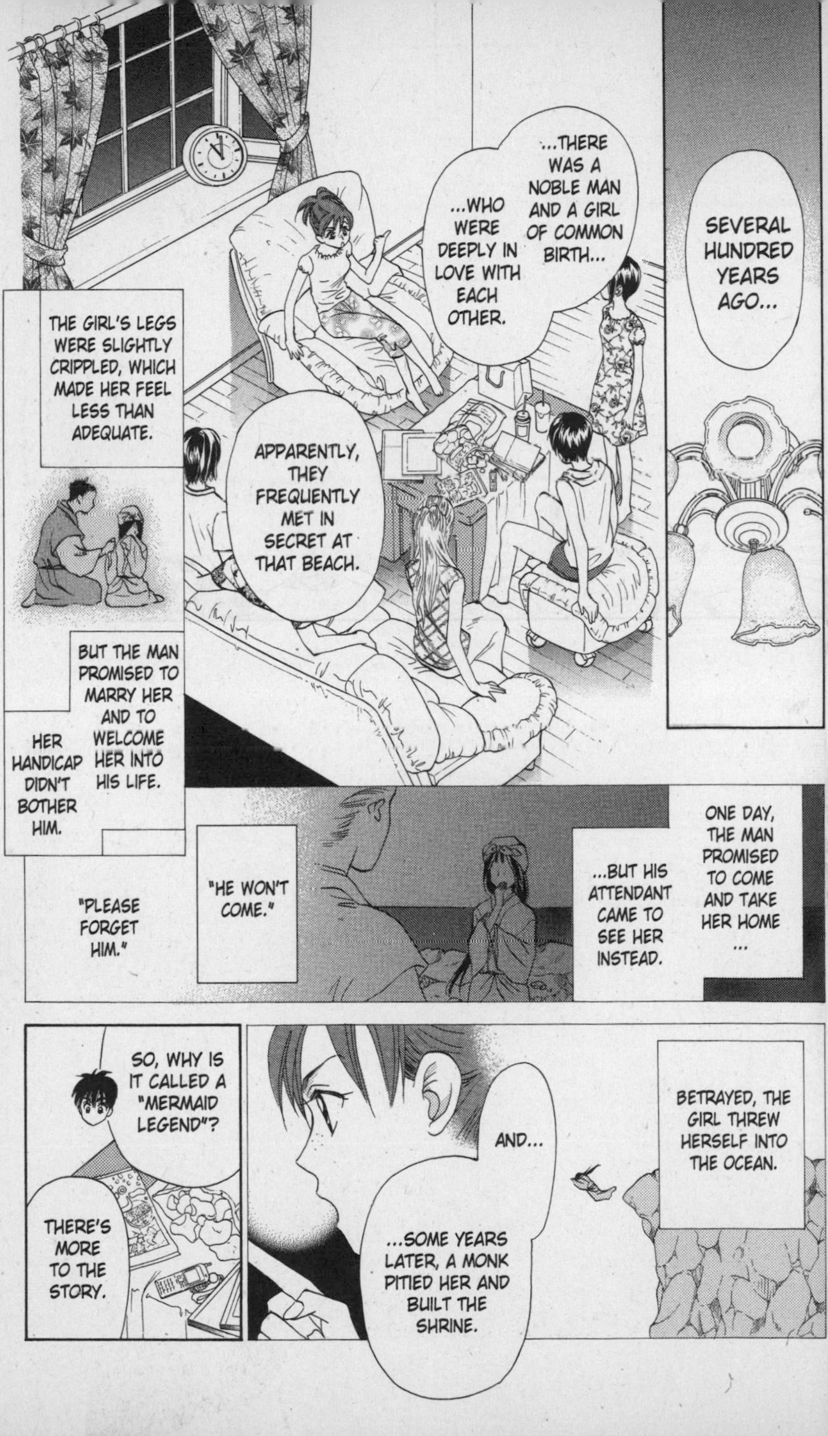
SEVERAL HUNDRED YEARS AGO...
...THERE WAS A NOBLE MAN AND A GIRL OF COMMON BIRTH...
...WHO WERE DEEPLY IN LOVE WITH EACH OTHER.
APPARENTLY, THEY FREQUENTLY MET IN SECRET AT THAT BEACH.
THE GIRL'S LEGS WERE SLIGHTLY CRIPPLED, WHICH MADE HER FEEL LESS THAN ADEQUATE.
BUT THE MAN PROMISED TO MARRY HER AND TO WELCOME HER INTO HIS LIFE.
HER HANDICAP DIDN'T BOTHER HIM.
ONE DAY, THE MAN PROMISED TO COME AND TAKE HER HOME ...
...BUT HIS ATTENDANT CAME TO SEE HER INSTEAD.
"HE WON'T COME."
"PLEASE FORGET HIM."
BETRAYED, THE GIRL THREW HERSELF INTO THE OCEAN.
AND...
...SOME YEARS LATER, A MONK PITIED HER AND BUILT THE SHRINE.
SO, WHY IS IT CALLED A "MERMAID LEGEND"?
THERE'S MORE TO THE STORY.

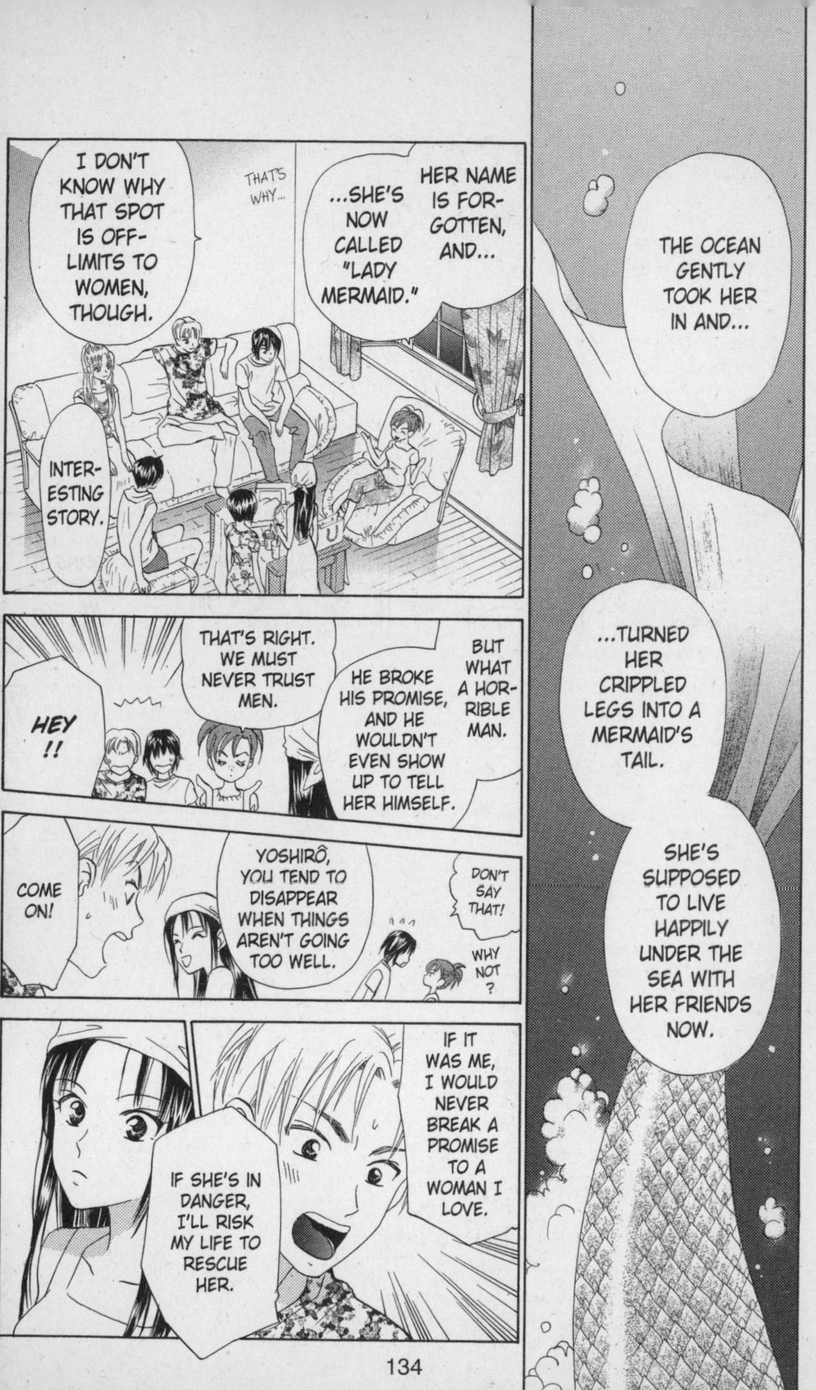
THE OCEAN GENTLY TOOK HER IN AND...
...TURNED HER CRIPPLED LEGS INTO A MERMAID'S TAIL.
SHE'S SUPPOSED TO LIVE HAPPILY UNDER THE SEA WITH HER FRIENDS NOW.
HER NAME IS FOR-GOTTEN, AND...
...SHE'S NOW CALLED "LADY MERMAID."
THAT'S WHY...
I DON'T KNOW WHY THAT SPOT IS OFF-LIMITS TO WOMEN, THOUGH.
INTER-ESTING STORY.
BUT WHAT A HOR-RIBLE MAN.
HE BROKE HIS PROMISE, AND HE WOULDN'T EVEN SHOW UP TO TELL HER HIMSELF.
THAT'S RIGHT. WE MUST NEVER TRUST MEN.
HEY !!
DON'T SAY THAT!
WHY NOT ?
YOSHIRÔ, YOU TEND TO DISAPPEAR WHEN THINGS AREN'T GOING TOO WELL.
COME ON!
IF IT WAS ME, I WOULD NEVER BREAK A PROMISE TO A WOMAN I LOVE.
IF SHE'S IN DANGER, I'LL RISK MY LIFE TO RESCUE HER.

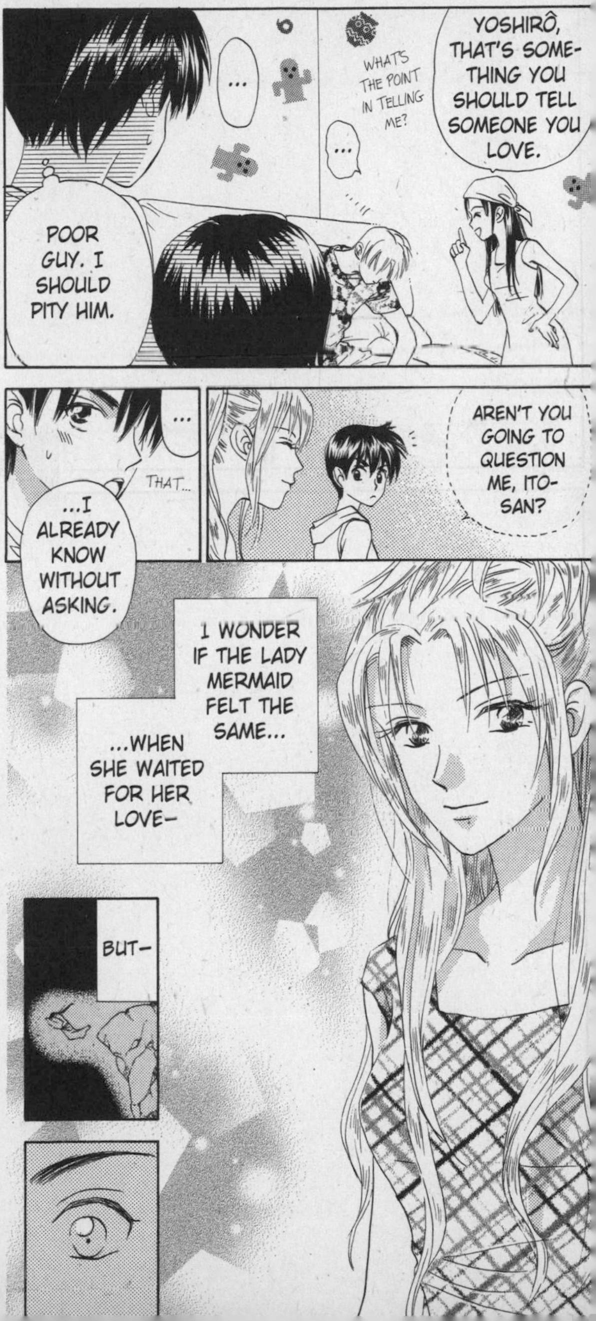
YOSHIRÔ, THAT'S SOMETHING YOU SHOULD TELL SOMEONE YOU LOVE.
WHAT'S THE POINT IN TELLING ME?
...
...
POOR GUY. I SHOULD PITY HIM.
AREN'T YOU GOING TO QUESTION ME, ITO-SAN?
...
THAT...
...I ALREADY KNOW WITHOUT ASKING.
I WONDER IF THE LADY MERMAID FELT THE SAME...
...WHEN SHE WAITED FOR HER LOVE–
BUT–

STORY ON MANGA (2)

So, it's not true that I never read Shô jo manga. It's just that I mainly focus on fantasy.

Shô jo manga
↓

- Reiko Shimizu
- Kyoko Hikawa
- Saki Hiwatari
- Kei Kusunoki
- Ryo Ikuemi
- Natsuki Takaya
- Karin Mochizuki
- Banri Hidaka
- Miyuki Yamaguchi
- Yumi Tamura
- Kaori Ozaki

Ummm, I'm totally warped-- I am definitely a *Hana to Yume* child! Once I became a *Hana to Yume* manga-ka, I added more favorites. Recently, I've been totally hooked on love comedy. I mean, is it because I'm writing one, too?!

It's true I became more aware of Shô jo manga once I started drawing *W Juliet*.

I admire those manga-ka who have a beautiful touch with their pen.

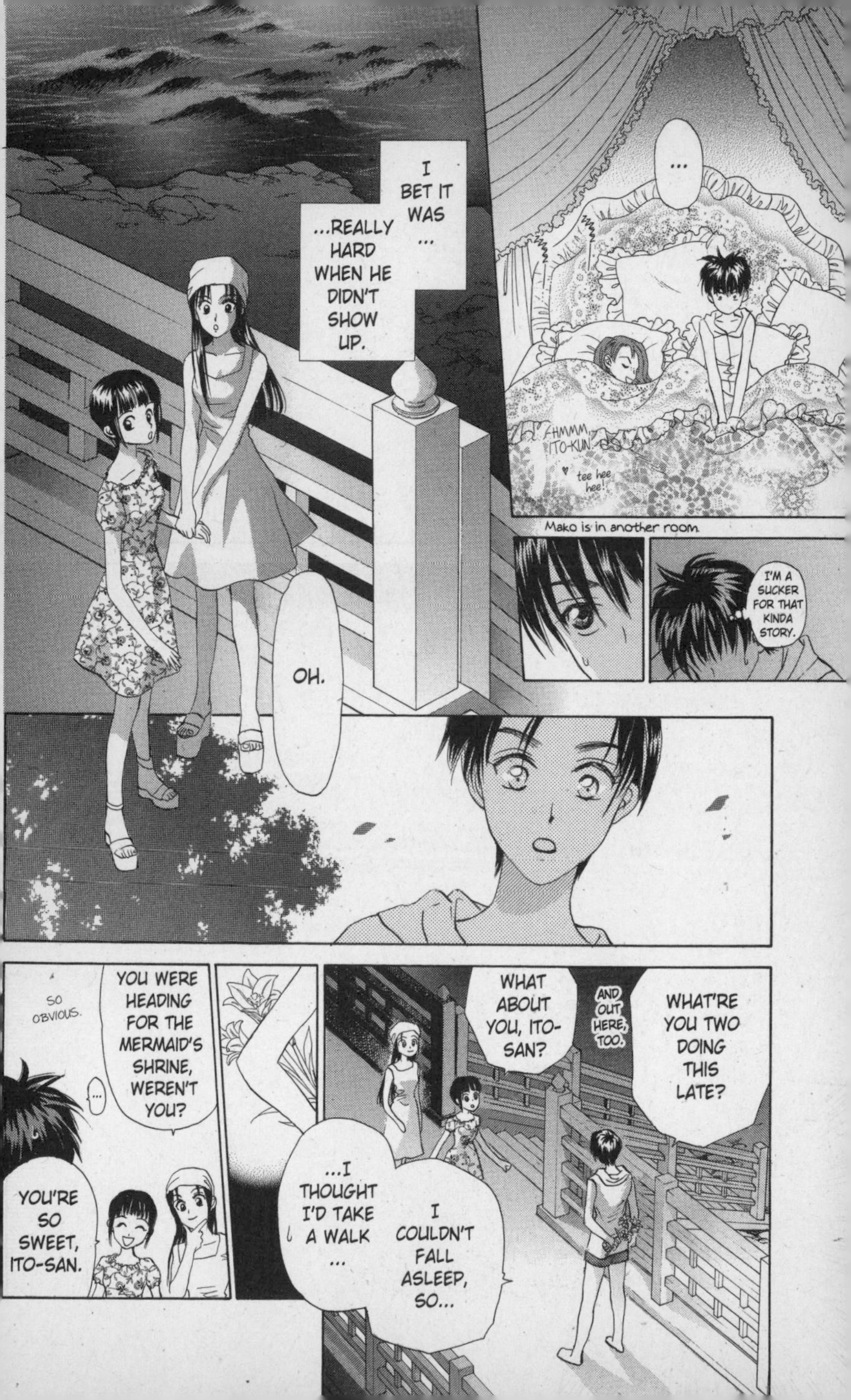
...
HMMM, ITO-KUN.
tee hee hee!
Mako is in another room.
I'M A SUCKER FOR THAT KINDA STORY.
I BET IT WAS ...
...REALLY HARD WHEN HE DIDN'T SHOW UP.
OH.
WHAT'RE YOU TWO DOING THIS LATE?
AND OUT HERE, TOO.
WHAT ABOUT YOU, ITO-SAN?
I COULDN'T FALL ASLEEP, SO...
...I THOUGHT I'D TAKE A WALK ...
YOU WERE HEADING FOR THE MERMAID'S SHRINE, WEREN'T YOU?
SO OBVIOUS.
...
YOU'RE SO SWEET, ITO-SAN.

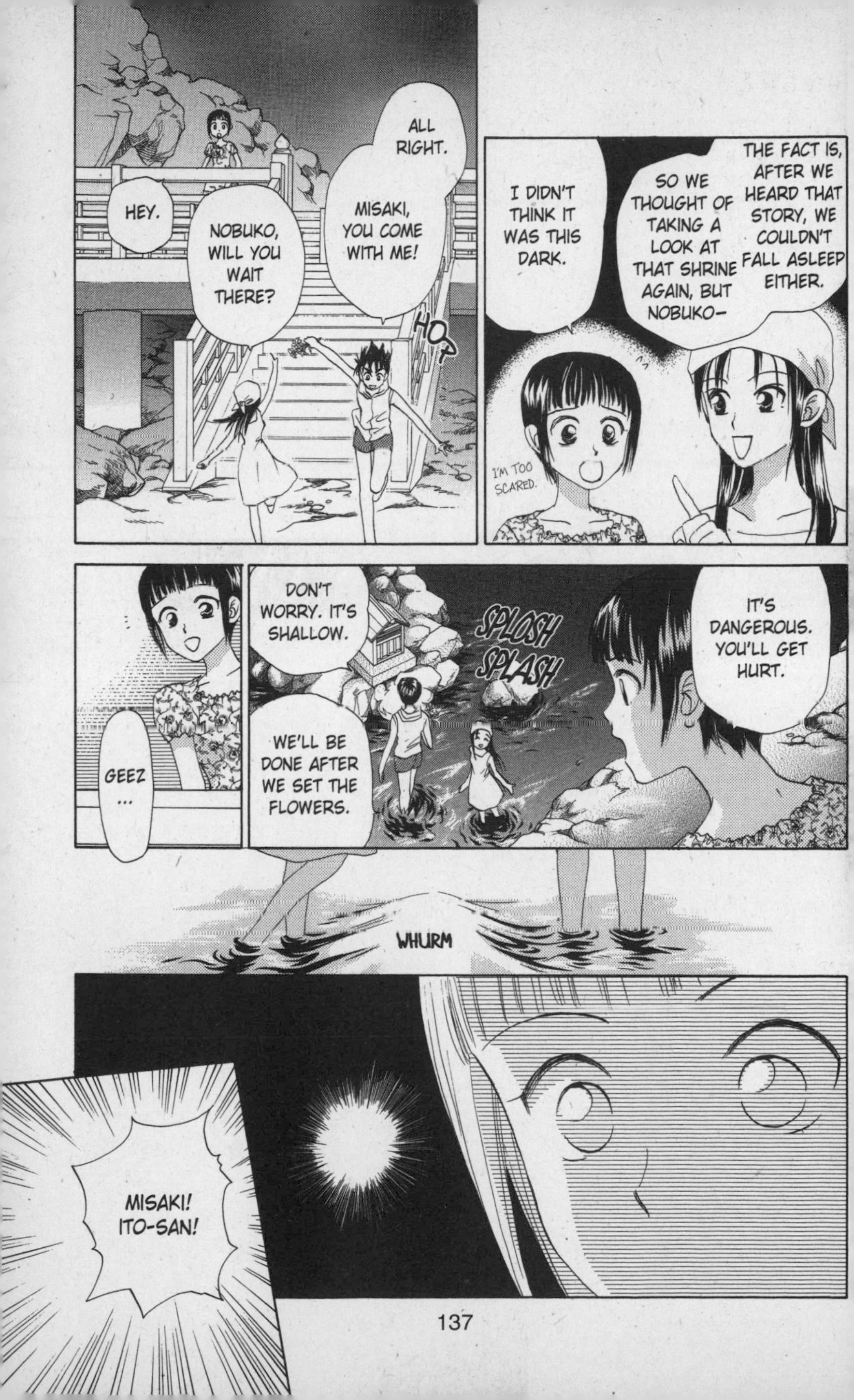
THE FACT IS, AFTER WE HEARD THAT STORY, WE COULDN'T FALL ASLEEP EITHER.
SO WE THOUGHT OF TAKING A LOOK AT THAT SHRINE AGAIN, BUT NOBUKO—
I DIDN'T THINK IT WAS THIS DARK.
I'M TOO SCARED.
ALL RIGHT.
MISAKI, YOU COME WITH ME!
HOP
NOBUKO, WILL YOU WAIT THERE?
HEY.
IT'S DANGEROUS. YOU'LL GET HURT.
SPLOSH SPLASH
DON'T WORRY. IT'S SHALLOW.
WE'LL BE DONE AFTER WE SET THE FLOWERS.
GEEZ ...
WHURM
MISAKI! ITO-SAN!

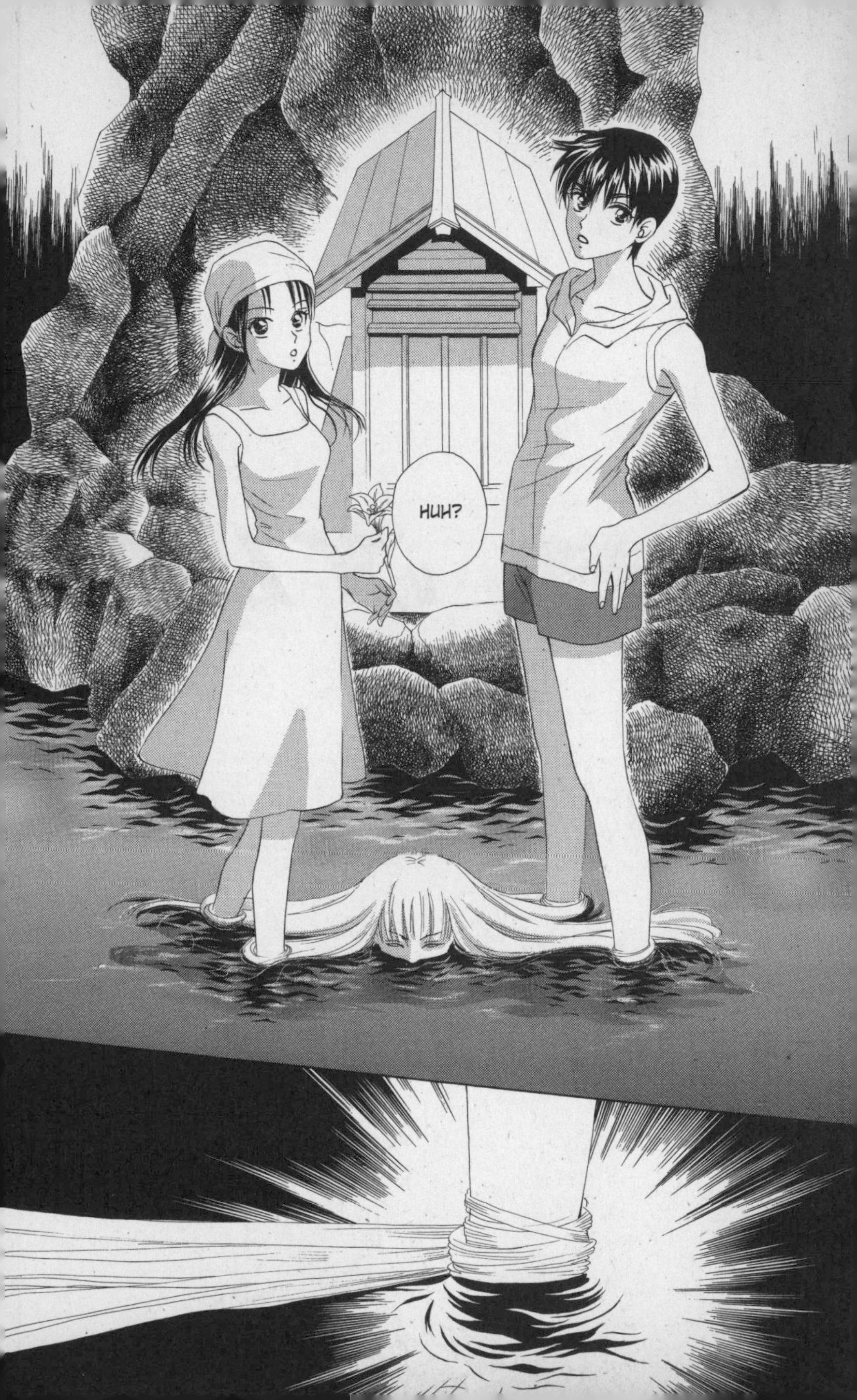
HUH?

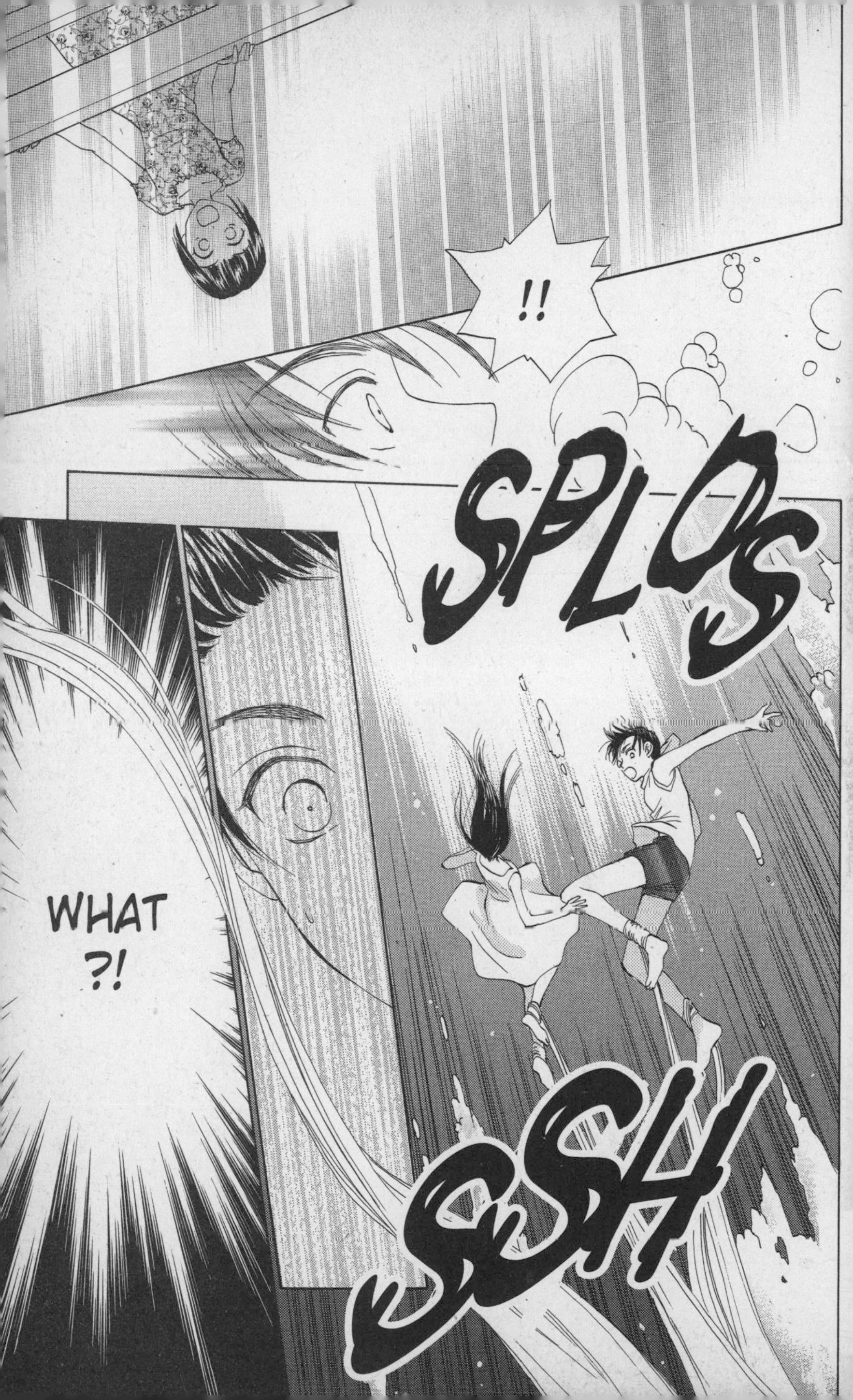
!!
SPLOS
SSH
WHAT ?!

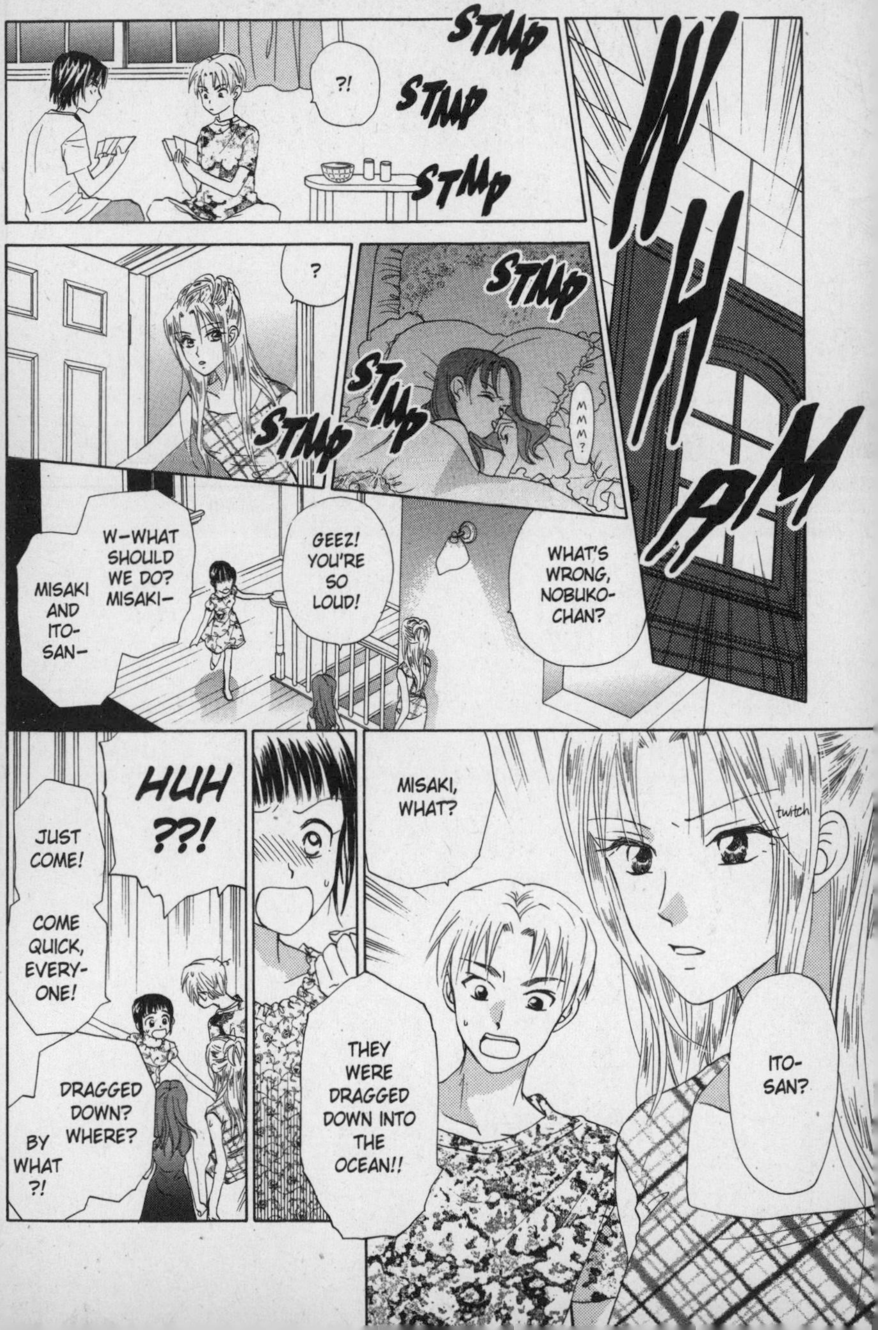
WHAM
?!
STMP
STMP
STMP
STMP
STMP
MMM?
STMP
?
WHAT'S WRONG, NOBUKO-CHAN?
GEEZ! YOU'RE SO LOUD!
W-WHAT SHOULD WE DO? MISAKI-
MISAKI AND ITO-SAN-
twitch
MISAKI, WHAT?
ITO-SAN?
THEY WERE DRAGGED DOWN INTO THE OCEAN!!
HUH ??!
JUST COME!
COME QUICK, EVERY-ONE!
DRAGGED DOWN? WHERE?
BY WHAT ?!

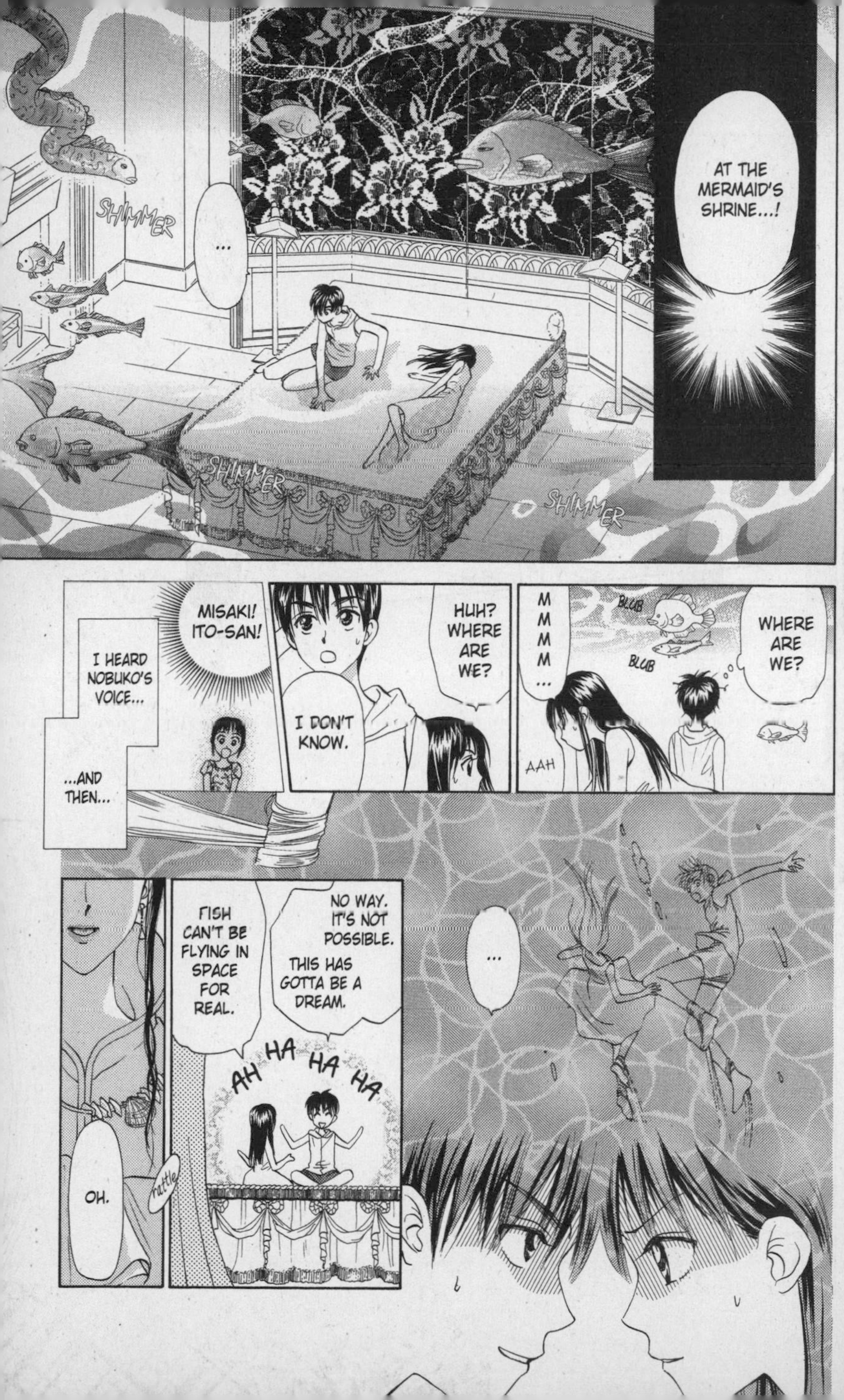
AT THE MERMAID'S SHRINE...!
...
SHIMMER
SHIMMER
SHIMMER
WHERE ARE WE?
BLUB
BLUB
MMMM...
AAH
HUH? WHERE ARE WE?
I DON'T KNOW.
MISAKI! ITO-SAN!
I HEARD NOBUKO'S VOICE...
...AND THEN...
...
NO WAY. IT'S NOT POSSIBLE.
FISH CAN'T BE FLYING IN SPACE FOR REAL.
THIS HAS GOTTA BE A DREAM.
AH HA HA HA
rattle
OH.

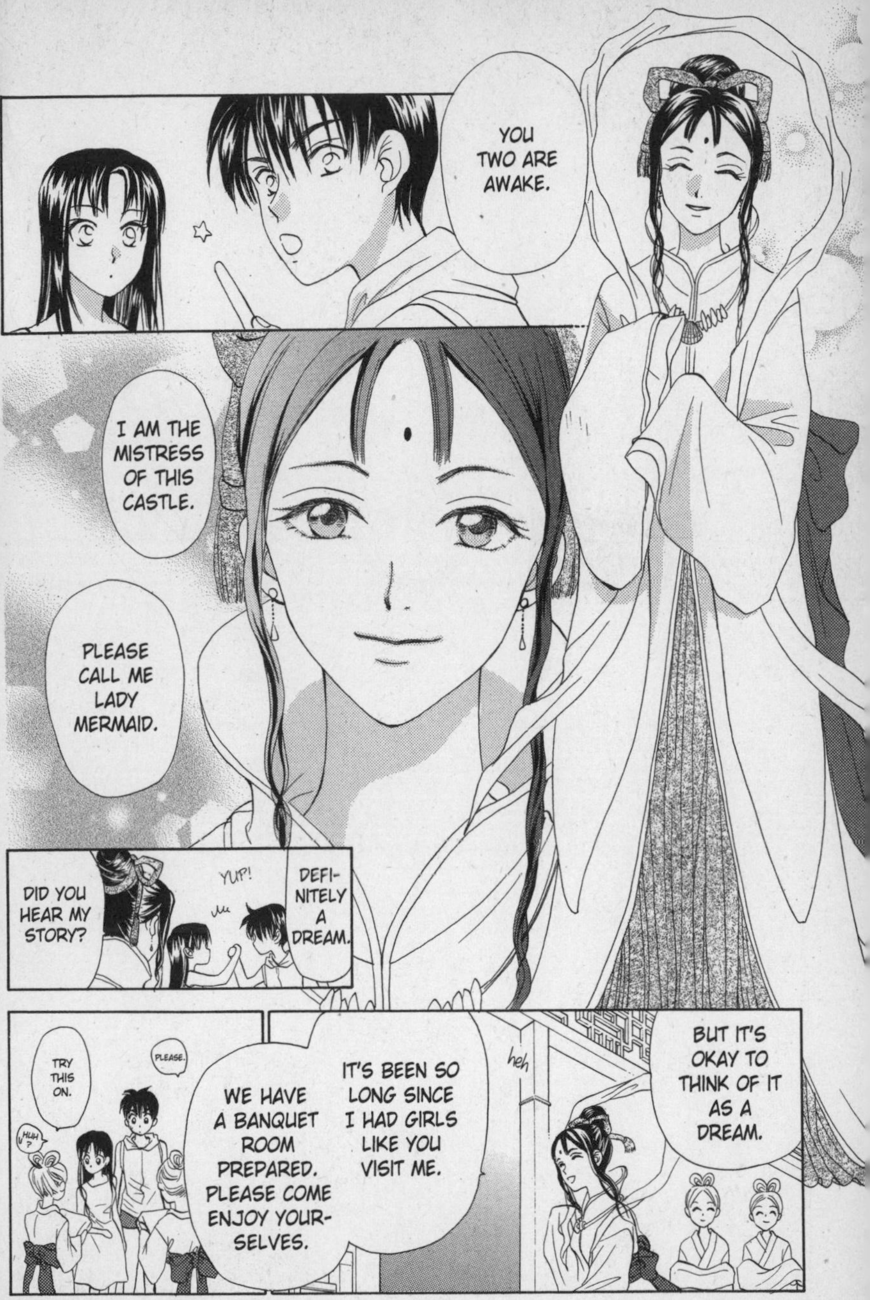
YOU TWO ARE AWAKE.
I AM THE MISTRESS OF THIS CASTLE.
PLEASE CALL ME LADY MERMAID.
DEFI-NITELY A DREAM.
YUP!
DID YOU HEAR MY STORY?
BUT IT'S OKAY TO THINK OF IT AS A DREAM.
heh
IT'S BEEN SO LONG SINCE I HAD GIRLS LIKE YOU VISIT ME.
WE HAVE A BANQUET ROOM PREPARED. PLEASE COME ENJOY YOUR-SELVES.
PLEASE.
TRY THIS ON.
HUH?

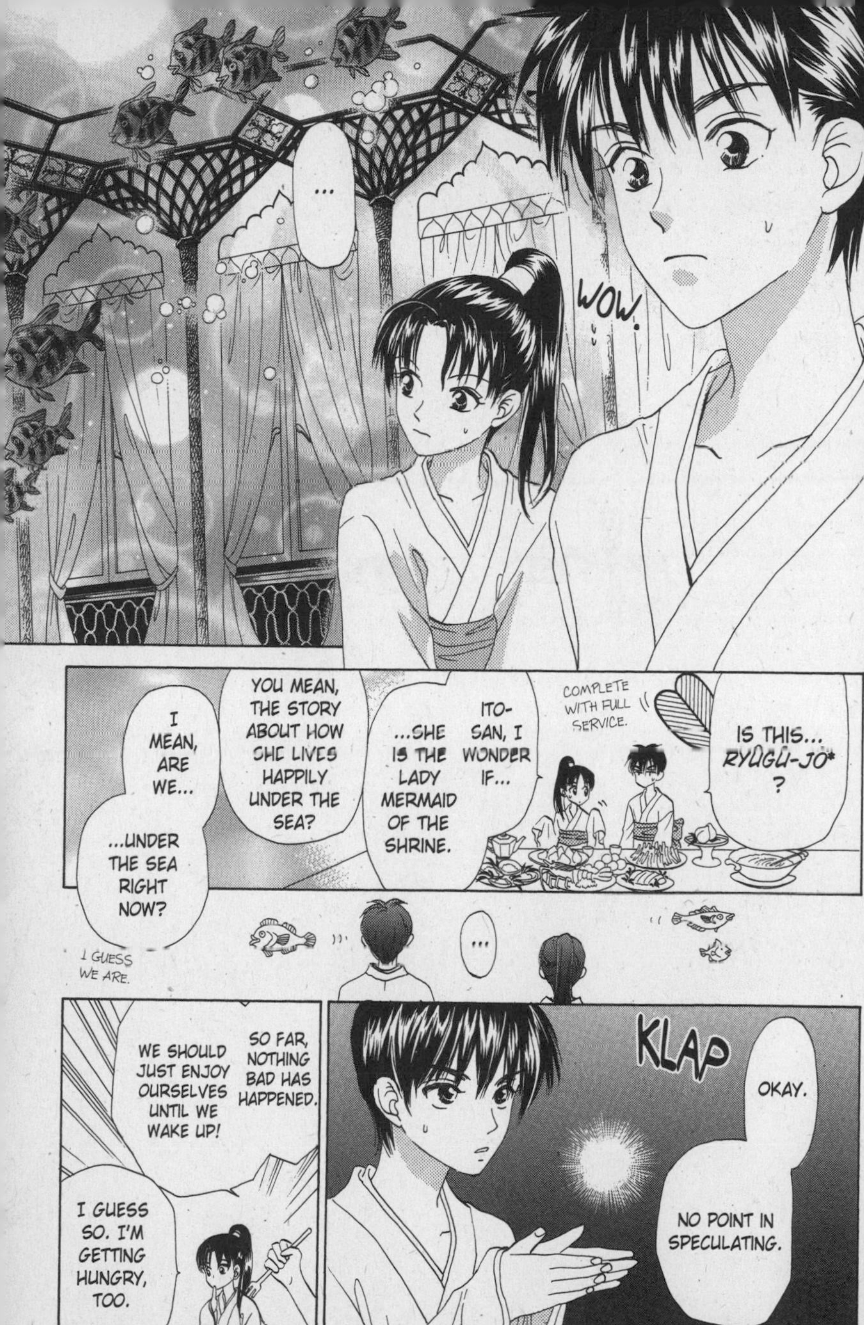
WOW.
...
IS THIS... RYŪGŪ-JŌ* ?
COMPLETE WITH FULL SERVICE.
ITO-SAN, I WONDER IF...
...SHE IS THE LADY MERMAID OF THE SHRINE.
YOU MEAN, THE STORY ABOUT HOW SHE LIVES HAPPILY UNDER THE SEA?
I MEAN, ARE WE...
...UNDER THE SEA RIGHT NOW?
...
I GUESS WE ARE.
KLAP
OKAY.
NO POINT IN SPECULATING.
SO FAR, NOTHING BAD HAS HAPPENED.
WE SHOULD JUST ENJOY OURSELVES UNTIL WE WAKE UP!
I GUESS SO. I'M GETTING HUNGRY, TOO.

*UNDERSEA PALACE OF DRAGON GODS

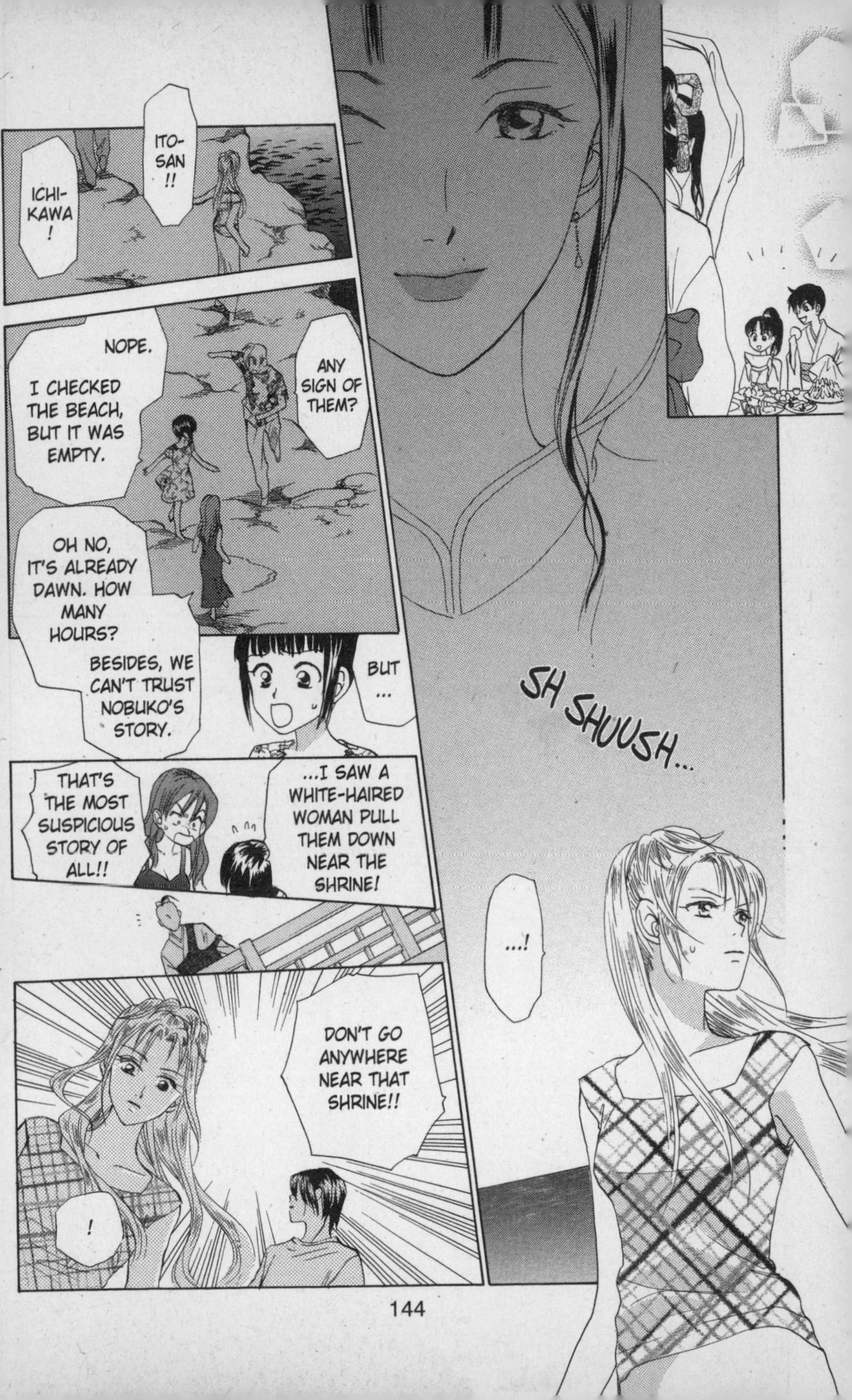
SH SHUUSH...
...!
ITO-SAN !!
ICHI-KAWA !
ANY SIGN OF THEM?
NOPE.
I CHECKED THE BEACH, BUT IT WAS EMPTY.
OH NO, IT'S ALREADY DAWN. HOW MANY HOURS?
BUT ...
BESIDES, WE CAN'T TRUST NOBUKO'S STORY.
...I SAW A WHITE-HAIRED WOMAN PULL THEM DOWN NEAR THE SHRINE!
THAT'S THE MOST SUSPICIOUS STORY OF ALL!!
DON'T GO ANYWHERE NEAR THAT SHRINE!!
!

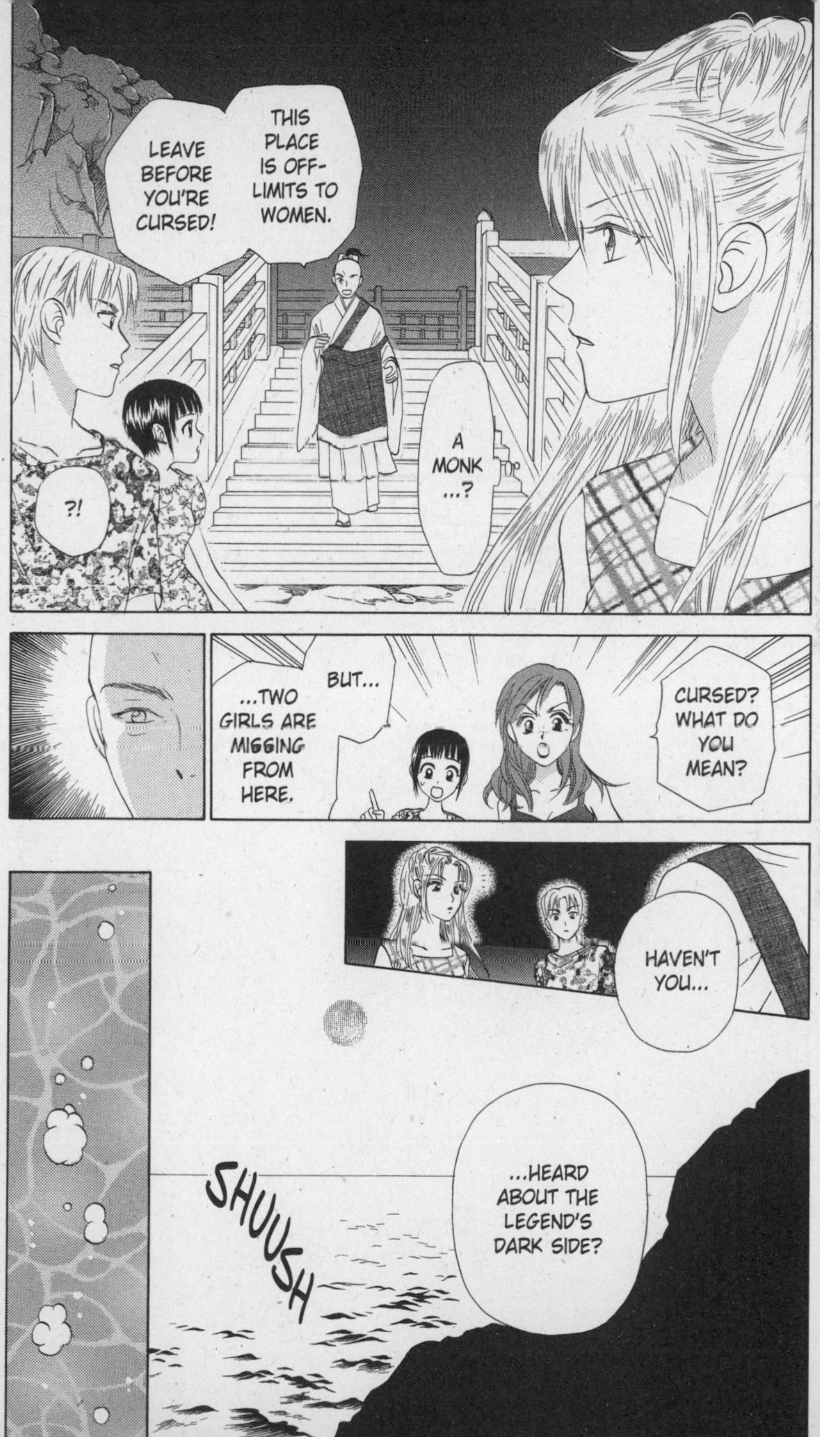
THIS PLACE IS OFF-LIMITS TO WOMEN.
LEAVE BEFORE YOU'RE CURSED!
A MONK ...?
?!
CURSED? WHAT DO YOU MEAN?
BUT...
...TWO GIRLS ARE MISSING FROM HERE.
HAVEN'T YOU...
...HEARD ABOUT THE LEGEND'S DARK SIDE?
SHUUSH

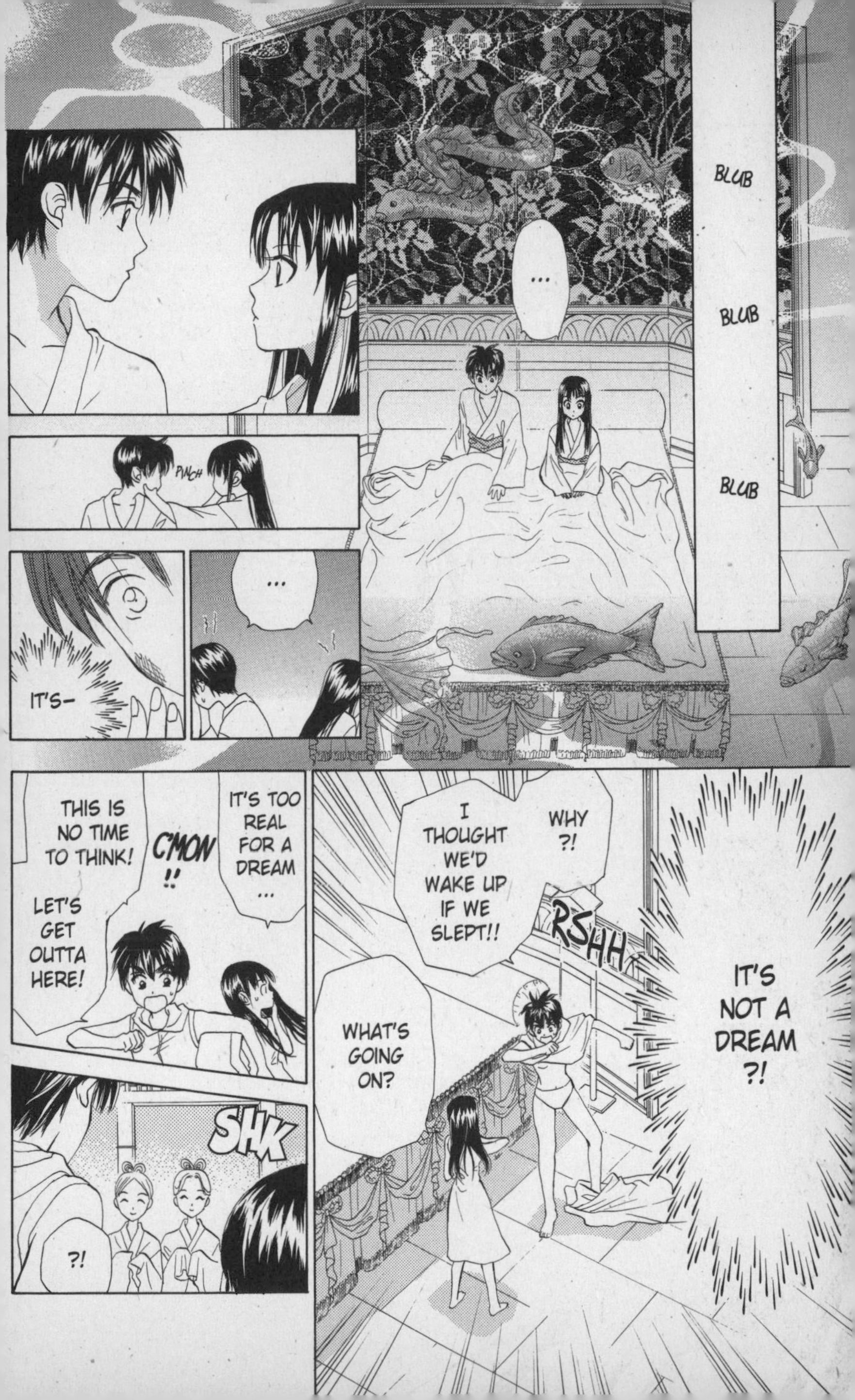
BLUB
BLUB
BLUB
...
PINCH
...
IT'S-
IT'S NOT A DREAM ?!
RSHH
WHY ?!
I THOUGHT WE'D WAKE UP IF WE SLEPT!!
WHAT'S GOING ON?
IT'S TOO REAL FOR A DREAM ...
C'MON !!
THIS IS NO TIME TO THINK!
LET'S GET OUTTA HERE!
SHK
?!

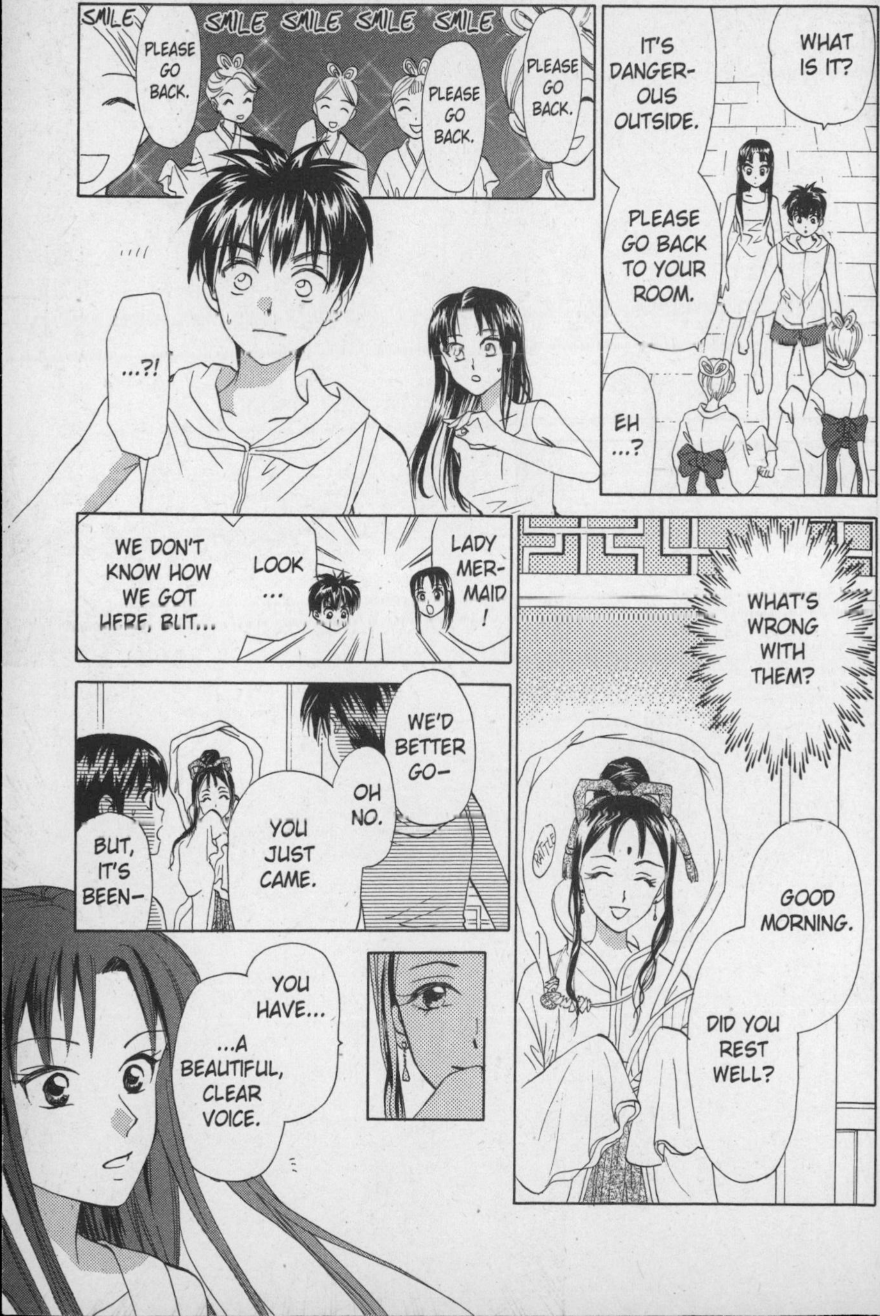
WHAT IS IT?
IT'S DANGER-OUS OUTSIDE.
PLEASE GO BACK TO YOUR ROOM.
EH ...?
PLEASE GO BACK.
SMILE SMILE SMILE SMILE
PLEASE GO BACK.
SMILE
PLEASE GO BACK.
...?!
WHAT'S WRONG WITH THEM?
GOOD MORNING.
DID YOU REST WELL?
LADY MER-MAID!
LOOK ...
WE DON'T KNOW HOW WE GOT HERE, BUT...
WE'D BETTER GO—
OH NO.
YOU JUST CAME.
BUT, IT'S BEEN—
YOU HAVE...
...A BEAUTIFUL, CLEAR VOICE.

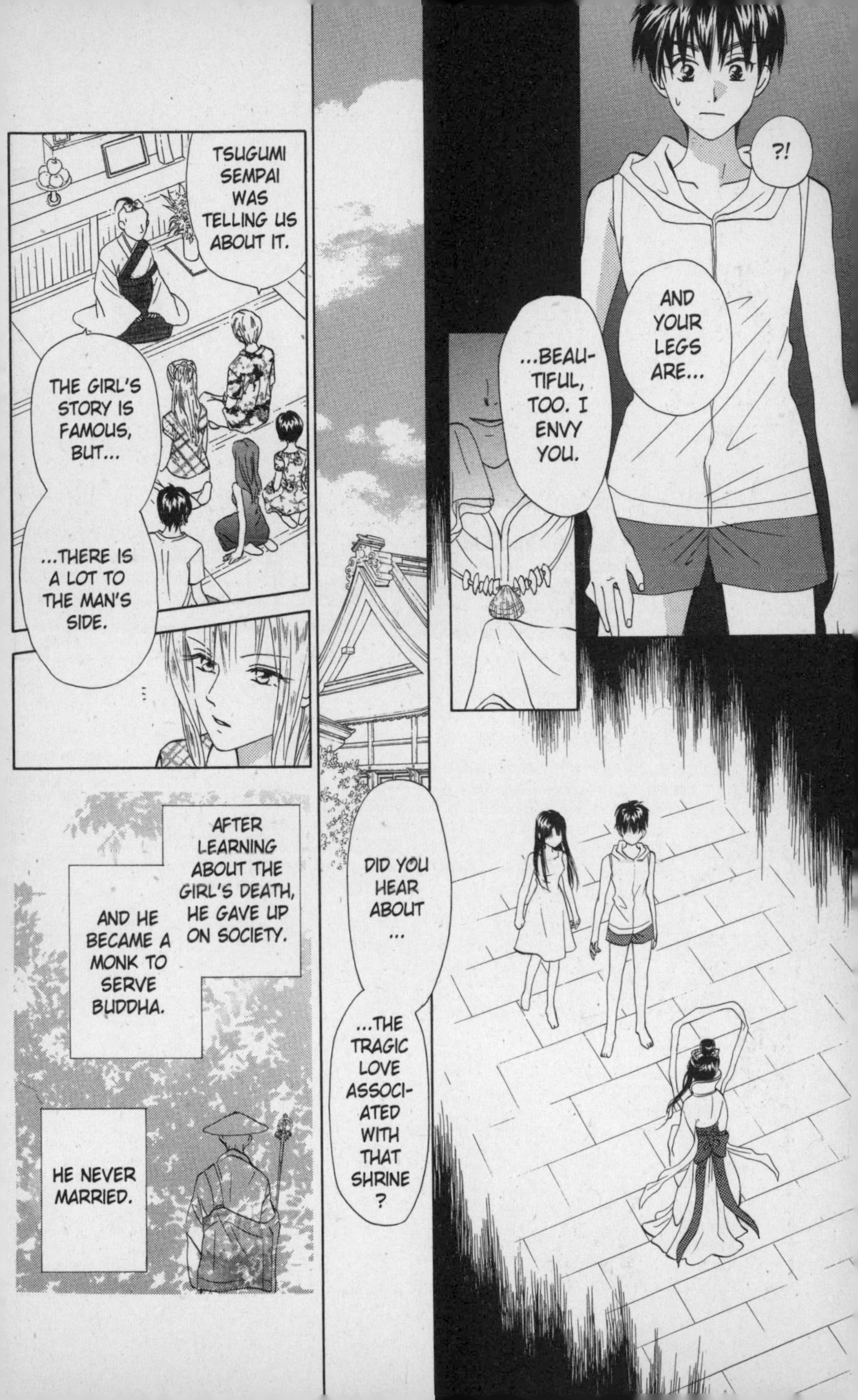
AND YOUR LEGS ARE...
...BEAUTIFUL, TOO. I ENVY YOU.
?!
DID YOU HEAR ABOUT ...
...THE TRAGIC LOVE ASSOCIATED WITH THAT SHRINE?
TSUGUMI SEMPAI WAS TELLING US ABOUT IT.
THE GIRL'S STORY IS FAMOUS, BUT...
...THERE IS A LOT TO THE MAN'S SIDE.
...
AFTER LEARNING ABOUT THE GIRL'S DEATH, HE GAVE UP ON SOCIETY.
AND HE BECAME A MONK TO SERVE BUDDHA.
HE NEVER MARRIED.

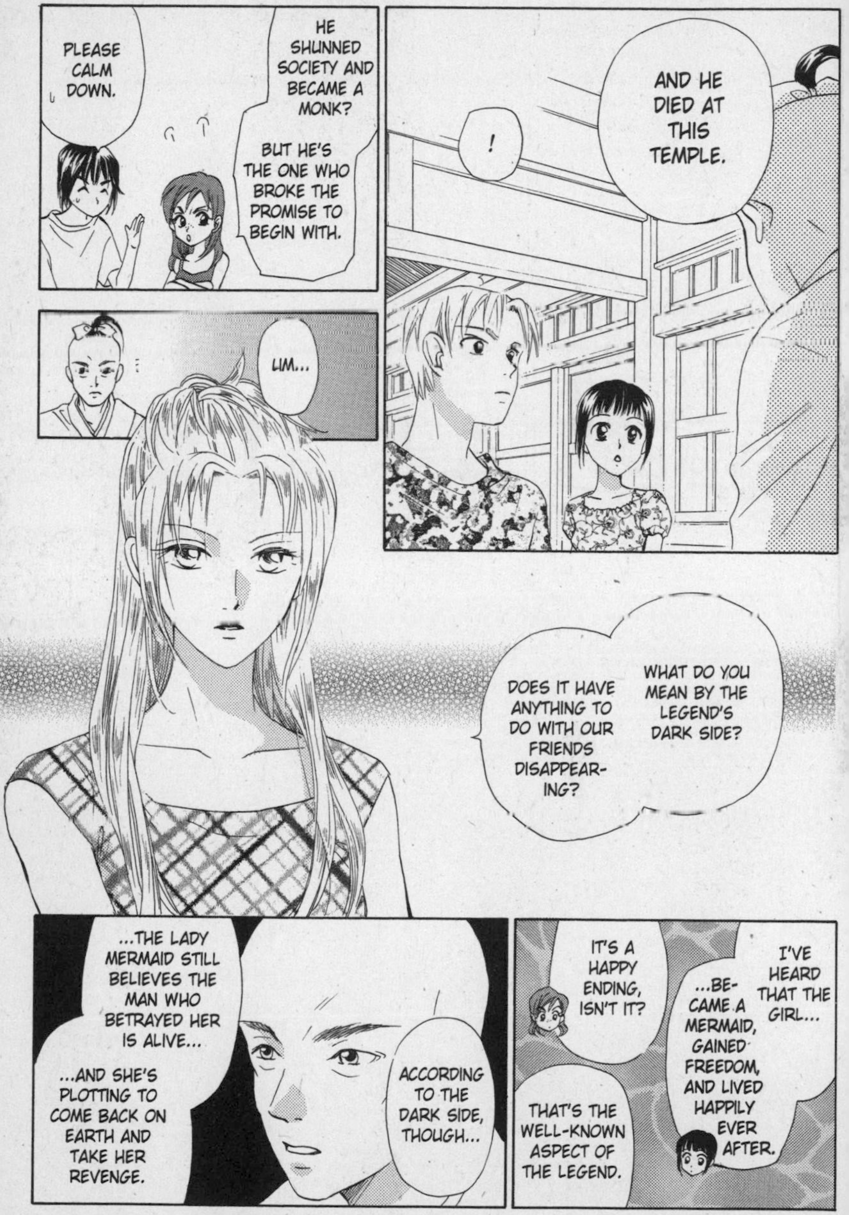
AND HE DIED AT THIS TEMPLE.
!
HE SHUNNED SOCIETY AND BECAME A MONK?
BUT HE'S THE ONE WHO BROKE THE PROMISE TO BEGIN WITH.
PLEASE CALM DOWN.
UM...
WHAT DO YOU MEAN BY THE LEGEND'S DARK SIDE?
DOES IT HAVE ANYTHING TO DO WITH OUR FRIENDS DISAPPEAR-ING?
I'VE HEARD THAT THE GIRL...
...BE-CAME A MERMAID, GAINED FREEDOM, AND LIVED HAPPILY EVER AFTER.
IT'S A HAPPY ENDING, ISN'T IT?
THAT'S THE WELL-KNOWN ASPECT OF THE LEGEND.
ACCORDING TO THE DARK SIDE, THOUGH...
...THE LADY MERMAID STILL BELIEVES THE MAN WHO BETRAYED HER IS ALIVE...
...AND SHE'S PLOTTING TO COME BACK ON EARTH AND TAKE HER REVENGE.

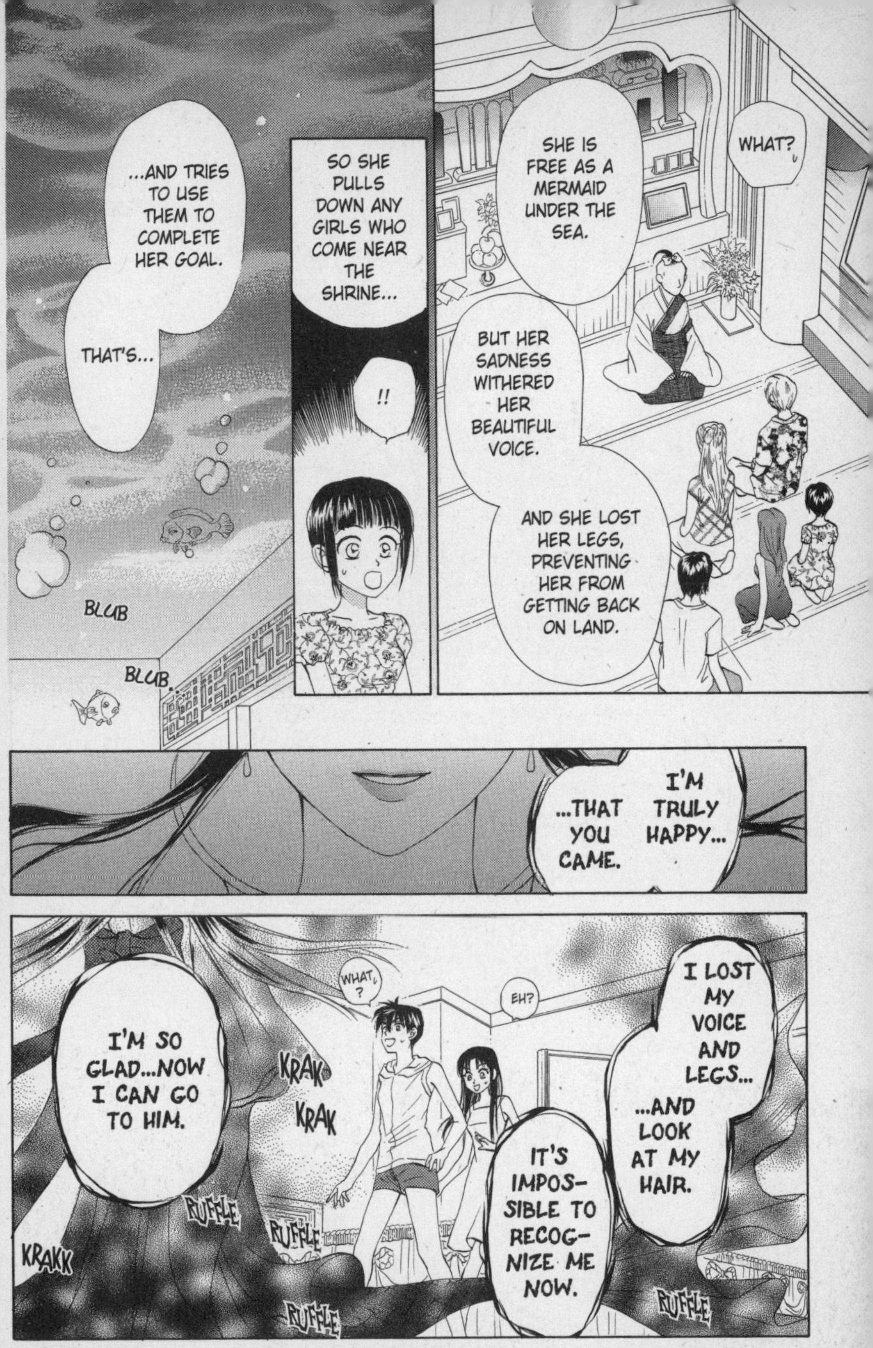
WHAT?
SHE IS FREE AS A MERMAID UNDER THE SEA.
BUT HER SADNESS WITHERED HER BEAUTIFUL VOICE.
AND SHE LOST HER LEGS, PREVENTING HER FROM GETTING BACK ON LAND.
SO SHE PULLS DOWN ANY GIRLS WHO COME NEAR THE SHRINE...
!!
...AND TRIES TO USE THEM TO COMPLETE HER GOAL.
THAT'S...
BLUB
BLUB
I'M TRULY HAPPY...
...THAT YOU CAME.
I LOST MY VOICE AND LEGS...
...AND LOOK AT MY HAIR.
IT'S IMPOSSIBLE TO RECOGNIZE ME NOW.
EH?
WHAT?
I'M SO GLAD...NOW I CAN GO TO HIM.
KRAK
KRAK
RUFFLE
RUFFLE
KRAKK
RUFFLE
RUFFLE

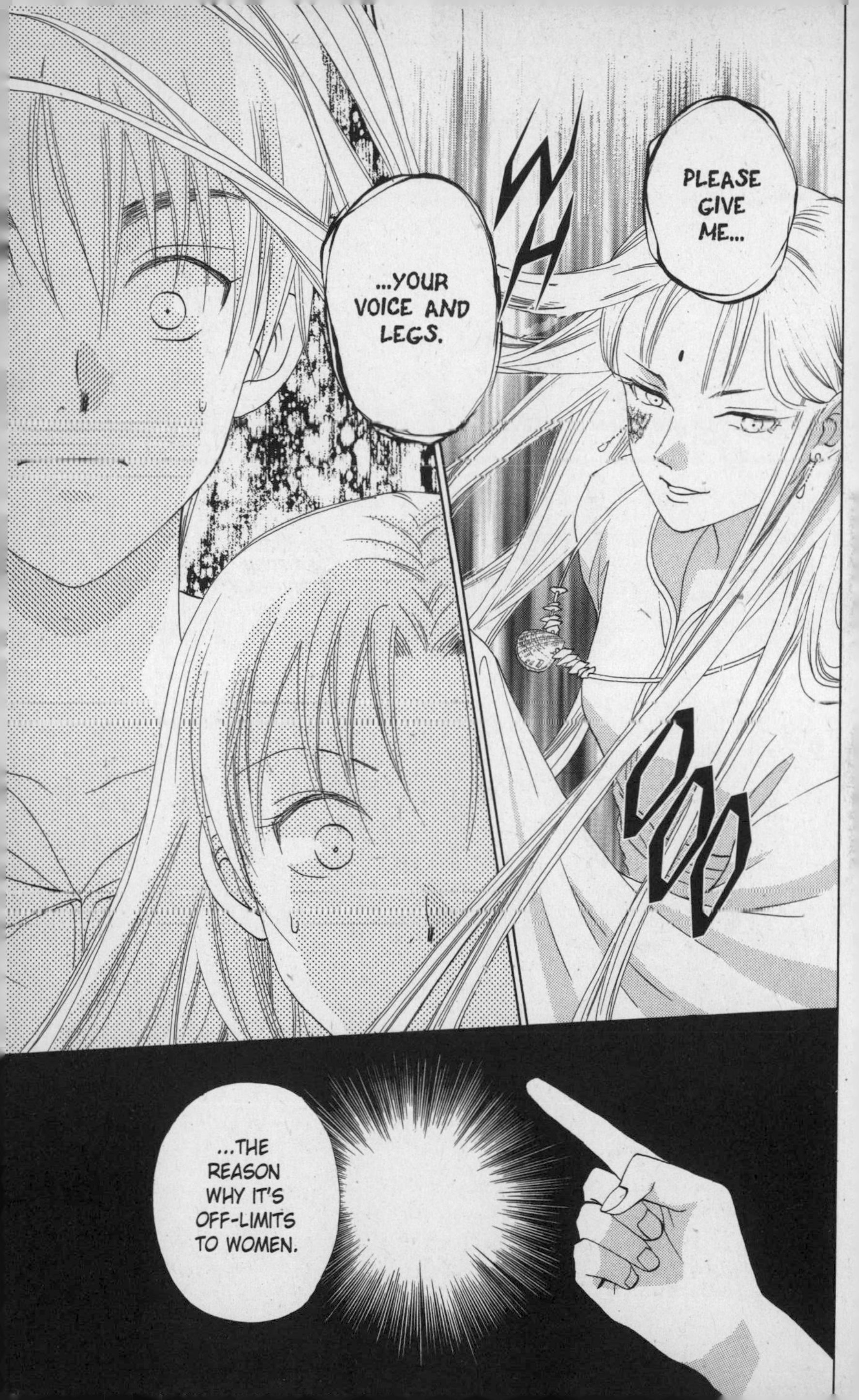
PLEASE GIVE ME...
...YOUR VOICE AND LEGS.
...THE REASON WHY IT'S OFF-LIMITS TO WOMEN.

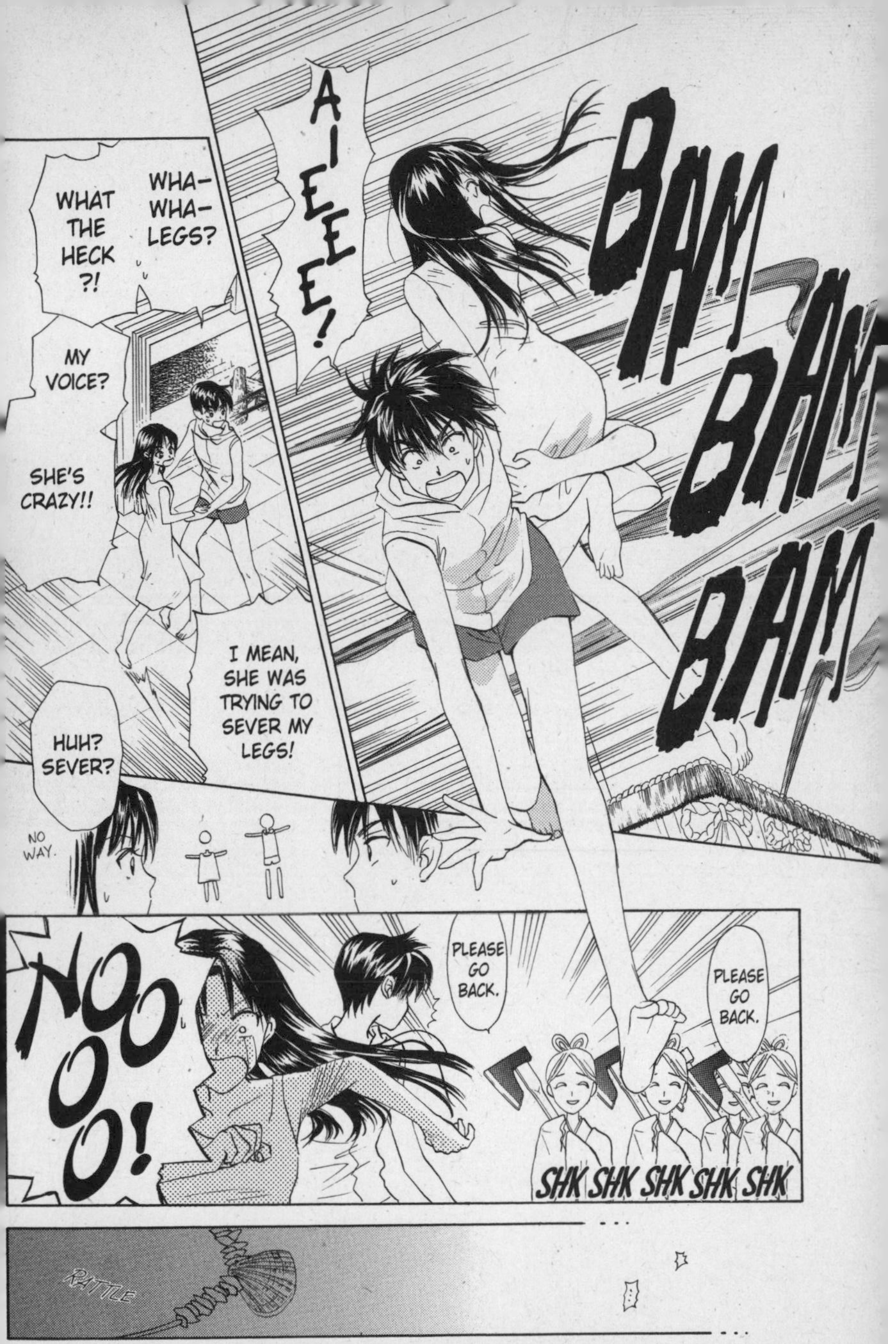
BAM BAM BAM BAM
AIEEE!
WHA-WHA-LEGS?
WHAT THE HECK ?!
MY VOICE?
SHE'S CRAZY!!
I MEAN, SHE WAS TRYING TO SEVER MY LEGS!
HUH? SEVER?
NO WAY.
PLEASE GO BACK.
PLEASE GO BACK.
NOOOOO!
SHK SHK SHK SHK SHK
RATTLE

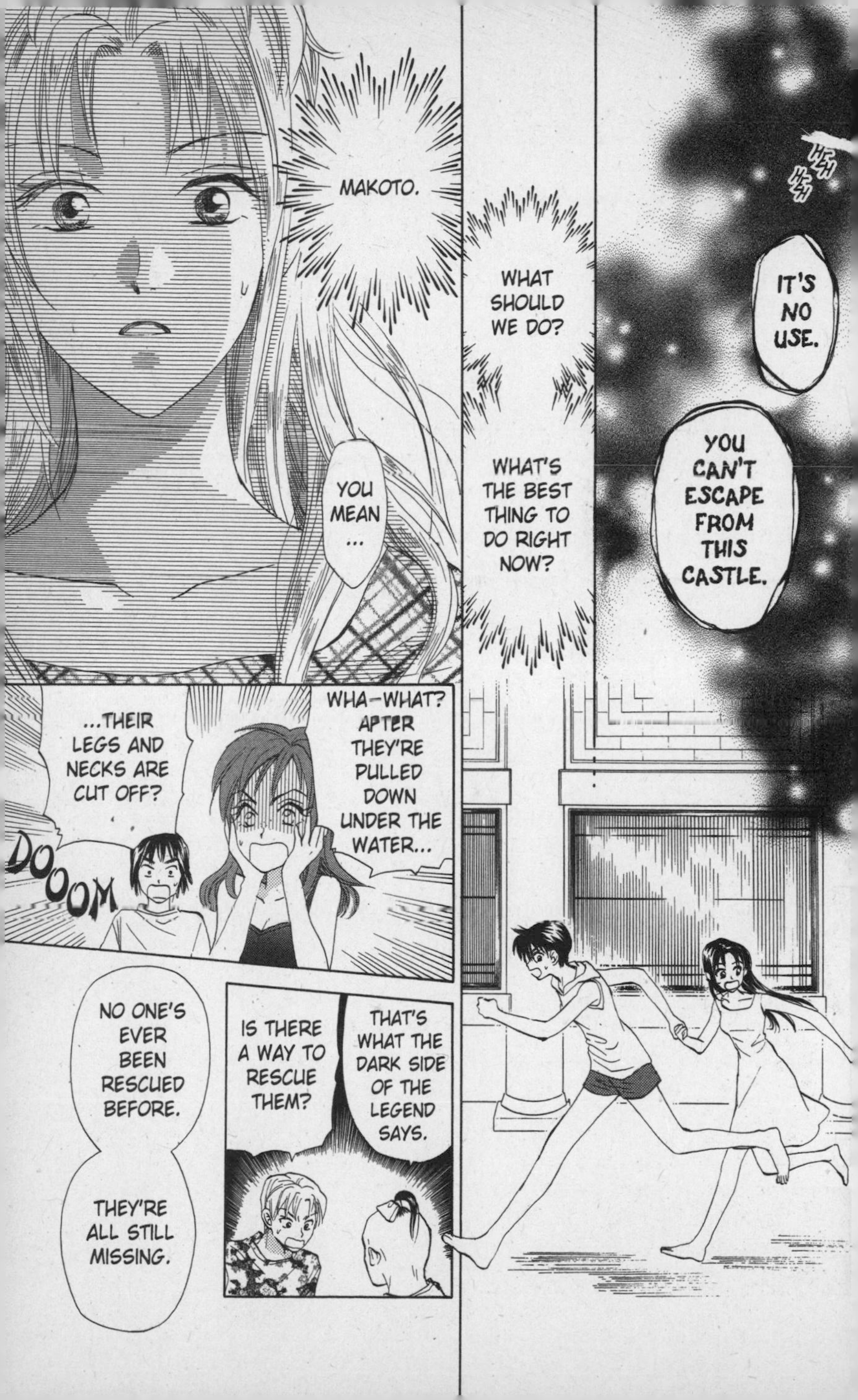
HEH HEH
IT'S NO USE.
YOU CAN'T ESCAPE FROM THIS CASTLE.
WHAT SHOULD WE DO?
WHAT'S THE BEST THING TO DO RIGHT NOW?
MAKOTO.
YOU MEAN ...
WHA-WHAT? AFTER THEY'RE PULLED DOWN UNDER THE WATER...
...THEIR LEGS AND NECKS ARE CUT OFF?
DOOOM
THAT'S WHAT THE DARK SIDE OF THE LEGEND SAYS.
IS THERE A WAY TO RESCUE THEM?
NO ONE'S EVER BEEN RESCUED BEFORE.
THEY'RE ALL STILL MISSING.

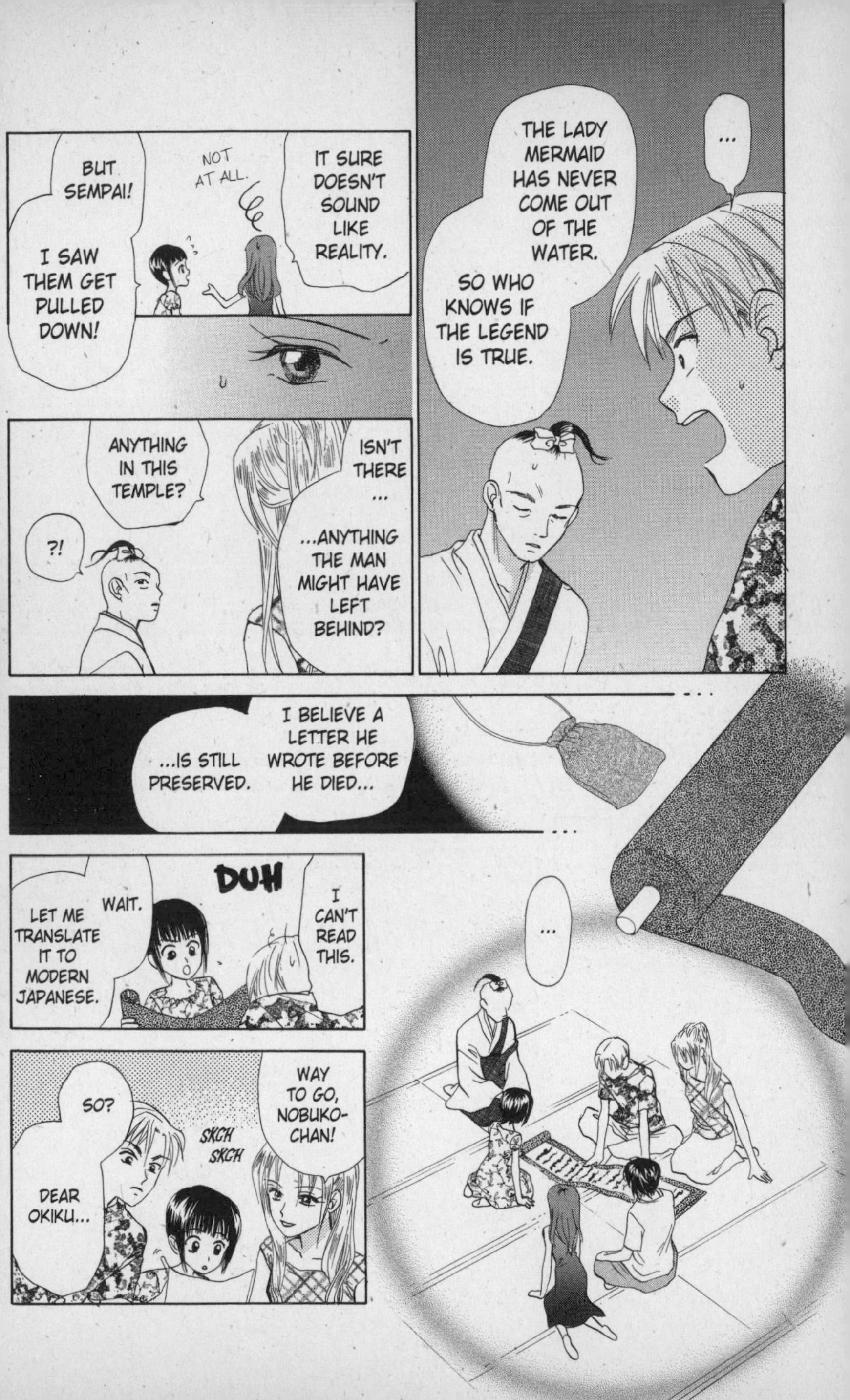
...
THE LADY MERMAID HAS NEVER COME OUT OF THE WATER.
SO WHO KNOWS IF THE LEGEND IS TRUE.
IT SURE DOESN'T SOUND LIKE REALITY.
NOT AT ALL.
BUT SEMPAI!
I SAW THEM GET PULLED DOWN!
ISN'T THERE ...
...ANYTHING THE MAN MIGHT HAVE LEFT BEHIND?
ANYTHING IN THIS TEMPLE?
?!
I BELIEVE A LETTER HE WROTE BEFORE HE DIED...
...IS STILL PRESERVED.
...
I CAN'T READ THIS.
DUH
WAIT.
LET ME TRANSLATE IT TO MODERN JAPANESE.
WAY TO GO, NOBUKO-CHAN!
SKCH SKCH
SO?
DEAR OKIKU...

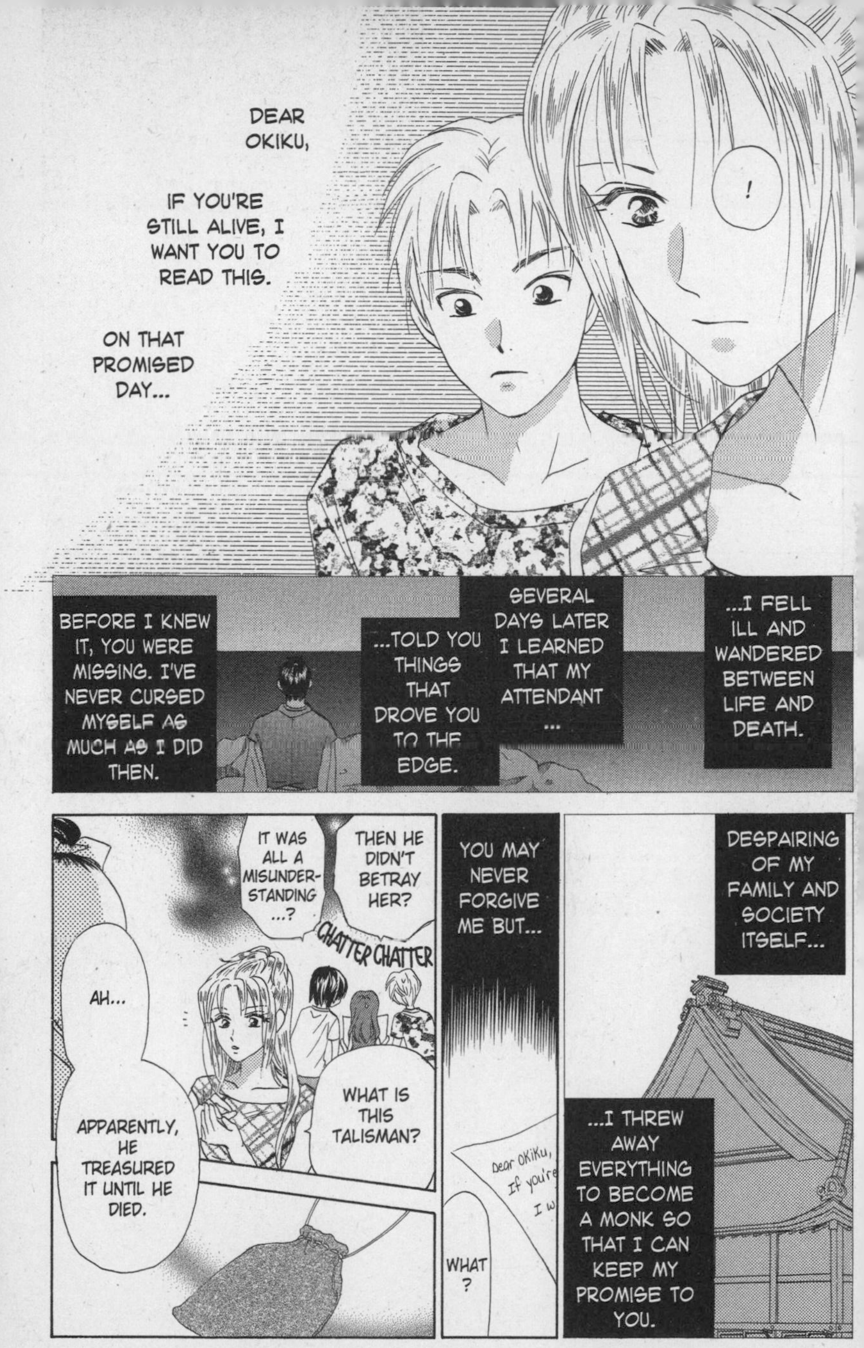
!
DEAR OKIKU,
IF YOU'RE STILL ALIVE, I WANT YOU TO READ THIS.
ON THAT PROMISED DAY...
...I FELL ILL AND WANDERED BETWEEN LIFE AND DEATH.
SEVERAL DAYS LATER I LEARNED THAT MY ATTENDANT ...
...TOLD YOU THINGS THAT DROVE YOU TO THE EDGE.
BEFORE I KNEW IT, YOU WERE MISSING. I'VE NEVER CURSED MYSELF AS MUCH AS I DID THEN.
DESPAIRING OF MY FAMILY AND SOCIETY ITSELF...
...I THREW AWAY EVERYTHING TO BECOME A MONK SO THAT I CAN KEEP MY PROMISE TO YOU.
YOU MAY NEVER FORGIVE ME BUT...
Dear OKiKu,
WHAT ?
THEN HE DIDN'T BETRAY HER?
IT WAS ALL A MISUNDER-STANDING ...?
CHATTER CHATTER
AH...
WHAT IS THIS TALISMAN?
APPARENTLY, HE TREASURED IT UNTIL HE DIED.

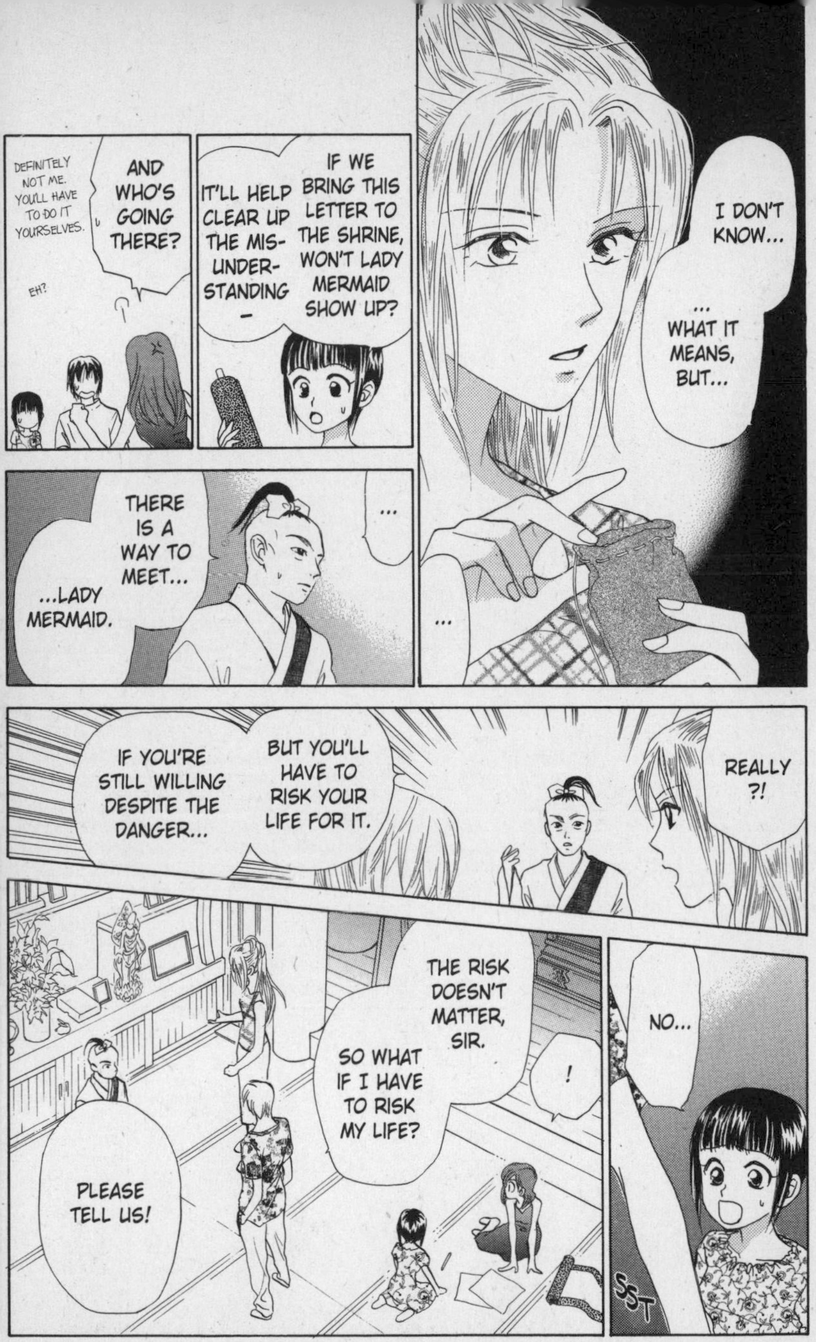
I DON'T KNOW...
... WHAT IT MEANS, BUT...
...
IF WE BRING THIS LETTER TO THE SHRINE, WON'T LADY MERMAID SHOW UP?
IT'LL HELP CLEAR UP THE MIS-UNDER-STANDING —
AND WHO'S GOING THERE?
DEFINITELY NOT ME. YOU'LL HAVE TO DO IT YOURSELVES.
EH?
...
THERE IS A WAY TO MEET...
...LADY MERMAID.
REALLY ?!
BUT YOU'LL HAVE TO RISK YOUR LIFE FOR IT.
IF YOU'RE STILL WILLING DESPITE THE DANGER...
NO...
SST
!
THE RISK DOESN'T MATTER, SIR.
SO WHAT IF I HAVE TO RISK MY LIFE?
PLEASE TELL US!

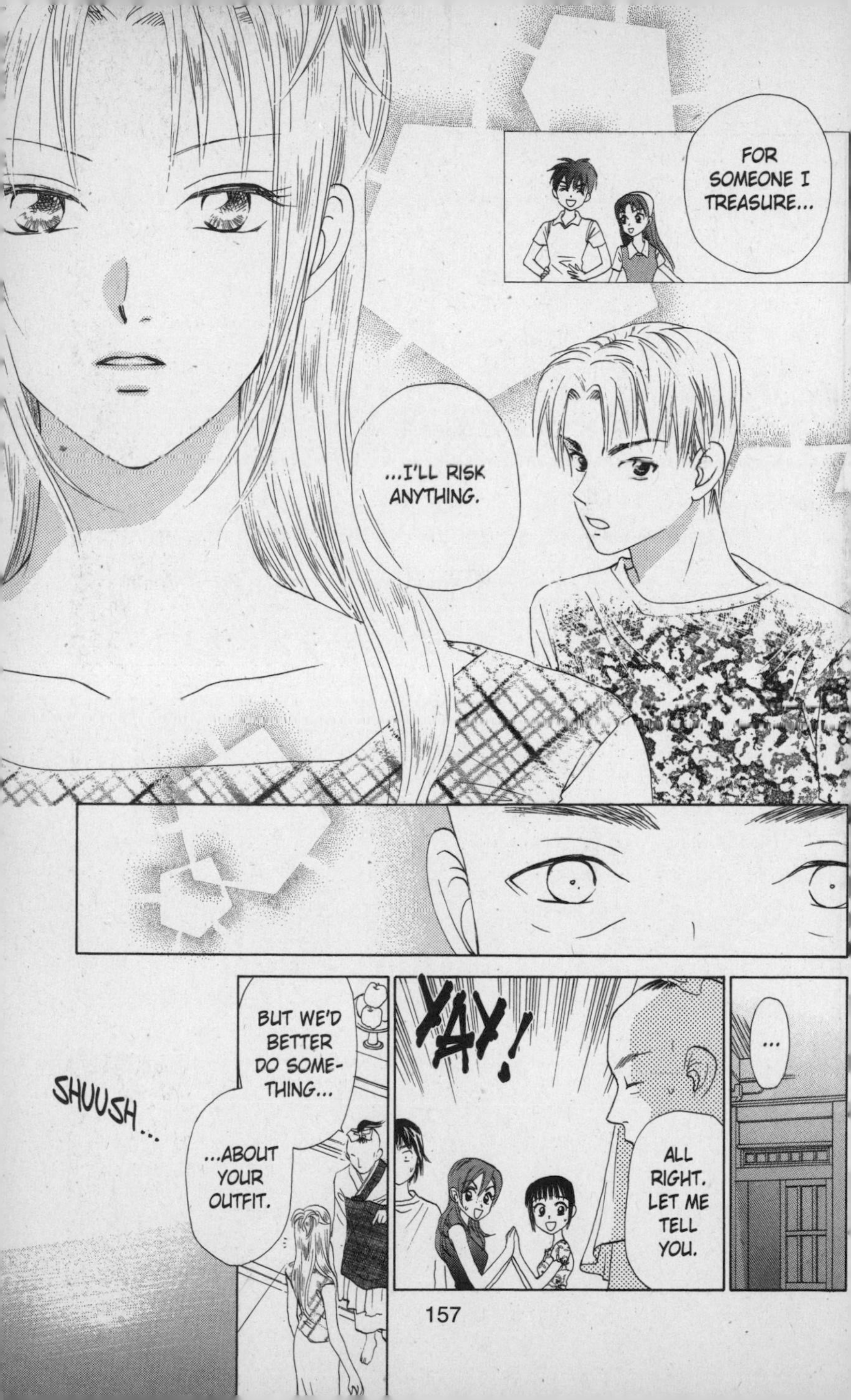
FOR SOMEONE I TREASURE...
...I'LL RISK ANYTHING.
...
ALL RIGHT. LET ME TELL YOU.
YAY!
BUT WE'D BETTER DO SOME-THING...
...ABOUT YOUR OUTFIT.
SHUUSH...

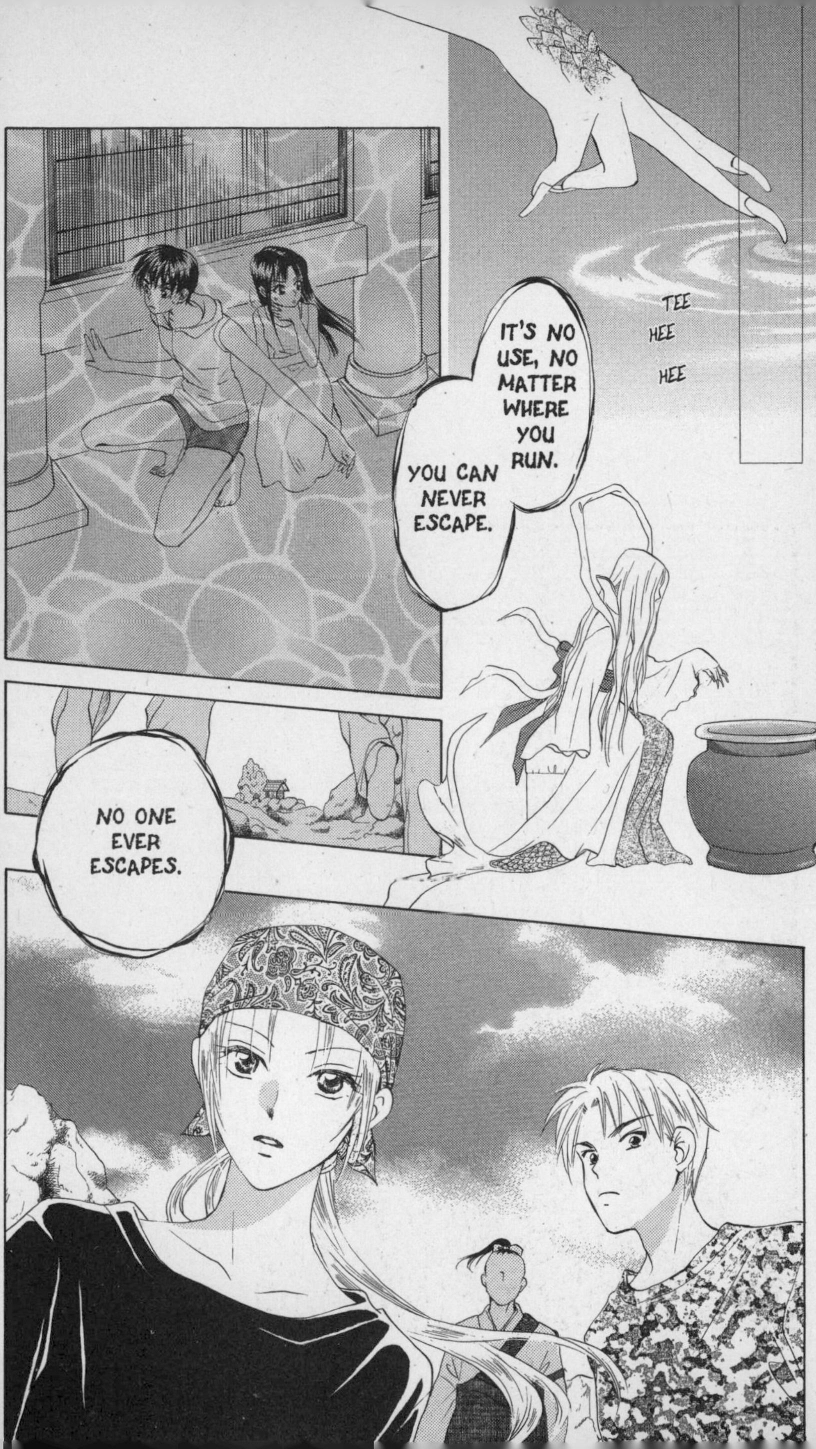
TEE HEE HEE
IT'S NO USE, NO MATTER WHERE YOU RUN.
YOU CAN NEVER ESCAPE.
NO ONE EVER ESCAPES.

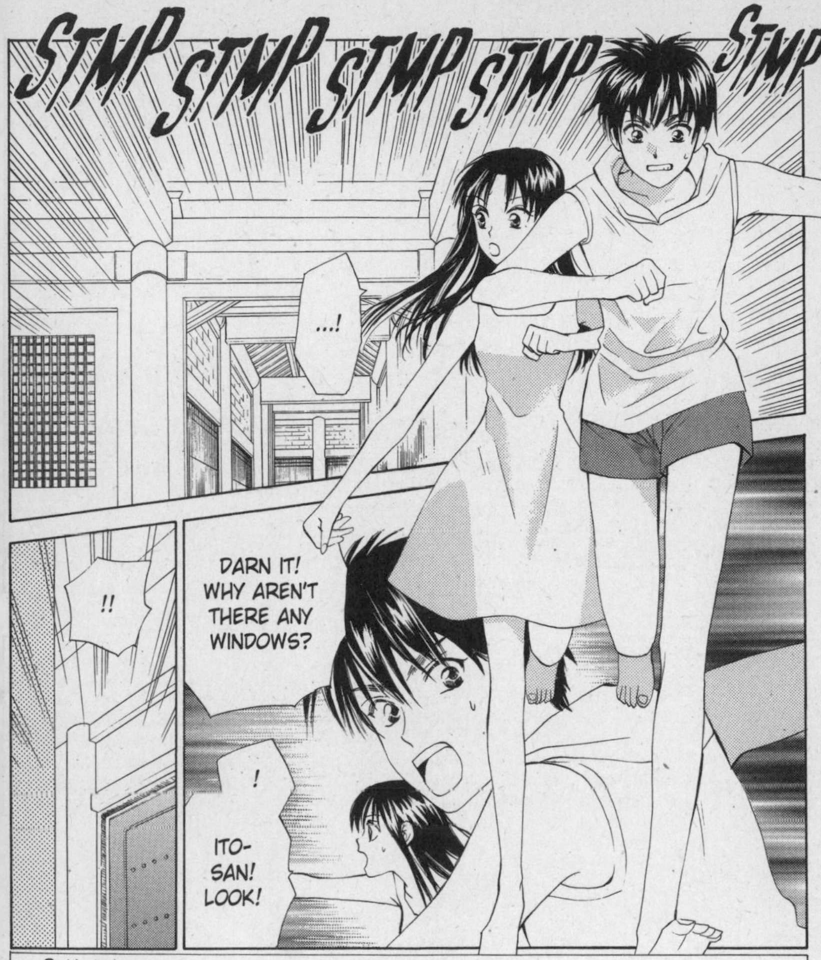
STMP STMP STMP STMP STMP
...!
DARN IT! WHY AREN'T THERE ANY WINDOWS?
!
ITO-SAN! LOOK!
!!

-Behind the Scenes Story- ⑥

Poor Yoshirô. But he'll get another chance someday!!
To tell the truth, I enjoyed drawing a story about Ito and Yoshirô. They're both simple-minded fools.
Their gender difference is nothing. You know what Ito is like to begin with. Yoshirô treats Ito like a man, and they're like guy friends to each other anyway.

Besides, Yoshirô is attracted to girls like Misaki. Makoto knows that very well, and that's why no matter how close Ito and Yoshirô become, Makoto is not at all concerned.

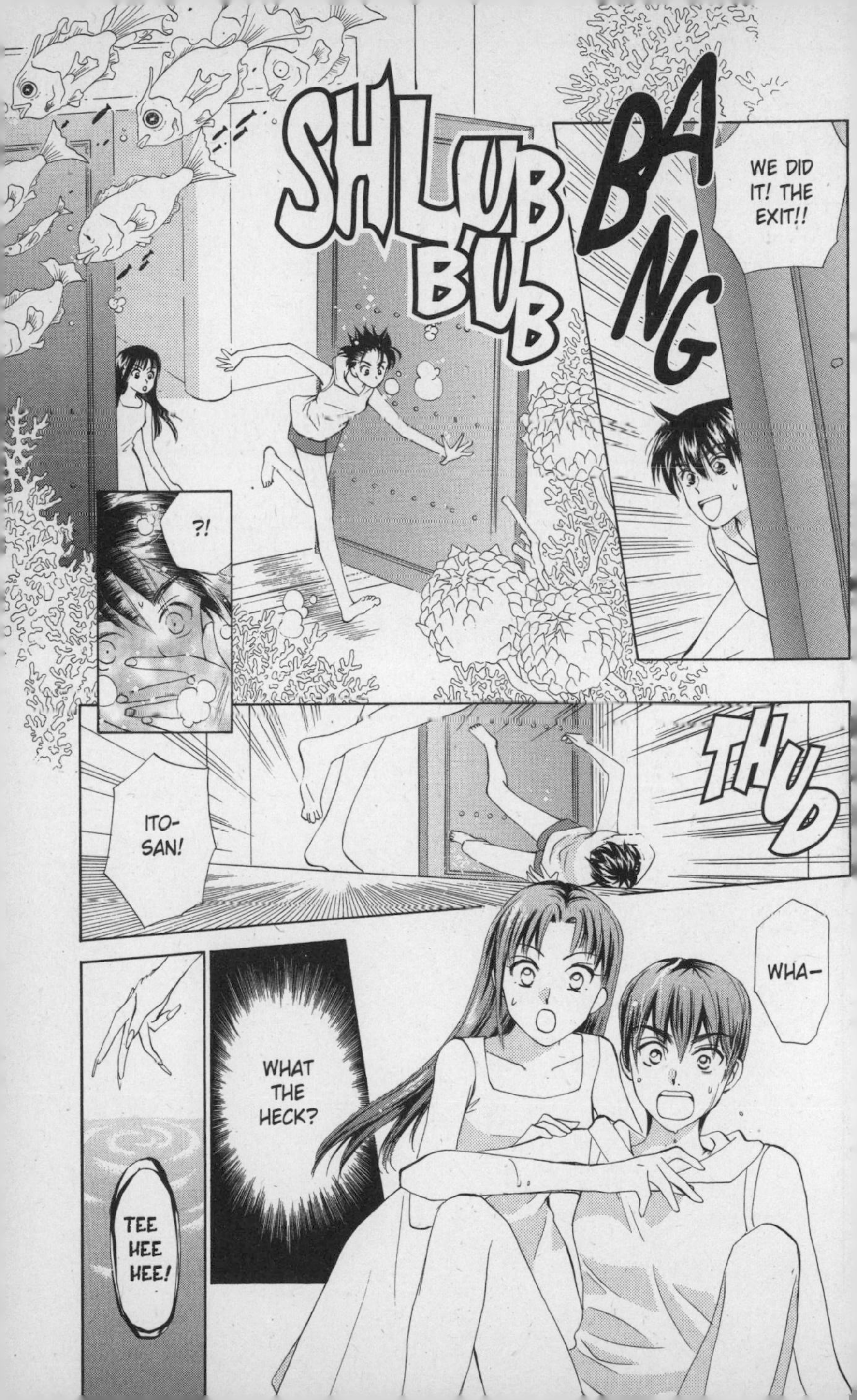
BANG
WE DID IT! THE EXIT!!
SHLUB BUB
?!
THUD
ITO-SAN!
WHA-
WHAT THE HECK?
TEE HEE HEE!

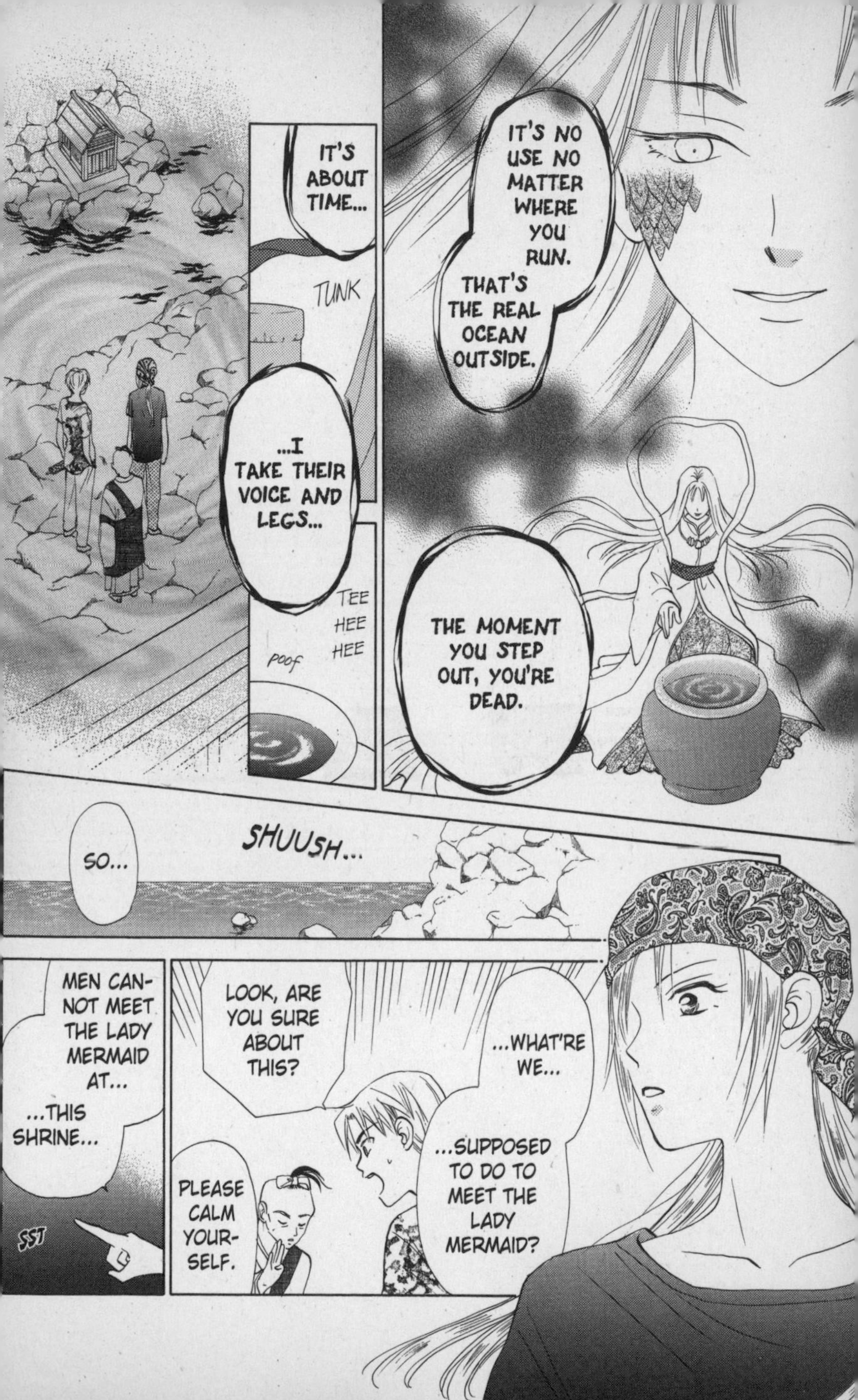
IT'S NO USE NO MATTER WHERE YOU RUN.
THAT'S THE REAL OCEAN OUTSIDE.
THE MOMENT YOU STEP OUT, YOU'RE DEAD.
IT'S ABOUT TIME...
TUNK
...I TAKE THEIR VOICE AND LEGS...
TEE HEE HEE
poof
SHUUSH...
SO...
...WHAT'RE WE...
...SUPPOSED TO DO TO MEET THE LADY MERMAID?
LOOK, ARE YOU SURE ABOUT THIS?
PLEASE CALM YOURSELF.
MEN CAN-NOT MEET THE LADY MERMAID AT...
...THIS SHRINE...
SST

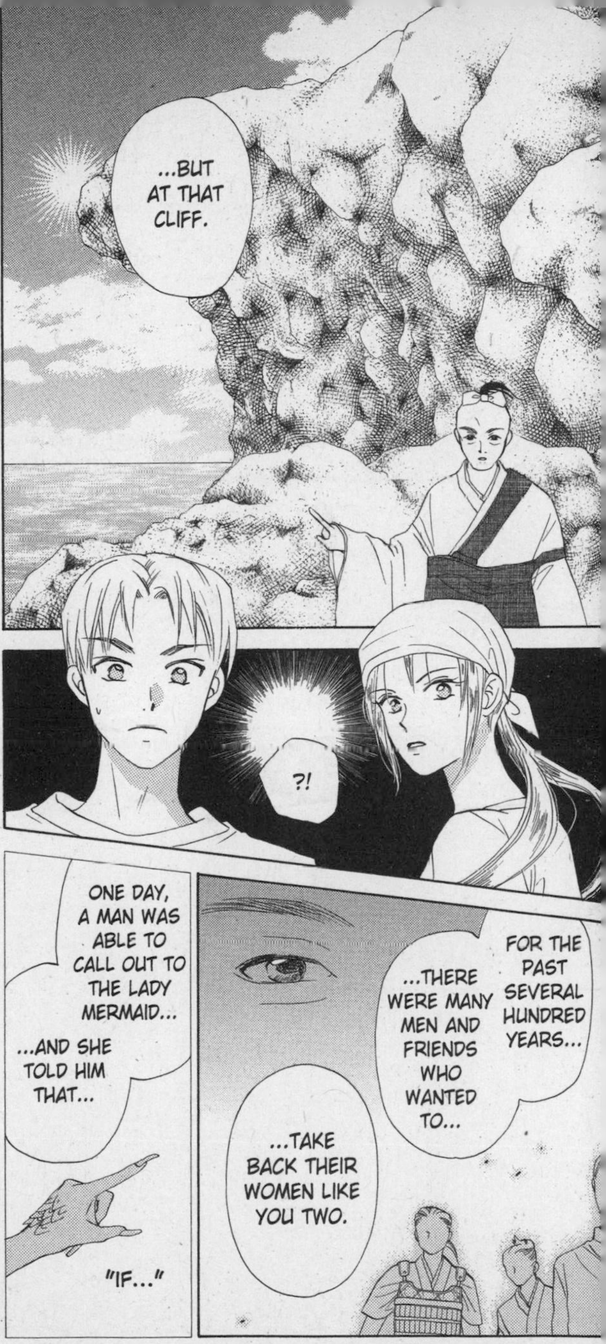
...BUT AT THAT CLIFF.
?!
FOR THE PAST SEVERAL HUNDRED YEARS...
...THERE WERE MANY MEN AND FRIENDS WHO WANTED TO...
...TAKE BACK THEIR WOMEN LIKE YOU TWO.
ONE DAY, A MAN WAS ABLE TO CALL OUT TO THE LADY MERMAID...
...AND SHE TOLD HIM THAT...
"IF..."

Q+A CORNER

Oh dear, there aren't many vertical spaces in this volume. Anyhow, let me answer one of the most often-asked questions, which is:

- "Are you friends with Banri Hidaka?"

Ⓔ Yes, absolutely. ♥ But since we live far away from each other, we can only get together once or twice a year. (Banri-san lives in Aichi Prefecture, while I live in Kanagawa Prefecture.) That's why we usually have a long phone conversation.

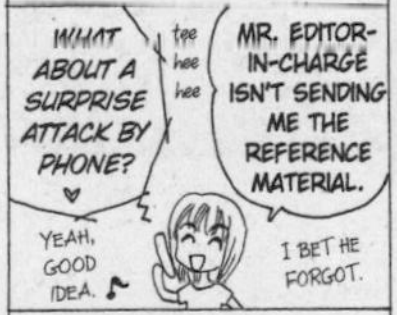
MR. EDITOR-IN-CHARGE ISN'T SENDING ME THE REFERENCE MATERIAL.
tee hee hee
WHAT ABOUT A SURPRISE ATTACK BY PHONE? ♥
YEAH, GOOD IDEA. ♪
I BET HE FORGOT.

Don't know what we're talking about. Sorry about that, Andy.

She is—how should I say it—exactly like her work. Sweet and bright and funny. (Laugh) And super pretty!! For a couple years after I first made my debut, she faxed me detailed information about drawing materials and all. It made me so happy.

Let's have a long phone conversation again, Banri-san ♪

Anyhow, I'll see you again in volume 9.

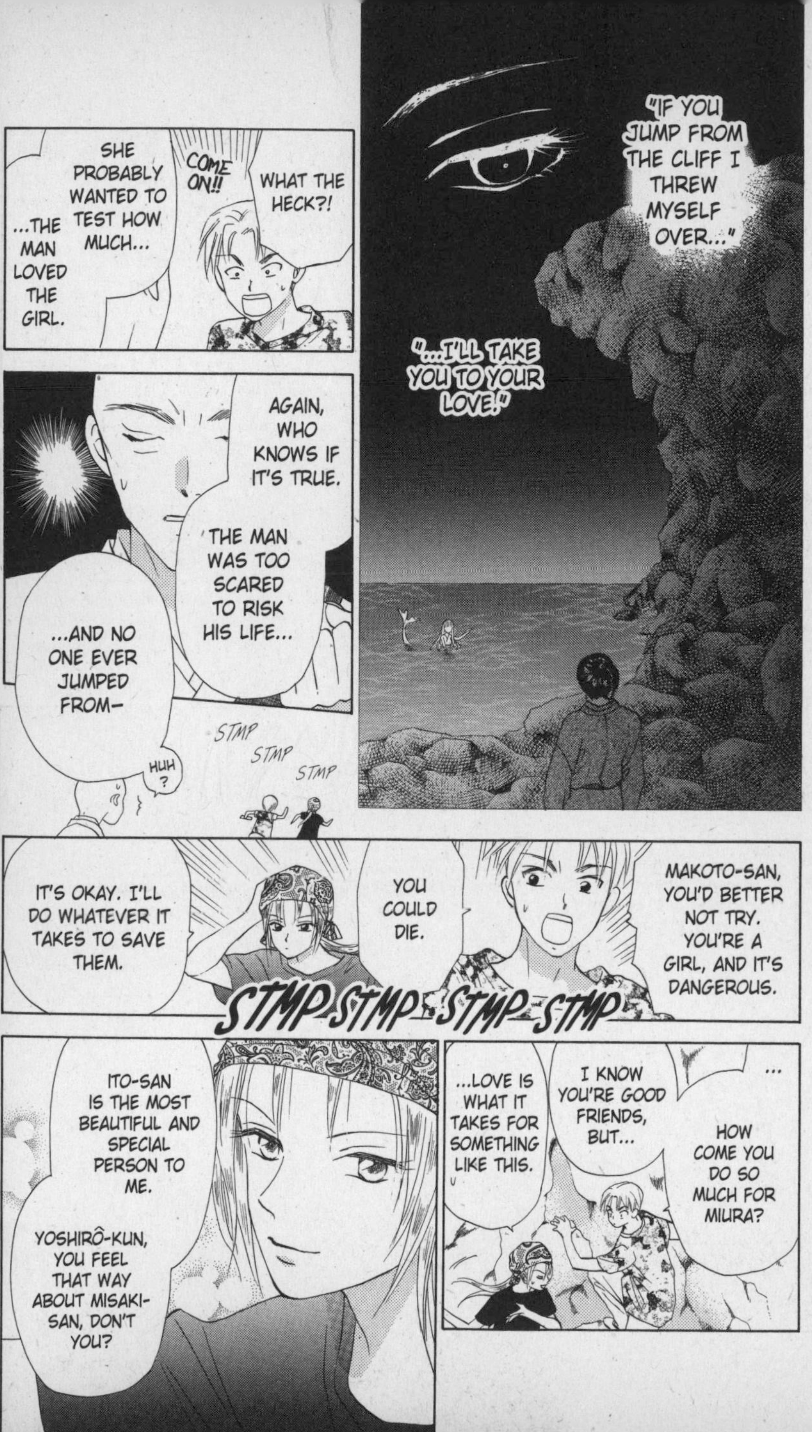
"IF YOU JUMP FROM THE CLIFF I THREW MYSELF OVER..."
"...I'LL TAKE YOU TO YOUR LOVE."
WHAT THE HECK?!
COME ON!!
SHE PROBABLY WANTED TO TEST HOW MUCH...
...THE MAN LOVED THE GIRL.
AGAIN, WHO KNOWS IF IT'S TRUE.
THE MAN WAS TOO SCARED TO RISK HIS LIFE...
...AND NO ONE EVER JUMPED FROM—
STMP STMP STMP
HUH?
MAKOTO-SAN, YOU'D BETTER NOT TRY. YOU'RE A GIRL, AND IT'S DANGEROUS.
YOU COULD DIE.
IT'S OKAY. I'LL DO WHATEVER IT TAKES TO SAVE THEM.
STMP STMP STMP STMP
...
HOW COME YOU DO SO MUCH FOR MIURA?
I KNOW YOU'RE GOOD FRIENDS, BUT...
...LOVE IS WHAT IT TAKES FOR SOMETHING LIKE THIS.
ITO-SAN IS THE MOST BEAUTIFUL AND SPECIAL PERSON TO ME.
YOSHIRÔ-KUN, YOU FEEL THAT WAY ABOUT MISAKI-SAN, DON'T YOU?

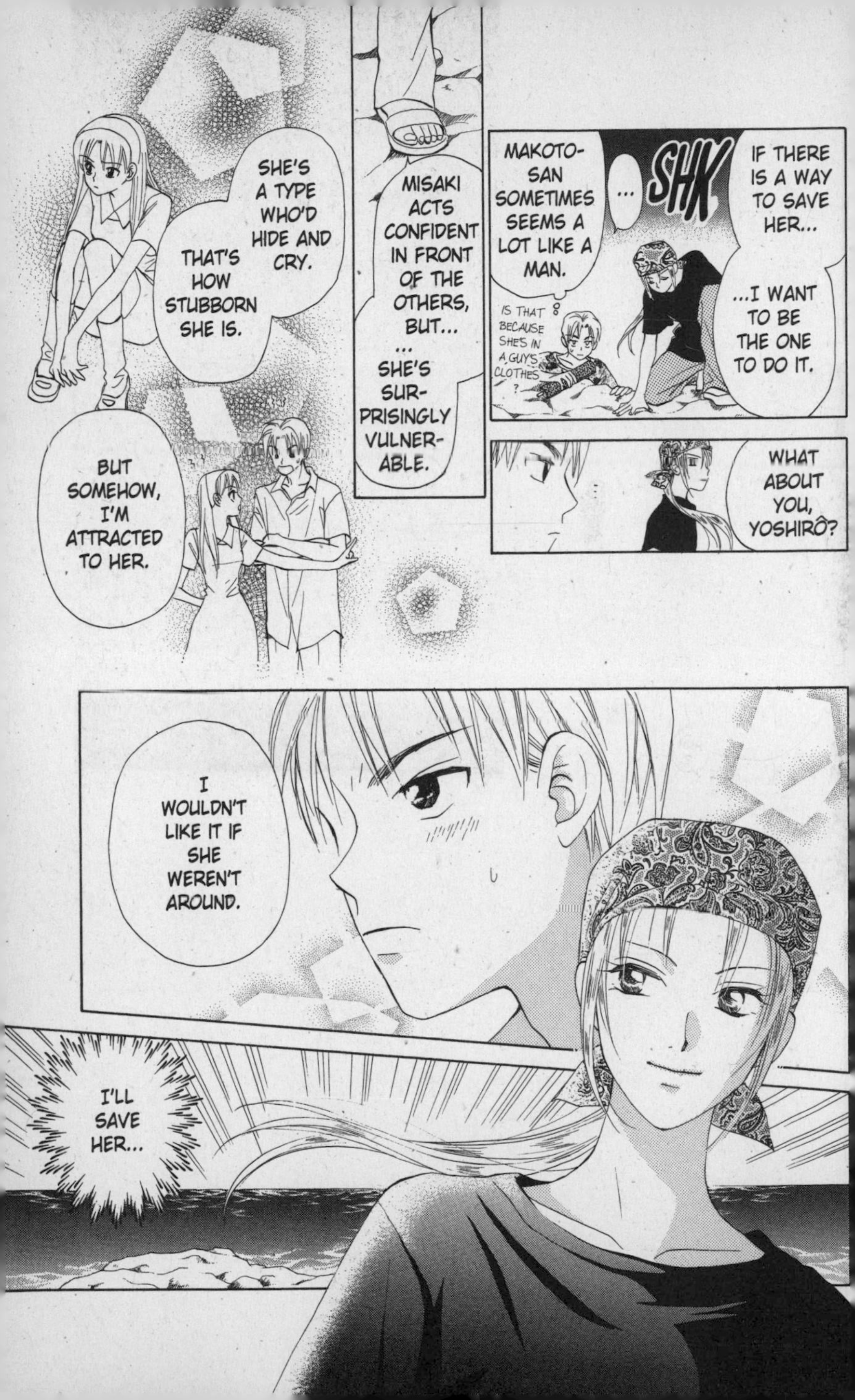
IF THERE IS A WAY TO SAVE HER...
SHK
...
MAKOTO-SAN SOMETIMES SEEMS A LOT LIKE A MAN.
...I WANT TO BE THE ONE TO DO IT.
IS THAT BECAUSE SHE'S IN A GUY'S CLOTHES?
WHAT ABOUT YOU, YOSHIRÔ?
MISAKI ACTS CONFIDENT IN FRONT OF THE OTHERS, BUT... ... SHE'S SURPRISINGLY VULNERABLE.
SHE'S A TYPE WHO'D HIDE AND CRY.
THAT'S HOW STUBBORN SHE IS.
BUT SOMEHOW, I'M ATTRACTED TO HER.
I WOULDN'T LIKE IT IF SHE WEREN'T AROUND.
I'LL SAVE HER...

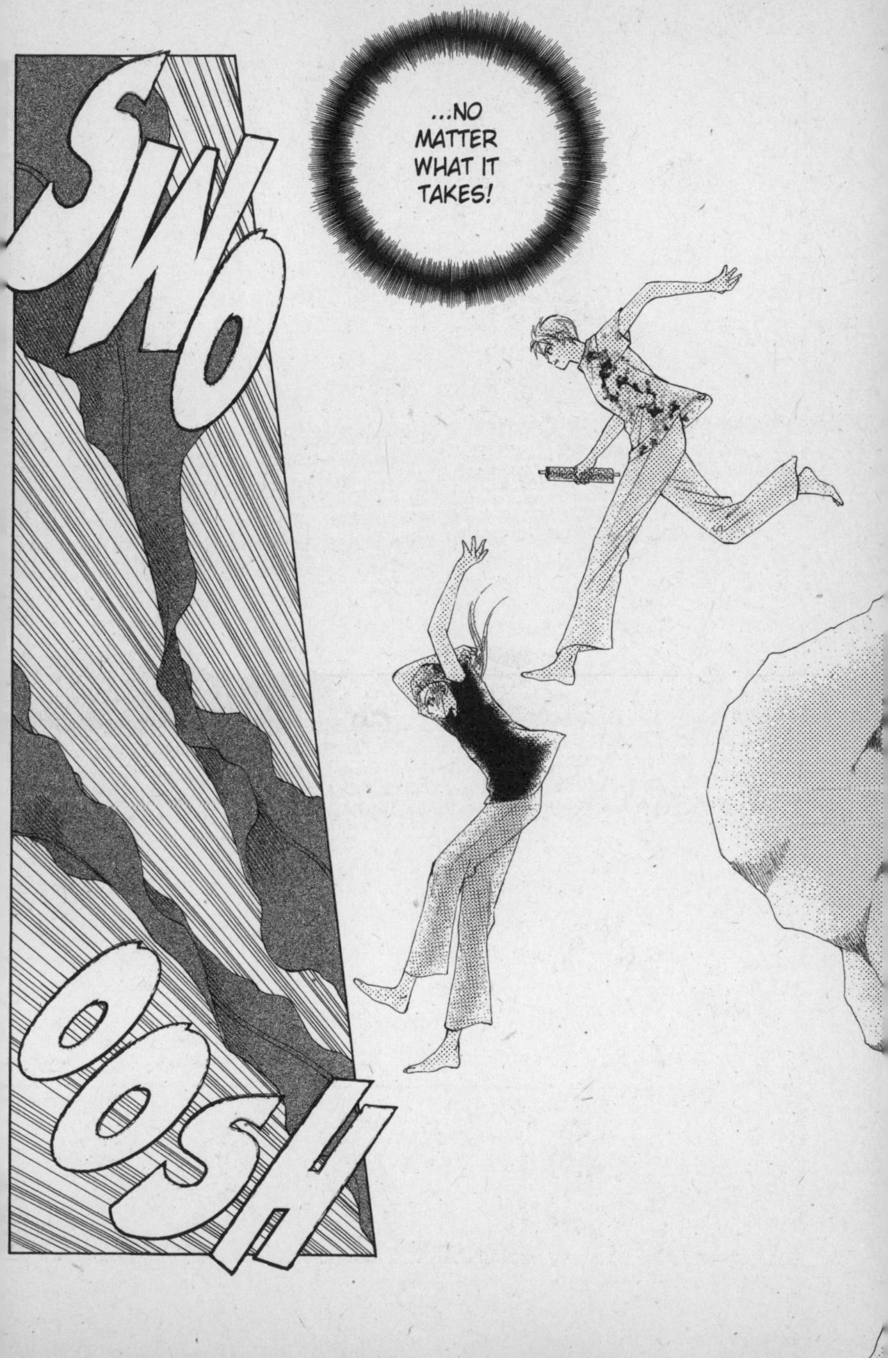
...NO MATTER WHAT IT TAKES!
SWOOOSH

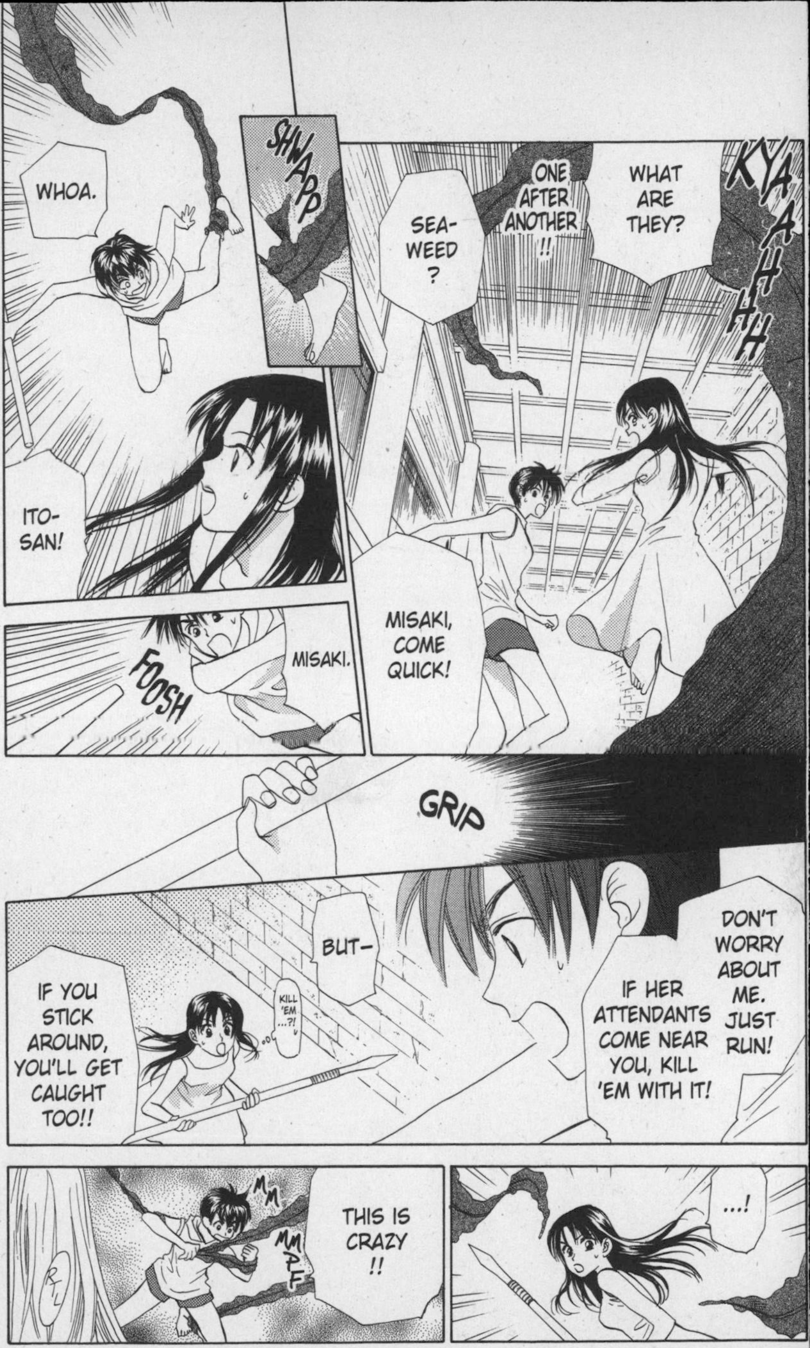
KYAAHHHH
WHAT ARE THEY?
ONE AFTER ANOTHER !!
SEA-WEED ?
MISAKI, COME QUICK!
WHOA.
SHWAPP
ITO-SAN!
MISAKI.
FOOSH
GRIP
DON'T WORRY ABOUT ME. JUST RUN!
IF HER ATTENDANTS COME NEAR YOU, KILL 'EM WITH IT!
BUT–
KILL 'EM ...?!
IF YOU STICK AROUND, YOU'LL GET CAUGHT TOO!!
...!
THIS IS CRAZY !!
MM
MMPF

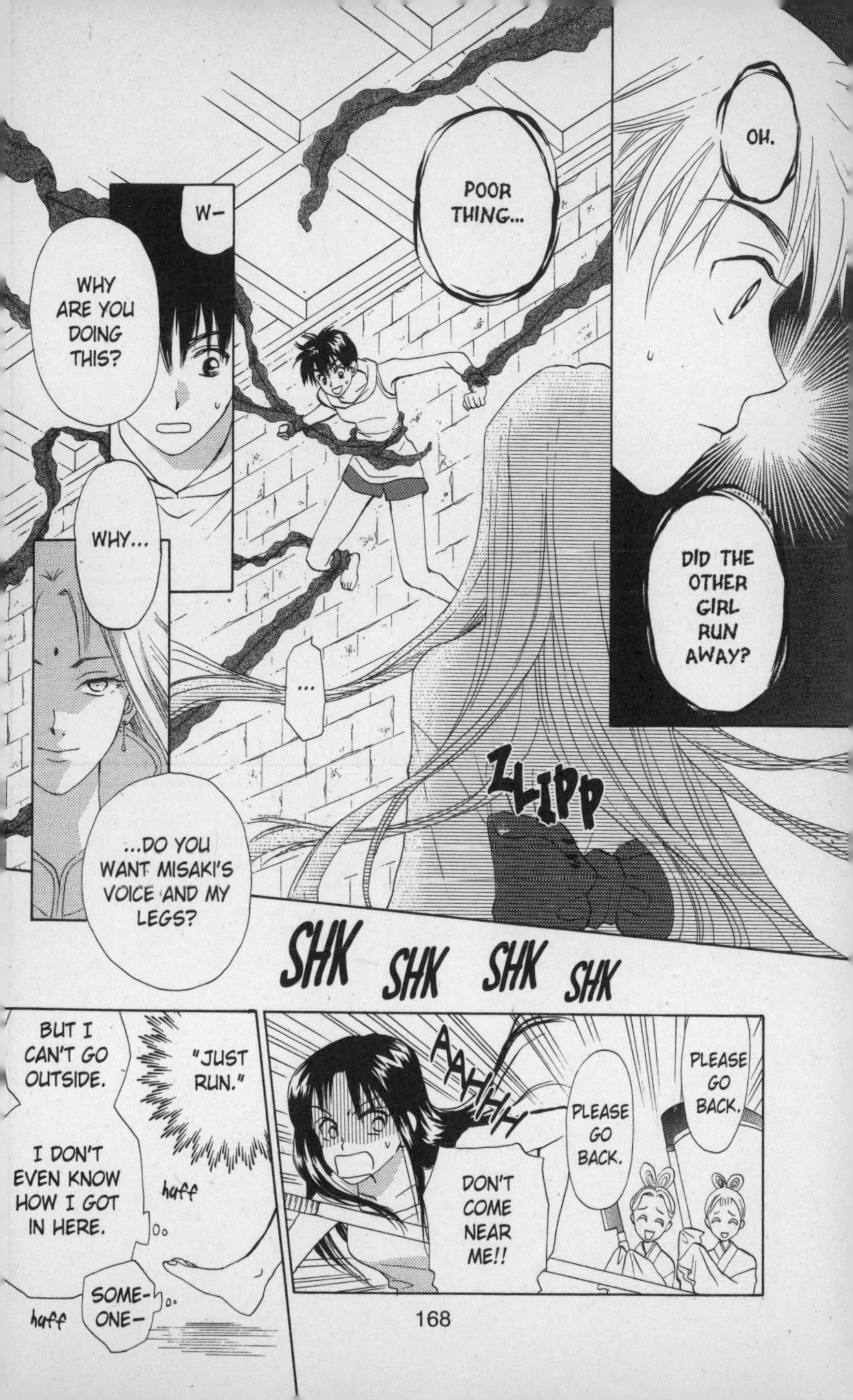
OH.
DID THE OTHER GIRL RUN AWAY?
POOR THING...
W-
WHY ARE YOU DOING THIS?
WHY...
...
...DO YOU WANT MISAKI'S VOICE AND MY LEGS?
ZLIPP
SHK SHK SHK SHK
PLEASE GO BACK.
PLEASE GO BACK.
AAHHHH
DON'T COME NEAR ME!!
"JUST RUN."
BUT I CAN'T GO OUTSIDE.
I DON'T EVEN KNOW HOW I GOT IN HERE.
huff
SOME-ONE-
huff

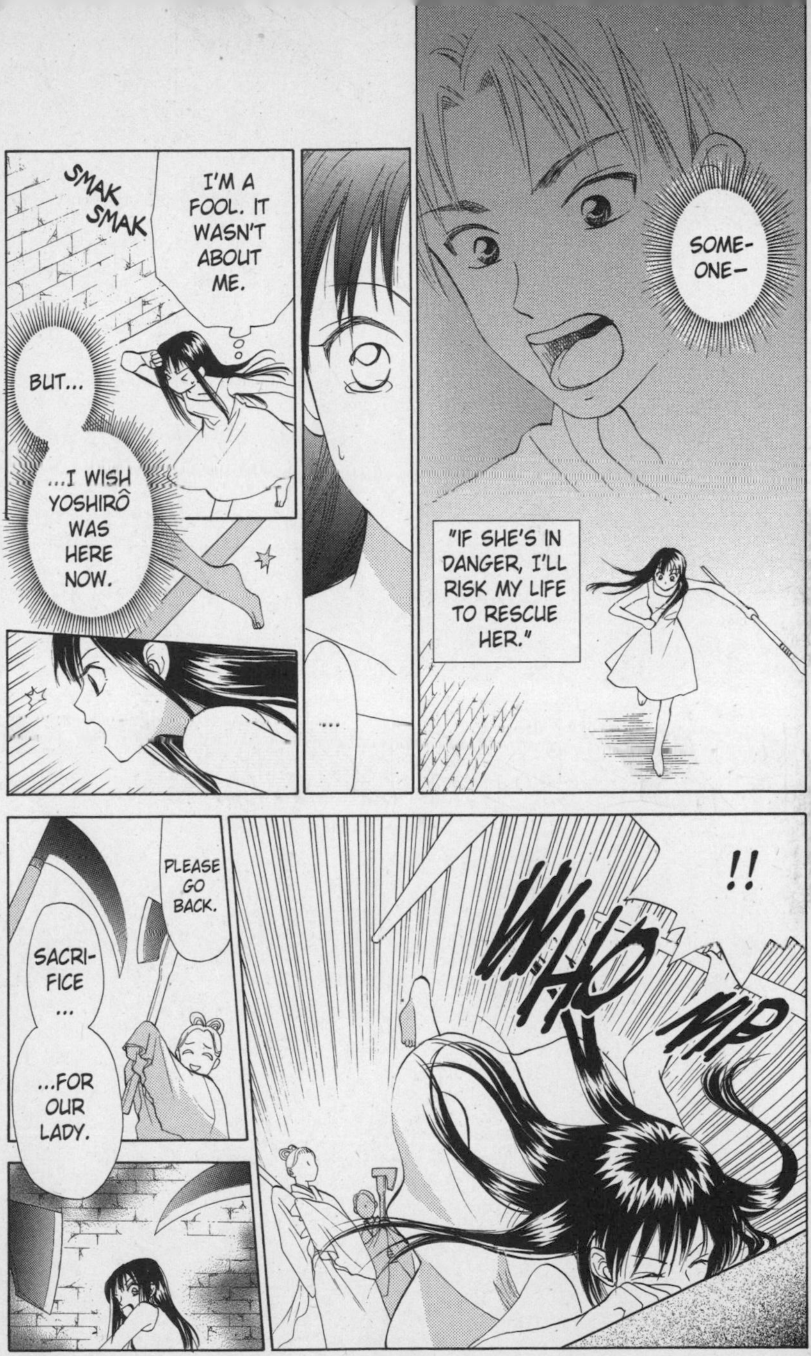
SOME-ONE-
"IF SHE'S IN DANGER, I'LL RISK MY LIFE TO RESCUE HER."
....
I'M A FOOL. IT WASN'T ABOUT ME.
SMAK SMAK
BUT...
...I WISH YOSHIRÔ WAS HERE NOW.
!!
WHOMP
PLEASE GO BACK.
SACRI-FICE...
...FOR OUR LADY.

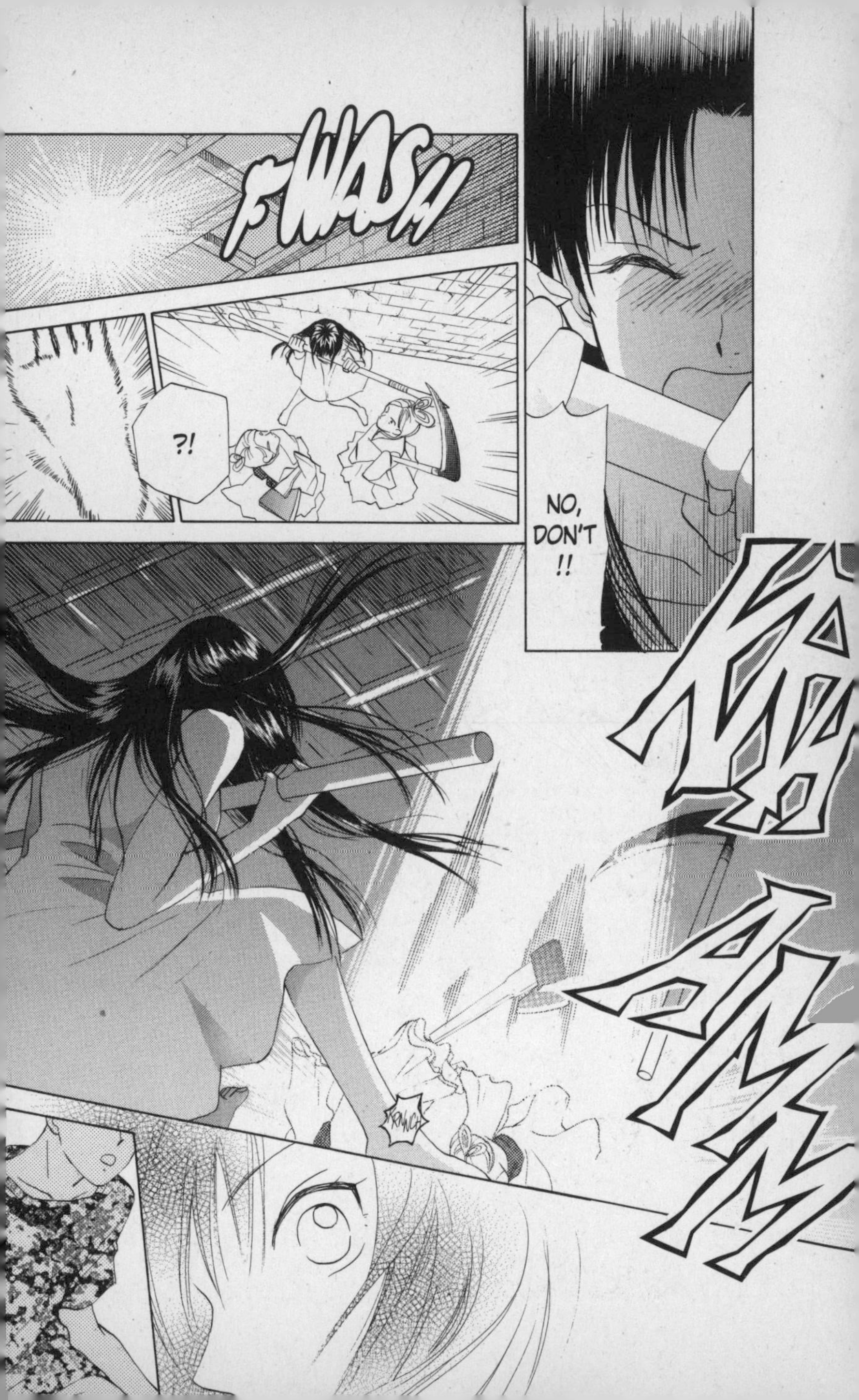
NO, DON'T !!
FWASH
?!

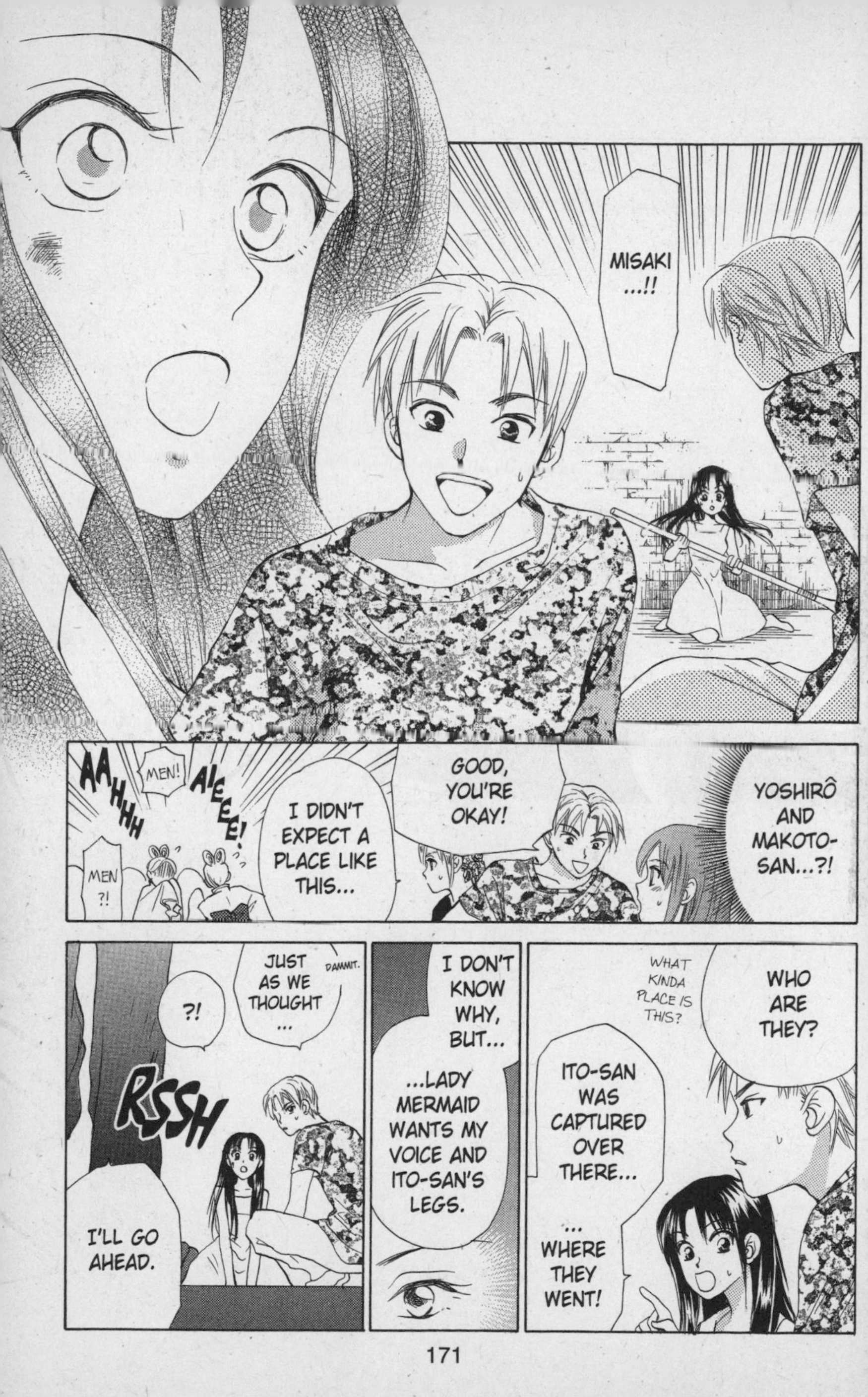
MISAKI ...!!
YOSHIRÔ AND MAKOTO-SAN...?!
GOOD, YOU'RE OKAY!
I DIDN'T EXPECT A PLACE LIKE THIS...
AIEEE!
MEN!
AAHHHH
MEN ?!
WHO ARE THEY?
WHAT KINDA PLACE IS THIS?
ITO-SAN WAS CAPTURED OVER THERE...
... WHERE THEY WENT!
I DON'T KNOW WHY, BUT...
...LADY MERMAID WANTS MY VOICE AND ITO-SAN'S LEGS.
JUST AS WE THOUGHT ...
DAMMIT.
?!
RSSH
I'LL GO AHEAD.

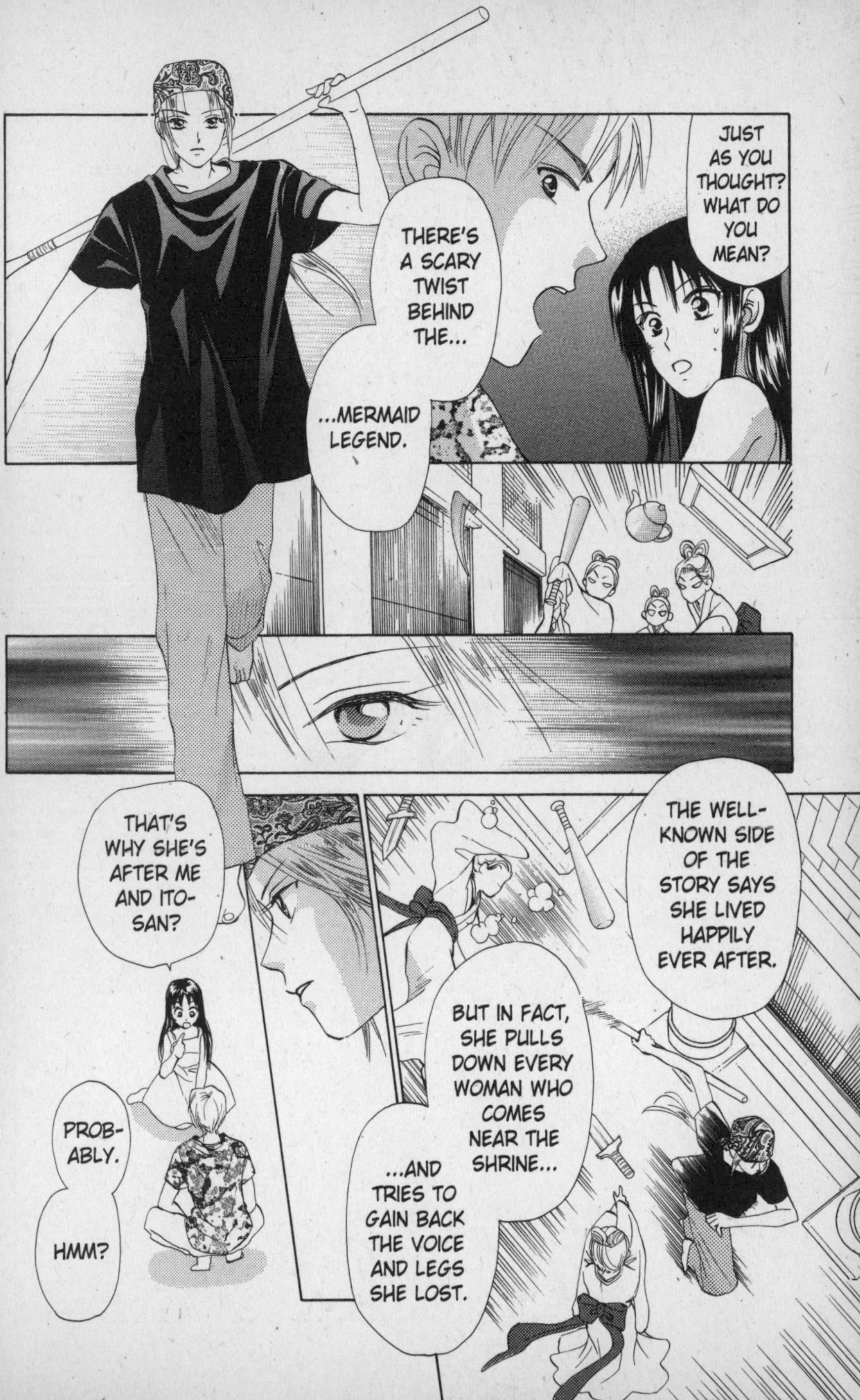
JUST AS YOU THOUGHT? WHAT DO YOU MEAN?
THERE'S A SCARY TWIST BEHIND THE...
...MERMAID LEGEND.
THE WELL-KNOWN SIDE OF THE STORY SAYS SHE LIVED HAPPILY EVER AFTER.
BUT IN FACT, SHE PULLS DOWN EVERY WOMAN WHO COMES NEAR THE SHRINE...
...AND TRIES TO GAIN BACK THE VOICE AND LEGS SHE LOST.
THAT'S WHY SHE'S AFTER ME AND ITO-SAN?
PROB-ABLY.
HMM?

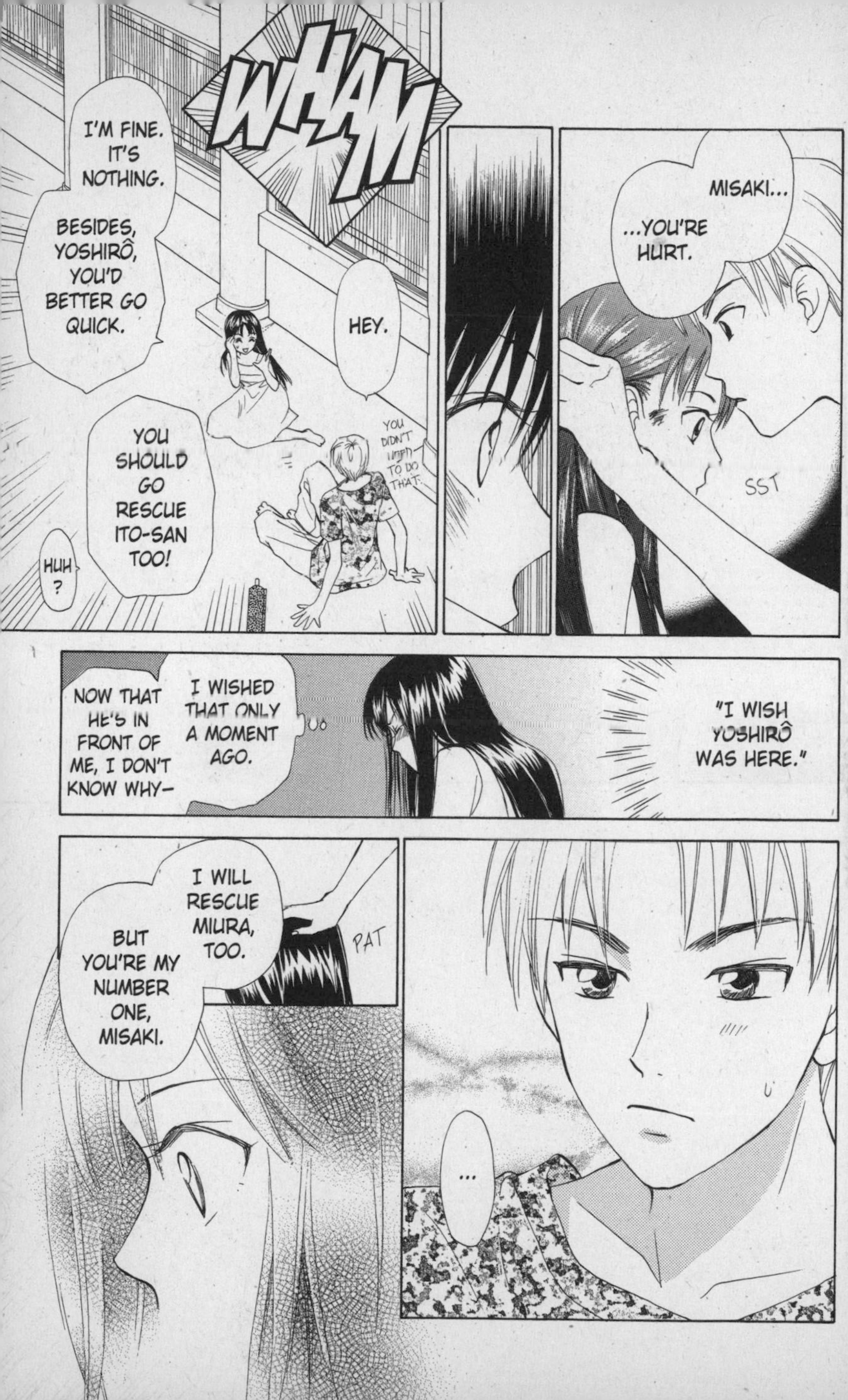
MISAKI...
...YOU'RE HURT.
SST
WHAM
HEY.
YOU DIDN'T NEED TO DO THAT.
I'M FINE. IT'S NOTHING.
BESIDES, YOSHIRÔ, YOU'D BETTER GO QUICK.
YOU SHOULD GO RESCUE ITO-SAN TOO!
HUH?
"I WISH YOSHIRÔ WAS HERE."
I WISHED THAT ONLY A MOMENT AGO.
NOW THAT HE'S IN FRONT OF ME, I DON'T KNOW WHY-
...
I WILL RESCUE MIURA, TOO.
PAT
BUT YOU'RE MY NUMBER ONE, MISAKI.

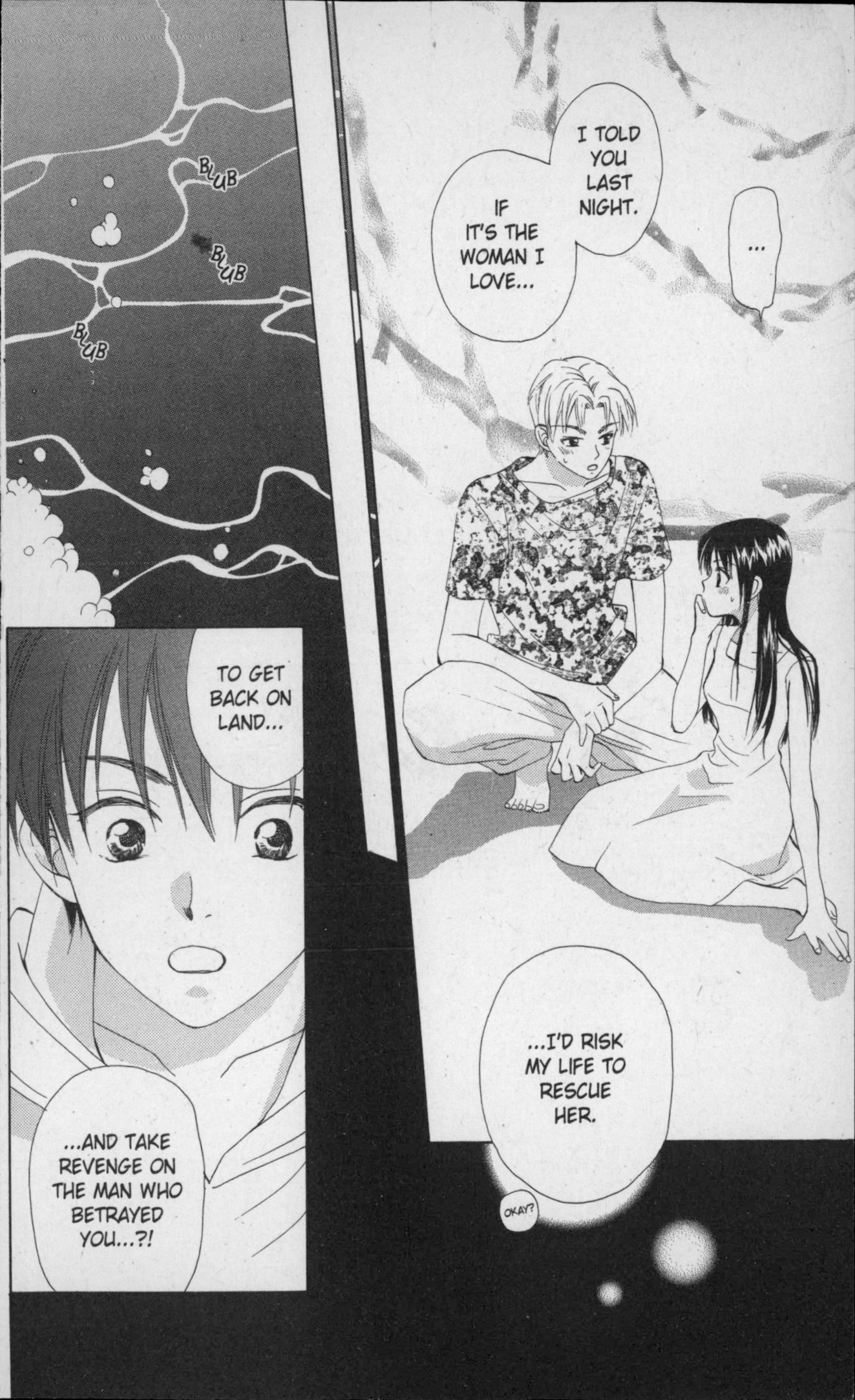
...
I TOLD YOU LAST NIGHT.
IF IT'S THE WOMAN I LOVE...
...I'D RISK MY LIFE TO RESCUE HER.
OKAY?
BLUB
BLUB
BLUB
TO GET BACK ON LAND...
...AND TAKE REVENGE ON THE MAN WHO BETRAYED YOU...?!

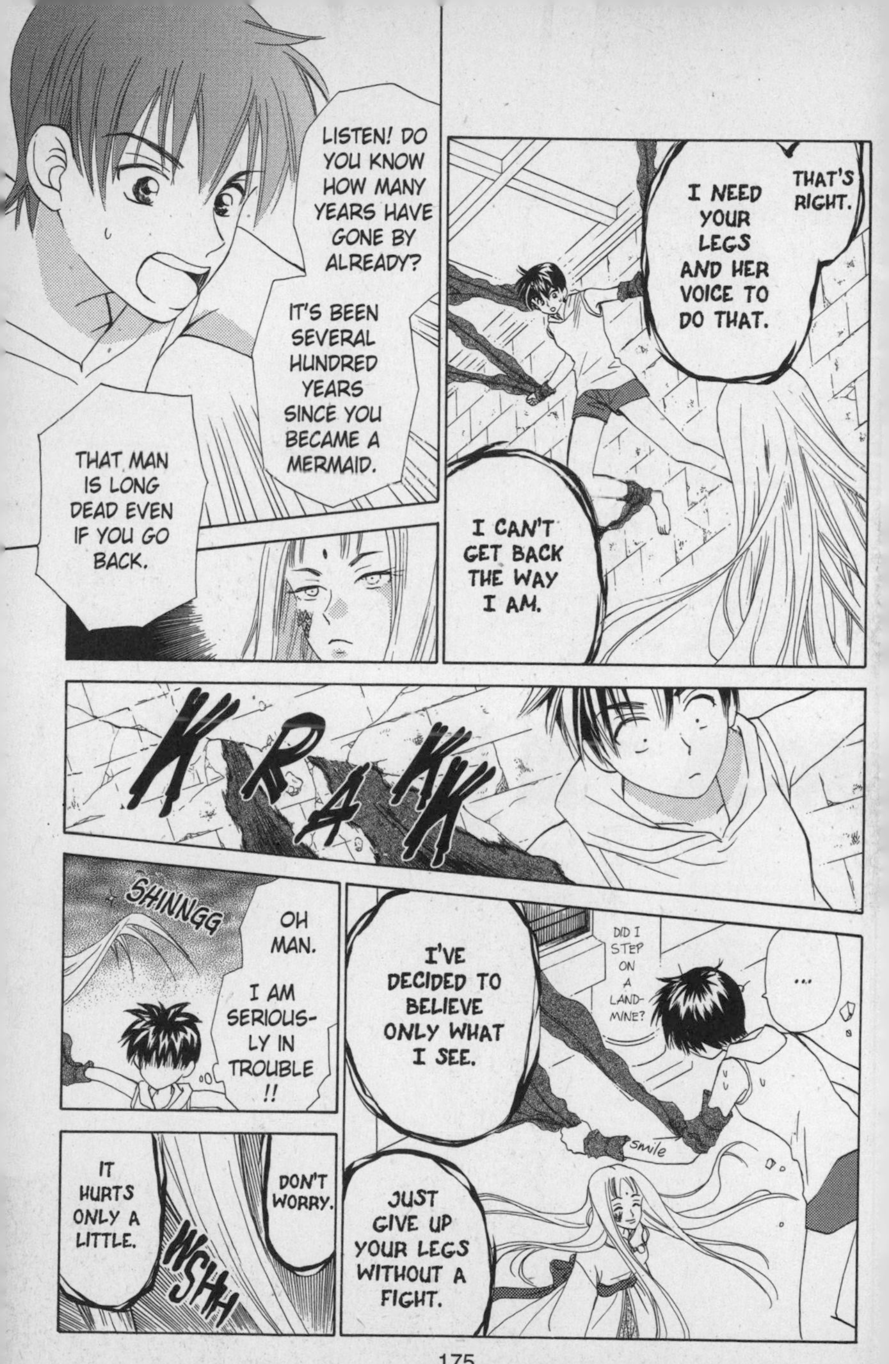
THAT'S RIGHT.
I NEED YOUR LEGS AND HER VOICE TO DO THAT.
I CAN'T GET BACK THE WAY I AM.
LISTEN! DO YOU KNOW HOW MANY YEARS HAVE GONE BY ALREADY?
IT'S BEEN SEVERAL HUNDRED YEARS SINCE YOU BECAME A MERMAID.
THAT MAN IS LONG DEAD EVEN IF YOU GO BACK.
KRAWK
...
DID I STEP ON A LAND-MINE?
I'VE DECIDED TO BELIEVE ONLY WHAT I SEE.
smile
JUST GIVE UP YOUR LEGS WITHOUT A FIGHT.
OH MAN.
I AM SERIOUS-LY IN TROUBLE!!
SHINNGG
DON'T WORRY.
IT HURTS ONLY A LITTLE.
WSHH

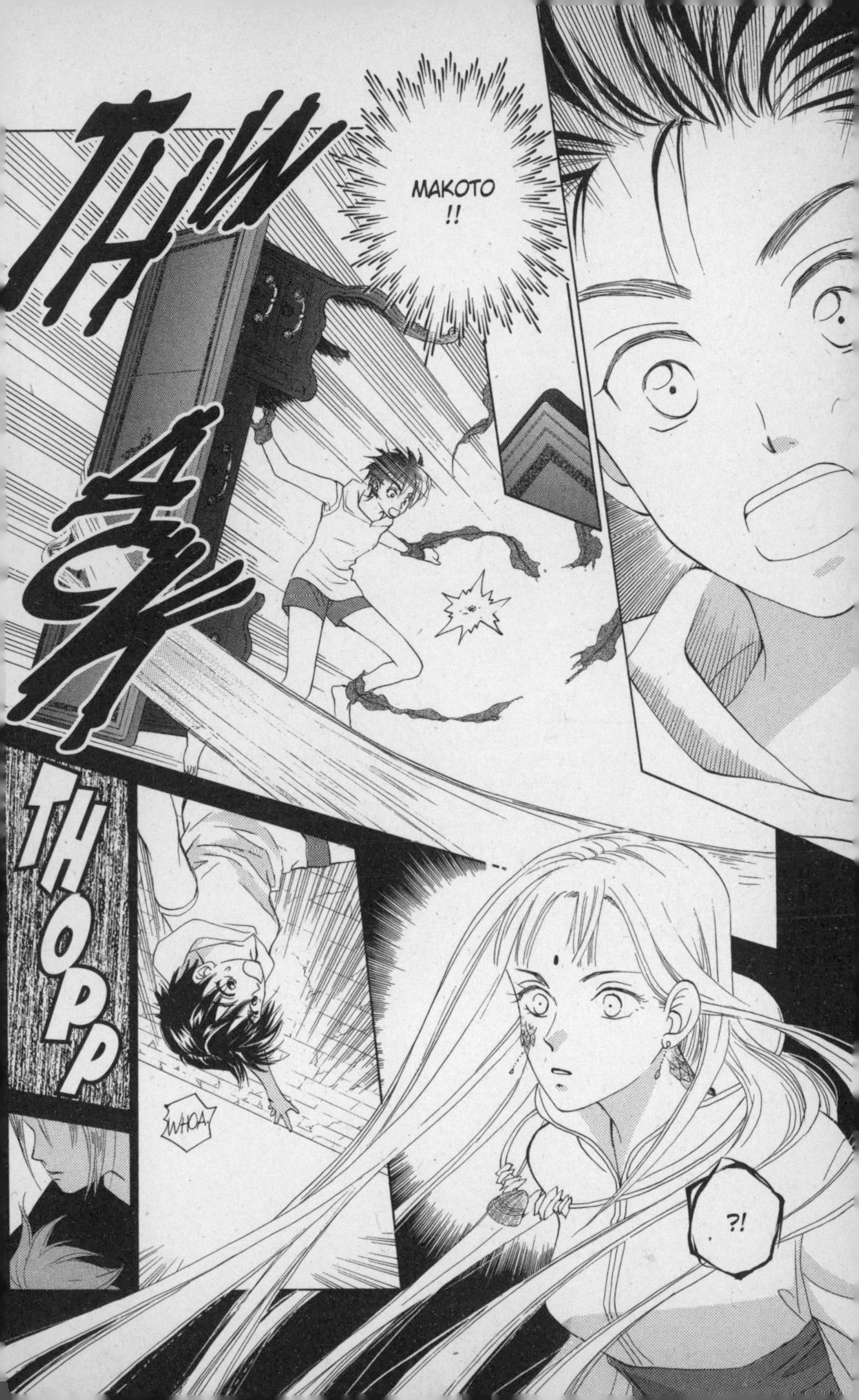
MAKOTO !!
THWACK
?!
WHOA
THOPP

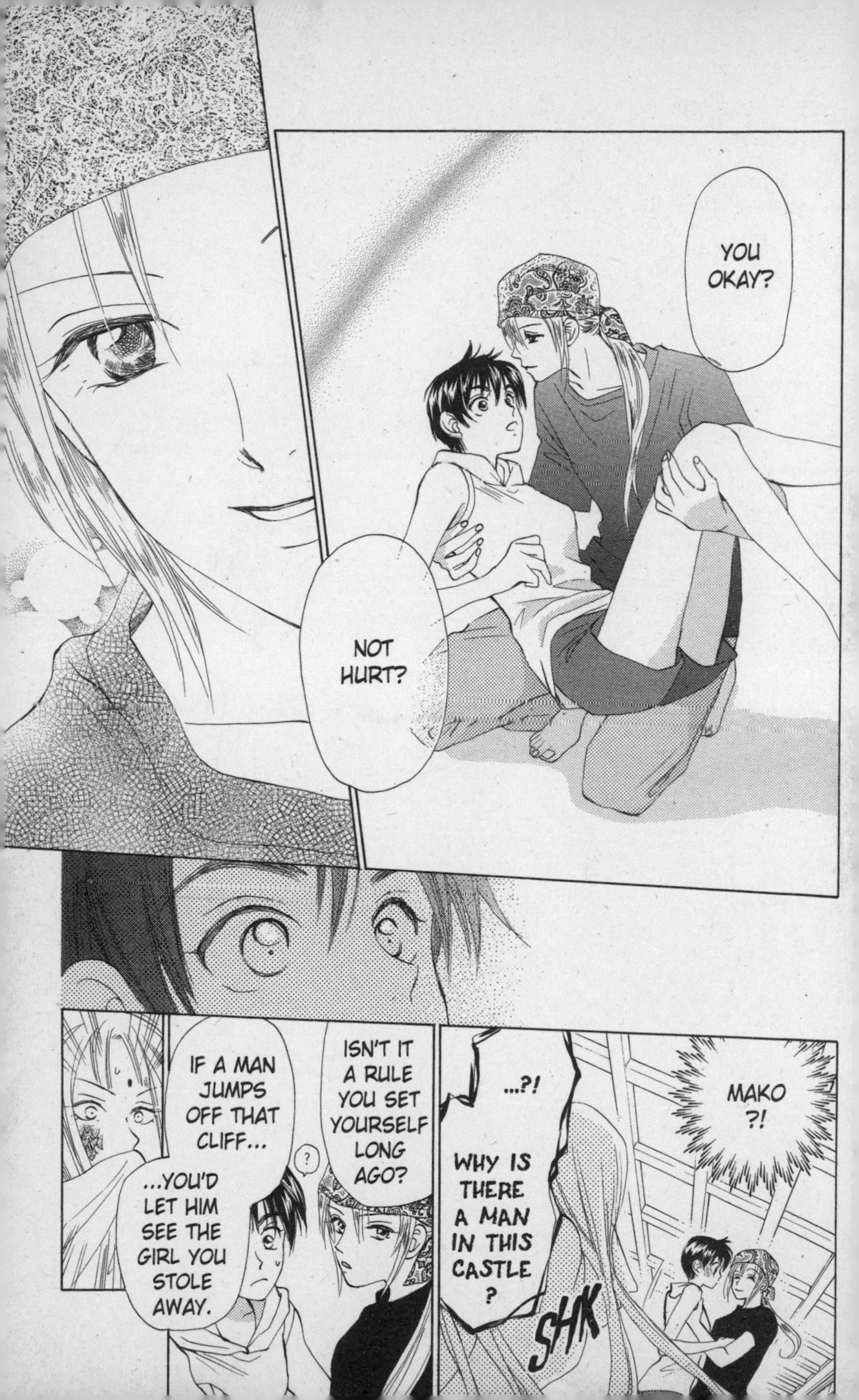
YOU OKAY?
NOT HURT?
MAKO ?!
...?!
WHY IS THERE A MAN IN THIS CASTLE ?
SHK
ISN'T IT A RULE YOU SET YOURSELF LONG AGO?
?
IF A MAN JUMPS OFF THAT CLIFF...
...YOU'D LET HIM SEE THE GIRL YOU STOLE AWAY.

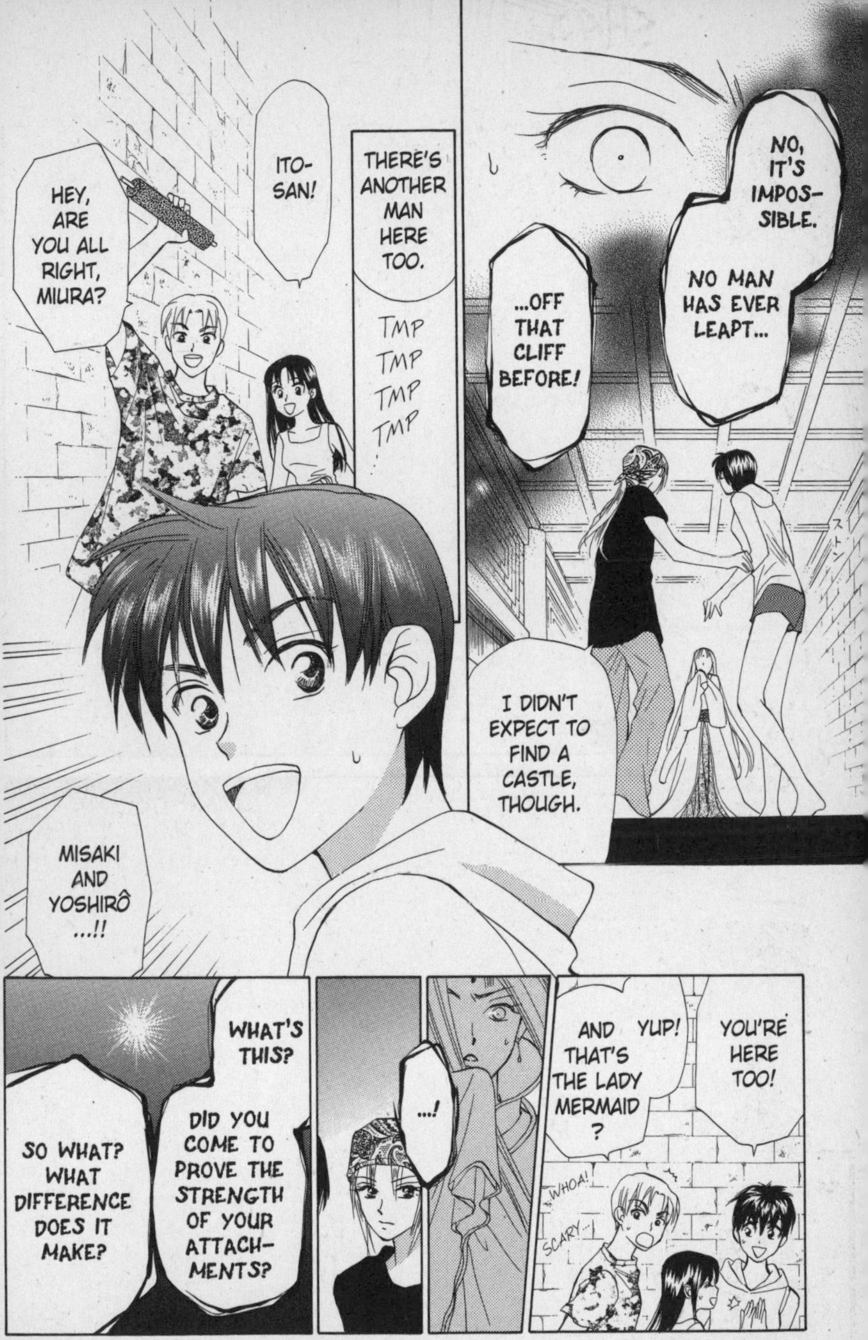
NO, IT'S IMPOSSIBLE.
NO MAN HAS EVER LEAPT...
...OFF THAT CLIFF BEFORE!
ストン
I DIDN'T EXPECT TO FIND A CASTLE, THOUGH.
THERE'S ANOTHER MAN HERE TOO.
TMP TMP TMP TMP
ITO-SAN!
HEY, ARE YOU ALL RIGHT, MIURA?
MISAKI AND YOSHIRÔ ...!!
YOU'RE HERE TOO!
YUP!
AND THAT'S THE LADY MERMAID ?
WHOA!
SCARY...
...!
WHAT'S THIS?
DID YOU COME TO PROVE THE STRENGTH OF YOUR ATTACH-MENTS?
SO WHAT? WHAT DIFFERENCE DOES IT MAKE?

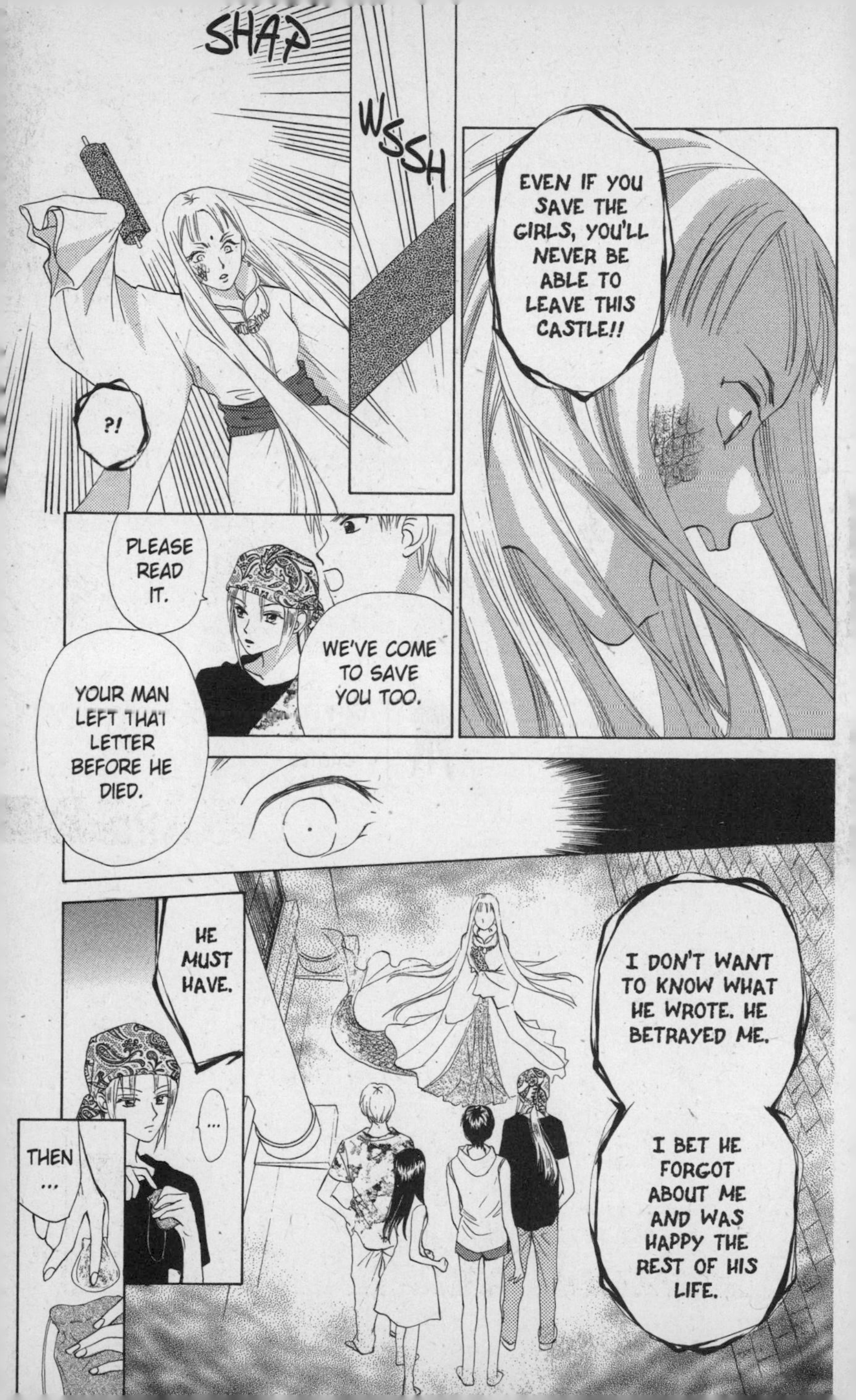
EVEN IF YOU SAVE THE GIRLS, YOU'LL NEVER BE ABLE TO LEAVE THIS CASTLE!!
WSSH
SHAP
?!
WE'VE COME TO SAVE YOU TOO.
PLEASE READ IT.
YOUR MAN LEFT THAT LETTER BEFORE HE DIED.
I DON'T WANT TO KNOW WHAT HE WROTE. HE BETRAYED ME.
I BET HE FORGOT ABOUT ME AND WAS HAPPY THE REST OF HIS LIFE.
HE MUST HAVE.
...
THEN ...

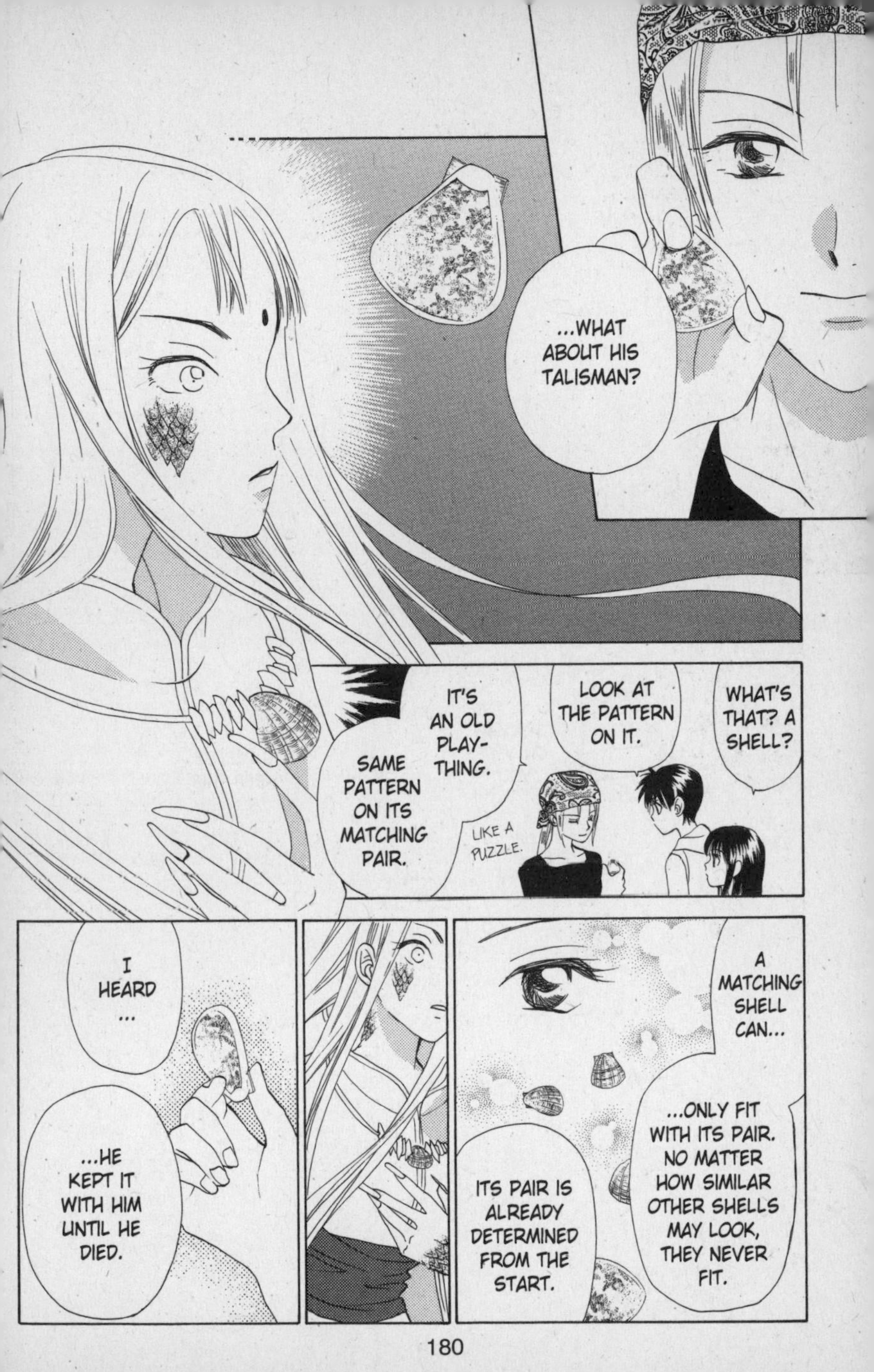
...WHAT ABOUT HIS TALISMAN?
WHAT'S THAT? A SHELL?
LOOK AT THE PATTERN ON IT.
IT'S AN OLD PLAY-THING.
LIKE A PUZZLE.
SAME PATTERN ON ITS MATCHING PAIR.
A MATCHING SHELL CAN...
...ONLY FIT WITH ITS PAIR. NO MATTER HOW SIMILAR OTHER SHELLS MAY LOOK, THEY NEVER FIT.
ITS PAIR IS ALREADY DETERMINED FROM THE START.
I HEARD ...
...HE KEPT IT WITH HIM UNTIL HE DIED.

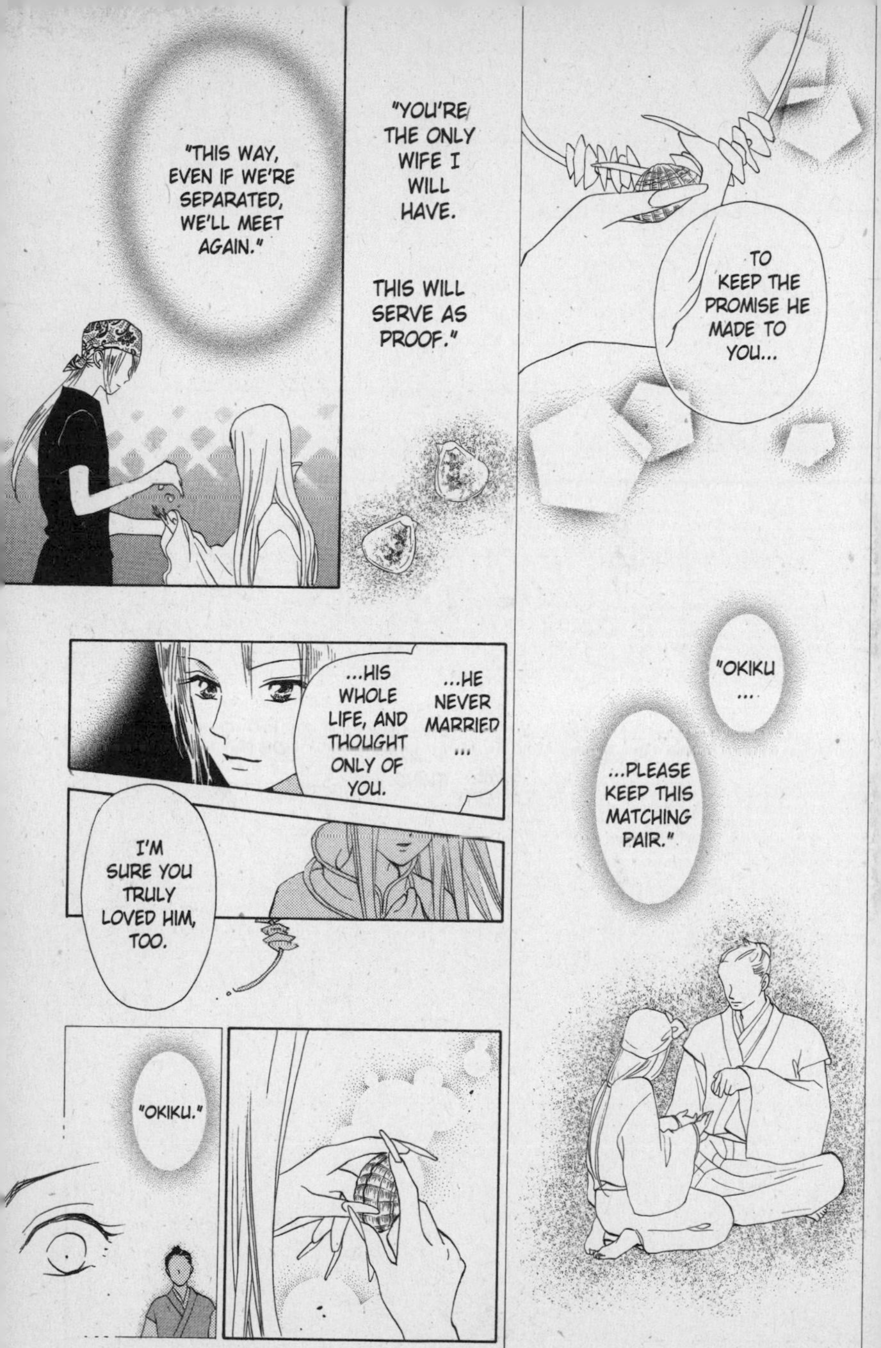
TO KEEP THE PROMISE HE MADE TO YOU...
"OKIKU ...
...PLEASE KEEP THIS MATCHING PAIR."
"YOU'RE THE ONLY WIFE I WILL HAVE.
THIS WILL SERVE AS PROOF."
"THIS WAY, EVEN IF WE'RE SEPARATED, WE'LL MEET AGAIN."
...HE NEVER MARRIED ...
...HIS WHOLE LIFE, AND THOUGHT ONLY OF YOU.
I'M SURE YOU TRULY LOVED HIM, TOO.
"OKIKU."

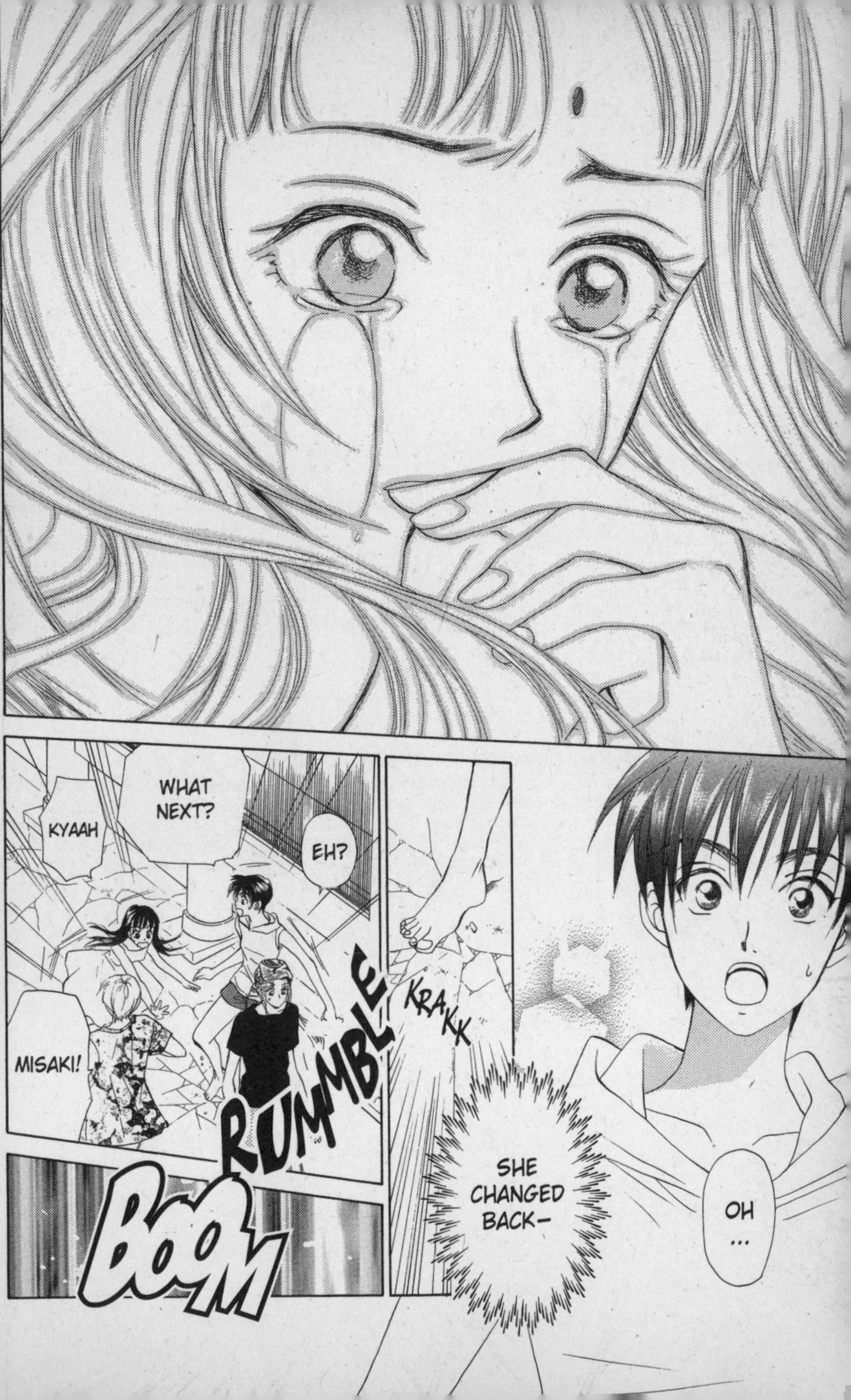
OH ...
SHE CHANGED BACK-
KRAKK
EH?
WHAT NEXT?
KYAAH
MISAKI!
RUMMBLE
BOOM

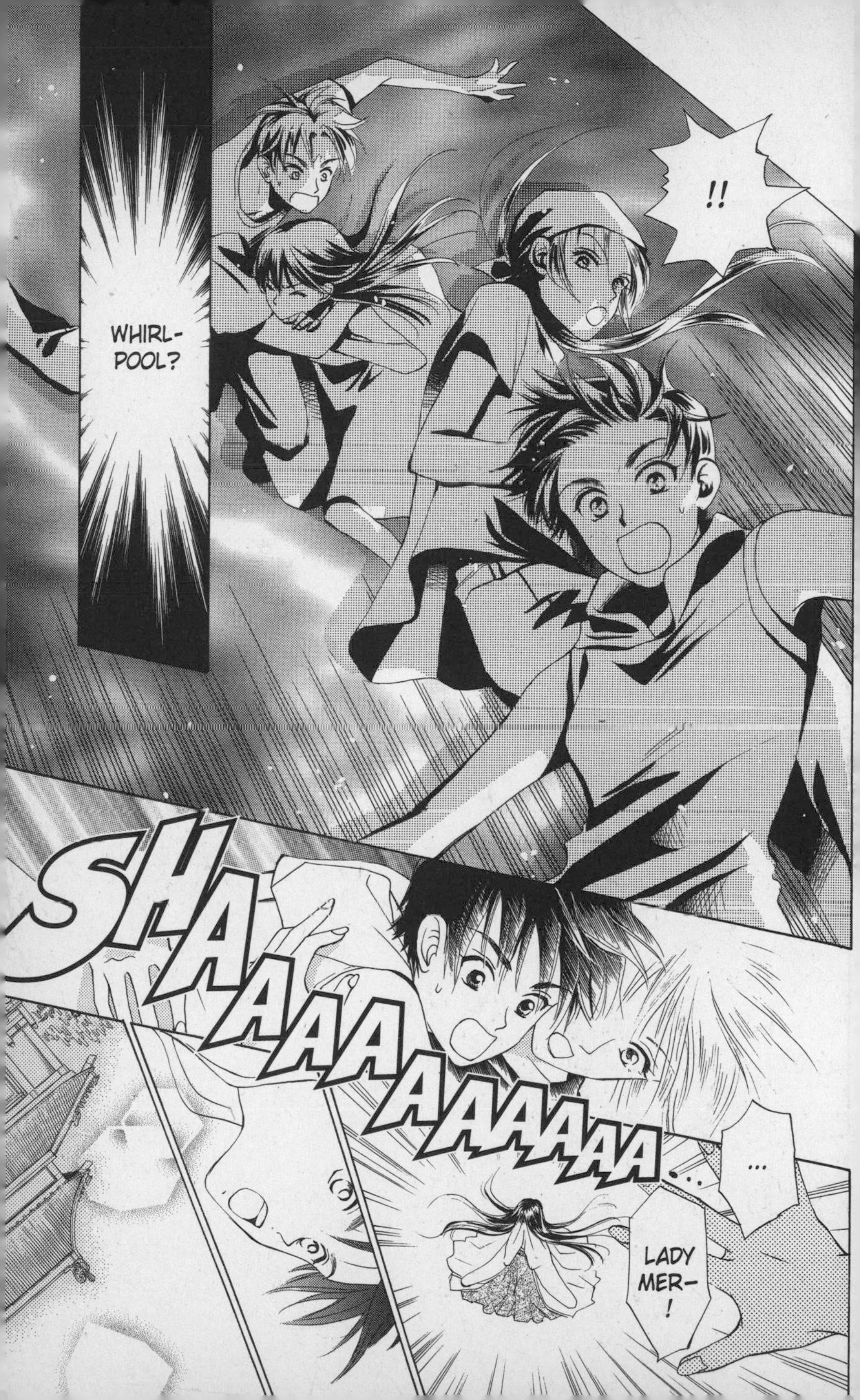
!!
WHIRL-POOL?
SHAAAAAAAAAAAA...
...
LADY MER-!

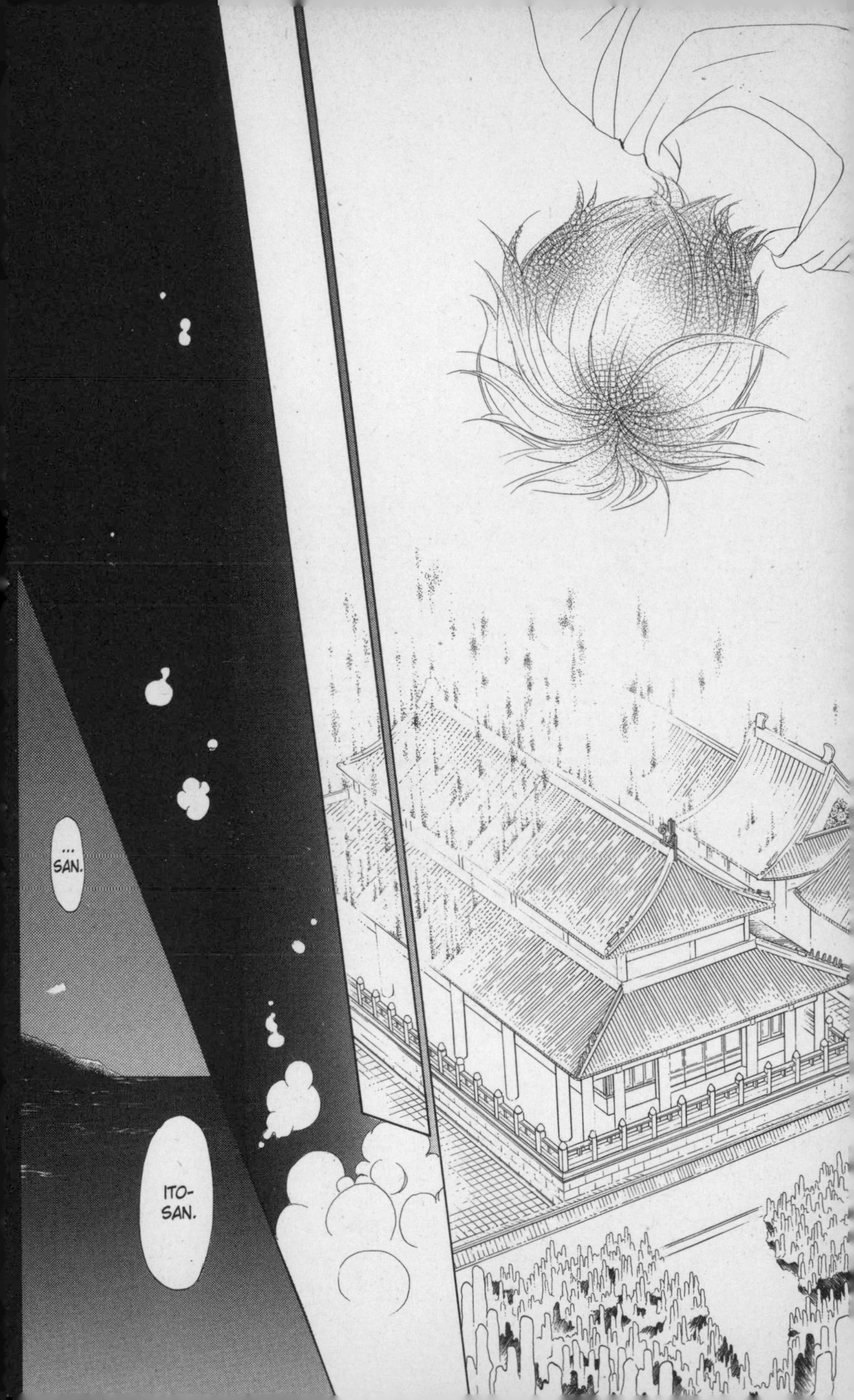
...SAN.
ITO-SAN.

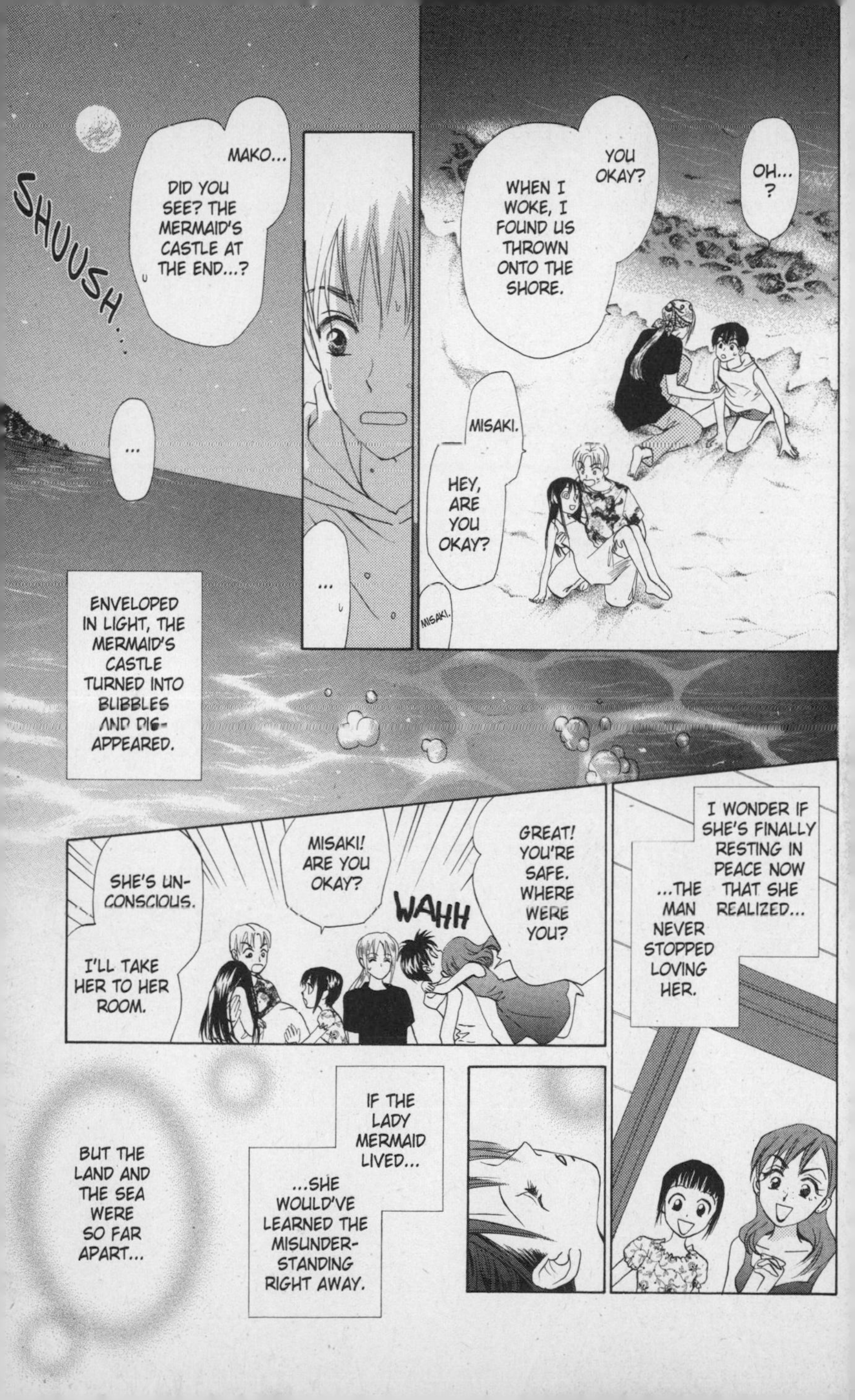
OH...?
YOU OKAY?
WHEN I WOKE, I FOUND US THROWN ONTO THE SHORE.
MISAKI.
HEY, ARE YOU OKAY?
MISAKI.
...
MAKO...
DID YOU SEE? THE MERMAID'S CASTLE AT THE END...?
SHUUSH...
...
ENVELOPED IN LIGHT, THE MERMAID'S CASTLE TURNED INTO BUBBLES AND DIS-APPEARED.
I WONDER IF SHE'S FINALLY RESTING IN PEACE NOW THAT SHE REALIZED...
...THE MAN NEVER STOPPED LOVING HER.
GREAT! YOU'RE SAFE. WHERE WERE YOU?
WAHH
MISAKI! ARE YOU OKAY?
SHE'S UN-CONSCIOUS.
I'LL TAKE HER TO HER ROOM.
IF THE LADY MERMAID LIVED...
...SHE WOULD'VE LEARNED THE MISUNDER-STANDING RIGHT AWAY.
BUT THE LAND AND THE SEA WERE SO FAR APART...

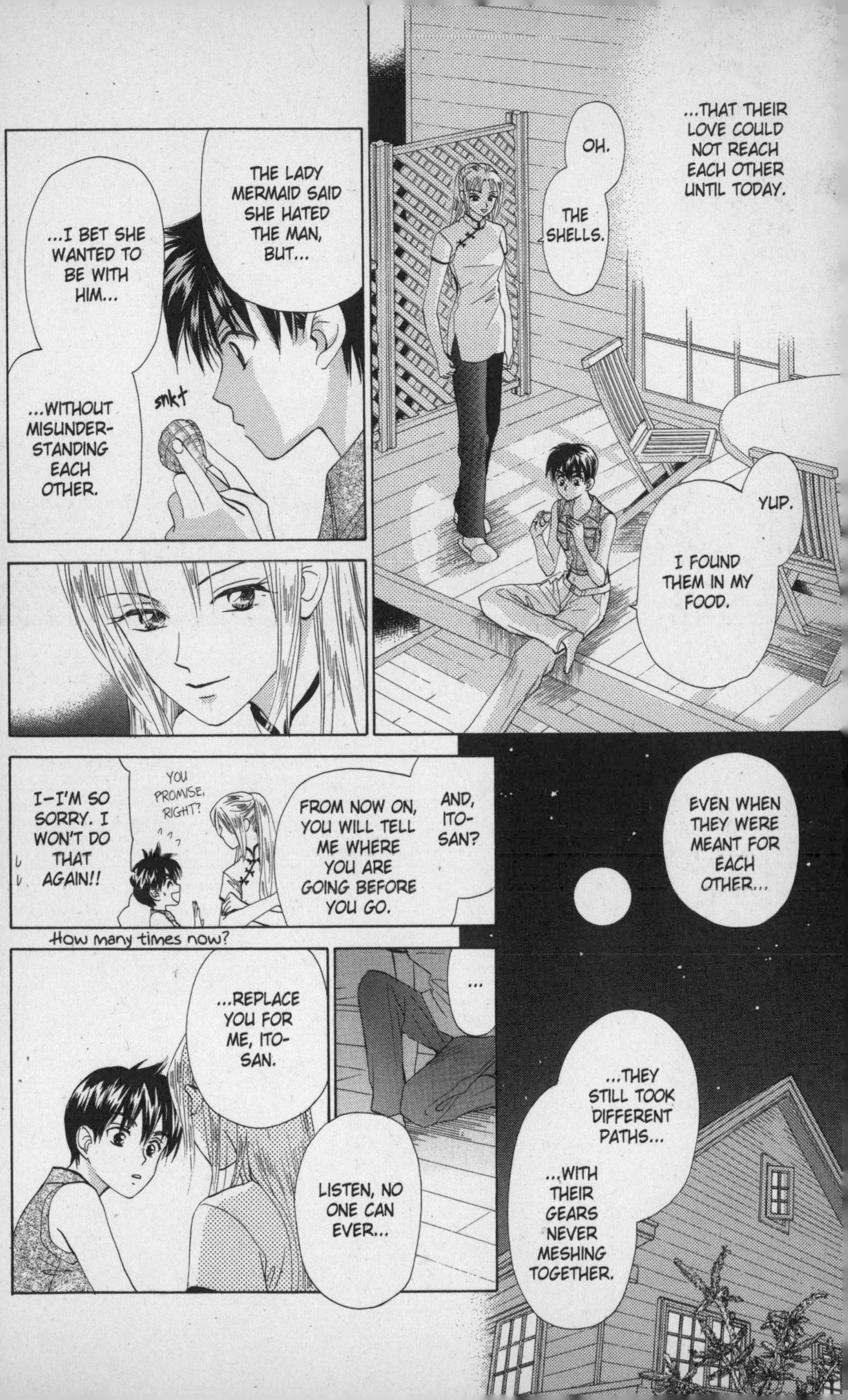
...THAT THEIR LOVE COULD NOT REACH EACH OTHER UNTIL TODAY.
OH.
THE SHELLS.
YUP.
I FOUND THEM IN MY FOOD.
THE LADY MERMAID SAID SHE HATED THE MAN, BUT...
...I BET SHE WANTED TO BE WITH HIM...
snkt
...WITHOUT MISUNDERSTANDING EACH OTHER.
EVEN WHEN THEY WERE MEANT FOR EACH OTHER...
...THEY STILL TOOK DIFFERENT PATHS...
...WITH THEIR GEARS NEVER MESHING TOGETHER.
AND, ITO-SAN?
FROM NOW ON, YOU WILL TELL ME WHERE YOU ARE GOING BEFORE YOU GO.
YOU PROMISE, RIGHT?
I-I'M SO SORRY. I WON'T DO THAT AGAIN!!
How many times now?
...
LISTEN, NO ONE CAN EVER...
...REPLACE YOU FOR ME, ITO-SAN.

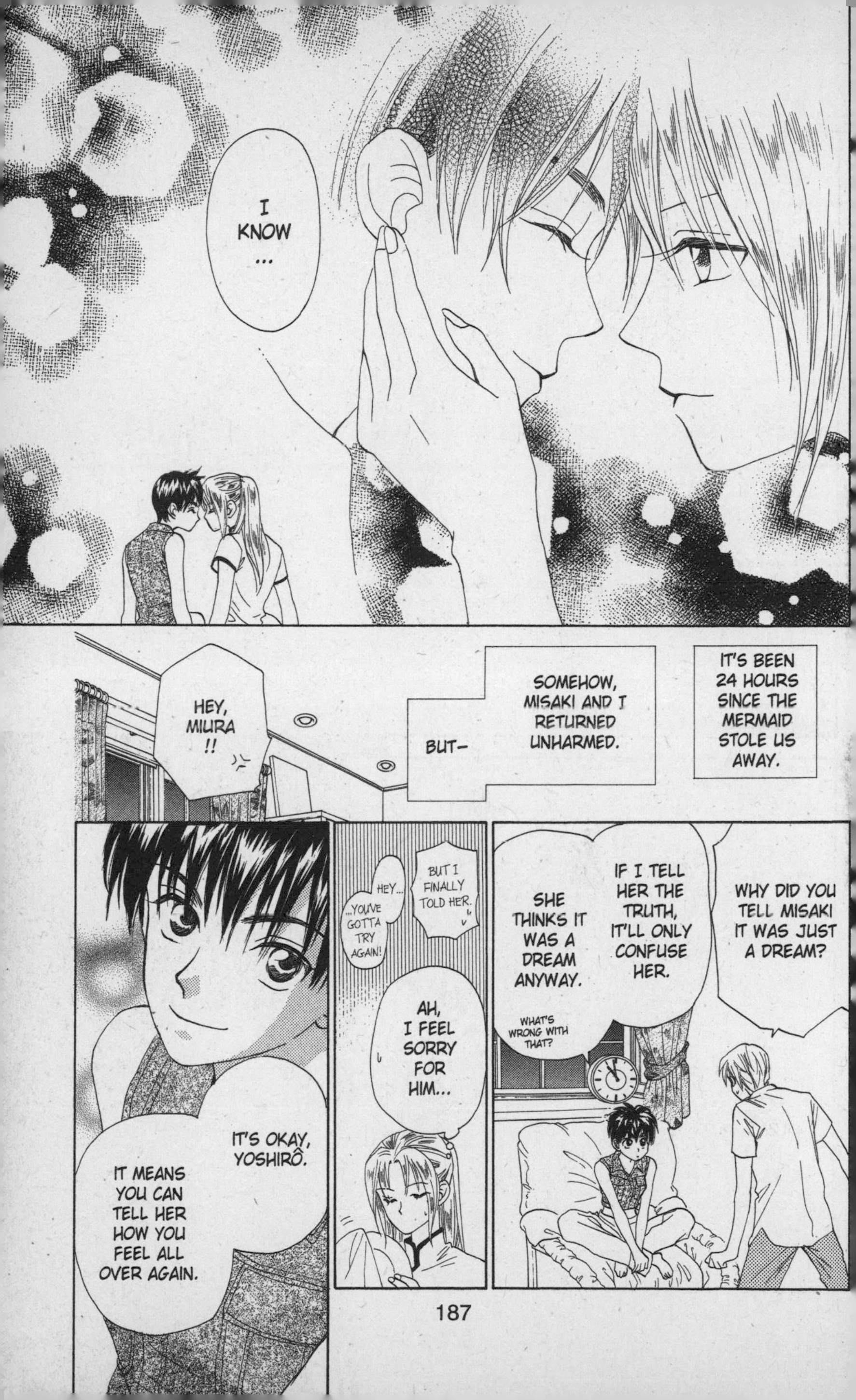
I KNOW ...
IT'S BEEN 24 HOURS SINCE THE MERMAID STOLE US AWAY.
SOMEHOW, MISAKI AND I RETURNED UNHARMED.
BUT—
HEY, MIURA !!
WHY DID YOU TELL MISAKI IT WAS JUST A DREAM?
IF I TELL HER THE TRUTH, IT'LL ONLY CONFUSE HER.
SHE THINKS IT WAS A DREAM ANYWAY.
WHAT'S WRONG WITH THAT?
BUT I FINALLY TOLD HER.
HEY... ...YOU'VE GOTTA TRY AGAIN!
AH, I FEEL SORRY FOR HIM...
IT'S OKAY, YOSHIRÔ.
IT MEANS YOU CAN TELL HER HOW YOU FEEL ALL OVER AGAIN.

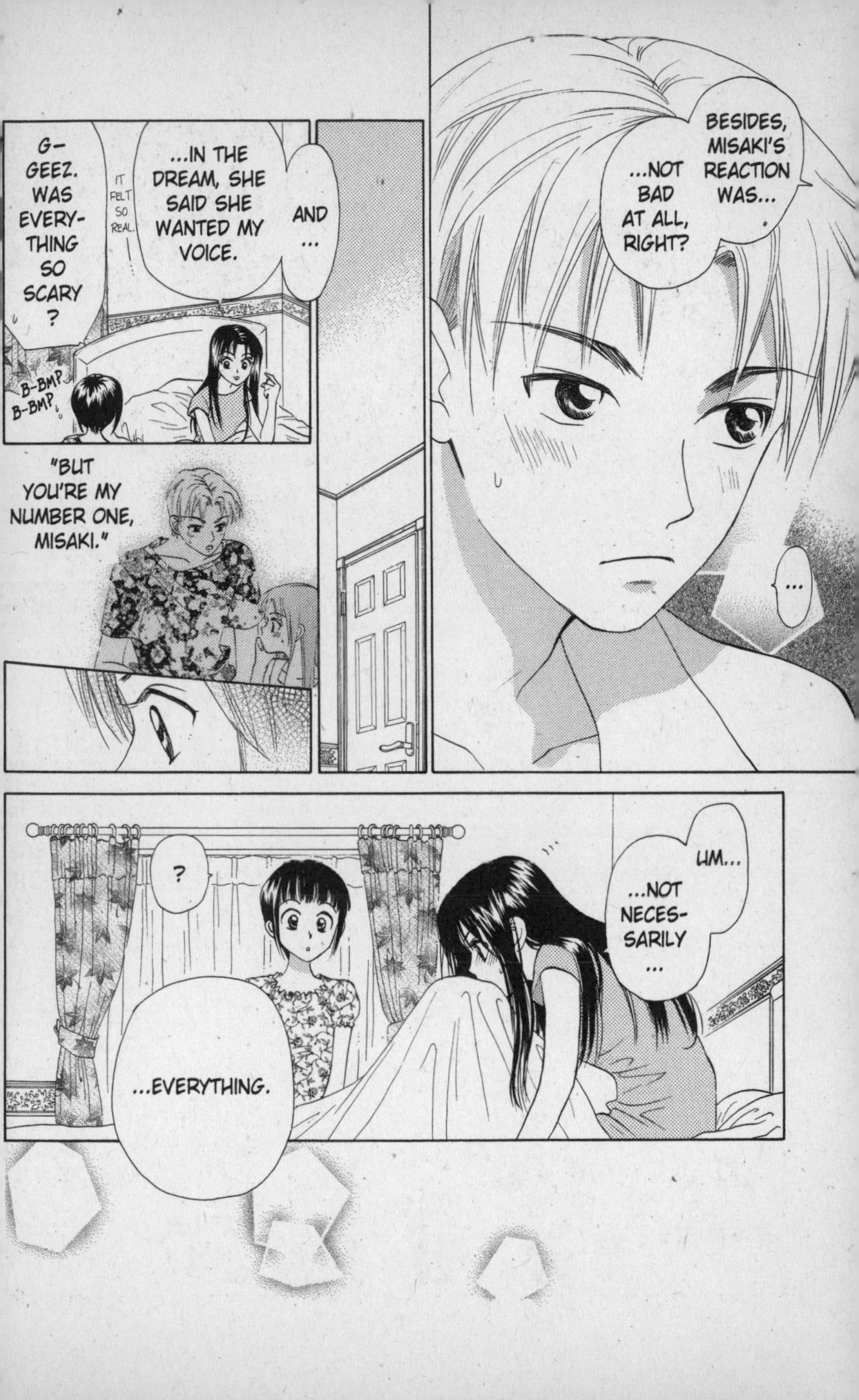
BESIDES, MISAKI'S REACTION WAS...
...NOT BAD AT ALL, RIGHT?
...
AND ...
...IN THE DREAM, SHE SAID SHE WANTED MY VOICE.
IT FELT SO REAL.
G-GEEZ. WAS EVERY-THING SO SCARY?
B-BMP B-BMP
"BUT YOU'RE MY NUMBER ONE, MISAKI."
UM...
...NOT NECES-SARILY ...
?
...EVERYTHING.

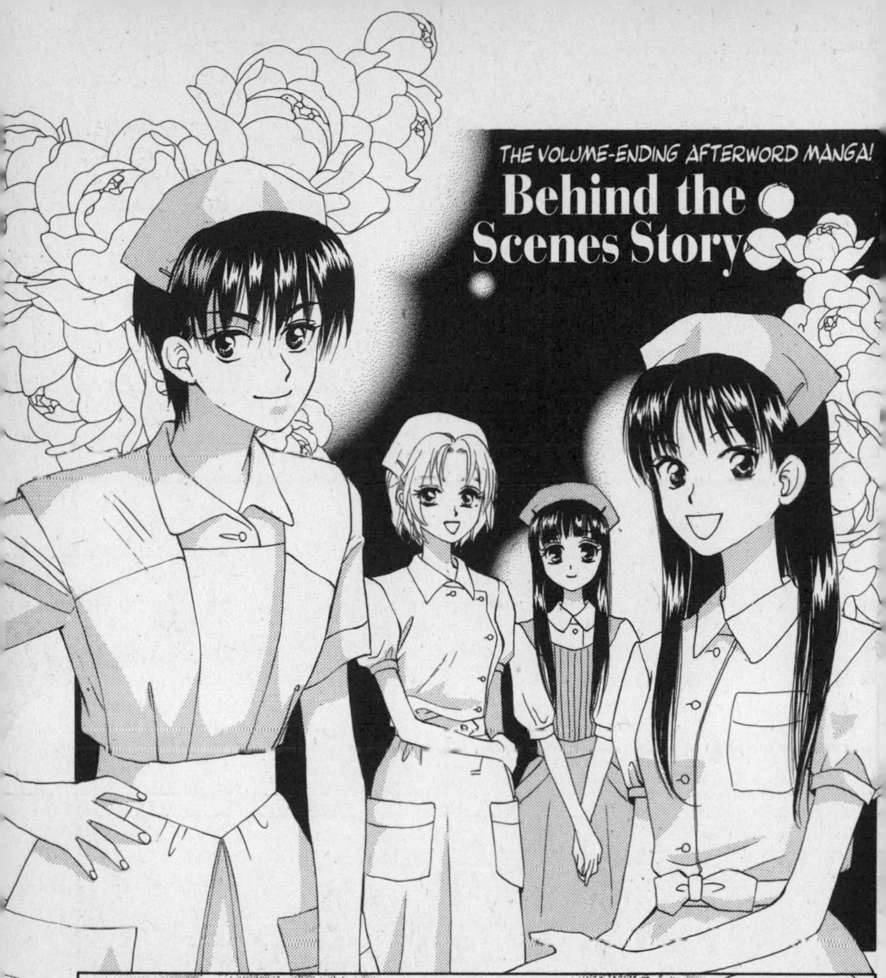
THE VOLUME-ENDING AFTERWORD MANGA!
Behind the Scenes Story

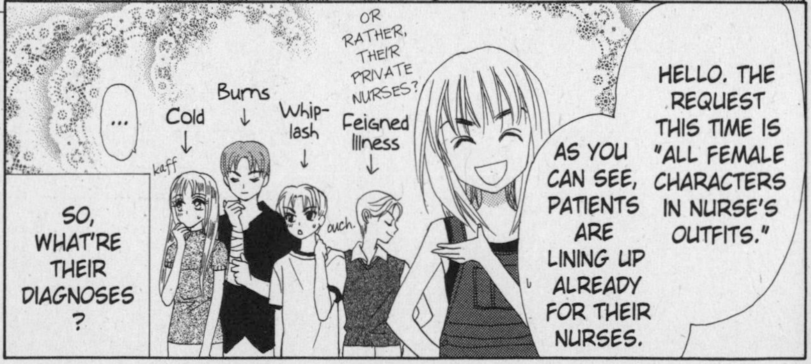
HELLO. THE REQUEST THIS TIME IS "ALL FEMALE CHARACTERS IN NURSE'S OUTFITS."
AS YOU CAN SEE, PATIENTS ARE LINING UP ALREADY FOR THEIR NURSES.
OR RATHER, THEIR PRIVATE NURSES?
Feigned Illness
Whip-lash
ouch.
Burns
Cold
kaff
...
SO, WHAT'RE THEIR DIAGNOSES?

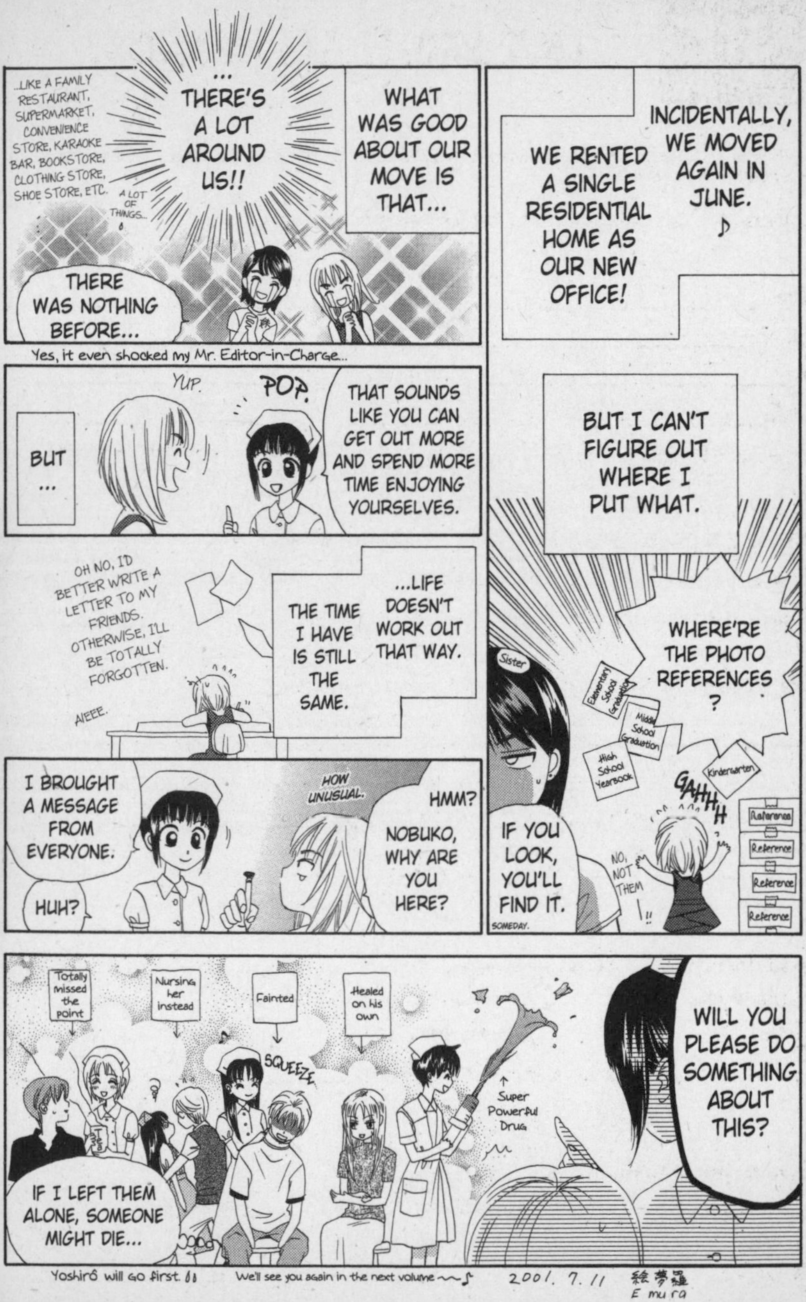
INCIDENTALLY, WE MOVED AGAIN IN JUNE. ♪
WE RENTED A SINGLE RESIDENTIAL HOME AS OUR NEW OFFICE!
BUT I CAN'T FIGURE OUT WHERE I PUT WHAT.
WHERE'RE THE PHOTO REFERENCES?
Sister
Elementary School Graduation
Middle School Graduation
High School Yearbook
Kindergarten
GAHHH
Reference
Reference
Reference
Reference
NO, NOT THEM!!
IF YOU LOOK, YOU'LL FIND IT.
SOMEDAY.
WHAT WAS GOOD ABOUT OUR MOVE IS THAT...
...THERE'S A LOT AROUND US!!
...LIKE A FAMILY RESTAURANT, SUPERMARKET, CONVENIENCE STORE, KARAOKE BAR, BOOKSTORE, CLOTHING STORE, SHOE STORE, ETC.
A LOT OF THINGS...
THERE WAS NOTHING BEFORE...
Yes, it even shocked my Mr. Editor-in-Charge...
THAT SOUNDS LIKE YOU CAN GET OUT MORE AND SPEND MORE TIME ENJOYING YOURSELVES.
POP.
YUP.
BUT...
...LIFE DOESN'T WORK OUT THAT WAY.
THE TIME I HAVE IS STILL THE SAME.
OH NO, I'D BETTER WRITE A LETTER TO MY FRIENDS. OTHERWISE, I'LL BE TOTALLY FORGOTTEN.
AIEEE.
HMM?
NOBUKO, WHY ARE YOU HERE?
HOW UNUSUAL.
I BROUGHT A MESSAGE FROM EVERYONE.
HUH?
WILL YOU PLEASE DO SOMETHING ABOUT THIS?
Super Powerful Drug
Healed on his own
Fainted
SQUEEZE
Nursing her instead
Totally missed the point
IF I LEFT THEM ALONE, SOMEONE MIGHT DIE...
Yoshirô will go first.
We'll see you again in the next volume ~
2001. 7. 11 絵夢羅 E mura

LOVE SHOJO? LET US KNOW!

☐ Please do NOT send me information about VIZ Media products, news and events, special offers, or other information.

☐ Please do NOT send me information from VIZ' trusted business partners.

Name: _____

Address: _____

City:_____ State:_____ Zip:_____

E-mail: _____

☐ Male ☐ Female   Date of Birth (mm/dd/yyyy): ___ / ___ / _____   (Under 13? Parental consent required)

What race/ethnicity do you consider yourself? (check all that apply)

☐ White/Caucasian   ☐ Black/African American   ☐ Hispanic/Latino

☐ Asian/Pacific Islander   ☐ Native American/Alaskan Native ☐ Other: _____

What VIZ shojo title(s) did you purchase? (indicate title(s) purchased)

_____

What other shojo titles from other publishers do you own? _____

_____

Reason for purchase: (check all that apply)

☐ Special offer   ☐ Favorite title / author / artist / genre

☐ Gift   ☐ Recommendation   ☐ Collection

☐ Read excerpt in VIZ manga sampler   ☐ Other _____

Where did you make your purchase? (please check one)

☐ Comic store   ☐ Bookstore   ☐ Mass/Grocery Store

☐ Newsstand   ☐ Video/Video Game Store

☐ Online (site:_____)   ☐ Other _____

How many shojo titles have you purchased in the last year? How many were VIZ shojo titles?
(please check one from each column)

SHOJO MANGA

☐ None
☐ 1 – 4
☐ 5 – 10
☐ 11+

VIZ SHOJO MANGA

☐ None
☐ 1 – 4
☐ 5 – 10
☐ 11+

What do you like most about shojo graphic novels? (check all that apply)

☐ Romance
☐ Comedy
☐ Other _____

☐ Drama / conflict
☐ Real-life storylines

☐ Fantasy
☐ Relatable characters

Do you purchase every volume of your favorite shojo series?

☐ Yes! Gotta have 'em as my own
☐ No. Please explain: _____

Who are your favorite shojo authors / artists? _____

_____

What shojo titles would like you translated and sold in English? _____

_____

THANK YOU! Please send the completed form to:

NJW Research
ATTN: VIZ Media Shojo Survey
42 Catharine Street
Poughkeepsie, NY 12601